A house of prayer

A house of prayer

The message of 2 Chronicles

Andrew Stewart

 EVANGELICAL PRESS

EVANGELICAL PRESS
Faverdale North Industrial Estate, Darlington, DL3 0PH, England

Evangelical Press USA
P. O. Box 84, Auburn, MA 01501, USA

e-mail: sales@evangelicalpress.org

web: http://www.evangelicalpress.org

First published 2001

British Library Cataloguing in Publication Data available

ISBN 0 85234 480 5

Printed and bound in Great Britain by Creative Print & Design Wales, Ebbw Vale

To the members of
Glenmanus Reformed Presbyterian Church,
where I ministered from 1990–1998.
Their response to the Scriptures at our midweek Bible study
has helped to shape this volume.

Contents

Introduction to 2 Chronicles

The book of Chronicles is one book and needs to be read as such. However, for the sake of reference and convenience it has been divided into two volumes, 1 and 2 Chronicles. This commentary seeks to explain the message of 2 Chronicles. A survey of the whole book of Chronicles is found in the Welwyn Commentary on 1 Chronicles, *A Family Tree*; it covers such issues as the authorship, date, theology and contents of Chronicles. Readers of this commentary may benefit from reading that introduction before beginning to study 2 Chronicles.

It is worthwhile explaining the title of this volume, *A House of Prayer*. It seeks to highlight the distinctive focus of the history covered by 2 Chronicles, which is the place of the temple in the life of the nation of Israel (and later the southern kingdom of Judah). 2 Chronicles commences with the building of the temple during the reign of King Solomon and in its closing verses it envisages the rebuilding of the temple after the return of the exiles to Judah in the time of Zerubbabel. Much of the action described in 2 Chronicles — apostasy as well as reformation — took place within the temple precincts. The temple was a place where God had placed his name; it was a place towards which God's people would pray; it provided a geographical forum for God's redemptive actions during the period of the Israelite monarchy.

The prophets of the Old Testament saw the significance of such a place. They knew that places and buildings do not, in themselves, guarantee salvation (Jer. 7:1-7). However, God's redemptive acts are *historical* and that means they are located in space and time. When God redeemed his people he would send his promised Messiah to a place where a sacrifice was to be offered: ' "Then suddenly the Lord you are seeking will come to his temple, the messenger of the covenant, whom you desire, will come," says the Lord Almighty' (Mal. 3:1). When God proclaimed salvation he would send his gospel from that place of sacrifice:

> Many nations will come and say,
> 'Come let us go up to the mountain of the LORD,
>   to the house of the God of Jacob.
> He will teach us his ways,
>   so that we may walk in his paths.'
> The law will go out from Zion,
>   the word of the LORD from Jerusalem
>
> (Micah 4:2).

Since the resurrection of Jesus Christ redemption is now a completed work and the place where the great sacrifice of atonement took place is no longer the focus of our attention. Our focus is on the *person* who offered himself as the final and all-sufficient sacrifice for sinners. 'Let us fix our eyes on Jesus, the author and perfecter of our faith, who for the joy set before him endured the cross, scorning its shame, and sat down at the right hand of the throne of God' (Heb. 12:2). He does not now minister in an earthly temple, for he sits at the right hand of God the Father in heaven.

Rejoicing in the completed work of Christ does not mean that we must forget those Old Testament believers who worshipped and ministered in an earthly temple. In fact as we follow the faith and, yes, the failures too, of these worshippers we are pointed to Christ, the everlasting Temple. That is why God has given us the book of Chronicles. It is good for us to learn about their struggles to be faithful to God. It is good for us to take heed when we read of their descent into disobedience. It is good for us to be exhilarated when we read about godly leaders who called the nation back to the grace of God.

Much of this book was written as an encouragement to ordinary Israelites who were struggling to be faithful in daily and mundane matters. Much of the post-exilic period in Israel's history seemed like the 'day of small things' which Zechariah urged his readers not to despise (Zech. 4:10). Surely modern readers can relate to these challenges and discouragements! Yet there is a great hero who towers above all these struggles, and that is the Lord Jesus Christ, the Lamb of God who, at the place of God's choosing and appointment, took away the sins of the world.

1.
A test for Solomon

Please read 2 Chronicles 1:1-17

Our first attempts to do something new are very important, for they establish our patterns and habits of behaviour, and once those habits are established it is very difficult to change them. Every golfer knows that if he is going to play well he needs a good stance at the tee and a good grip on his golf club. If, as an inexperienced player, he developed a wrong way of holding his club and positioning his feet, these seemingly trivial mistakes can ruin his game. After a few years it is hard to break old habits and learn a new way of playing. In any area of life a bad start is hard to remedy, but a good start is a great blessing.

That is why the early days of the reign of King Solomon were so important. To the Chronicler (who wrote this history after the return of the Jewish people from exile in Babylon) Solomon was the model king. During his reign the temple in Jerusalem was built and the kingdom of Israel reached its zenith. Solomon presided over a truly golden age in biblical history to which subsequent generations of Israelites looked back with awe and envy. They also looked back to learn lessons about what the Lord was doing in their own day. The history of Solomon taught them about the everlasting covenant that God had made with his people, the importance of true worship and the glory of God's kingdom, but it also taught them about the need to make a good start.

Like every leader, Solomon had to make many decisions, and some of them were demanding (see 1 Kings 3:16-28), but in this chapter we read of the most important decision that he was called to make as King of Israel. In 1:7 God appeared to Solomon and said to him, **'Ask for whatever you want me to give you.'** The answer that Solomon gave to this question would determine what the rest of his reign would be like.

The background to Solomon's reign (1:1-6)

In some ways the break between 1 and 2 Chronicles is an artificial one. Both books were written by the same author, at the same time, and as one book. For the sake of convenience this book was divided into two parts by the scribes who copied the text of the Old Testament onto scrolls for people to read. It would have required two of the scrolls typically used in Old Testament times to copy out the whole book of Chronicles, so an informal division was made. This division was formalized by the translators of the Old Testament into Greek (a version which came to be known as the Septuagint), for in this translation Chronicles appears as two separate books.

The division is, however, not an arbitrary or unhelpful one, for it marks an important milestone in Israel's history. David, the great warrior king, had laid a strong foundation for the kingdom, and now Solomon sought to build upon it. Threats from within and without had been subdued and a strong central government had been set up. David had wanted to go further and build a temple for the Lord in Jerusalem (1 Chr. 17), but God had prevented David from building the temple, because it was not appropriate that he, a man of war, should build it (1 Chr. 22:6-10). Solomon, a man of peace, would build the temple, while David devoted the rest of his reign to setting aside the materials which Solomon would use in its construction (1 Chr. 28; 29). With these preparations made, it was Solomon's task to build. The temple and the kingdom are the themes that bind the message of Chronicles together. Preparation is the theme of 1 Chronicles, while dedication and reformation are the themes of 2 Chronicles.

We are reminded of this transition in the opening words: **'Solomon son of David established himself firmly over his kingdom, for the LORD his God was with him and made him exceedingly great'** (1:1). The verb translated 'established himself firmly' is a strong, or intensive, one. We get an insight into what this involved for Solomon from 1 Kings chapters 1-2, which are sometimes called 'the succession narrative'. Here we are told about Solomon's rival for the throne, his half-brother Adonijah. As David lay dying, Adonijah sought to stage a palace coup to displace Solomon, David's chosen heir. Only the courageous actions of Bathsheba (Solomon's mother), Nathan the prophet and Zadok the priest prevented him from succeeding. When it became clear that Solomon would indeed take the throne David advised him, 'Be strong, show yourself [to be] a man' (1 Kings 2:2).

The Chronicler begins his account of Solomon's reign with the new king firmly in control of his kingdom. The setting is an assembly of national leaders and representatives of all the people (**'the commanders of thousands and commanders of hundreds ... the judges and ... all the leaders in Israel, the heads of families'**) at Gibeon. Gibeon was ten kilometres (just over six miles) north-west of Jerusalem in the territory of the tribe of Benjamin. It had been one of the royal cities before the Israelite conquest of Canaan and its inhabitants had deceived Joshua to ensure their survival (Josh. 9:3-6; 10:2). After the conquest Gibeon's central location made it a focal point for national gatherings. It had a **'high place'** where sacrifices were offered to the Lord, and **'God's Tent of Meeting'** was there (1:3).

As well as inheriting David's kingdom, Solomon inherited institutions of worship that went back to the time of Moses. These institutions were now to be renewed.

At Gibeon there was the tabernacle **'which Moses the Lord's servant had made in the desert'**. Also there was the **'bronze altar that Bezalel son of Uri'** had made (1:5). Bezalel was the skilled craftsman specially equipped by God to make the bronze altar and many other items used in the tabernacle. In Exodus 31:2-5 God told Moses, 'See I have chosen Bezalel son of Uri, the son of Hur, of the tribe of Judah, and I have filled him with the Spirit of God, with skill, ability and knowledge in all kinds of crafts — to make artistic designs for work in gold, silver and bronze, to cut and set stones, to work in wood, and to engage in all kinds of craftsmanship.' This is significant in view of the gift that God would later give to Solomon. He would be endowed with wisdom so that he could complete the temple.

There was one very glaring irregularity about the tabernacle that Solomon found at Gibeon. When Moses built the tabernacle, it contained both the bronze altar and the ark of the covenant. The ark (the symbol of the covenant between God and his people) was kept in the Most Holy Place, or the inner room of the tabernacle. When the tabernacle was built and commissioned, the Shekinah glory of God came down and rested over the ark (Exod. 40:34). The route to the ark went past the altar of burnt offering upon which the sacrificial animal died in the place of the sinner. There was no forgiveness, and hence no acceptance with God, apart from the shedding of blood on the altar of burnt offering. However, by the time that Solomon became king, the altar and the ark had been separated. The 'bronze altar' was at Gibeon while the 'ark' was in Jerusalem.

Something of the recent history of the ark is indicated by the short account in 1:4. After Hophni and Phinehas, the godless sons of Eli, the high priest, had lost the ark to the Philistines in battle (1 Sam. 4:1-11), it was eventually returned to Israel and by stages brought up to Jerusalem by King David (1 Chr. 13; 15). However, the ark was never returned to its rightful place inside the Most Holy Place of the tabernacle. There it symbolized the blessings enjoyed through the atonement accomplished by the shedding of the blood of the sacrificial substitute. It was Solomon's task to build a temple in which the altar and the ark would be brought together permanently. By this means the symbols of atonement and acceptance would be contained in close proximity within one building. It is important that believers see the clear link between what Christ has done for them and the privileges they enjoy.

Solomon entered into his life's work knowing that this had been mapped out for him by God. For hundreds of years God had been preparing for this work. Solomon was entering upon a path that was unknown to him, but not to God. He went up to Gibeon to accept the responsibilities of his office (charge over the people of Israel) and to seek God's blessing as he worshipped. **'Solomon went up to the bronze altar before the LORD in the Tent of Meeting and offered a thousand burnt offerings on it'** (1:6).

The testing of Solomon's character (1:7-10)

We often think that testing times are also difficult times. Bereavement, illness, unemployment, or strained relationships are, to be sure, times when a believer's faith is tested. However, times of blessing can also be times of testing. Some people will readily cry to God when they have no one else to turn to, but they very quickly forget about him after he has answered their prayers.

In these verses Solomon was tested by an offer from God: **'That night God appeared to Solomon and said to him, "Ask for whatever you want me to give you"'** (1:7). Solomon's response (recorded in 1:8-10) is significant for two reasons.

Firstly, *he acknowledged God's goodness* to him and his family before he went on to ask for more: **'You have shown great kindness to David my father and have made me king in his place.'** There should always be thanksgiving as well as intercession in our prayers. In fact it is a good discipline in our praying to consider how God has answered our past requests before we bring new ones.

Another reason why Solomon's response is significant is because of *the request he made* to God. It may be helpful to consider how we might have answered that question had it been put to us. It is interesting to listen to children talking about the presents they hope to receive, perhaps for their birthday or at Christmas. Some of them, in their naïveté, imagine that everything is there for the asking — and how their imagination runs riot! Doesn't our imagination similarly run riot as we think of the enormity of the offer that God set before Solomon — 'Ask for whatever you want'?

What might Solomon have asked for? In 1:11 God lists some of the blessings that the young king might have sought from him. Solomon might have asked for 'wealth, riches or honour', or 'the death of [his] enemies', or 'long life'. All of these were legitimate things for a king to seek. As the Lord's anointed over Israel, Solomon was responsible for maintaining the security and stability of his kingdom. The peace and prosperity of the nation were closely tied to his own well-being. There were also many unworthy requests that Solomon might have made, or he could have asked for good things with an unworthy motive, but he did not. Instead, he asked God for **'wisdom and knowledge'** (1:10).

Two words are used in this verse to describe the blessing Solomon sought from God. There are two sides to true biblical wisdom. The first word describes 'prudence', or 'shrewdness'. It is the ability to digest the facts and respond appropriately. This is wisdom undergirded by the moral law of God. We should never confuse this wisdom with the hard-nosed pragmatism of the calculating man of the world. According to Job 28:28, 'The fear of the Lord — that is wisdom.'

The second word that Solomon used means 'knowledge'. It describes information that has been amassed. Daniel and his young friends in the Babylonian training school had this kind of knowledge, for they were 'handsome, showing aptitude for every kind of *learning*, well informed, quick to understand, and qualified to serve in the king's palace' (Dan. 1:4). 1 Kings 4:29-33 draws attention to this aspect of Solomon's wisdom: 'God gave Solomon wisdom and very great insight, and a breadth of understanding as measureless as the sand on the seashore... He described plant life, from the cedar of Lebanon to the hyssop that grows out of walls. He also taught about animals and birds, reptiles and fish.'

Scripture brings together these two ideas to describe the wisdom that God gives (see Deut. 4:6; Ps. 49:3; Prov. 2:2; Isa. 11:2; Eph. 1:8). It is a wisdom that is interested in the world which God has created and in which we live. It is a wisdom that grapples with the problems of our world. Christians can take great delight, as Solomon did, in learning about the world of nature, and in applying their minds to understanding human nature. It is good to learn about these things, but as we study them we must recognize that without the gift of discernment none of our enquiries will lead very far. We need this wisdom from God.

Solomon recognized this at the beginning of his reign when he asked God for 'wisdom and knowledge'. He recognized his need for wisdom and he recognized that wisdom comes from God. 'For the LORD gives wisdom...' (Prov. 2:6). 'The fear of the LORD is the beginning of wisdom' (Prov. 9:10; cf. 1:7). 'If any of you lacks wisdom, he should ask God, who gives generously to all without finding fault, and it will be given to him' (James 1:5).

On the other hand, there is such a thing as human, or worldly, wisdom. Often it is purely pragmatic; people say that a course of action is wise simply because it 'works' for them. For instance, the world often tells us to 'look after number one', or that money in the bank is what gives our lives real security. This is the 'wisdom' that governs the lives of many people around us, but it is not God's wisdom. Divine wisdom (like the gospel itself) appears foolish to the world (1 Cor. 1:20-21), but it is far greater than the wisdom of the world, for it is vindicated by God's eternal judgement. God's 'Well done!' is bestowed upon those who live their lives according to his wisdom. This is the wisdom that Solomon seeks.

The purpose of Solomon's wisdom (1:10-13)

With a great sense of his own inadequacy for the task ahead of him, Solomon asked for wisdom (1:10). He asked God, **'Who is able to govern this great people of yours?'** At a similar point in his life, C. H. Spurgeon felt a similar sense of inadequacy. In 1854, at the age of nineteen, when he moved from his first pastorate in the small Cambridgeshire village of Waterbeach to the prestigious pulpit of New Park Street Baptist Church in London, he described his fear as follows: 'Who was I that I should lead so great a multitude? I would betake myself to my village obscurity... It was just then that the curtain was rising upon my life work, and I dreaded what it might reveal.'

Solomon was taking up the heavy responsibilities as the Lord's anointed king over the people of Israel. Perhaps only someone who has experienced the loneliness that comes with power can really understand what a burden this is. Shakespeare's King Henry V, on the eve of the Battle of Agincourt, describes the burden that rests on the shoulders of a king:

Upon the King! Let us our lives, our souls,
Our debts, our careful wives,
Our children, and our sins, lay on the King!
We must bear all. O hard condition,
Twin-born with greatness, subject to the breath
Of every fool, whose sense no more can feel
But his own wringing! What infinite heart's ease
Must kings neglect that private men enjoy!
(*Henry V,* Act IV, Scene I, lines 222-30).

The demands upon King Solomon were immense. He was following in the footsteps of David, the great warrior king, and would have to control David's fierce generals, who sometimes were too difficult even for David himself to handle (see 2 Sam. 3:39). He would have to work with wily politicians, cunning diplomats from powerful neighbours and a host of officials at home. Then, too, there were thousands upon thousands of ordinary people who would come to Solomon for justice and advice. The happiness of their daily lives would rest upon him.

As well as these demanding tasks, there was the work of building the temple in Jerusalem. This great work would dominate Solomon's reign. It was for this purpose that Solomon was made to sit on the throne of his father David. The temple would be no ordinary building, for it was the place where God would meet with his covenant people. Many of the blessings that God stored up for his chosen nation of Israel would be enjoyed within its walls. It was to be a building set aside for the worship of the true and holy God of heaven. Human wisdom alone would not be sufficient to plan and carry out the construction of such a building. It would require God's wisdom.

With this in mind Solomon prayed for wisdom. His desire for wisdom did not arise out of curiosity, or a yearning for praise. He sought wisdom so that he might do the work that God had laid upon him. The eyes of the whole nation were upon Solomon. Everything he did and said was seen by his people and the surrounding nations. As a result of his actions God would either be greatly honoured or greatly dishonoured; God's people would either be greatly blighted or greatly blessed. What a heavy burden to rest upon the heart of a young king! Is it any wonder he prayed, **'Give me wisdom and knowledge, that I may lead this people'**? (1:10).

The two marks of a pure heart are the desire to *do the right thing* and the desire to *do it for the right reason*. Solomon desired a good thing (wisdom from God) and he desired it for the right reason (so that he could do the great work that God had laid upon him). What an excellent start to his reign! This was a prayer that pleased God, and God showed his great pleasure by promising to answer it in abundance — **'Therefore wisdom and knowledge will be given you'** (1:12) — and by also promising Solomon the blessings he had not asked for: **'And I will also give you wealth, riches and honour, such as no king who was before you ever had and none after you will have.'**

The priorities of God's people must always be like those of Solomon — kingdom-centred priorities. Our Lord expressed it this way: 'Seek first [God's] kingdom and his righteousness, and all these things will be given to you as well' (Matt. 6:33). This will express itself in the prayers we pray, the plans we make, the ambitions we cherish and the way we set about our daily lives. Our first goal will be to be useful servants of God. And if our ambitions are in line with God's purposes, not only shall we see them being realized, but we shall enjoy far greater blessings than we even dared seek for in prayer.

The magnificence of Solomon's kingdom (1:14-17)

These verses describe how God did in fact bless Solomon. The tokens of the king's wealth and influence were impressive. They fall into four categories.

First of all, we are told that **'Solomon accumulated chariots and horses; he had fourteen hundred chariots and twelve thousand horses'** (1:14). In the book of Kings we read of the cities that Solomon constructed to accommodate this impressive military force (1 Kings 9:17-19; 10:26).

Secondly, we are told of Solomon's role in international trade. He was greatly helped by Israel's strategic location within the fertile crescent, between Egypt and Asia Minor. Egypt, lying to the south, is mentioned in 1:16,17 as a source for chariots and horses. **'Kue'**, lying to the north, is Cilicia in south-east Asia Minor. It too was a source from which Solomon's merchants purchased horses. It was also the route through which these merchants would have exported their chariots to the **'kings of the Hittites'**. According to one commentator, Solomon's position on the main trade routes between Asia and Africa 'made him the middleman in the contemporary arms race' — a very lucrative position indeed.

The third indication of the great blessing bestowed upon Solomon is the abundance of **'silver and gold'** in his kingdom. These precious metals have always been a symbol of national wealth, and even today central banks store bars of silver and gold in heavily fortified underground vaults as a safeguard for national currencies. The fabulous wealth of Solomon's kingdom is vividly illustrated by the fact that **'The king made silver and gold as common in Jerusalem as stones'** (1:15).

Then fourthly, the abundance of **'cedar'** wood is mentioned (1:15). This sturdy wood was a valuable building material. In the twentieth century it was accepted that 'Steel is power' because no powerful economy could prosper without a plentiful supply of such a basic building material. In Solomon's time a supply of cedar wood was an equally valuable commodity. That there was no shortage of cedar wood in Solomon's kingdom is made clear by the comment that cedar was **'as plentiful as sycamore-fig trees in the foothills'**. We should not confuse these 'sycamore-fig trees' with the stately timber-bearing trees of cool temperate climates. They were scrubby fig trees grown in great numbers in the Mediterranean lands for their fruit rather than their timber.

In 9:25-28 the Chronicler makes further reference to these material blessings enjoyed by Solomon, this time by way of retrospect rather than anticipation. God was faithful to the promises he made to Solomon during those early 'honeymoon' years of his reign. That faithfulness continued throughout the forty years that Solomon was king in Israel. These two accounts of the material blessings that God gave to Solomon constitute the introduction and conclusion to the Chronicler's account of his reign. In between comes what was most significant about Solomon's life — the construction of the temple in Jerusalem. Even Hiram, the heathen King of Tyre, could discern that the God of Israel had a special purpose in establishing God's kingdom: 'Because the LORD loves his people, he has made you their king' (2:11).

What Solomon has to teach us

We cannot all expect to be blessed exactly as God blessed Solomon; nor ought we to expect material blessing as a matter of course. Solomon certainly did not expect these blessings as a matter of course. He was a king in Israel and had a unique task to do for God (building the temple in Jerusalem) which required unique blessings. Today Christian believers are 'God's fellow-workers' (1 Cor. 3:9) in the building up of the church of Christ. This work takes forms that are often very different from the work given to Solomon and, as a result, 'The weapons of our warfare are not carnal but mighty in God for pulling down strongholds' (2 Cor. 10:4, NKJV). God, however, is no less faithful to his believing people today. Let us conclude with some lessons that we can learn from the blessings that prepared Solomon for his life's work.

1. God moulds our lives

We are all shaped by our backgrounds, as was Solomon. This brings with it many blessings, some handicaps and sometimes heavy responsibilities. Perhaps we may be daunted by the responsibilities and burdens that we have inherited and look back with resentment in our hearts. Solomon was frightened, but he was not resentful that God had placed a heavy responsibility on his shoulders. He recognized that God had brought him to that day, and so God is at work in our lives too.

2. God gives good gifts

Whether it was the wisdom that Solomon had asked for, or whether it was the riches, long life or honour that he had not requested, it was God who gave good things to Solomon.

'Every good and perfect gift is from above, coming down from the Father of the heavenly lights, who does not change like shifting shadows' (James 1:17).

3. We are stewards of the gifts God gives

Just as God gave Solomon wisdom for a reason (so that he might build the temple), so God gives us good things so that we might dedicate them to his service. Whether it is our money, our homes, our time, our talents, or our very lives — everything that God has given to us will be accounted for to him. Are you using God's gifts with wisdom? May God give us hearts to seek that wisdom to guide all that we do.

4. God bestows upon us the gift of wisdom through the Lord Jesus Christ

He is the most perfect demonstration of the wisdom of God. As the Old Testament unfolded its promises of a Messianic King, it was shown that this King would be even wiser than Solomon: 'And he will be called Wonderful Counsellor...' (Isa. 9:6). 'The Spirit of the LORD will rest on him — the Spirit of wisdom and of understanding, the Spirit of counsel and of power' (Isa. 11:2). Just as the Queen of Sheba 'came from the ends of the earth to listen to Solomon's wisdom', so many will come to the Lord Jesus because he is the 'one greater than Solomon' (Matt. 12:42).

The Lord Jesus demonstrated his wisdom by his words and actions all through his earthly life. Even from childhood he demonstrated the wisdom of God: 'And the child grew and became strong; he was filled with wisdom, and the grace of God was upon him... And Jesus grew in wisdom and stature, and in favour with God and men' (Luke 2:40,52). However, it is as the Redeemer that he most fully demonstrates the wisdom of God. By offering himself as the mediator between God and man he illuminates the divine wisdom of the gospel. 'For the foolishness of God is wiser than man's wisdom... It is because of him that you are in Christ Jesus, who has become for us wisdom from God' (1 Cor. 1:25,30).

How do we come to receive that wisdom? Solomon asked God, and God gave him the gift of wisdom directly and immediately. The people in turn went to Solomon for advice. Today Christ Jesus (the source of all wisdom for his people) gives the gift of wisdom through the Scriptures: '... from infancy you have known the holy Scriptures, which are able to make you wise for salvation through faith in Christ Jesus' (2 Tim. 3:15). By faith we are united to Christ. When we are united to Christ the regular ministry of his Word makes us wise. 'We proclaim him, admonishing and teaching everyone with all wisdom, so that we may present everyone perfect in Christ ... in whom are hidden all the treasures of wisdom and knowledge' (Col. 1:28; 2:3).

2.
Building the temple

Please read 2 Chronicles 2:1 – 4:22

King Solomon is renowned as the wisest of all men. His wisdom was a gift from God, given for a very special purpose. After describing how Solomon received his wisdom in chapter 1, the Chronicler goes on to describe in the chapters that follow how he used it to glorify God. There are many interesting episodes in the life of Solomon that are not recorded in Chronicles. This is not because these incidents were unimportant, but because the writer had a very specific goal in mind. He wrote this history to encourage the Jews who had returned from exile in Babylon as they worshipped God in the rebuilt temple.

Solomon's reign was the golden age of the Israelite kingdom, and his achievements were numerous, but the most important of them all was building a house for the Lord. This project had been in the planning stages for many years. The book of Chronicles has already described how Solomon's father, King David, brought the ark to its resting-place in Jerusalem and wanted to build a house for the Lord. The Lord's somewhat unexpected reply is found in 1 Chronicles 17:4-12: 'You are not the one to build me a house to dwell in... When your days are over and you go to be with your fathers, I will raise up your offspring to succeed you, one of your own sons, and I will establish his kingdom. He is the one who will build a house for me...' David accepted God's will and started to lay aside the resources that Solomon would need to build the temple. God himself completed Solomon's preparation by giving him the gift of wisdom and understanding. Now in 2 Chronicles 2-4 the work commences.

Ancient history records many impressive building projects. The pharaohs of ancient Egypt constructed great pyramids and tombs along the valley of the River Nile. Nebuchadnezzar was another great builder king, taking especial pride in the Hanging Gardens of Babylon. In terms of size Solomon's temple was rivalled by that of Herod the Great, who ruled Judea from 40–4 B.C. Herod started to reconstruct the Jerusalem temple in 19 B.C. and although the main structure was completed within ten years, work continued until A.D. 64. He built many other impressive public buildings in Jerusalem and Judea, including great fortresses at Herodion (where he removed a whole mountain in the process) and Masada (a citadel that still impresses all who visit its ruins today). All these building projects are of interest to historians and archaeologists, but the construction of the temple in Jerusalem is what captures the attention of the biblical historians. This was no ordinary building. It had a central place in the unfolding of God's redemptive plans.

The Chronicler's history sought to show the importance of the temple to God's people in the heyday of the Israelite kingdom. A nation that honoured God's house would in turn be honoured by God. The care and attention that were given to the building of the temple should also be devoted to the daily worship of Jehovah. In these chapters the Chronicler sought to show the people of Judah the importance of their heritage, and the temple was an important part of that heritage. The temple taught the people many lessons about their God and his dealings with them. It illustrated truths that never change. It was worthy of their interest — and it is worthy of ours!

The people involved in building the temple (2:1-18)

Solomon's plans are summarized in 2:1: **'Solomon gave orders to build a temple for the Name of the LORD and a royal palace for himself.'** In Chronicles we read nothing more about the building of a palace for the king, but we have an account of its construction in 1 Kings 7:1-12. It took thirteen years to build Solomon's palace, whereas the temple of the Lord was built first and took seven years to build (see 1 Kings 6:38). Matthew Henry gives a fitting comment on Solomon's order of priorities: 'It is fit that he who is the first should be first served — first a temple and then a palace... Those are the wisest men that lay out themselves most for the honour of the name of the Lord and the welfare of communities.'

To construct these buildings a large army of labourers was needed: **'He conscripted seventy thousand men as carriers and eighty thousand as stonecutters in the hills and thirty-six hundred as foremen over them'** (2:2). This was a huge army of workmen. The 'carriers' did the most menial kinds of manual labour. The 'stonecutters' were skilled labourers. They are described in the Hebrew text as 'those who hew out of the mountains'. Some take this as a reference to felling and trimming trees growing in the mountains, but most understand it as referring to quarrying stone out of the mountainside.

Solomon's building projects depended heavily on forced labour. 150,000 labourers were 'conscripted' into the royal work force (2:2). Most of these labourers were from Gentile backgrounds. **'Solomon took a census of all the aliens who were in Israel... He assigned 70,000 of them to be carriers and 80,000 to be stonecutters in the hills'** (2:17-18). These labourers are described in 8:7-8 as the descendants of 'the Hittites, Amorites, Perizzites, Hivites and Jebusites ... whom the Israelites had not destroyed'. Their contribution to the building of the temple was a conquest of sorts, for they bowed in service to Jehovah.

In time, many Israelites were conscripted into the bands of forced labourers and Solomon came to rely heavily upon them (see 1 Kings 5:13-14). This left a legacy of bitterness for Rehoboam to deal with, as we shall see in 10:3-4. However, in these verses the Chronicler refers to the Gentiles and their involvement in the building of the temple.

Solomon wanted the temple of the Lord to be perfect in every way, so he set out to find the very best of materials and craftsmen. He wrote to Hiram, King of Tyre, asking for **'a man skilled to work in gold and silver'** and other materials (2:7). This man would train Solomon's **'skilled craftsmen'** so that they might do their work better. This was the golden age of Phoenician craftsmanship; their craftsmen had centuries of experience in the delicate work of carving wood and precious metals and Solomon turned to them for the skills lacking among his own people. **'Send me also cedar, pine and algum logs from Lebanon...'** (2:8). Solomon wanted this timber from Lebanon because he knew that Hiram's workmen were **'skilled in cutting timber'**. He wanted **'plenty of timber'** because the temple was to be **'large and magnificent'**. Only the very best was good enough for the house of God (2:3-10).

Solomon's letter to Hiram explained why he wanted to build such a magnificent temple for the Lord his God (2:4-6). He told Hiram that Jehovah is the only God, and totally unlike other gods: **'Our God is greater than all other gods'** (2:5). Solomon was not ashamed to make exclusive claims for Jehovah in a way that seems almost offensive to modern ears, used to the more accommodating ideas of religious pluralism. Yet those same claims are the essence of the gospel (see John 14:6; Acts 4:12). Knowing that Jesus Christ is the only Saviour and that his gospel is the only way to God ought to make us more confident and compelling in our witness.

Solomon was aware that even his very best efforts would never be sufficient to contain the Lord of glory: **'Who is able to build a temple for him, since the heavens, even the highest heavens, cannot contain him? Who then am I to build a temple for him, except as a place to burn sacrifices before him?'** (2:6). This is a theme to which Solomon would return in his prayer of dedication after the temple had been built (see 6:18). This exalted view of God is taken up in other parts of Scripture (e.g., Isa. 66:1; Acts 7:48-49). The God of Israel is not limited to one nation or city, and certainly not to one building. Anything that finite men give to the Lord will be flawed and inadequate. That was true of Solomon's great temple, just as much as it was true of the temple that was built after the exile. However, God looks at the generosity of the heart rather than the outward grandeur of the gift. However limited our means may be, we should always give of our best to the Lord and he will be pleased with a 'cheerful giver'.

Solomon's reason for building the temple was not because God needed it to dwell in. No matter how grand its appearance, it could never be grand enough for God! The purpose for its construction is found in 2:6, where Solomon describes it as **'a place to burn sacrifices before him'**. The temple was to be a place where sinners would come and approach a holy God through the shed blood of the sacrifice offered in their place. The ordinances of worship that God had commanded are mentioned in 2:4: **'... for burning fragrant incense before him, for setting out the consecrated bread regularly, and for making burnt offerings...'** The building was to be beautiful because God's name was to be associated with it, but the building itself was merely a means to an end. The objective in view was that God should be glorified when his people gathered for worship.

Too often people lose sight of this important fact and the buildings in which they gather to worship become almost as important as God himself. In fact the building can become an idol. We always need to remember that God's greatness does not depend on the beauty or decor of the buildings in which his people worship. God does not need elaborate buildings. In fact he does not need buildings at all!

During the summer of 1843 there was a great movement of God in Scotland which came to be known as the Disruption. This followed a period of controversy within the Church of Scotland over the appointment of parish ministers. Put simply, the question was whether Christ Jesus would be free to rule his own church, or whether that authority would be usurped by the civil powers. When the General Assembly met in Edinburgh, 478 ministers and their elders left the Established Church to form the Free Church of Scotland. For many ministers and congregations this step involved great sacrifices, because the ministers had to leave their manses and the congregations had to give up their meeting houses. That summer nearly 500 new congregations gathered for worship throughout Scotland, many of them worshipping in rented halls, or barns, or even the open air. God blessed this faithful stand and there was a mighty movement of grace in the hearts of many within those congregations. Buildings where God's people can meet for worship and fellowship are useful, but they are not essential to the work of the kingdom. They should be carefully designed and well built, but they must never become expressions of pride and affluence. If they do, they have become idols in our thinking.

Hiram's reply is found in 2:11-16. Hiram was obviously impressed by Solomon's devotion to God. He saw that God was blessing Solomon: **'Praise be to the Lord, the God of Israel... He has given King David a wise son, endowed with intelligence and discernment, who will build a temple for the Lord and a palace for himself'** (2:12). Furthermore, he could see that Solomon had been given wisdom for the purpose of building the temple.

Hiram agreed to Solomon's request. As well as selling Solomon the timber he needed (2:15-16), he sent a skilled craftsman called Huram-Abi (2:13). The suffix *Abi* means 'my father' and may indicate that he was a master craftsman who had a 'family' of apprentices who would have looked up to him as a father figure.

Huram's tribal origin is noted. His **'mother was from Dan'** (2:13). Jewish people record their ancestry through their mother, so this made him an Israelite from the tribe of Dan. This was the tribe of Oholiab the son of Ahisamach, who was the skilled craftsman appointed to work alongside Bezalel son of Uri in the construction of the tabernacle (see Exod. 31:1-6). This link between Huram's work and that of Bezalel and Oholiab serves to emphasize the importance of the building work now in hand, for the tabernacle was being renewed to provide a place of God's own choosing to bless his people.

The employment of Gentiles in the construction of the temple was also a significant pointer to the future. When God established his covenant with Abraham he promised:

> I will bless those who bless you,
>   and whoever curses you I will curse;
> and all peoples on earth
>   will be blessed through you
>
> (Gen. 12:3).

Often the covenant people forgot that God's plans included a place for the Gentiles. 'This is what the LORD Almighty says: "In those days ten men from all languages and nations will take firm hold of one Jew by the hem of his robe and say, 'Let us go with you, because we have heard that God is with you'"'(Zech. 8:23). Three aspects of God's promises of blessing for the Gentiles are illustrated in this chapter.

1. Kings will come to the aid of God's people

This is an indication of how the whole world will come to be in submission to Christ. Rulers will be brought to bow the knee to him and serve the advancement of his kingdom. This is prophesied in many Old Testament passages. For example, in Psalm 72 we read:

> The kings of Tarshish and of distant shores
> > will bring tribute to him;
> the kings of Sheba and Seba
> > will present him gifts.
> All kings will bow down to him
> > and all nations will serve him
> > (vv. 10-11; see also Ps. 2:1-12; Isa. 49:7,23; 60:10).

We should pray for the day when, just as Hiram responded heartily to Solomon's appeal for loyalty and help, our earthly rulers will submit to the claims of a greater King than Solomon — King Jesus.

2. Gentiles will dedicate their wealth to the building of God's house

This again is a symbol of God's kingdom extending over all nations. The prophets spoke of gifts from the nations after the people of Israel returned from exile to rebuild the temple (Isa. 60:13; 61:6; 66:12; Hag. 2:6-9). The task of rebuilding would be expensive, but God is not short of resources because the nations of the world belong to him. Hiram, who gave timber and craftsmen for the building of the temple, was a forerunner of many more who would dedicate their wealth and talents to the service of King Jesus.

3. People will be drawn from all nations to serve God in the temple

The Gentile labourers of 2:2,17-18 came to carry burdens and to carve stone, but many others would come to the temple to pray and to worship the Lord (see Isa. 2:2-3; 56:6-7; Zech. 8:20-21). This promise was confirmed by our Lord (Mark 11:17) and came to glorious fulfilment on the Day of Pentecost (Acts 2:8-11). It is still being fulfilled today as the church's great commission to 'make disciples of all nations' continues. Christ Jesus is the foundation stone of a new temple, and believers are not just workmen but 'living stones ... built into a spiritual house to be a holy priesthood, offering spiritual sacrifices acceptable to God through Jesus Christ'. Through faith in Jesus Christ many who 'once ... were not a people' are now called 'the people of God' (1 Peter 2:5,10).

The place where God was to be worshipped (3:1-17)

The temple was the building where God would dwell. In 2 Chronicles 7 we read of the day when Solomon dedicated the temple and the glory of God came down like a cloud and filled the building. There is no greater privilege for the believer than being one of his redeemed and able to stand in his presence.

> One thing I ask of the LORD,
>   this is what I seek:
> that I may dwell in the house of the LORD
>   all the days of my life,
> to gaze upon the beauty of the LORD
>   and to seek him in his temple
>
> (Ps. 27:4).

The temple was the one place on earth that God was pleased to call his dwelling so that he might reveal himself to his people. The very details of its construction and layout were intended to teach the people about God. That is why God was so concerned about every detail of the plans for the construction of the temple. Let us now take a closer look at some of those details.

1. Its historical associations (3:1-2)

The temple was established on a site of God's choosing which had very significant historical associations. **'Then Solomon began to build the temple of the LORD in Jerusalem on Mount Moriah, where the LORD had appeared to his father David'** (3:1). Mount Moriah was the scene of two important events in both of which the death of a substitutionary sacrifice spared the lives of others.

On the first of these occasions Abraham had taken Isaac to the top of Mount Moriah to offer a sacrifice to the Lord (see Gen. 22). Unknown to Isaac, he himself was to be the sacrifice, according to God's command, until the Lord provided a ram to be sacrificed in his place: ' "Abraham! Abraham! ... Do not lay a hand on the boy" ... Abraham looked up and there in a thicket he saw a ram caught by its horns. He went over and took the ram and sacrificed it as a burnt offering instead of his son. So Abraham called that place The LORD Will Provide. And to this day it is said, "On the mountain of the LORD it will be provided" ' (Gen. 22:11-14).

On the same site, which had been a threshing-floor belonging to Araunah (or Ornan) the Jebusite, David offered a sacrifice to the Lord just as the angel of destruction was about to strike Jerusalem (see 1 Chr. 21:26). The lives of many Israelites were spared from destruction in a terrible plague. David cried out to God for mercy and offered a sacrifice to appease his anger. As a result of the sacrifice on the altar that David had erected there, the Lord restrained the destroying angel and spared his people.

The temple was built on this site to continue the work of atonement. It was to be a place where sacrifices were to be offered by sinners under the wrath of God. It was also a place where sinners were assured of forgiveness, because of the death of the sacrificial victim. Each one of these sacrifices pointed to an even greater sacrifice, which would also be made on a hill overlooking Jerusalem — the sacrifice made by Jesus Christ. He 'did not enter by means of the blood of goats and calves; but he entered the Most Holy Place once for all by his own blood, having obtained eternal redemption' (Heb. 9:12). He alone can rescue sinners from God's anger and offer them the forgiveness of sins. He is the fulfilment of all the hopes of the Old Testament. His sacrifice is linked to each and every sacrifice offered on that sacred site.

2. The approach to it (3:15-17)

As the worshipper approached the entrance to the temple, he would pass two pillars about sixteen metres high, capped with an ornamental decoration on top. These pillars were festooned with chains on which were pomegranates crafted out of metal. Pomegranates were a sign of fruitfulness, and the land into which God led his people was plentifully supplied with pomegranates and other fruits (see Num. 13:23; Deut. 8:7-9). Thus, as the worshipper entered the temple, he was reminded of the material blessings that God had given to his people, as was King David in Psalm 65:9-13.

These pillars were free-standing structures, rather than supports for the main structure of the temple. Free-standing pillars were common in ancient cities and were often dedicated to pagan gods, or to the memory of great men. This has led some commentators to suggest that these pillars were the first signs of the creeping influence of pagan worship in Solomon's reign. (For the development of this trend see 1 Kings 11:1-8.) However, this is unlikely at this stage, because Solomon followed strict instructions from God (1 Chr. 28:11-19) so that the temple he built might truly be an earthly copy of heavenly things (Heb. 9:23).

The great significance of these pillars can be found in their names they bore, **'Jakin'** and **'Boaz'**. The name 'Jakin' means 'He establishes.' The name of the second pillar means 'In him is strength'. It is interesting to note that this is the same name as that of Solomon's ancestor in the book of Ruth, who was such a tower of strength to Ruth and Naomi, at a time when they were in dire circumstances, by becoming their kinsman-redeemer.

The names of the pillars are symbolic of God who, by his great strength, establishes a way of salvation for his people. God himself was a pillar of cloud by day and a pillar of fire by night for his people during their journey through the wilderness. God strengthened them throughout the journey until at last he established them in the land (see Exod. 13:21-22; Num. 14:14). When Moses constructed the tabernacle, the Lord stood as a pillar at its door (Num. 12:5; Deut. 31:15). The worshippers of Solomon's day were reminded of God's faithfulness over many years as they approached the temple and passed these pillars.

3. *Its appearance inside and out* (3:3-9)

As the worshipper approached the temple, he would have been impressed by the beauty of the building. It was well proportioned, laid out in an orderly fashion and richly decorated. Its dimensions are given in verses 3-4 and 8 and they show that, although not a massive structure by modern standards, it had a geometric regularity. As Matthew Henry comments, 'The dimensions were given by divine wisdom.'

A great quantity of gold was used to decorate the temple: **'He overlaid the inside with pure gold'**, **'with six hundred talents of fine gold. The gold nails weighed fifty shekels'** (3:4,8-9). 600 talents of gold was the price that David had originally paid Araunah for the temple site and the wood and oxen needed to sacrifice to the Lord (1 Chr. 21:25). Nothing inside was left untouched by gold! **'And the gold he used was gold of Parvaim'** (3:6). Parvaim was in Arabia, and the gold that came from there was renowned for its fine quality. **'He also overlaid the upper parts with gold'** (3:9). Even the exterior structures of the temple (the roof, or the panelling where the roof met the walls) were overlaid with gold. This would have been a dazzling sight for pilgrims as they caught sight of the temple on their approach to Jerusalem.

Inside the temple, **'He panelled the main hall with pine and covered it with fine gold and decorated it with palm tree and chain designs. He adorned the temple with precious stones...'** (3:5-6). The craftsmen produced intricate work that must have been fascinating to the eye. When John the apostle saw a vision of the heavenly city he described it in terms that are reminiscent of the interior of Solomon's temple (see Rev. 21:18-21). Although most Israelites would never see this beauty for themselves, it was an important symbol of God's glory. They would read about it in the Scriptures. They would learn the lesson that only the very best is fit for God's service. We must not give to God gifts that cost us nothing. This had a ready application to the returning exiles who rebuilt the temple in Jerusalem. It presented a challenge to the following generations who worshipped in the temple and were tempted to bring worthless offerings to the Lord (Mal. 1:9-10). It is a challenge to us if we hold back our tithe to the Lord, or offer God our second-best, or worship him with our lips but not with our hearts. God expects the very best.

4. The sanctuary within the temple (3:10-14)

Inside the temple was a room that the ordinary worshipper never saw. It was called the Holy of Holies, or the Most Holy Place. Most of the priests never saw the inside of it either, except the high priest on the Day of Atonement. So these verses gave their readers a unique insight into the sanctuary: **'In the Most Holy Place he made a pair of sculptured cherubim and overlaid them with gold... They stood on their feet, facing the main hall'** (3:10,13).

Cherubim are heavenly beings whose beauty complements the glory of God. They are the inner circle of God's heavenly courtiers and, like the seraphim of Isaiah 6:2-3, they stand before God to worship him and do his bidding (Ps. 103:20-21). They stand while God sits, because he is worthy of all honour and they are his creatures. Scripture often speaks of God as dwelling between the cherubim (Ps. 80:1; 99:1; Isa. 37:16; Ezek. 10:1-22) because they have the special honour of heralding God when he reveals his glory. Just as a herald indicates the approach of someone important, so these cherubim tell us that God was pleased to dwell in this sanctuary.

The sanctuary was hidden behind a curtain. **'He made the curtain of blue, purple and crimson yarn and fine linen, with cherubim worked into it'** (3:14). This curtain represents the partial darkness in which Old Testament believers lived. They longed to know more of God's purposes (1 Peter 1:10-12) and to experience more of his presence, but they had to wait until the coming of the Messiah. Only when the Lord Jesus died at Calvary to offer the last and greatest sacrifice was this curtain torn open to allow sinful men to join with the angels in the presence of a holy God (Matt. 27:51).

The furnishings inside the temple (4:1-22)

This chapter describes the furnishings and tools that were used in the life and worship of the temple. Solomon was concerned that even these apparently trivial items should be prepared with a view to the glory of God.

The most important of all the temple furnishings is described first of all: **'He made a bronze altar twenty cubits long, twenty cubits wide and ten cubits high'** (4:1). Central to everything that happened in the temple was the provision of *atonement*. By the shedding of blood God's forgiveness and salvation were enjoyed. Everything that the priests and other Levites did in carrying out the rituals of the temple related back to this central truth. Upon this atonement rested every other blessing that God's people enjoyed.

After mentioning the altar the Chronicler goes on to describe the sea: **'He made the Sea of cast metal, circular in shape, measuring ten cubits from rim to rim and five cubits high'** (4:2). This was a large water-container which the priests used for ceremonial washing (4:6). Old Testament ritual laid great stress on the ceremonial *purity* of those who drew near to God (Exod. 30:19-21; 40:30-32). Yet the Old Testament also emphasized that a clean heart was just as important as clean hands:

> Who may ascend the hill of the LORD?
>   Who may stand in his holy place?
> He who has clean hands and a pure heart,
>   who does not lift up his hands to an idol
>   or swear by what is false.
> He will receive blessing from the LORD
>   and vindication from God his Saviour
>
> (Ps. 24:3-5).

The New Testament develops this theme: 'Come near to God and he will come near to you. Wash your hands, you sinners, and purify your hearts, you double-minded' (James 4:8; see also Mark 7:1-23; Heb. 10:22).

What, then, can make a person clean before God? We have an indication in the foundation upon which the sea rested: **'The Sea stood on twelve bulls, three facing north, three facing west, three facing south and three facing east. The Sea rested on top of them, and their hindquarters were towards the centre'** (4:4). These bulls represented the sacrifices brought by the twelve tribes of Israel as an atonement for their sin. Upon this atonement rests the cleansing of God's people.

Ritual cleansing was an external sign, but the spiritual reality of which it speaks is a deep and lasting change of heart. On account of this cleansing the apostle Paul was able to tell the Corinthian believers, 'You were washed, you were sanctified, you were justified in the name of the Lord Jesus Christ and by the Spirit of our God' (1 Cor. 6:9). If you are not yet a believer, pursue this cleansing with all your soul because without it you can never hope to enter the joy of God's presence. If you are trusting in the Lord Jesus, rejoice in his words of reassurance: 'You are already clean because of the word I have spoken to you' (John 15:3).

Other blessings were signified by the furnishings of the temple: **'He made ten gold lampstands according to the specifications for them and placed them in the temple'** (4:7). These lampstands shed *light* upon those who worked and worshipped in the temple. They represent the light that guides and directs the people of God. The Lord Jesus is the lampstand who gives light to the world, and in the shadow of the great lampstand in the temple he drew attention to his ministry: 'I am the light of the world. Whoever follows me will never walk in darkness, but will have the light of life' (John 8:12).

'He made ten tables and placed them in the temple...' (4:8). These tables held the shewbread, or 'Bread of the Presence', which was continuously on display in the temple and replaced with fresh loaves each Sabbath. This ritual spoke of *the grace that sustains in every situation*, just as the Lord provided manna for the people every day on their journey through the wilderness. The Lord Jesus also provides nourishment for our souls. He urges us, 'Do not work for food that spoils, but for food that endures to eternal life' (John 6:27). He is also the 'bread of life', and declares that 'He who comes to me will never go hungry, and he who believes in me will never be thirsty' (John 6:35).

When we study the temple furnishings we can see *the development of God's plans*. Compared with the furnishings of the tabernacle (built in the time of Moses), those of Solomon's temple were bigger and more numerous. The bronze altar, for instance, measured **'twenty cubits long, twenty cubits wide and ten cubits high'**, compared with three cubits by five cubits by five cubits for the altar used in the tabernacle (Exod. 27:1). Instead of one lampstand with seven branches which lit the sanctuary of the tabernacle (Exod. 25:31-40), there were **'ten gold lampstands'** in the temple. Instead of one table for the shewbread (Exod. 25:23), there were **'ten tables'**. Instead of twelve silver sprinkling bowls and twelve gold dishes (Num. 7:84), there were **'a hundred gold sprinkling bowls'** (4:8). The Chronicler records his amazement at the quantity of bronze used to furnish the temple: **'All these things that Solomon made amounted to so much that the weight of the bronze was not determined'** (4:18).

These figures show that Solomon's temple was, in material terms at least, an improvement upon the tabernacle that had preceded it. The whole period of the Old Covenant was a time of progressive development as God revealed, in carefully planned stages, more and more of his plan of redemption. It was a period of preparation for the gospel in Christ, when God, like a wise teacher, brought out 'new treasures as well as old' (Matt. 13:52). Yet even the temple was not perfect. For all its wealth and beauty, Solomon's temple looked forward to an even more glorious temple, which, according to our Lord's words, would be built in three days (John 2:19; Matt. 26:61; 12:6).

While the temple utensils show development and improvement, they also serve to illustrate *the continuity of God's plans*. The utensils used by the priests, such as **'pots, shovels, meat forks'**, **'wick trimmers, sprinkling bowls, dishes and censers'** (4:16,22) were essentially the same as those made for the tabernacle (Exod. 31:8-9; 35:12-14; 38:8; 39:36). They were used throughout the time of the monarchy and some of them survived the exile to be used in the second temple.

Although this second temple was less impressive than its predecessor, the furnishings and utensils used in its ministry were the same. According to Ezra 1:7-11 and 8:24-34, many of these treasures that had been taken by the Babylonians at various times when they ransacked Jerusalem (Dan. 1:2; 2 Chr. 36:7,10,18) were restored when the exiles returned to Jerusalem in 538 B.C. Although the setting and circumstances of those post-exilic generations were very different from Solomon's golden age, these utensils were a tangible link with the past. But they were more than just a link with the nation's history, for they reminded the people that the worship of God was to continue unaltered because the covenant of mercy was an everlasting covenant.

As in the days of Moses, when the tabernacle was being constructed, God did not leave the details of his worship to be dreamt up by men. Worship is far too important for that! God showed in great detail how the temple was to be furnished and how the sacrifices were to be offered. Detailed specifications were given to David as a guide for Solomon: 'He gave him the plans of all that the Spirit had put in his mind for the courts of the temple of the LORD and all the surrounding rooms, for the treasuries of the temple of God and for the treasuries of the dedicated things' (1 Chr. 28:11-12; cf. 28:19). Even the weight of gold to be used for all these articles had been specified in advance (see 1 Chr. 28:14-18).

Another lesson to be learned as we consider the furnishing of the temple is that *God's plans were detailed*. The construction and furnishing of the temple were regulated, right down to the last detail. The lampstands were made **'according to the specifications for them'** (4:7). This was true of everything connected with the temple. God gave creative gifts to men and women that were to be used for his glory, but even a craftsman like Huram did not have total freedom to indulge his imagination. This is a reminder that God knows how he wants us to worship him and he shows us in his Word how we are to go about it. We have no right to offer him that which he has not sought.

The construction of the temple was costly. This teaches us one final lesson: *redemption is costly*. Freedom from sin is blood-bought. It was purchased at a great cost, but it brings great blessing (1 Peter 1:18). The temple and its furnishings were a constant reminder of the cost, not just because of what it cost to construct and furnish, but because of the constant shedding of blood (Ezek. 36:38; Heb. 9:22). We do well constantly to remember how costly and precious our salvation is. At a lunch party hosted by a Christian businessman one of the guests asked, rather insensitively, how much the meal had cost. It was obvious that it must have cost a good deal to provide the meal, as only the best of food was laid on the table, and there was plenty of it. The reply was: 'Well, it is like the gospel, free to you!' Yes, our salvation is like that — free at the point of reception, but extremely costly to the provider. Never let its freeness at the point of reception blind us to what it cost our precious Redeemer.

3.
Final preparations

Please read 2 Chronicles 5:1 – 6:11

Putting together a jigsaw puzzle can be a frustrating process. The disconnected pieces seem to form no recognizable picture and one wonders if some of them might be missing. Yet as the puzzle comes together, piece by piece, there is a sense of achievement, and even excitement. Solomon must have known a similar excitement as he supervised the final preparations for the opening of the temple of the Lord in Jerusalem. The temple was a demonstration of God's covenant grace to his people. It had taken seven years to build (1 Kings 6:38) and had been many more years in the planning. Solomon had the joy of seeing the project finally brought to completion.

Completeness is the thread that runs through these chapters. Most importantly, it was God's plans that were being brought to completion. Many generations before either David or Solomon, God had told Moses that a house would be built for the worship of his name. This house would be an object lesson in the redemption that God provides for his chosen people. When the people of Israel wandered in the wilderness and first settled in the promised land, that house was a portable tent. This temporary measure would, in time, be replaced by a more permanent structure, located at a place which God would show his people (see Deut. 12:5).

This promise had encouraged David to plan the building of such a house. The king was distressed to see the ark of the Lord kept in a tent, while he dwelt in a palace of stone and cedar, but he had to be content with laying aside the building materials for the construction of the temple. It was his appropriately named son, Solomon, who completed the temple building project. Solomon's name means 'peace', or 'completeness'. Not only was Solomon a king whose reign was blessed with peace and prosperity, but during his reign a house of worship was built where God's people could experience the blessings of spiritual peace. So when Solomon gathered his people for the dedication of the temple he reminded them of the faithfulness of God. Not one of God's promises had failed! Each one had been brought to completeness. This is what the people were called to celebrate.

The finishing touches to the temple (5:1-10)

After the external structure of the temple had been completed, Solomon brought into the building **'the things his father David had dedicated — the silver and gold and all the furnishings — and he placed them in the treasuries of God's temple'** (5:1). Then Solomon called an assembly of the **'elders of Israel ... to bring up the ark of the LORD's covenant from Zion, the City of David'** (5:2). These dedicated furnishings and the ark of the covenant (dating back to the time of David and Moses respectively) were reminders of God's dealings with his people over many years.

The 'things ... David had dedicated' dated back to the time when David had wanted to build a house for the Lord, but the Lord had checked his ambition. In the meantime David had laid up treasure for Solomon: 'I have taken great pains to provide for the temple of the LORD a hundred thousand talents of gold, a million talents of silver, quantities of bronze and iron too great to be weighed, and wood and stone' (1 Chr. 22:14). These treasures came from David's personal wealth, the generous giving of God's people (1 Chr. 29:2-5) and the spoils of conquered nations: 'King David dedicated these articles to the LORD, as he had done with the silver and gold from all the nations he had subdued: Edom and Moab, the Ammonites and the Philistines, and Amalek. He also dedicated the plunder taken from Hadadezer son of Rehob, King of Zobah' (2 Sam. 8:11-12).

They were 'dedicated' to the Lord. The Hebrew word *(qadeshe)* that is used to describe David's action speaks of a solemn religious action. He 'sanctified' them to the Lord. This means that they were set apart from common use and given over to the service of the temple. David appointed stewards to make sure that they were not used for profane purposes (1 Chr. 26:26). There is no more fitting response to God's goodness to us than sacrificial obedience.

The 'ark of the LORD's covenant' had been kept in a tent in 'Zion, the City of David' ever since the time David had brought it up from Kiriath Jearim to the very heart of his kingdom at Jerusalem. It was the realization that the ark was kept in a tent while he lived in a palace (1 Chr. 17:1) that prompted David to enquire about building the temple in the first place. The ark's progress towards a fitting resting-place was begun by David (see 1 Chr. 13; 15), but brought to a conclusion by Solomon (5:2-10). There is a series of similarities between 1 Chronicles 13 and 15 and 2 Chronicles 5 which emphasize the fact that David's work is now being brought to completion.

Firstly, the setting is *a gathering of the leaders of all the tribes and the whole assembly of Israel* (see 1 Chr. 13:2; 15:3; 2 Chr. 5:2,3,6). This was a movement that united the tribes in acknowledging God's goodness.

Secondly, *the priests had consecrated themselves and the Levites led the praise of the people* (see 1 Chr. 15:12-24; 2 Chr. 5:11-13). After the tragedy of 1 Chronicles 13:9-10, there was a great concern to do everything as God commanded, so the ark was carried by the priests bearing it on two poles (1 Chr. 15:2,15; 2 Chr. 5:7).

Thirdly, *many sacrifices were offered* in recognition of God's abundant goodness to his people (see 1 Chr. 15:26; 2 Chr. 5:6). The record of 5:6 may seem rather extravagant: **'King Solomon and the entire assembly of Israel that had gathered about him were before the ark, sacrificing so many sheep and cattle that they could not be recorded or counted.'** Yet this abundance was entirely appropriate because they were acknowledging all the blessings of God's covenant that the ark symbolized.

On this occasion the ark came to its final resting-place: **'The priests then brought the ark of the LORD's covenant to its place in the inner sanctuary of the temple, the Most Holy Place, and put it beneath the wings of the cherubim. The cherubim spread their wings over the place of the ark and covered the ark and its carrying poles'** (5:7-8).

As we noted in the previous chapter, the 'cherubim' are the most glorious of God's angels who know most intimately the presence and glory of God. When God speaks to his people, his voice comes 'from between the cherubim' (Num. 7:89; Ps. 80:1; Isa. 37:16). As the ark was a symbol of God's presence among his people there was no more fitting place for it to stay. The Most Holy Place in the temple sanctuary was an earthly replica (see Heb. 9:23-24) of the throne room of God in heaven where the cherubim surrounded God as heavenly courtiers. In this central sanctuary of the temple God would make his presence known by filling the room with a cloud of glory. Images of these 'cherubim' were made at God's command (Exod.

25:18-22) as a constant reminder that God was present among his people in the temple.

Inside the ark were **'the two tablets that Moses had placed in it at Horeb'** (5:10). Horeb was the place **'where the LORD made a covenant with the Israelites after they came out of Egypt'**, better known as Sinai. The law of God constituted the terms of that covenant. The tablets were the blocks of stone on which the finger of God had written the Ten Commandments as a summary of his law. For those who are redeemed by grace God's law is not superfluous, but a guide for living and a daily reminder of the covenant bonds that bind the Redeemer and his people together.

At various times other reminders of God's covenant had been placed within the ark, according to Hebrews 9:4: 'This ark contained the gold jar of manna, Aaron's staff that had budded, and the stone tablets of the covenant.' The jar of manna reminded the people that God had fed them during their wilderness wanderings (Exod. 16:33-34). The rod testified to the fact that God had vindicated Aaron and his family when challenged by Korah and the others in Numbers 17:8-11. In Exodus 16:34 and Numbers 17:10, God had commanded that the jar and the rod be 'put ... in front of the Testimony', rather than actually in the ark. In Solomon's time only the tablets of stone were in the ark.

Psalm 132 (which may have been written when David brought the ark to Jerusalem, or when Solomon placed the ark in the temple) reflects on the significance of the ark as a symbol of God's presence. The psalmist saw the coming of the ark to its final resting-place as a confirmation of the covenant that God had made at Sinai all those years before. God is faithful to his covenant promises and he requires obedience from those who enjoy his goodness in every age:

Let us go to his dwelling place;
    let us worship at his footstool —
arise, O LORD, and come to your resting-place,
    you and the ark of your might...

The LORD swore an oath to David,
    a sure oath that he will not revoke:
'One of your own descendants
    I will place on your throne —
if your sons keep my covenant
    and the statutes I teach them,
then their sons shall sit
    on your throne for ever and ever'

                       (Ps. 132:7-8,11-12).

The priests who experienced God's faithfulness (5:11-14)

The Chronicler took a great interest in the ministry of the priests and Levites. This has always been acknowledged by those who have studied the distinctive features of this book. However, in the nineteenth century critical scholars of the Old Testament put forward the theory that, over a long period of time both during and after the exile, a group of priestly scholars produced a body of literature with a specifically liturgical slant. The theory goes on to suggest that this body of religious literature (known as the Priestly Code) was woven together with other documents to produce the Old Testament.

These claims that books of Scripture evolved from communities of men who wove together their diverse religious insights contradict the biblical teaching that the inspired books of Scripture were written by men who spoke as they were moved by the Holy Spirit (2 Peter 1:20-21). The effect of this documentary analysis of the Old Testament was to cast doubt upon its reliability and unity. If (as was alleged) parts of the Pentateuch were written by priestly historians after the exile, then Moses' claim to have written them is untenable, and with it fall the doctrines of biblical inspiration and inerrancy.

We need not, however, deny that the perspective of the whole book of Chronicles (together with Ezra and Nehemiah) is a *priestly* one. The life of post-exilic Judaism was dominated by the concerns of the priests and Levites. The Chronicler gives us a priest's-eye view of Solomon's temple. An example of this is found in 5:9, which describes the poles on which the ark was carried into the Most Holy Place. They 'were so long that their ends, extending from the ark, could be seen from in front of the inner sanctuary, but not from outside the Holy Place'. Only a priest serving in the temple could have made this observation.

This account emphasizes the role of the priests and Levites in bringing the ark and the treasures into the temple. 'The Levites took up the ark' (5:4). 'The priests, who were Levites, carried them up' (5:5). 'The priests then brought the ark of the LORD's covenant to its place in the inner sanctuary of the temple' (5:7). 'The priests then withdrew from the Holy Place' (5:11). The preparations of the priests are described in the latter part of 5:11. The music of the Levites is described in 5:12-13. Yet far from making Chronicles a book of little relevance for Christians today, this feature provides us with the key to unlocking the message of this passage.

1. The priests had a first-hand opportunity to witness the glory of God and his faithfulness to his people

They were like the civil servants who work closely with national leaders and who gain an insight into the affairs of state. The priests and Levites were able to see how God worked in the midst of his chosen nation. They saw sights that most people will never see, such as the cloud of glory descending and the smoke of the sacrifices and incense ascending to God (5:13-14). Every day they saw the signs and seals of God's covenant love as they were enacted in the ordinances of the Old Covenant.

As a result, the priests led the nation in the praise of God. They **'raised their voices in praise to the Lord and sang: "He is good; his love endures for ever"'** (5:13). These words were frequently used as a refrain in the psalms (Ps. 100:5; 106:1; 107:1; 118:1 are but a few examples). It is repeated twenty-six times throughout Psalm 136, which lists many instances of God's faithfulness in the history of Israel. We also find these words in 1 Chronicles 16:34, when David rejoiced that the ark had at last come to Jerusalem; 2 Chronicles 5:13, when Solomon brought the ark to its final resting-place in the temple; and 2 Chronicles 20:21, when King Jehoshaphat led the people into battle against the Moabites and Ammonites.

On account of their privileged position, the priests were equipped to lead the people in worship. They were in a position to observe that the Lord **'is good'** to his people. Their words rang true because they reflected their experience of God's grace. How important it is for those who lead the worship of God's people to know God's grace and greatness as they feed on his Word and walk with him day by day!

2. The priests served in a mediatorial role between God and the people

They represented the whole nation before God. It is the function of a priest to be a mediator between God and men. This was symbolized by the priestly procession in 5:12. As the Levites entered from the courtyard outside the sanctuary where the rest of the nation was gathered, they **'stood on the east**

side of the altar', facing the Most Holy Place where the cloud representing God's presence was to settle. Physically they stood between the people and the cloud.

These **'Levites who were musicians'** led the people in offering worship as a 'sacrifice of praise'. When the people brought a sacrifice to God they offered it through the priests. This was true, not just of the sin offerings and burnt offerings which were consumed on the altar, but also of the sacrifices of praise with which they worshipped God. At all times God relates to men through a mediator. Sinners need a mediator through whom they can come to God for salvation. When we pray, or gather for worship, or 'present our bodies as a living sacrifice', it is only because of the mediation of the Lord Jesus that our actions can ever be pleasing to God.

3. The priests consecrated themselves (5:11)

'All the priests who were there had consecrated themselves, regardless of their divisions.' The word 'consecrate' means 'to separate', and that was what the Israelites did when they consecrated themselves at Mount Sinai. God had told Moses that the people were to consecrate themselves before the Lord came down upon the mountain (Exod. 19:10). They did this by washing their clothes, abstaining from sexual relations and fencing themselves away from the slopes of the mountain.

When priests were anointed and ordained they were also consecrated, or set apart from ordinary work (see Exod. 28:41; 30:30). In consecrating themselves the priests recognized that they were sinful men and that everything they touched was defiled because of their sinful natures. That is why even our righteous actions are like 'filthy rags' before God (Isa. 64:6). Like the rest of the people, they came before God as defiled men and needed to be separated from their sin. Their ritual consecration reminded them of this spiritual truth, and fostered a broken and contrite spirit among them as they drew near to God.

4. The priests and Levites were dressed in fine linen (5:12)

This was another requirement of those who served as priests. Moses was told, 'Make sacred garments for your brother Aaron, to give him dignity and honour... Make them use gold, and blue, purple and scarlet yarn, and fine linen' (Exod. 28:2-5). The significance of the **'fine linen'** is explained in Revelation 19:8, which describes the beauty of the redeemed multitude of God's people: 'Fine linen, bright and clean, was given her to wear. (Fine linen stands for the righteous acts of the saints.)' These are the righteous actions that God's people are enabled to perform; they are the fruit of redeeming grace.

We are reminded that holiness of life is not an optional extra for God's people. Righteous actions are to be like a garment that covers our lives and marks us out as God's people. 'Let your light shine before men, that they may see your good deeds and praise your Father in heaven' (Matt. 5:16). 'Make every effort to live in peace with all men and to be holy; without holiness no one will see the Lord' (Heb. 12:14).

5. The Levites came together in harmony (5:13)

'The trumpeters and singers joined in unison, as with one voice, to give praise and thanks to the LORD.' Twice in this verse the Chronicler mentions the harmony that was evident in what they did. They 'joined in unison', 'as with one voice', to give thanks to the Lord. This musical harmony represents the deeper spiritual harmony that is always found in the hearts of those awakened by the Holy Sprit. Paul urged the Ephesians: 'Make every effort to keep the unity of the Spirit through the bond of peace. There is one body and one Spirit — just as you were called to one hope when you were called — one Lord, one faith, one baptism; one God and Father of all...' (Eph. 4:3-6). This unity is rooted in salvation. It ought to be a priority for all who love the Lord Jesus Christ, whose prayer was: 'May they be brought to complete unity to let the world know that you sent me and have loved them even as you have loved me' (John 17:23). This is the unity that God delights to bless (Ps. 133:1-3) and it was found among the priests who went up with the ark to the temple.

6. The priests united to acknowledge God's faithfulness to Israel (5:13)

'He is good; his love endures for ever.' As we have already noted, this is a phrase that was used many times to express thankfulness to God (see comment on 5:13 on page 55). Here it is used to express the delight of the priests that God was pleased to fill Solomon's temple with his glory. The temple was a constant reminder that God loved his people. The cloud of verse 14 is a powerful symbol that tells us much about the God for whom the temple had been built.

7. The priests were driven from the temple because of the cloud (5:13-14)

'The temple of the LORD was filled with a cloud and the priests could not perform their service because of the cloud, for the glory of the LORD filled the temple of God.'
This cloud was associated with *God's anger*. A holy God cannot bear to let evil continue in his presence. He will certainly

punish the wicked. When the people of Israel came into the promised land, in the time of Joshua, there was often a pall of smoke hanging over the land because of God's judgement upon the notoriously sinful inhabitants of the land (Josh. 8:20; see also Gen. 19:28). In Revelation 19:3 this smoke of divine judgement becomes an occasion of rejoicing for the redeemed as they see the city of evil destroyed in the final judgement: 'Again they shouted: "Hallelujah! The smoke from her goes up for ever and ever."'

This cloud was associated with *the mystery surrounding God*. At Sinai smoke hid the face of God so that the people could not see him. Only Moses and Joshua went onto the mountain and into the cloud so that they could speak with God; but to the people God was a hidden mystery, who revealed himself through a mediator. Both in Exodus 40:34-35 and in 2 Chronicles 5:11-14 even the priests were driven from God's presence when the cloud came into the Most Holy Place.

This cloud also represented *the awesomeness and majesty of God*. This aspect of God's character is not appreciated as it ought to be by many Christians today. Many churches focus almost exclusively on the love of God and have little to say about the fear of God. Yet it is impossible to know God as he really is without being awestruck by his infinite greatness. When God draws back the curtain of his mystery to reveal what is normally hidden from our gaze, we recoil because of our fallen humanity. That was the experience of Isaiah when he saw the Lord 'seated on a throne, high and exalted' (Isa. 6:1). When Peter, James and John saw our Lord transfigured upon the mountain, and heard the Father's voice, 'They fell face down to the ground, terrified' (Matt. 17:6).

There must come a moment in our lives when we stand still and realize our helplessness. All the work of our hands is fruitless unless the Lord is also at work to make our labours fruitful.

At times the Lord has to stop us in our tracks to teach us that lesson, just as these priests were stopped in theirs. Yet, far from being frustrated at their temporary idleness, we can be sure that they would have been rejoicing in the knowledge that God had drawn near to his people.

8. In Christ all believers enjoy the status and privileges of priests (1 Peter 2:5,9; Rev. 1:6; 5:10)

The privileges which the priests enjoyed (that is, being able to draw near to a holy God) are now enjoyed by all God's people, and not just by a privileged caste of priests. We should not view the event recounted in 2 Chronicles 5:11-14 as a mystical experience linked to Israelite sacrificial rituals, but as a gracious encounter between God and his people. This was an extraordinary manifestation of God's presence. Such was the intensity of God's glory that the priests 'could not perform their service because of the cloud, for the glory of the LORD filled the temple of God' (5:14). However, this revelation of the glory of God to the priests indicates the kind of God we serve and the impact that his presence makes upon sinful men (see Matt. 14:33; Luke 5:8; Rev. 1:17).

The king acknowledging God's faithfulness (6:1-11)

After the temple treasures had been put in their place and the priests had completed their ministrations, Solomon came forward to lead the assembly in prayer. He explained to the people the significance of the events that were unfolding before them.

Solomon began by acknowledging a great mystery: **'The LORD has said that he would dwell in a dark cloud; I have**

built a magnificent temple for you, a place for you to dwell for ever' (6:1-2). He was genuinely amazed that God should be willing to dwell in a temple built by man. These verses are a personal — almost private — reflection upon a theme to which Solomon would return in his prayer of dedication (see, for example, 6:18-19). The combination of God's majesty and his condescension took hold of Solomon's mind and he meditated upon it in prayer.

Personal communion with God involves taking delight in the truths that God has revealed to us. Godly meditation is not a process of emptying our minds, but of delving deeper into God's truth, wrestling with it and reflecting upon what we find. We are to take delight in these truths and allow them to transform our thinking.

In 6:3 Solomon turned to bless the whole nation: **'While the whole assembly of Israel was standing there, the king turned round and blessed them.'** Solomon then returned to the theme of God's covenant faithfulness, which came to a climax on that day. The language that Solomon uses in 6:4 is striking for the figures that he employs: **'Praise be to the LORD, the God of Israel, who with his hands has fulfilled what he promised with his mouth to my father David.'** Of course, Solomon knew that God is a Spirit and that he does not have hands or a mouth, as we have. The language is anthropomorphic. Solomon speaks figuratively of God having a mouth to speak to his people, and hands with which to bless them. God is not distant from the lives of his people; for his hand is continually upon them.

God's words and actions were the outworking of his sovereign plan. In this blessing Solomon lays stress upon that fact. God's sovereignty became, for him, a reason to praise God and an encouragement to trust God. That application is also made in the *Westminster Confession of Faith*: 'So shall this doctrine afford matter of praise, reverence, and admiration of God, and of humility, reverence and abundant consolation, to all that sincerely obey the gospel' (Chapter 3, 'On God's Eternal Decree', para. VIII).

Solomon indicates three aspects of God's decree that cause him to praise God.

1. God has chosen a place of worship for his people (6:3-6)

It had been the practice of Abraham, Isaac and Jacob to set up altars from time to time while God's people were still a single family. This privilege had been greatly abused over the years and the heads of many families introduced idolatrous practices into their worship. The construction of the tabernacle as a centralized way of worshipping God was intended to check this tendency to fall into sin. Yet even the tabernacle did not prevent do-it-yourself religion. Therefore God promised Moses that he would designate a central place of worship: 'You are to seek the place the LORD your God will choose from among all your tribes to put his Name there for his dwelling. To that place you must go; there bring your burnt offerings and sacrifices, your tithes and special gifts, what you have vowed to give and your freewill offerings' (Deut. 12:5-6).

Jerusalem was the chosen place to which the tribes ought to bring their sacrifices to the Lord. According to Psalm 122:4:

> That is where the tribes go up,
>   the tribes of the LORD,
> to praise the name of the LORD
>   according to the statute given to Israel.

Jerusalem was to be a unifying focus for an often divided people.

In every age it is important for God's people to come together for fellowship with each other and to draw near to God. Today there is not one special place which God has appointed as a sanctuary to hold believers together. God has appointed his Son as the sanctuary for his people. Wherever his truth is preached his people will be drawn together in true gospel unity. Being together as God's people is a blessing that focuses our attention on God our Saviour. 'Let us not give up meeting together, as some are in the habit of doing, but let us encourage one another — and all the more as you see the Day approaching' (Heb. 10:25).

2. God has chosen men to do his work (6:7-11)

Solomon reminded the people that David had been chosen by God to be their king: '...and I have chosen David to rule my people Israel' (6:6). David had been chosen by God to be a warrior and a king, but David had not been God's choice to build the temple that was about to be dedicated. **'But the Lord said to my father David, "... you are not the one to build the temple."'** Solomon was chosen by God to bring God's building plans to a climax: **'Your son, who is your own flesh and blood — he is the one who will build the temple for my Name'** (6:8-9). The name 'Solomon' is derived from a Hebrew verb meaning 'to complete'. Significantly, the same verb is used in 5:1: 'When all the work Solomon had done for the temple of the Lord was finished...'

God calls some to tear down while he appoints others to build his people up. He chooses some for work that requires patience and tenacity, while he selects others for tasks that call for rapid and creative action. It was not because Solomon was a great man that God blessed him. It was because God chose him to complete this great work that he blessed him with such singular giftedness. God chose him to do a great work and equipped him for his calling. It is important for us to find the place that God has appointed for us to serve. Whether that role is glorious or humble, we are to do our work with all the might that God has given us.

4.
A house of prayer

Please read 2 Chronicles 6:12-42

Times of crisis draw people to pray. In the dark days of the
Second World War, King George VI, at the behest of his
prime minister Sir Winston Churchill, led the people of Britain in national prayer, seeking God's deliverance from a
deadly peril. The king's words were broadcast over the
radio, into every home in the British Isles, and the nation
was united in prayer. Even in more secular times, people
will seek God in a time of crisis. They may know little about
the one to whom they pray and their prayers may be confused, but their religious instinct remains. The thanksgiving service after the Falklands War in 1982 and the funeral
service for Diana, Princess of Wales, in 1997 are examples
of this instinctive recourse to prayer.

Solomon prayed when the building of the temple was
completed. The dedication of the temple was a grand
national occasion in Israel, and it was natural that the king
should acknowledge God's mercies in prayer. Solomon represented the covenant people as he stood up to pray. His
prayer teaches us about prayer and about God himself.

How Solomon prayed (6:12-13)

1. Solomon prayed submissively

The postures he adopted tell us about his attitude as he drew near to God: **'Then Solomon stood ... and spread out his hands.'** Standing with his hands lifted to heaven emphasized the solemnity of the occasion. Solomon was approaching the mighty and exalted God. If it is appropriate to rise as a mark of respect to an older person, it is surely right to demonstrate respect for God.

As Solomon was about to open his lips in prayer, he **'knelt down before the whole assembly'** (6:13). It must have amazed the people to see their king, who bowed to no man, bowing on his knees before God. Many of them came to him for counsel, and some came to plead for mercy. In those days ordinary people came before their king on their knees. Yet Solomon acknowledged that his royal authority came from 'one greater than Solomon', the 'King of kings'. As he prayed, Solomon opened, or **'spread out his hands towards heaven'** (6:13) to receive whatever the Lord would give. He was saying, 'Your will be done, for it is always good.'

2. Solomon prayed through a mediator

'Solomon stood before the altar' (6:12). The altar was central to everything that took place in the temple. The priests ministered 'before the altar' and the people came to offer their sacrifices upon the altar. So too, Solomon's prayer was offered 'before the altar'.

He stood on a **'bronze platform'** that had been specially constructed for the occasion and **'placed ... in the centre of the outer court'**. It stood between 'the courtyard of the priests' and 'the large court' (4:9) where the worshippers would gather with their offerings. Solomon took care not to trespass on the duties of the priests who ministered *at* the altar (as Uzziah would later do, see 26:16-18). After the priests had sacrificed the burnt offerings Solomon took his stand *before* the altar. His work of intercession followed their work of mediation. This is the essential prelude to every prayer. Before we can be heard by God, the way must be opened by atonement (Heb. 10:19-22). That is why our every prayer is to be offered through our great High Priest, the mediator who has opened for us that 'new and living way' of coming to our heavenly Father.

3. Solomon prayed on behalf of the whole community

This was corporate prayer. Twice in 6:12-13 we find the phrase, **'the whole assembly of Israel'**. The bronze platform was set up in the outer courtyard to make Solomon visible as the people's spokesman. It placed him 7½ feet (or 2.3 metres) above the people, and even when he knelt to pray all who were there could see him kneeling and hear the words of his prayer.

Private prayer is a very important part of the life of the believer. It is encouraged by our Lord's example (Matt. 14:23; Mark 1:35) and by his command (Matt. 6:5-13). Congregational or corporate prayer is also commanded by our Lord. This is clearly in view when our Lord taught his disciples to pray, '*Our* Father in heaven'. From this the *Westminster Shorter Catechism* drew the lesson 'that we should pray with and for others' (Answer to Question 100). In corporate prayer one person prays aloud, but the whole congregation prays with him. **'Hear the supplications of your servant and of your people Israel when they pray towards this place'** (6:21).

The ministry of leading congregational prayer is a very important one among God's people, for by this means the thoughts of many individuals are brought together like the various threads which make up a tapestry. The petitions of many believers are bound together like many hands knocking on heaven's door. This was Solomon's important ministry when he called the whole nation together for prayer.

4. Solomon prayed heavenwards

He **'spread out his hands towards heaven'** (6:13). His opened and outstretched hands were an acknowledgement of need. In holding out his opened hands towards heaven Solomon was drawing the people's thoughts beyond the temple, its builders and the worshippers. His focus was on the God who dwells in heaven. What follows in this chapter is not a sermon directed to the people, but a prayer addressed to God. R. C. Sproul has described secularism (the mindset of many people today) as the belief that 'What matters is now and only now. All access to the above and beyond is blocked. There is no exit from the confines of this present world.' Solomon's prayer and the actions that accompany them are the perfect antidote to secularism. His whole heart is directed to 'the above and beyond'.

Solomon really did expect God in heaven to hear his prayer and act in response to it. Eight times in his prayer he pleads with the Lord to **'Hear from heaven and act'** (6:23; see also 6:21,25,27,30,33,35,39). Prayer requires a heavenly mindset. We are to have a lively awareness of eternal realities that transcend time and space. In prayer we enjoy fellowship with God, who is eternal and infinite. We ask him to bring heavenly influences to bear upon the day-to-day activities of our lives. If not, are we really praying to the God of heaven? Could it be that we are just musing within our hearts? Solomon's prayer was expectant prayer! Solomon's action in holding up his hands shows that he was waiting for an answer from God in heaven.

Why Solomon prayed (6:14-21)

After preparing himself, Solomon opened his lips to speak to God. His words were not a matter of form, well rehearsed for a great national occasion. They were reverent, but they were also personal and direct. Solomon was speaking to a God whose blessings he had often enjoyed, and he expressed his great confidence that God would hear his prayers and answer them.

In the opening verses of this prayer Solomon explains the reasons that had prompted him to lead the nation in prayer.

1. Who God is

God is unique, for **'There is no God like you in heaven or on earth'** (6:14). No other god is able to hear and answer prayer. The Hebrew Bible uses a very interesting word to describe the heathen gods. The word *hebel* means 'mist' or 'vapour'. It describes something which appears to exist, but which upon closer examination disappears as rapidly as a morning mist. These gods are nothing more than a figment of the imagination:

> They know nothing, they understand nothing;
> > their eyes are plastered over so that they cannot see,
> > and their minds closed so that they cannot understand
> > > > > > (Isa. 44:18).

Elijah taunted the prophets of Baal as they danced around his altar on Mount Carmel, but their prayers elicited no response: 'Perhaps he is deep in thought, or busy, or travelling. Maybe he is sleeping and must be awakened' (1 Kings 18:27). The God of Israel is unique because he is able to hear and to see and to answer the prayers of his people.

2. What the Lord has done

The Lord had made a covenant with his people. Solomon acknowledged the Lord as the one **'who keep[s] your covenant of love with your servants who continue wholeheartedly in your way'** (6:14-17). In these words Solomon brings together two aspects of God's covenant of mercy. On the one hand, the covenant is unconditional, for it is founded upon God's sovereign mercy, which is freely given. God makes promises to his chosen people simply because he is merciful. On the other hand, the covenant is conditional in its application, for there must be a willing response to God's mercy. God expects wholehearted faithfulness, not as a way of earning his favour, but as a way of continuing in his mercies. When men and women faithfully claim the promises of God's covenant they will never be let down.

Solomon thought back to God's promise to his father David: **'You have kept your promise to your servant David my father'** (6:15). Solomon thought of the promise to David that **'You shall never fail to have a man to sit before me on the throne of Israel'** (6:16) and that one of his sons would build a temple for the Lord. He saw that promise fulfilled in this own lifetime: **'You have kept your promise to your servant David my father; with your mouth you have promised and with your hand you have fulfilled it — as it is today.'** Everything that Solomon saw around him that day — the royal robes he wore, the palace in which he lived, the temple in which he worshipped, the priests and the sacrifices and the people willingly assembled — all this was a reminder that God keeps his promises.

There were many more promises that God would keep. When we move into verses 22-39 (which is the main section of this prayer) Solomon recounts those promises. However, lest anyone should think that Solomon's prayers have become too bold, here he explains why he is so bold in making these requests. God has already demonstrated that he is abundantly faithful to all his many promises: **'And now, O Lord, God of Israel, let your word that you promised your servant David come true'** (6:17).

3. The pledge that God has given (6:18-20)

In these verses Solomon answers a pressing question: **'But will God really dwell on earth with men?'** Sometimes people ask the question: 'Why bother praying at all? Why should God ever listen to such an insignificant person as me?' Do you ever secretly doubt that your prayers are heard? Many Christians go through periods when they feel that their prayers are not heard. It can be helpful for such struggling believers to know that they are not the only ones to be assailed by such doubts.

Perhaps some of those in the assembly gathered before Solomon doubted that the prayers offered in this newly built temple would be heard. In these verses Solomon echoed their question: **'But will God really dwell on earth with men? The heavens, even the highest heavens, cannot contain you. How much less this temple that I have built!'** (6:18). They were asking, 'Will the great God of heaven come to dwell in this temple so that he will hear our prayers?' Solomon acknowledges that God could not be contained in a temple built by mere men. This has often been acknowledged by those who knew something of the majesty of God (see 2:6; Ps. 50:9-12; Isa. 40:16; 66:1; Acts 7:49-50).

The significance of the temple was that it was the one place on earth where God had promised to meet with his people. **'May your eyes be open towards this temple day and night, this place of which you said you would put your Name there'** (6:20). This meant that God associated himself and his glory with the place and with the worship that was offered there. The magnificence of the building pointed to God's heavenly majesty. The construction of such a building was a visible symbol that God was interested in the affairs of people on earth. The temple itself was a pledge that God would listen to the prayers of his people. Solomon took that pledge to heart when he prayed, **'May your eyes be open... May you hear the prayer your servant prays towards this place'** (6:20). Solomon was assured that **'... your servant is praying in your presence'** (6:19).

4. The forgiveness that God offers

'Hear the supplications of your servant and of your people Israel when they pray towards this place ... and when you hear, forgive' (6:21). When God hears the prayers of his people he is moved to respond to them. 'If we confess our sins, he is faithful and just and will forgive us our sins and purify us from all unrighteousness' (1 John 1:9). 'This is the confidence we have in approaching God: that if we ask anything according to his will, he hears us' (1 John 5:14). God hears the prayers of his people in the way that parents hear the cries of their infants. Even in a room full of crying children a mother will recognize the cry of her own child, and will not rest content within herself until she has put right what is upsetting the infant. This was how God listened to the cry of the Israelites while they were slaves in Egypt: 'I have heard them crying out because of their slave drivers, and I am concerned about their suffering. So I have come down to rescue them' (Exod. 3:7-8).

What a blessed linkage between God's hearing the prayers of his people and God's initiative to relieve their distress! Divine interest leads to divine action. **'Hear from heaven, your dwelling-place; and when you hear, forgive'** (6:21). The prayer that God listens to is the prayer of a broken and contrite heart. It must include confession of sin, because 'There is no one who does not sin' (6:36). Many of the situations that Solomon would go on to mention in the rest of his prayer were instances of disaster following as a result of sin. Yet when God's people acknowledge their sin they find that he is a forgiving God.

The Hebrew word which the Chronicler uses to describe God's forgiveness is *salah*. In the Old Testament it is used only with reference to God's pardon for sinners. In Exodus 34:9 and Numbers 14:19-20 it describes how God acted in two of the darkest moments of Israel's history. The heart of the gospel is that the same gracious Lord is still willing to forgive:

> Let the wicked forsake his way
>> and the evil man his thoughts.
> Let him turn to the LORD, and he will have mercy on
>> him,
>> and to our God, for he will freely pardon
>>>> (Isa. 55:7).

> If you, O LORD, kept a record of sins,
>> O LORD, who could stand?
> But with you there is forgiveness;
>> therefore you are feared
>>>> (Ps. 130:3-4).

As a result Solomon was able to pray that God would 'hear ... and ... forgive'.

When the people would pray (6:22-40)

It is often easier to talk about praying than actually to pray. This is especially true when the situations about which we pray are particularly unpromising. It is interesting to consider the sort of situations in which Solomon envisaged that future generations would come to the temple to pray. He prayed that God would hear them, and as he did so he applied the principles of prayer that he had just outlined to seven very testing situations. These were situations in which the perseverance of a child of God would be tested severely. Solomon described these situations in turn and followed them with the plea to God that he would **'hear from heaven'** and act accordingly.

1. Taking judicial oaths (6:22-23)

Every legal system has ways of resolving 'hard cases', and the Mosaic law listed several in Exodus 22:1-15 (a passage which governed civil disputes over property). It was laid down that if an animal died in the custody of another person and there was no way of either proving or denying misconduct, then, 'The issue between them will be settled by the taking of an oath before the Lord that the neighbour did not lay hands on the other person's property. The owner is to accept this, and no restitution is required' (Exod. 22:11). This is the oath referred to here in 6:22. It would be taken in the temple and the matter would be laid before the Lord. Both parties would pray that God would bring judgement on any party that swore deceitfully, thus **'repaying the guilty by bringing down on his head what he has done'**. Both parties could accept the justice of this resolution because they were assured that the Judge of all the earth would assuredly do what was right (see Gen. 18:25).

2. Defeat in war (6:24-25)

This happened many times in the history of Israel, and the book of Judges contains many examples of defeat followed by repentance and deliverance. Solomon summarized the principle: **'When your people Israel have been defeated by an enemy because they have sinned against you and when they turn back and confess your name ... then hear from heaven and forgive...'** Such distress was often the Lord's way of bringing sinners to repentance. The same can be said of those who will not listen to the preaching of the gospel. Eventually they must 'heed the rod and the One who appointed it' (Micah 6:9).

3. *Drought* (6:26-27)

Drought is a recurring problem in Bible lands and it can bring untold suffering to whole communities. Solomon clearly saw God's hand in such disasters: **'When the heavens are shut up and there is no rain because your people have sinned against you...'** On other occasions God told his people that drought was his way of punishing them (see 1 Kings 17:1; Joel 1:10-11) and that their unaided efforts would bring little relief. Only the Lord who hears and answers prayers could open the windows of heaven to bring rain (see Deut. 28:12; James 5:18). Solomon was confident of God's power to answer such prayers and to relieve the people of their suffering: **'Teach them the right way to live, and send rain on the land that you gave your people for an inheritance.'**

4. *Natural disaster* (6:28-31)

Solomon has in view a range of natural disasters that might follow in the wake of drought to make a bad situation worse. **'When famine or plague comes to the land, or blight or mildew, locusts or grasshoppers, or when enemies besiege them in any of their cities, whenever disaster or disease may come...'** These disasters would come upon Israel because they were slow to learn from God's chastisements. Sometimes God brings disaster after disaster upon sinners because they are slow to recognize the sinfulness of their actions. Saul, the proud Pharisee, kicked for a long time against the goads, before he humbled himself before the Lord Jesus (Acts 26:14). Only after he had lost everything by squandering his wealth in the 'distant country' did the prodigal son 'come to his senses' and return to his father (Luke 15:13,17).

According to Solomon, we see that it is only when **'each one [is] aware of his afflictions and pains'** (6:29) that he will spread out his hands towards this temple. Only when he is fully aware of the evil and destructiveness of sin will the sinner repent. Often it takes the painful experience of chastening to realize the glorious purpose outlined in 6:31: **'so that they will fear you and walk in your ways all the time they live in the land that you gave our fathers'**.

5. Foreigners come to the Lord (6:32-33)

Post-exilic Judaism (that of the generation for whom the Chronicler compiled this history) was a proselytizing, missionary faith. This missionary vision was encouraged by prophecies of the nations coming to the Lord (see Isa. 19:24-25; 60:3,10; Zech. 8:20-22). Significantly, too, Isaiah described the temple as a house of prayer for all nations:

'... for my house will be called
   a house of prayer for all nations.'
The Sovereign Lord declares —
   he who gathers the exiles of Israel:
'I will gather still others to them
   besides those already gathered'

(Isa. 56:7-8).

Solomon describes these 'others' who will be gathered as 'foreigners': **'As for the foreigner who does not belong to your people Israel but has come from a distant land because of your great name and your mighty hand and your outstretched arm...'** (6:32). The Hebrew word for 'foreigner' describes one who goes to live as an alien in a strange land. In the years after the exile many Gentiles were drawn to the faith of the Jews by its focus on one almighty God (as opposed to many petty gods) and moral purity (as opposed to pagan debauchery). How would these foreigners be received by pious Jews?

This question was not satisfactorily answered until the New Testament. The apostle Paul described the condition of the Gentiles: 'At that time you were separate from Christ, excluded from citizenship in Israel and foreigners to the covenants of promise, without hope and without God in the world.' Paul then went on to speak of their acceptance in Christ: 'Consequently you are no longer foreigners and aliens, but fellow-citizens with God's people and members of God's household' (Eph. 2:12,19). Yet, amazingly, speaking a thousand years before Paul, Solomon talks of their being accepted: **'... when he comes and prays towards this temple, then hear from heaven, your dwelling-place, and do whatever the foreigner asks of you, so that all the peoples of the earth may know your name and fear you.'**

6. Going to war (6:34-35)

These verses describe the nation of Israel on the offensive rather than on the defensive. Not only in times of disaster, but also in times of national expansion, they were to look towards the temple and seek the Lord's blessing. It was not every military venture that God would bless in answer to prayer, but only those directed by the Lord himself: **'When your people go to war against their enemies, wherever you send them...'** King Jehoshaphat saw the importance of seeking the Lord in such a situation (18:6; 20:6-12). The Reubenites and the other Transjordan tribes knew such help from the Lord when they went up to possess the land at the time of the conquest: 'God handed the Hagrites and all their allies over to them, because they cried out to him during the battle. He answered their prayers, because they trusted in him' (1 Chr. 5:20). Similarly, our prayers for God's blessing will be assured of a positive answer only when we are in submission to God's will.

7. Captivity and exile (6:36-40)

The far-off prospect of exile was the context in which Solomon developed the themes of sin and repentance. Sin is a universal fact: **'For there is no one who does not sin'** (6:36; see also Rom. 3:23). It is primarily directed against God: **'when they sin against you'** (see Ps. 51:4). And it provokes God to holy anger and retribution: **'... and you become angry with them and give them over to the enemy, who takes them captive to a land far away...'**

Solomon applied these principles to the nation in exile. His words had a particular relevance to those whose task it was to rebuild the temple and the city of Jerusalem after the exile. Even though the city might be destroyed, its people deported and the temple in ruins, there was a promise to be claimed: **'When they sin against you ... and you ... give them over to the enemy who takes them captive ... and if they have a change of heart in the land where they are held captive, and repent and plead with you in the land of their captivity and say, "We have sinned, we have done wrong and acted wickedly" ... then from heaven, your dwelling-place,**

**hear their prayer and their pleas, and uphold their cause.
And forgive your people, who have sinned against you.'**
This was the climax of Solomon's prayer.

The only way to avoid God's anger is repentance, which is
described in 6:37 as 'a change of heart'. Repentance is more
than a change of mind resulting from a pang of regret. It is a
new way of thinking that God infuses into the sinners by means
of a total transformation. As a result of regeneration the newly
born child of God will plead to the Lord for mercy. He will
acknowledge his wrongdoing, and totally renounce it. When
God hears such prayers, his mercy freely flows to restore those
that are cast away in exile.

By way of summary, there are two lessons we can learn
from Solomon's prayer.

First of all, *God's pledges do not make our prayers redundant.* God's promises encouraged Solomon to pray. In the seven
situations listed in 6:22-40 Solomon reminded the nation of
the promises that God had made to Israel. God knew the needs
of his people even before they brought them to him. He knows
the desires of their hearts: **'For you alone know the hearts
of men'** (6:30). Yet this does not take away the urgency of
our prayers. Men and women 'should always pray and not
give up' (Luke 18:1). This is because the mercies of God require a covenant response from us. God is faithful to his promises when we claim them in our prayers. We should not overlook the short but very important word **'if'** in 6:38.

Throughout this prayer Solomon has emphasized God's
mercy. God is willing to forgive sinners, but are you willing to
repent? God is willing to bless his people, but are you willing
to plead for this blessing? An exalted view of God will always
lead to fervent praying. This is how C. H. Spurgeon described
the praying of the New Park Street congregation in London

during a time of spiritual awakening: 'Every man seemed like a crusader besieging the New Jerusalem, each one appeared determined to storm the Celestial City by might of intercession; and soon the blessing came upon us in such abundance that we had not room to receive it.' May the Lord find more of such praying among his people today!

Then secondly, *our failings make prayer essential.* There is no greater block to effective prayer than unacknowledged or unrepented sin (Ps. 66:18). Yet Solomon did not allow any room for spiritual defeatism in his thinking. Some will plead their unworthiness as an excuse for not exerting themselves in prayer before God. In 2 Chronicles 6:36 we find one of the great acknowledgements of human sinfulness in the Scriptures. Yet far from being a reason for hiding from God and neglecting intercessory prayer, this truth spurred on national repentance. In all the situations that Solomon surveyed in his prayer there was sin to be acknowledged. Yet the appropriate response was prayer offered to God, towards his holy place.

Conclusion (6:41-42)

Solomon concluded his prayer with a paraphrased version of Psalm 132:8-10. This psalm had a personal significance for him. Solomon himself was a living fulfilment of the promises in verses 11-12 that David would have a son to sit upon his throne, and in verses 13-14 that the Lord would make his dwelling with those who keep his covenant. The portions of Psalm 132 which Solomon quotes in 6:41-42 are a direct appeal to God to vindicate the theology which undergirded his prayer throughout.

Solomon appealed to the Lord to make his dwelling-place within the temple that had just been dedicated as a house of prayer: '**Now arise, O LORD God, and come to your resting-**

place, you and the ark of your might' (6:41). The presence of the ark in the temple (a symbol of God's presence among his people) was a reminder that God hears the prayers of those who cry out to him. Often God's people would mourn before God in prayer. They would mourn when they were afflicted by drought, disaster and captivity. But after they had prayed they would rise from their knees and rejoice. Solomon looked forward to answered prayer and the rejoicing that follows: **'May your priests, O LORD God, be clothed with salvation, may your saints rejoice in your goodness'** (6:41).

In particular, Solomon rejoiced at the promise of the Messiah: **'O LORD God, do not reject your anointed one. Remember the great love promised to David your servant'** (6:42). David was the Lord's anointed (or messiah). David's son (who would sit upon his throne and build a temple for the Lord) would also be anointed as a messiah. Yet this is a reference to the divine Messiah, the Lord Jesus Christ. All God's promises are fulfilled in him, and to him are given 'the sure mercies of David'.

Commentators differ over the best translation of the words at the end of 6:42. Some translate the phrase as, 'Remember David's faithfulness to God', while others translate it as 'Remember God's faithfulness to David.' The latter is preferable because the constant theme of Solomon's prayer has been God's faithfulness to the promises he has made to his servants. This continues right to the petition at the end of 6:42, where the prepositions used are significant. Solomon pleads that God would not turn his face *from* his anointed one, but would remember his mercies *towards* his servant. Hence the translation: **'Remember the great love promised to David your servant.'**

We find the same phrase again in Isaiah 55:3-4, which refers to the divine initiative of mercy to David, the chosen leader of God's people:

Give ear and come to me;
   hear me, that your soul may live.
I will make an everlasting covenant with you,
   my faithful love promised to David.
See, I have made him a witness to the peoples,
   a leader and commander of the peoples.

Nothing can diminish the importance of our faithfulness to God. Solomon has taken pains to call God's people to be faithful and fervent in prayer. In his letter James reminds us of this call: 'Therefore confess your sins to each other and pray for each other so that you may be healed. The prayer of a righteous man is powerful and effective' (James 5:16). So too does Paul: 'Pray continually; give thanks in all circumstances, for this is God's will for you in Christ Jesus' (1 Thess. 5:17-18). But this is not the note upon which Solomon's prayer begins and ends!

The divine initiative of grace was to the fore in Solomon's mind as he prayed to God back in 6:6, and it still is here in 6:41-42. This is the truth that he left in the minds of the people of Israel as his voice fell silent. He leaves us to ponder the marvellous faithfulness of God. Without a grasp of this truth our prayers will quickly seem pointless, and we may even give up praying altogether. But because God is faithful to his promises, prayer is an activity that moves mountains!

5.
Answered prayer

Please read 2 Chronicles 7:1-22

One of the great blessings of the Christian life is the knowledge that God really does answer prayer. God's answers may come promptly, or they may come 'after many days'. We bring many requests to God, and to some of them he gives the answer, 'No'; to others, 'Not yet'; while in response to others he says, 'There is a better way.' Whatever the answer, we can be assured that God hears our prayers and relieves our distress.

In 2 Chronicles 6:14-42 Solomon led the nation of Israel in prayer to dedicate the temple and claim the mercies of God's covenant. In the following chapter God's answer is recorded and we discover how Solomon's prayer was answered. Solomon had asked, 'But will God really dwell on earth with men?' (6:18). Solomon received his answer when 'Fire came down from heaven and consumed the burnt offering and the sacrifices, and the glory of the LORD filled the temple' (7:1). But that was not all. Solomon received a further answer from God when 'The LORD appeared to him at night' and assured him that his prayer had been heard (7:12-22).

This chapter contains some of the best-known portions from the book of Chronicles. The Chronicler presents the Lord as a God who is full of mercy, even to sinners. We see that God is 'a very present help in trouble' (Ps. 46:2, NKJV) both in his actions and his promises. God bestows his presence upon his people.

What is the 'presence of God'? We speak of God as *omni-present*. This means that God is an infinite Spirit, who is present in all places at the same time:

> Where can I go from your Spirit?
>> Where can I flee from your presence?
> If I go up to the heavens, you are there;
>> if I make my bed in the depths, you are there.
> If I rise on the wings of the dawn,
>> if I settle on the far side of the sea,
> even there your right hand will guide me,
>> your right hand will hold me fast
>
> (Ps. 139:7-10).

Yet it is a presence more intense than God's universal presence that is described in this psalm.

There are times when God draws especially near to men and women in order to accomplish his purposes. At conversion a person becomes very aware of the fact that he has offended God and has fallen far short of the glory of God. At first God's presence is a terror to him; but through the saving grace of God this sense of his presence becomes a great pleasure. Before his conversion C. S. Lewis had been aware of the idea of God, but when he looked back on that experience he described how that 'idea' 'began to stir and heave and throw off its gravecloth and stood upright and became a living presence'. We might call this God's *saving presence*, and this is a blessing that the believer will never lose.

Moreover, there is a *special presence* of God that is from time to time enjoyed by believers for a season. It is known during periods of revival within the church and within the individual believer. At such times God's presence is felt in a very palpable way. The weight of God's glory rests upon his people, and it is significant that the Old Testament word for 'glory' is derived from the verb which means 'to be heavy', even to the point of being burdensome.

This special presence of God was associated with the cloud that filled the temple when the priests brought the ark of the covenant into the temple. This was no ordinary cloud, for it was the glory that had descended upon the tabernacle when the Lord came down to dwell in it (Exod. 40:34-35). This cloud hung in the air like a heavy weight, for 'The glory of the Lord filled the temple' (5:14). As a result, 'The priests could not perform their service.' It is an awesome thing to be in the presence of the living God. It is an unspeakable blessing when God hears our prayers and comes down into our lives to answer them. Let us consider how God answered Solomon's prayers.

God's presence is symbolized by fire from heaven (7:1-11)

'When Solomon finished praying, fire came down from heaven and consumed the burnt offering and the sacrifices, and the glory of the Lord filled the temple.' God's response was immediate. It came in the form of fire that consumed the sacrifices upon the altar. The temple was where the people's offerings were brought to God and the fire was God's demonstration that he had accepted them. When the Aaronic priesthood was inaugurated in Leviticus 8 and 9, Moses and Aaron went to the Tent of Meeting and offered sacrifices to the Lord. The sign that the Lord endorsed Aaron's priestly ministry came in Leviticus 9:24: 'Fire came out from the presence of the Lord and consumed the burnt offering and the fat portions on the altar. And when all the people saw it, they shouted for joy and fell face down.'

Fire was also a sign of God's approval in 1 Chronicles 21:26 when David built an altar on the threshing-floor of Araunah, and made an offering to the Lord. The purpose of this sacrifice was to turn back the destroying angel whose sword was approaching Jerusalem: 'David built an altar to the LORD there and sacrificed burnt offerings and fellowship offerings. He called on the LORD, and the LORD answered him with fire from heaven on the altar of burnt offering' (1 Chr. 21:26).

Many years later, on the same site, after Solomon had built the temple, God showed his approval by sending fire from heaven to consume the sacrifices offered to him. God's approval of the temple and his answer to Solomon's prayer were dramatic and unmistakable. There could be no doubt that this was the place of God's choosing. Nor could there be any doubt that God was in the midst of his people, for **'The glory of the LORD filled the temple. The priests could not enter the temple of the LORD because the glory of the LORD filled it'** (7:1-2).

This was a national occasion. **'All the Israelites'** (or at least all the Israelites who came to Jerusalem representing all the tribes of Israel) **'saw the fire coming down and the glory of the LORD above the temple'** (7:3). As a result, the whole people **'knelt on the pavement with their faces to the ground, and they worshipped and gave thanks to the LORD, saying, "He is good; his love endures for ever."'** It was a truly national response. There were Israelites **'from Lebo Hamath to the Wadi of Egypt'** (7:8). These were the northern and southern boundaries of Israel. The fact that so many came from so far afield shows that this was a powerful movement in the spiritual life of God's people. This was an awakening that spread throughout the nation and touched every aspect of national life. Oh for such a movement in our nations today!

Solomon's leadership

We cannot overlook the significance of Solomon's leadership: **'Then the king and all the people offered sacrifices...**

And King Solomon offered a sacrifice of twenty-two thousand head of cattle and a hundred and twenty thousand sheep and goats' (7:4-5). In military circles it is said that there is no such thing as a bad soldier; there are only badly led soldiers. If men will not fight, it is because they have not been trained, motivated or led properly by their officers. The same principle frequently applies among the people of God. God's people are often as zealous as the leadership they are given. In these verses Solomon was an outstanding example of leadership.

Those who serve as leaders in the church could learn much from Solomon's bold initiative. The impact of such leadership was described in Judges 5:2:

> When the princes in Israel take the lead,
>   when the people willingly offer themselves —
>   praise the LORD!

God's people are more likely to offer themselves for service when their leaders give clear directions and lead by example. These verses reveal a happy combination of popular zeal and effective leadership. Both were the spontaneous response of people who knew the presence of God among them.

> O greatly bless'd the people are
>   the joyful sound that know.
> In brightness of thy face, O Lord,
>   they ever on shall go
>   (Ps. 89:15, Scottish Metrical Version).

Solomon's leadership was *sacrificial*. Vast numbers of animals were sacrificed on the newly consecrated altar: **'King Solomon offered a sacrifice of twenty-two thousand head of cattle and a hundred and twenty thousand sheep and**

goats' (7:5). Because of the numbers of animals being sacrificed, an additional part of the temple courtyard (outside the main temple building) had to be set aside and an additional altar erected **'because the bronze altar ... could not hold the burnt offerings, the grain offerings and the fat portions'** (7:7).

The role of the priests and Levites

The Chronicler draws our attention to the important role of the priests and Levites. They **'took their positions'** (as men appointed by God) and directed the people according to God's revealed commands. From this we learn that zeal alone does not make the worship of God's people acceptable and pleasing to him. There is such a thing as 'zeal ... not based on knowledge' which is not according to 'the righteousness that comes from God' (Rom. 10:2,3).

In this festival the Levites used **'the LORD's musical instruments, which King David had made for praising the LORD'** (7:6). God had given David great skill as a musician so that he might arrange the pattern of Israel's praise for the coming generations. As well as being 'the sweet psalmist of Israel' (2 Sam. 23:1, NKJV), David was a 'prophet' (Acts 2:30). God used David to lay down his ordinances to regulate the worship of his people. At God's command musical instruments were used to accompany the Levitical sacrifices. The zeal of the worshippers was always directed and channelled by specific precepts.

The people's praise at this great festival was taken from the Psalms of David: **'He is good; his love endures for ever'** (7:3). See the explanation of these words in the comment on 7:13 on page 55; they remind us that God acted on many occasions to demonstrate his covenant faithfulness to Israel. God never forgets those he saves! What wonderful words with which to praise God! God wants our praise to be instructive as well as heart-warming; these words teach us about God's gracious attributes and they express adoration for his person.

The link with the Feast of Tabernacles

The dedication of the temple was linked to one of the great pilgrim festivals — the Feast of Tabernacles. It took place at 'the festival of the seventh month' (so called because it was normally celebrated between the fifteenth and twenty-second days of Tisri, the seventh month, see 5:3). Its purpose was to remind the Israelites of the forty years that their forefathers had spent wandering in the wilderness (see Lev. 23:39-43). When the Israelites entered the promised land they needed a regular reminder of those unsettled times when they had to rely upon God every day to provide them with manna and to lead them on to their next encampment. 'When the LORD your God brings you into the land he swore to your fathers, to Abraham, Isaac and Jacob, to give you — a land with large, flourishing cities you did not build, houses filled with all kinds of good things you did not provide, wells you did not dig, and vineyards and olive groves you did not plant — then when you eat and are satisfied, be careful that you do not forget the LORD, who brought you out of Egypt, out of the land of slavery' (Deut. 6:10-12).

Now that the ark had come to its resting-place in the temple, and its days of wandering had come to an end, Solomon linked the dedication of the temple to the Feast of Tabernacles. He called the people together on the eighth day of the seventh month and **'celebrated the dedication of the altar for seven days and the festival for seven days more'** (7:9). After the 'seven days' of dedication, the 'festival' of Tabernacles was celebrated for seven more days, lasting from the fifteenth until the twenty-second day of the seventh month.

Then, on the twenty-third day of the month, Solomon **'sent the people to their homes, joyful and glad in heart for the good things the LORD had done for David and Solomon and for his people Israel'** (7:10). They were joyful because God had given them a place of rest. The temple was a symbol of that rest, because there the ark had entered its resting-place. The temple was the place to which all Israel would go to seek the Lord, and represents the blessings enjoyed by those who are justified by faith in Christ (see Rom. 5:1-5). Today our temple and resting-place are found in the person of the Lord Jesus Christ. At the cross of Christ we find everlasting rest: 'Come to me, all you who are weary and burdened, and I will give you rest' (Matt. 11:28).

Paradoxically, this rest leads on to further activity, rather than inactivity. Those who enjoy the rest of the gospel go on to be the most zealous servants of God. After a building programme lasting many years and a week-long festival of worship we could have understood it if Solomon and his people had decided to go home and take it easy. Yet they resolved to worship God 'for seven days more'. Even then they were not weary, but 'joyful and glad in heart'.

The Israelites did not find worship a burden. They delighted to worship God because they had an appreciation of what God had done for them. They were willing to go the extra mile (except in this case it was an extra week!). What a rebuke to Christians who find it too much of a burden to attend an evening service, or a midweek Bible study, or a prayer meeting! Consider 'what good things the Lord [has] done ... for his people' living in the age of grace. Does our Lord not warn us that those to whom much has been given will find that much is expected from them? May we give ourselves gladly!

God's answer to a praying people (7:11-18)

Yes, God answers prayer — but when? We often want God to answer our prayers yesterday! God sometimes asks us to wait. There was a time-gap between the answer by fire in 7:1-10 and the night vision in 7:11-18. God appeared to Solomon in that night vision **'when Solomon had finished the temple of the LORD and the royal palace'**. According to 1 Kings 7:1, it took a further thirteen years to construct the royal palace. This long delay shows us how long it can take for God to answer prayer. It reminds us that God's timescale is not ours. Where we can see only inexplicable delay, God has a wise and loving purpose (see 2 Peter 3:8-9). When we think that God has forgotten our prayers he is, in fact, preparing to teach us important lessons.

'The LORD appeared to him at night...' (7:12). Perhaps Solomon was reminded of that night in Gibeon, early in his reign, when God had offered him whatever his heart desired (1:7; cf. 1 Kings 9:2, where the linkage is made). At that time Solomon had asked for wisdom, and God had given it to him because the task that lay ahead of him required great wisdom. Now that Solomon's great building projects were behind him, God appeared to him again to remind him not to take his blessing for granted. God confirmed what Solomon had acknowledged in his prayer of dedication — that God would hear their prayers 'if they turn ... to [him] with all their heart'.

God's response to Solomon's prayer is found in 7:12-22. It begins with explicit references to the situations Solomon describes in his prayer: **'When I shut up the heavens so that there is no rain, or command locusts to devour the land or send a plague among my people...'** (see 6:26,28). Here is direct evidence that the Lord 'knows the thoughts of man' (Ps. 94:11) and that 'The righteous cry out, and the LORD hears them; he delivers them from all their troubles' (Ps. 34:17).

The account of God's response to Solomon's prayer of dedication is more complete here than that in 1 Kings 9:3-9, and the well-known message of 7:14-16 is found only in Chronicles: **'If my people, who are called by my name, will humble themselves and pray and seek my face and turn from their wicked ways, then I will hear from heaven and will forgive their sin and will heal their land.'** These words summarize the message of the book of Chronicles, for God's response to Solomon's prayer gave the Chronicler his basis for understanding the whole history of Israel. When the nation suffered invasion, drought and defeat, it was a consequence of their refusal to seek the Lord. When the nation enjoyed times of revival, reformation, peace and prosperity, it was because they humbled themselves and sought the Lord. Centuries later the Chronicler and his generation were able to look at their experience of exile and restoration in the light of this principle.

Christians today can find encouragement in this promise. God looks upon the church as his covenant people, enjoying the same promises of grace as were given to Israel in the Old Testament. Those promises are expanded to embrace every nation, and they speak of great things for the church (see Matt. 16:18; Acts 1:8; Eph. 1:22-23; 2:19-22). One of the first signs that God is fulfilling these great promises is when he moves his people to pray earnestly and with true repentance. Little happens until they are convicted of their sin and the urgency of crying out to God to claim his promises. Then when the spiritual life of the church is renewed, the blessings ripple out to heal the wounds inflicted by sin on the wider community.

Central to this passage is the requirement that God's people should seek him in his temple: **'Now my eyes will be open and my ears attentive to the prayers offered in this place. I have chosen and consecrated this temple so that my Name may be there for ever. My eyes and my heart will always be there'** (7:15-16). This is an endorsement of the place of the temple in the life of God's people. Truly it was the place chosen by God for his dwelling, and the sacrifices offered there were means of grace for those who worshipped. When the temple was faithfully maintained as a place of worship, the nation prospered. When the temple was neglected or defiled with heathen worship, then the nation declined. The rest of 2 Chronicles is an illustration of this truth, and it reminded the returning exiles of the importance of rebuilding the temple in Jerusalem.

As Christians we shall remember the words of our Lord identifying himself as the temple of the new covenant: 'Destroy this temple, and I will raise it again in three days... The temple he had spoken of was his body' (John 2:19,21; cf. Heb. 10:20). The Lord Jesus is the person upon whom our heavenly Father looks with constant delight (Matt. 3:17), so that when God's people draw near to God through the Lord Jesus Christ they can be certain that their prayers will be heard.

God's response to Solomon's prayer was an encouragement to the Israelites to continue earnestly in prayer (7:14-15). An essential element of true prayer is repentance. In these verses the Lord pointed out four aspects of repentant prayer: humbling before God, petitioning God for mercy, seeking God and turning from evil. Each of these raises a searching question. Are we willing to humble ourselves by acknowledging that we have done evil? Are we willing to be honest about our sins and seek forgiveness? Do we really want to have our lives changed by God? Are we willing to give up our sins, just as the Thessalonians were willing to turn 'from idols to serve the living and true God'? (1 Thess. 1:9).

God's response to such prayers would be twofold. First of all, God would **'hear from heaven and ... forgive their sin'** (7:14). As individuals and collectively as a nation, they would know the removal of the burden of guilt. What a blessing! 'Blessed is he whose transgressions are forgiven, whose sins are covered' (Ps. 32:1). 'You will again have compassion on us; you will tread our sins underfoot and hurl all our iniquities into the depths of the sea' (Micah 7:19).

Then, secondly, God would **'heal their land'**. Many were the wounds inflicted upon the nation of Israel because of their sins. Drought had turned their farmland into a dust-bowl; famine had turned their people into skeletons; civil war had divided the kingdom into two; invading armies had turned Jerusalem into a ruin. These wounds would be healed when God's people turned to him in prayer: 'But for you who revere my name, the sun of righteousness will rise with healing in his wings' (Mal. 4:2).

As a result of this promise God's people will have a view of God's kingdom that stretches far beyond their personal salvation and anticipates the healing of nations from the effects of sin. The consequences of sin against God include crime and poverty, environmental disaster and economic instability, wars and other man-made disasters. The whole creation groans because of human sin, but God will deliver it from the consequences of sin. 'Then the angel showed me the river of the water of life, as clear as crystal, flowing from the throne of God and of the Lamb down the middle of the great street of the city. On each side of the river stood the tree of life, bearing twelve crops of fruit, yielding its fruit every month. And the leaves of the tree are for the healing of the nations' (Rev. 22:1-2).

God's solemn warning (7:19-22)

God's response to Solomon's prayer ended on a solemn note. If Israel was unfaithful the temple would be taken from them: **'But if you turn away ... then I will uproot Israel from my land, which I have given them, and will reject this temple** which I have consecrated for my Name' (7:19-20). To the Chronicler and his contemporaries this was no idle threat, but something which had actually happened.

The Israelites forgot that their privileges were God's to give and God's to take away. In 7:20 God describes the land of Israel as 'my land'. Similarly the temple was 'consecrated for my Name'. These were covenant blessings and they came with conditions attached. God's people were to serve him only: **'But if you turn away and forsake the decrees and commands I have given you and go off to serve other gods and worship them, then I will uproot Israel from my land, which I have given them, and will reject this temple which I have consecrated for my Name'** (7:19-20). In spite of many warnings these are exactly the sins that the people of Israel committed. Generation after generation of provocation was brought to a conclusion when Nebuchadnezzar captured Jerusalem in 587 B.C. and destroyed the city and the temple.

However, even the destruction of the temple served God's purpose to speak to the nations. Its charred ruins became an object lesson to all who saw them: **'And though this temple is now so imposing, all who pass by will be appalled and say, "Why has the LORD done such a thing to this land and to this temple?"'** (7:21). The Lord had indeed made it **'a byword and an object of ridicule among all peoples'** (7:20).

For many years one of the grandest hotels in the seaside town of Portrush in Northern Ireland was the Northern Counties. In its heyday it had entertained King Edward VII (when he was Prince of Wales). However, in 1990 it was burnt to the ground, and its charred ruins remained an eyesore for many years. Those who remembered its former grandeur were saddened to pass by and would say to themselves, 'What a shame!' Similarly, the temple had been a demonstration of God's mercy to his people, but after its destruction it became a public eyesore and a national disgrace. Once a jewel in Israel's crown, it became a millstone around her neck. Once a place of atonement, it became a public display of God's wrath.

The majestic ruins of the temple forced people from many nations (not just the people of Judah) to ask questions. Why had the Lord done this to his own people? The answer is to be found in the justice of God. God will never overlook sin, not even the sin of his own people. If men will not worship God as he has commanded, then they cannot continue to enjoy the blessings that he bestows. Those blessings will be turned into crumbling ruins as a public demonstration of the truth that sin is 'a disgrace to any people'.

Sometimes we see the ruins of the lives of men and women who were once so full of promise for the Lord, but they have disintegrated because of spiritual failure. Or perhaps we see the ruins of a congregation that had once been faithful to the truth of Scripture, but has fallen away. Or we may see in our own lives the ruins of plans that we once cherished, but we did not walk close to the Lord. These ruins are a daily reminder that God will hold us to account for unfaithfulness. This is a truth that God will not allow us to gloss over.

In this solemn warning God's grace is still evident. In years to come the warnings God had given them were brought back to the memory of his people and helped them to understand (and therefore to profit from) their plight. When the temple was destroyed the Israelites asked why God had done such a thing. The Chronicler wrote his history to give them an answer. He could see that his people's tribulations were not arbitrary and meaningless, and that helped him to see light at the end of the tunnel.

If our trials are random acts of cruelty on God's part, then all we can do is to bear them in silence, while we keep out of God's way and hope he will leave us alone. But if our afflictions are the actions of a just and holy God, then we can see that there is a reason for God's chastisements. He is visiting the consequences of our unfaithfulness upon us. Since God is a covenant-making God, he is being faithful to his word when he punishes us. We can also see that, even when he punishes, God is merciful. When God's people listen to his warnings, they will discover that he '[does] not stay angry for ever but [delights] to show mercy' (Micah 7:18).

> You will again have compassion on us;
>> you will tread our sins underfoot
>> and hurl all our iniquities into the depths of the sea.
> You will be true to Jacob,
>> and show mercy to Abraham,
> as you pledged on oath to our fathers
>> in days long ago
>>
>>> (Micah 7:19-20).

6.
Solomon's splendour

Please read 2 Chronicles 8:1 – 9:31

How often have we heard that life was better in the 'good old days'? The pound in your pocket was worth something; people worked harder; the streets were safer places, and children were not so cheeky. Someone has said that even nostalgia is not what it used to be! Yes, there has always been a temptation to look on the past through rose-tinted spectacles and to long for better times than the present.

This must have been a temptation that faced the Chronicler when he wrote this history of Israel. He lived five centuries after Solomon, by which time the kingdom of Israel was a shadow of its former glory. The people of Judah had been taken into exile as God's judgement upon their disobedience. However Cyrus, King of Persia, had decreed that they should return to Jerusalem to rebuild the temple. The Jerusalem they saw when they returned was very different from the Jerusalem we read about in these chapters where 'Nothing was made of silver, because silver was considered of little value in Solomon's day' (9:20; cf. 9:27). Jerusalem was no longer a city of imposing public buildings and luxurious palaces. Few foreign dignitaries came to visit because it was no longer even the administrative centre of a province within the Persian Empire. Its wealth had been wasted, its buildings destroyed; its pride had been reduced to shame.

The zenith of the Israelite monarchy was reached during the reign of King Solomon, and Solomon's glory is described by the Chronicler in 2 Chronicles 8-9. When we read these chapters we may be tempted to think that this is merely a piece of nostalgic reflection, looking back to the glorious reign of King Solomon. It would have been very easy for the Chronicler to turn to Israel's history to escape from the discouragements of his own generation. That, however, was not his purpose. Yes, we read of fortified cities (8:5), freedom from forced labour (8:9) and fantastic wealth (9:13). But, more importantly, we read about faithfulness to the worship of Jehovah (8:12-15) and to God's commission (8:16).

Faithfulness to the Lord was the foundation of Solomon's kingdom. God had raised up Solomon to sit on David's throne and to build a house of worship for the Lord. Solomon's kingdom was a temporal and earthly manifestation of something that transcends the boundaries of time and space — the everlasting kingdom of God. Jehovah is the Lord of all the nations of the earth, and Solomon reigned in submission to him. Solomon's kingdom set forth the principles and purposes that underlie God's everlasting kingdom in every age. Here we catch a glimpse of what is possible on earth when kings and kingdoms submit to the Lord God. Here we see how righteousness exalted Israel in Solomon's day. We shall see similar examples in subsequent reigns, but Solomon's reign was unique in that the Lord raised his kingdom to a level of greatness never to be repeated in Israel's history. It was a model for the kingdom of 'one greater than Solomon', and for that reason it is right that we should reflect on it with wonderment. As we look back to Solomon's splendour we are challenged to look forward to the reign of the Messianic King, Jesus Christ. We are also challenged to ask ourselves, are we faithfully devoted to the service of this great King?

Solomon consolidated his strength at home

1. Strengthening the frontiers (8:1-6)

'At the end of twenty years, during which Solomon built the temple of the Lord and his own palace…' These words place all Solomon's achievements in their proper perspective. The success of Solomon's reign was seen most clearly in his mature years. Before he could enjoy the benefits of success, there had been twenty years of hard work, building, first of all, the temple of the Lord, and then a palace for himself, and only then the cities described in these verses. During those years Solomon had to learn to put first things first.

It is not always easy to distinguish things that seem to be urgent from those that are essential. Some tasks may appear to be very important, but they are not. In a hospital casualty unit it is not always the patient who screams the loudest who needs the most urgent attention. Sometimes a superficial wound can bleed profusely, but it is the internal bleeding that is life-threatening. So, too, in daily life there are many issues that demand attention, but not all are equally important. We need to learn to put God's priorities first.

Solomon built a house of worship before he built his palace and the military defences of his kingdom. This was a lesson that many of the returning exiles had failed to learn. The prophet Haggai gave them a sharp rebuke: '"Is it a time for you yourselves to be living in your panelled houses, while this house remains a ruin? … Give careful thought to your ways. Go up into the mountains and bring down timber and build the house, so that I may take pleasure in it and be honoured," says the Lord' (Hag. 1:7-8). God's house had to come first. That meant sacrificing prestige projects such as palaces and public buildings, for the worship of God comes first.

Putting God first in our lives will involve sacrifices. It may mean sacrificing a sporting career rather than abandoning the sanctity of the Lord's Day. It may mean the 'sacrifice' of tithing, rather than spending 'our' money as we think best. It may involve the sacrifice of a good career so that we can devote ourselves more completely to the Lord's service. These are only some examples of how God's people have rearranged their priorities to put God first. 'But seek first his kingdom and his righteousness, and all these things will be given to you as well' (Matt. 6:33). Solomon proved the truth of this promise.

'**Solomon rebuilt the villages that Hiram had given him, and settled Israelites in them**' (8:2-6). These verses point to the political, military and commercial strength of Solomon's kingdom. How Hiram came to give these villages to Solomon is not made clear. 1 Kings 9:11-14 refers to Solomon giving twenty towns in Galilee (the strategically important area where their two kingdoms met) to Hiram, because Hiram supplied timber and gold for the building of the temple. According to this account, Hiram was not happy with them, so he called them disparagingly 'the Land of Cabul', or 'good for nothing'. He may have returned them to Solomon gratuitously in a fit of pique. On the other hand, these villages may have been the collateral for a loan to finance the building of the temple. Twenty years later, presumably with the loan paid off, Hiram then returned these Galilean towns to their rightful ruler. Whatever the circumstances, Solomon strengthened his control over this northerly region.

Solomon extended his influence far beyond the traditional boundaries of Israel: '**Solomon then went to Hamath Zobah and captured it. He also built up Tadmor in the desert and all the store cities he had built in Hamath**' (6:3-4). Zobah was the portion of Syria that lay between Damascus to the south and the Orontes River to the north; Hamath was its major town. Tadmor (later known as Palmyra) was 200 kilometres north-east of Damascus, on the main trade route east through the Syrian desert.

Closer to home were the places mentioned in 6:5-6: **'He rebuilt Upper Beth Horon and Lower Beth Horon as fortified cities ... as well as Baalath and all his store cities.'** Baalath may be another name for Kiriath Jearim. All these cities were located to the west of Jerusalem, where the Judean highlands started descending to the coastal plain. They were strategically important because they guarded the routes through which the Philistines and others had invaded Judah. In more peaceful times they were the routes through which flowed trade with the Mediterranean and lands further west.

In these towns Solomon constructed **'fortified cities, with walls and with gates and bars'**. These were **'cities for his chariots and for his horses'**, and in them Solomon deployed his military hardware. He also built **'store cities'** which provided centres of safety for his merchants. This ring of fortifications brought great benefits to Israel, for they enabled lucrative international trade to flourish.

2. Subjugating the Canaanites (8:7-10)

When God brought the people of Israel into the promised land of Canaan, he commanded them to drive out the heathen nations before them: 'My angel will go ahead of you and bring you into the land of the Amorites, Hittites, Perizzites, Canaanites, Hivites and Jebusites, and I will wipe them out... I will establish your borders from the Red Sea to the Sea of the Philistines, and from the desert to the River. I will hand over to you the people who live in the land and you will drive them out before you' (Exod. 23:23,31). God did not expect that this would happen overnight: 'I will not drive them out in a single year, because the land would become desolate and the wild animals too numerous for you. Little by little I will drive them out before you, until you have increased enough to take possession of the land' (Exod. 23:29-30). However, the Israelites were not to make peace with the heathen nations.

God's command that the Canaanites should be progressively removed from the land was never realized because of the disobedience of the Israelites. On occasions they violated God's clear command and intermarried with the people of the land, and as a result they adopted their pagan practices. On one notable occasion they were duped into making a covenant with the Gibeonites, who were allowed to live in the land on condition that they became servants of the Israelites (Josh. 9:23).

By Solomon's time the Canaanites had become an army of forced labourers: **'All the people left from the Hittites, Amorites, Perizzites, Hivites and Jebusites (these people were not Israelites), that is, their descendants remaining in the land, whom the Israelites had not destroyed — these Solomon conscripted for his slave labour force, as it is to this day'** (8:7-8). Reliance upon slave labour was to have tragic consequences for the kingdom (see 2 Chr. 10). This dependence on slave labour came about because the Israelites would not obey God's commands to remove the Canaanites from the land, preferring compromise and accommodation instead. However, this situation was turned to some benefit because the army of Canaanite slave labourers was put to use by Solomon 'for the house of [his] God'. Those who would not bend their hearts to God's law were at least made to bend their knee to his service.

What a marked contrast between the slavery of the Canaanites and the freedom of the Israelites! **'But Solomon did not make slaves of the Israelites for his work...'** (8:9). Much more prestigious tasks were assigned to the Israelites: **'They were his fighting men, commanders of his captains, and commanders of his chariots and charioteers. They were also King Solomon's chief officials.'** Here are the blessings that flow from submission to the Lord, and only those who abide by the terms of his covenant of mercy can expect to enjoy its blessings. One of the great blessings of the gospel is that it makes men and women of all nations free in Christ Jesus — free, that is, to serve the Lord. 'It is for freedom that Christ has set us free. Stand firm, then, and do not let yourselves be burdened again by a yoke of slavery' (Gal. 5:1).

3. Separating the heathen (8:11)

'Solomon brought Pharaoh's daughter up from the City of David to the palace he had built for her, for he said, "My wife must not live in the palace of David king of Israel, because the places the ark of the LORD has entered are holy."' This incident shows Solomon in a mixed light, illuminating both his strengths and weaknesses. The Chronicler is not, as some have suggested, a rather naïve historian who looked at Solomon through rose-tinted spectacles. His account of Solomon is like the portrait that Oliver Cromwell requested of himself, showing 'warts and all'.

Solomon's greatest failing was at home. He married many foreign wives and allowed them to bring the worship of heathen gods into his household (see 1 Kings 11:1-8). 'As Solomon grew old, his wives turned his heart after other gods, and his heart was not fully devoted to the LORD his God as the heart of David his father had been' (1 Kings 11:4). For this very reason the Lord had forbidden the people of Israel to intermarry with the heathen nations (Exod. 34:15-16). We can be quite sure that an Egyptian princess would not have brought a godly influence into Solomon's household. Many ordinary Israelites must have been confused by Solomon's example and some may have followed him in disregarding God's command to marry only the Lord's people.

At least Solomon had the wisdom to see the incongruity of bringing a heathen princess into the place where the ark of the

Lord had been stored. It was impossible to undo his marriage. The political ramifications, in terms of diplomatic relations with Egypt, would have been unthinkable. So too were the social implications of divorce (Mal. 2:10). Still, Solomon sought to limit the offence that his sinful marriage had caused to God. He built a palace specifically for her and her entourage to move them away from the place where his father had once kept the ark.

Solomon removed this heathen princess from a place which had sacred associations. No place on earth can be made holy because of the influence of mere men. However, the presence of God can make a place sacred (see Gen. 28:16-17; Exod. 3:5). The ark of the covenant was the symbol of God's presence among his people, and the inner sanctuary where it was kept was the most sacred room in the temple, into which only the high priest was permitted to enter. Many would have remembered that the ark had spent many years in the 'City of David' and it must have grieved them to think that David's palace had became a centre for the worship of Egyptian gods.

Solomon removed his wife from proximity to the temple of Jehovah. Jehovah is jealous for his own honour and the honour of his house. Such is his purity that he could not bear to have defilement *near* his temple. Ezekiel 43:8-9 (which describes the worship of heathen gods in Jerusalem just before the destruction of Jerusalem in 587 B.C.) casts some light on what lay behind Solomon's actions: 'When they placed their threshold next to my threshold and their doorposts beside my doorposts, with only a wall between me and them, they defiled my holy name by their detestable practices. So I destroyed them in my anger. Now let them put away from me their prostitution and the lifeless idols of their kings, and I will live among them for ever.' Surely this teaches us that if we want to enjoy God's blessing we need to seek reformation, not just in our homes and hearts, but in the public places of our nations as well.

4. Setting up the temple ministry (8:12-15)

'**On the altar of the L**ORD** that he had built in front of the portico, Solomon sacrificed burnt offerings to the L**ORD**, according to the daily requirement for offerings commanded by Moses**' (8:12). Here we see Solomon in his capacity as the leader of God's people. He was a regular worshipper at the temple. He supplied the sacrificial animals which the priests offered on the altar, and in doing so he threw his royal prestige behind the worship of Jehovah. Here is an example of a king being 'wise' as commanded in Psalm 2:10. In doing so Solomon was an encourager of true religion.

Solomon's leadership was thoroughly scriptural. In 8:13 we find a list of the sacrifices that were offered daily, weekly, monthly and annually. The pattern that Solomon's priests followed was 'commanded by Moses' in Numbers 28 and 29, which contain the regulations that governed the daily sacrifices (Num. 28:1-8), the Sabbath offerings (Num. 28:9-10), the monthly offerings made at each new moon festival (Num. 28:11-15) and at the three great annual pilgrim festivals — the Passover (Num. 28:16-25), the Feast of Weeks (Num. 28:26-31) and the Feast of Tabernacles (Num. 29:12-40). Solomon's leadership edified the people because he himself was under the direction of God's law. Here is a challenge to all those who hold positions of leadership among God's people. It should be clear to others that we are being directed by God in all that we do. We should be constantly seeking to hear what God has to say in the Scriptures and able at all times to point to the principles and precepts of God's Word that have directed us.

Solomon put in place a hierarchy to administer the temple: '**In keeping with the ordinance of his father David, he appointed the divisions of the priests for their duties and the Levites to lead the praise and assist the priests...**' (8:14).

The basic pattern had been drawn up by King David when he prepared for the building of the temple. Those plans were recorded in 1 Chronicles: the priestly divisions to minister in their turn in the sanctuary (1 Chr. 24), the Levites who were appointed to lead the praise in the temple (1 Chr. 25) and the gatekeepers (1 Chr. 26). David was a prophet through whom the Lord spoke (see Acts 2:30, 2 Sam. 23:3); therefore Solomon followed his directions carefully — **'in keeping with the ordinance of his father David'**. Solomon did not add to these regulations, but simply ensured that they were put into effect. If any of the Levitical families had become careless in performing the duties allocated to them we can be sure that Solomon would have brought them into line. Thus the worship of Jehovah was encouraged.

A matter of such importance as the worship of God was not left to Solomon's imagination or self-expression. God was not concerned to discover what new forms of worship Solomon could devise as an improvement on the worship of his father's age. God was pleased with Solomon's faithfulness when he followed the directions he had received from his father David. **'They did not deviate from the king's commands to the priests or to the Levites in any matter'** (8:15). This is a profound challenge to the idea of 'modern worship' that is revolutionizing the services of many churches today.

5. Completion of the work (8:16)

'All Solomon's work was carried out... So the temple of the LORD was finished.' The task was completed. God had been faithful to his promise and Solomon had been faithful to his commission. For this reason God blessed Solomon and his kingdom. All the blessings that Solomon enjoyed are to be seen in this light. God had promised that he would give Solomon wisdom and wealth to build a temple for his worship. To have taken these blessings from God and then to have used them for godless ends would have forfeited any hope of continuing in God's blessing. Solomon was faithful to God's commission and continued to enjoy his covenant mercies. In fact God made Israel into one of the wonders of the ancient world. The wealth and prestige of Solomon's Israel reached almost fabulous proportions.

In the lives of God's people today these blessings do not always take the material form that Solomon's splendour did. Very few of God's people are wealthy and powerful and noble (see 1 Cor. 1:26-28). However, every child of God who seeks God can be assured that he or she will enjoy many other blessings as well (Matt. 6:33; Mark 10:29-31). God is able to bless his people more richly than they realize: 'Now to him who is able to do immeasurably more than all we ask or imagine, according to his power that is at work within us, to him be glory in the church and in Christ Jesus throughout all generations, for ever and ever! Amen' (Eph. 3:20-21).

Solomon's standing abroad

1. The establishment of a merchant fleet (8:17-18; 9:21)

With the help of Hiram, Solomon established Israel as a maritime power. The people of Tyre were skilled seafarers, who had dominated the trade of the eastern Mediterranean for centuries. It was beneficial to them to join up with Solomon so that they could expand their trading activities southwards along the Arabian coastline. The venture was beneficial to Solomon as well, for the Israelites had never been a seafaring people. Solomon needed the technology and the expertise to launch a trading fleet, so **'Hiram sent him ships commanded by his own officers, men who knew the sea'** (8:18).

Solomon controlled the strategic ports of **'Ezion Geber and Elath'**, at the head of the Gulf of Aqaba. These may have been separate towns, or Ezion Geber may have been the port that was linked to the larger town of Elath. In either case, they were both in the area of the modern Israeli town of Eilat. From here Solomon sent out trading missions that sailed as far as Ophir. It has been suggested that Ophir was on the east coast of Africa, or as far away as India, though most probably it was in southern Arabia.

This trade reaped huge rewards for Solomon and his merchants. The first expedition **'brought back four hundred and fifty talents of gold, which they delivered to King Solomon'** (8:18). With the passage of time Solomon's fleet grew and became more adventurous. A **'fleet of trading ships'** (9:21) was able to travel longer distances. These 'ships of Tarshish' (as the Hebrew text describes them) were large trading vessels able to traverse the open sea. They did not necessarily go to Tarshish in the western Mediterranean, but they were equipped for long voyages. Regularly (**'once every three years'** according to 9:21) they returned with treasures and novelties previously unknown in Israel — **'gold, silver and ivory, and apes and baboons'**.

Overseas trade brought Israel into contact with many new peoples. Perhaps it created new enemies as Israelite merchants competed for the first time with these wealthy oriental merchants in gold, spices and ivory. Almost certainly it paved the way for a visit from one of the most powerful rulers of the lands lying to the south of Israel.

2. The Queen of Sheba and other rulers (9:1-14,22-24)

Sheba (or Saba) was an ancient kingdom at the southern tip of the Arabian peninsula, controlling the trade routes that converged on the Straits of Aden. In the Old Testament it is mentioned as one of the nations whose rulers will do homage to the Messianic King (Ps. 72:10,15; Isa. 60:6). Its most illustrious ruler was the queen whose visit to Solomon is described in this chapter.

She was drawn by what she had heard about Solomon (9:1)

'When the queen of Sheba heard of Solomon's fame, she came to Jerusalem...' Although Solomon's reputation was built upon many things, including his wealth, influence and military power, clearly it was his gift of wisdom from God that was of greatest interest to her: **'... she came to Jerusalem to test him with hard questions.'** These riddles, or enigmatic conundrums, were the issues of interest to ancient philosophers. Would Solomon be able to give her the answers that had eluded the wise men of her own land? Perhaps he might. Certainly it had become clear to her that Solomon was like no other king she knew. His kingdom was special, and so too was his wisdom.

Far beyond the boundaries of Israel people took notice of what the Lord was doing among his people. News spread and some were drawn to discover more. The lesson for God's people in every age — not least in the post-exilic age — is that faithfulness among God's people draws even unbelievers to seek the true God. 'This is what the LORD Almighty says: "In those days ten men from all languages and nations will take firm hold of one Jew by the hem of his robe and say, 'Let us go with you, because we have heard that God is with you'"' (Zech. 8:23). We should never blame the impotence of the modern church on the hardness of unbelievers around us. Rather we should look within and ask, have we been faithful to the Lord?

She was amazed by what she saw and heard (9:2-4)

She had come to test Solomon with her enigmatic riddles, but
Solomon answered her with straightforward words: **'Nothing
was too hard for him to explain.'** God's wisdom is like a
well of pure water; it is very deep, but crystal clear. God gave
Solomon the ability to fathom deep truths, but it was also the
sort of wisdom that 'makes the simple wise'. It was practical
wisdom that provided precepts for daily life. We find many
examples of Solomon's wisdom in the book of Proverbs:

The proverbs of Solomon son of David, king of Israel:

for attaining wisdom and discipline;
    for understanding words of insight;
for acquiring a disciplined and prudent life,
    doing what is right and just and fair;
for giving prudence to the simple,
    knowledge and discretion to the young —
let the wise listen and add to their learning,
    and let the discerning get guidance —
for understanding proverbs and parables,
    the sayings and riddles of the wise.
The fear of the LORD is the beginning of knowledge,
    but fools despise wisdom and discipline
                                            (Prov. 1:1-7).

The Queen of Sheba saw the fruit of Solomon's wisdom in
the way his kingdom was ordered: **'When the queen of Sheba
saw the wisdom of Solomon, as well as the palace he had
built, the food on his table, the seating of his officials, the
attending servants in their robes, the cupbearers in their
robes and the burnt offerings he made at the temple of the**

LORD, **she was overwhelmed'** (9:3-4). She was overwhelmed because these were manifestations of the same God-given wisdom.

She acknowledged God's goodness to Israel (9:5-8)

'The report I heard in my own country about your achievements and your wisdom is true. But I did not believe what they said until I came and saw with my own eyes.' She had to see it with her own eyes because mere words could not convey the greatness of what God had done for Solomon. Unbelievers are often very cynical about the claims made by God's people. That is why they need to be confronted, not just with claims made by Christians, but with the reality of lives surrendered to God's grace. That is why Paul described the Corinthian believers as 'our letter … known and read by everybody' (2 Cor. 3:2).

She praised God when she saw the happiness of Solomon's subjects (9:7-8)

She recognized that Solomon's kingdom was different from her own and from every other kingdom she had known.

Firstly, Solomon was not just *appointed by God* (as is every ruler according to Romans 13:1-2), but he also *reigned for God.* **'God … placed you on his throne as king to rule for the** LORD **your God.'** Solomon exercised a delegated, and not an absolute, monarchy. He was not a tyrant who used his authority to further his own interests and the interests of his family. He used his wisdom and power 'for the LORD'.

Secondly, Solomon was appointed by God as king over Israel as *an expression of divine favour* to Israel:

'**Because of the love of your God for Israel and his desire to uphold them for ever, he has made you king over them…**' As such, Solomon was a forerunner of an even greater King, whose reign is also an expression of God's love to his people (see John 3:16).

Thirdly, Solomon was also appointed by God *to advance the cause of godliness* among the people of Israel, '**… to maintain justice and righteousness**'. Although Solomon was not without his faults, he was a good and godly king. His greatest achievement was that he led the people to worship the Lord as the Lord had commanded. This was a great step forward in righteousness, and God's blessing followed it (Prov. 14:34).

She gave and received gifts (9:9,12)

'**Then she gave the king 120 talents of gold, large quantities of spices, and precious stones. There had never been such spices as those the queen of Sheba gave to King Solomon.**' Great as these gifts were, Solomon gave her even more in return, because he gave her from the riches of God's wisdom: '**King Solomon gave the queen of Sheba all she desired and asked for; he gave her more than she had brought to him**' (9:12).

The wisdom that God gives is precious:

Blessed is the man who finds wisdom,
     the man who gains understanding,
for she is more profitable than silver,
     and yields better returns than gold.
She is more precious than rubies;
     nothing you desire can compare with her
                                        (Prov. 3:13-15).

This wisdom cannot be bought with material riches, but according to Solomon, it buys something that money can never buy, for 'All her paths are peace' (Prov. 3:17). Only by seeking the Lord and submitting to him can we know the one who makes sinners wise unto salvation through the Lord Jesus Christ (2 Tim. 3:15).

She was not alone in honouring Solomon (9:13-14,22-24)

Although the Queen of Sheba was by far the best-known of the ancient rulers who came to visit Solomon, she was not the only one. Because of the lucrative trade that flowed through Solomon's kingdom (9:22), there were many who wanted to seek Solomon's favour (and perhaps trading concessions as well). Hence, **'All the kings of Arabia and the governors of the land brought gold and silver to Solomon'** (9:14). Other kings came to hear Solomon's words: **'All the kings of the earth sought audience with Solomon to hear the wisdom God had put in his heart'** (9:23). With them they brought gifts: **'articles of silver and gold, and robes, weapons and spices, and horses and mules'** (9:24). In all probability these gifts were tribute paid to Solomon as overlord, for we read that **'He ruled over all the kings from the River to the land of the Philistines, as far as the border of Egypt'** (9:26).

We know that Solomon was a forerunner of God's Messiah, who is given the title 'King of kings' (see 1 Chr. 17:13-14; Matt. 12:42). Moreover, the Queen of Sheba was a forerunner of those who would come from the nations of the world to honour Christ and seek divine wisdom from him (see Ps. 72:10,15; Isa. 60:6).

When the Lord Jesus was born into this world he was visited by wise men representing rulers from the east, bearing gifts as tribute, and asking the question: 'Where is the one who has been born king of the Jews? We saw his star in the east and have come to worship him' (Matt. 2:2). No doubt they sought wisdom as they followed the movement of heavenly bodies, but when they saw the Son of God they bowed to worship. Many people are willing to acknowledge that Jesus Christ is a wise teacher, but they will not submit to him as Lord and Saviour. Perhaps you are still seeking only advice from him. If so bow before him, acknowledge that he is the Lord and that you need his forgiveness and grace.

The signs and symbols of Solomon's splendour (9:15-21, 25-26)

In Old Testament times many truths were taught by signs and symbols. The details of Solomon's kingdom recorded here are signs and symbols that teach us about the glory of Christ's everlasting kingdom. The earthly power and glory described in these verses point towards the everlasting glory of the kingdom of King Jesus. With this in view, it is good for us to pause to reflect on the details of Solomon's grandeur.

Golden shields (9:15-16)

One of the first tasks of government is to provide safety for its people, and one of the blessings that Israel enjoyed when she was faithful to her Lord was safety from the attacks of her enemies. Through Solomon's leadership God gave peace and security to the people of Israel. The shields of gold and silver with which Solomon decorated his palace were a visible sign of that safety. A shield is a defensive weapon. Behind it a warrior knows a measure of protection. Under Solomon's rule Israel enjoyed safety from her enemies. Israel's golden age was symbolized by golden shields. Their later replacement with bronze shields (12:9-10) was a sign that the glory had departed and that political insecurity had taken its place.

A golden throne (9:17-19)

Even as we read these verses we marvel at what a sight this throne must have been. Precious materials were used to construct it — gold and ivory. It was *a symbol of Solomon's royal authority*, and the lions that stood on either side of the six steps represented his great power. It exalted Solomon high above all those who came to speak with him, and it exalted Solomon's kingdom far above every other kingdom: **'Nothing like it had ever been made for any other kingdom'** (9:19). In those days when even kings may not have been able to read, such symbols were used to convey powerful messages. Their message was unwritten, but clearly read.

Solomon's throne also represented *great hopes for the future*. The promise of an everlasting kingdom in 1 Chronicles 17:14 had been repeated to Solomon himself (see 6:10; 7:18). The writer of Solomon's wedding psalm recognized that God had appointed Solomon as his chosen ruler:

> Your throne, O God, will last for ever and ever;
> > a sceptre of justice will be the sceptre of your
> > kingdom.
> You love righteousness and hate wickedness,
> > therefore God, your God, has set you above your
> > companions
> > by anointing you with the oil of joy
>
> > > > > (Ps. 45:6-7).

This great hope is to be realized only by the Lord Jesus Christ, who is the Lord's Anointed. His throne is above all earthly thrones. His kingdom is a present (though opposed) reality in our world, and the focus of our hopes for the future.

Household articles (9:20)

Goblets and plates are humble items in themselves, but those used by King Solomon and his household were of the highest quality. They were made of **'pure gold. Nothing was made of silver, because silver was considered of little value in Solomon's day.'** If it was for the king's use, only the best would do. Do we apply that principle to the ordinary things we do for King Jesus?

Our Lord is not necessarily impressed by extravagance. On the contrary, he was impressed by the generous gift of even a few copper coins (see Mark 12:43-44). However, our Lord expects the best. Even the ordinary tasks we do for him are to be done well and reverently. When we offer hospitality, when we tidy the church grounds, when we prepare to give a message, let us be like workmen who do not need to be ashamed (see 2 Tim. 2:15).

Horses and chariots (9:25-28)

Archaeology has confirmed the size and scale of Solomon's stables. His stabling complexes were large, for **'Solomon had four thousand stalls for horses and chariots, and twelve thousand horses.'** It has been estimated that for every chariot, three horses were needed to keep the chariot regiments in prime condition. Solomon's military machine was not simply for show. It was powerful enough to inflict serious damage on his enemies.

Let people today realize that the kingdom of the Lord Jesus is not simply an empty cipher. Although he delays his Day of Judgement (see 2 Peter 3:8-9), that day of power will come.

Many who have said, 'We will not have this man to rule over us,' will be crushed by his power. Do not be deceived: the Lord reigns!

The end of Solomon's splendour (9:29-31)

In these concluding verses the Chronicler reminds his readers that Solomon's reign was not a mythical golden age, now lost in the mists of time. He points them to historical sources: '**... are they not written in the records of Nathan the prophet, in the prophecy of Ahijah the Shilonite and in the visions of Iddo the seer concerning Jeroboam the son of Nebat?**' The Chronicler gathered his sources as carefully as Luke did before he commenced his Gospel account (Luke 1:1-4). We have a reliable account of the life of Solomon that shows evidence of careful research. This is in stark contrast to the claims of liberal critics that the Chronicler gave himself a free hand to ignore and rewrite history as his prejudices dictated.

The Chronicler reminds us that Solomon's reign eventually came to an end. This rather obvious point needs to be made because Solomon, although he was such a great king, was only a man. What a disappointment this must have been to many of his subjects! How the Israelites of succeeding generations must have hankered after such a king! Yet we are told on the authority of our Lord himself that there is one greater than Solomon: 'The Queen of the South will rise at the judgement with this generation and condemn it; for she came from the ends of the earth to listen to Solomon's wisdom, and now one greater than Solomon is here' (Matt. 12:42).

The Lord Jesus is the only king who never dies (Ps. 16:9-10). His reign never comes to an end, for his kingdom is everlasting. He has established a throne of judgement before which he gathers all people. From that throne he issues many warnings to those who close their ears to his appeals and he makes many promises to those who take heed.

> Your kingdom is an everlasting kingdom,
>   and your dominion endures through all generations.
> The LORD is faithful to all his promises
>   and loving towards all he has made
>
>   (Ps. 145:13).

Have you bowed your knee to this one who is greater even than Solomon?

7.
Rehoboam: learning to listen

Please read 2 Chronicles 10:1 – 11:4

It is never easy to follow in the footsteps of a great man. The one who comes afterwards will never be exactly the same in all respects, and will often be compared unfairly and un- favourably with his predecessor. Ministers who come to new congregations often hear the words: 'Oh, but Mr So-and-so never did it that way!' Politicians face the same pressures. When Margaret Thatcher resigned as British prime minister and John Major was appointed as her successor, she made it clear that she would be keeping an eye on his performance, acting as the 'back-seat driver' of the new government.

It was inevitable that Rehoboam would be compared with his father, King Solomon. Rehoboam was probably as good as many of the kings who ruled Judah in the centuries that fol- lowed Solomon's death. However, he has been judged harshly because he stood in the shadow of his illustrious father. Solo- mon ruled over a great empire, but Rehoboam ruled over only the two tribes of Judah and Benjamin. Solomon was power- ful, but Rehoboam was weak. Solomon was the wisest of men, but Rehoboam made foolish decisions. People came from all over the world to see Solomon's splendour and to seek his counsel. Rehoboam, however, is remembered as the king who lost most of his kingdom because he did not know how to listen to good advice. In fact he sought out foolish advice and followed it, to his cost.

Rehoboam made some very foolish decisions early in his reign and they left a scar on the life of Israel that was never properly healed. As a result, the history of Israel became a history of two conflicting kingdoms. The Chronicler's history focuses almost exclusively upon the southern kingdom of Judah. He records the decline of a divided and weakened kingdom which was eventually conquered by the Babylonian King Nebuchadnezzar and taken into exile in 587 B.C.

A great man's legacy (10:1-4)

It is important to remember that great men are always only men. It used to be commonplace for people to hold their politicians in high esteem. Popular journalism, which delights in exposing the 'feet of clay' belonging to our public figures, has largely undermined that tendency today. Christians will esteem godly leaders whose ministry has brought them great blessing. They will recall great theologians, gifted preachers and godly pastors who have influenced them. We may thank God for these men, but we should remember that they are only men. It is not edifying to dwell upon their human failings, but they all possess them.

Solomon was a great king, but he left behind great problems. His ambitious programmes of public building had placed a huge burden on the nation's resources. The cost of building the temple, the palaces in Jerusalem, the garrison and store cities, throughout Israel and beyond, as well as maintaining an elaborate royal household, was immense. It was costly in terms of raw materials, finance and manpower.

Large armies of labourers worked on these building projects. At one stage there were over 150,000 men in forced labour (see 2:17-18), all of whom were non-Israelites. Solomon did not make slaves of the people of Israel, but he did recruit them into his civil service and his army (see 8:9). The demands of these and other duties must have increased steadily during Solomon's four decades on the throne, and as a result a crushing burden rested upon the people of Israel. Their appeal to Rehoboam was: **'Your father put a heavy yoke on us, but now lighten the harsh labour and the heavy yoke he put on us'** (10:4).

The prophet Samuel had warned the Israelites that this would happen when they asked God to appoint a king to reign over them. Until that time there had been no king to rule over the twelve tribes, because it was acknowledged that Jehovah was their King, ruling his people through the tribal elders and judges. Samuel was offended that the people should want to change this system. However, the greater offence was against the Lord, because his rule was being rejected. Furthermore, Samuel warned his hearers that they would be oppressed by the king they had requested and 'When that day comes, you will cry out for relief from the king you have chosen, and the LORD will not answer you in that day' (1 Sam. 8:18; cf. Deut. 17:16-17).

The 'heavy yoke' that Solomon placed upon the Israelites was an offence to God. It brought back memories of the years that the Israelites had spent as slaves in Egypt. 'The Israelites groaned in their slavery and cried out, and their cry for help because of their slavery went up to God' (Exod. 2:23-25). Now Solomon had started to treat God's people like another pharaoh of old. God is concerned for the labouring man (see Eph. 6:9; James 5:4). He commands that those who labour with their hands are to be paid fairly and promptly, and he detests the oppression of the powerless (see Lev. 25:17, Ps. 9:9; Prov. 14:31; Mal. 3:5).

Solomon's harsh treatment of the people provoked widespread discontent, and several troublemakers tried to turn the situation to their advantage. Even during his own lifetime there were stirrings of rebellion in Israel and Solomon had to act firmly to suppress several rebellions (see 1 Kings 11:14-25) and to drive one of their leaders, Jeroboam son of Nebat, into exile. **'He was in Egypt, where he had fled from King Solomon'** (10:2; cf. 1 Kings 11:26-40). However, the fundamental problem was not resolved and after Solomon died the people of Israel again sent for Jeroboam and asked him to be their mouthpiece: **'So they sent for Jeroboam, and he and all Israel went to Rehoboam'** (10:3). It was clear that, under the façade, all was not well with his kingdom, and that difficult times lay ahead.

In the light of this discouraging footnote to Solomon's reign, it is good to remember the Messianic King who is 'greater than Solomon'. The Lord Jesus makes his people servants (or 'bondslaves') and he puts a yoke upon them. Yet how different a yoke from that which Solomon put upon the Israelites! 'Come to me, all you who are weary and burdened, and I will give you rest. Take my yoke upon you and learn from me, for I am gentle and humble in heart, and you will find rest for your souls. For my yoke is easy and my burden is light' (Matt. 11:28-30). 'The blessing of the LORD brings wealth, and he adds no trouble to it' (Prov. 10:22).

A pressing problem for Rehoboam (10:1-5)

Solomon had been able to keep the lid on the cauldron of discontent that was coming to boiling point in his kingdom. Perhaps it was because he was respected as an older man who had achieved great things, or because of his skill in defusing difficult situations, or even because of his firm grip on the army. Rehoboam, however, did not have the respect, or the authority, or the wisdom, to handle the explosive situation that faced him when he became king. Yet he could not put it off until a more convenient time. The long-suppressed discontent could be contained no longer when Rehoboam came to the throne. The **'heavy yoke'** that rested upon the people was one of the first issues that confronted the new king, and he was forced to deal with it quickly.

'Rehoboam went to Shechem, for all the Israelites had gone there to make him king' (10:1). When Rehoboam went to Shechem to be acknowledged as king he was made fully aware of his people's feelings. Shechem was a traditional gathering-place for the tribes of Israel. Joshua had gathered the Israelites there to renew their covenant with the Lord (Josh. 24). At the beginning of Rehoboam's reign the people gathered at Shechem to make a covenant with their new king. Rehoboam came to Shechem expecting a coronation, but the Israelites came intent on negotiation.

We see the 'democratic' tradition of the monarchy in Israel. Jehovah was the King of Israel, and it was he who gave them a king in the first place (see 1 Sam. 8:22). However, the people of Israel gave their consent to the king's appointment, and ratified his authority in a covenant. At Shechem the people sought to restate the principle that the king did not possess absolute power, but must rule with the consent of the people and according to the laws of God. The accession of a new king gave them an opportunity to air their grievances, and they grasped it.

'So they sent for Jeroboam, and he and all Israel went to Rehoboam and said to him: "Your father put a heavy yoke on us, but now lighten the harsh labour and the heavy yoke he put on us, and we will serve you."' Although the seeds of rebellion were being sown here, their request was not, in itself, rebellious. The people's request was reasonable: they wanted freedom from oppression. Their terms were submissive: they offered their loyalty in return for fair treatment. 'We will serve you,' they promised, on condition that the 'harsh labour and the heavy yoke' were removed from them. These were the terms of the covenant between the king and his people. What would Rehoboam do? Rehoboam needed guidance.

Conflicting advice (10:6-14)

Rehoboam turned to his courtiers for advice. That was a good thing to do, because no one is so wise that he or she does not need advice. Even Solomon, with all his great wisdom, surrounded himself with men whose task it was to advise him. The first group of courtiers that Rehoboam approached were **'the elders who had served his father Solomon during his lifetime'** (10:6). Solomon often acknowledged his need for advice in the book of Proverbs: 'Pride only breeds quarrels, but wisdom is found in those who take advice.' 'For lack of guidance a nation falls, but many advisers make victory sure.' 'Plans fail for lack of counsel, but with many advisers they succeed' (Prov. 13:10; 11:14; 15:22).

As Christians we naturally turn to the Scriptures for guidance. We are taught that God's Word is 'a lamp to my feet and a light for my path' (Ps. 119:105). God has given us his Word so that, by careful study of its principles and prayerful application of its precepts to our lives, we might know God's direction. This Scripture-centred approach does not exclude a role for godly counsellors. Some take a very individualistic approach when they seek God's will and refuse to be guided by the 'words of men'. As a result they are not (as they imagine) being faithful to the Scriptures as their final authority; rather they are taking a blinkered view of how God directs his people by refusing to listen to others who might be able to shed light on truths in the Word of God which they have overlooked.

Rehoboam's situation was complicated by the fact that he received two very different sets of advice. First of all, he turned to the older men who had advised Solomon. These were the courtiers, rather than the tribal elders in the traditional sense of the word. They are called **'elders'** because of their years of accumulated experience. They had seen Solomon administer justice and they had heard the wise counsel he handed down to the many who sought him. They were a valuable resource for the young king to have at his side.

The counsel that these elders gave showed that they were perceptive men who realized that serious trouble was brewing in the kingdom. They could see that the people were reaching the limits of their endurance because of the 'heavy yoke' that rested upon them. As a result, they advised a conciliatory response to the people's request. **'They replied, "If you will be kind to these people and please them and give them a favourable answer, they will always be your servants"'** (10:7). The old men recognized the sincerity of the people's promise in 10:4, and advised Rehoboam to 'do good' and to 'show favour' to the people.

Not only was this a prudent response, it was also a righteous one. This is how God deals with all his creatures (Ps. 145:9), and he expects rulers to treat their subjects similarly (Prov. 14:35). The elders recognized that people have a right to expect fair treatment from their rulers, and that when their legitimate expectations are met they will give their loyalty willingly. 'If you will be kind to these people ... they will always be your servants' (10:7). Rehoboam's rights as king brought with them responsibilities towards his people.

Rehoboam did not like the advice he received from the elders. Even before he had the opportunity to listen to the alternatives, he rejected the advice of the old men: **'Rehoboam rejected the advice the elders gave him and consulted the young men who had grown up with him'** (10:8). Here is the first sign of the weaknesses that were to make Rehoboam an ineffective king. He did not want advisers who told him the truth, but people who would tell him what he wanted to hear.

Paul tells us that this is a characteristic of men and women whose hearts are unbroken before God, and that there are such people in the church in every generation: 'They will gather around them a great number of teachers to say what their itching ears want to hear. They will turn their ears away from the truth and turn aside to myths' (2 Tim. 4:3-4).

Rehoboam did not want to hear the advice of the older men, because it offended his pride. They told Rehoboam that, even though he was king, he could not behave in an arbitrary manner. They tried to impress upon him that he owed a duty of care to his subjects, just as they owed a duty of loyalty to him. They told him that, as king, he was the servant of his people, and that they were not slaves. They let him see that he had much to learn. Yet that was something Rehoboam was not willing to do.

How many spiritual problems flare up in our walk with God, in our relationships with other people and in the lives of many congregations because professing Christians are too proud to admit that they are wrong, listen to others and change their ways! Underlying this stubbornness is often something even more sinful — an unwillingness to listen to God. May we learn to repent of this!

Rehoboam set out to find advice more to his liking. He turned to **'the young men who had grown up with him and were serving him'** (10:8). The Hebrew word for 'young men' emphasizes their youthful inexperience. It must have been obvious that they were poor counsellors. They were Rehoboam's 'pals' from childhood. They were the friends with whom he had surrounded himself because he knew them well and felt comfortable in their company. Yet all too often such people will not tell us what we need to hear because it might be awkward or unpopular.

These young men came from the privileged, aristocratic classes of Jerusalem. They grew up amidst the opulence of Solomon's Jerusalem, where silver was considered of little value and household items were routinely made out of gold. They knew only an easy life, and would have had little sympathy with the struggles of the ordinary people. They were like Marie Antoinette, the Queen of France during the French Revolution. When she learned that the starving populace were rioting because of sheer hunger, she is reputed to have said, 'If they have no bread, let them eat cake.' Rehoboam's young companions gave advice that was simple and callous: **'Tell the people who have said to you, "Your father put a heavy yoke on us, but make our yoke lighter" — tell them, "My little finger is thicker than my father's waist. My father laid on you a heavy yoke; I will make it even heavier. My father scourged you with whips; I will scourge you with scorpions"'** (10:10-11). This was exactly the sort of advice that Rehoboam wanted to hear. Three days later when the people came to hear their king's answer they received, word for word, this crushing rebuke (10:12-14).

Why did Rehoboam seek out and follow this foolish advice? That answer is that he did not appreciate how much he still had to learn. Rehoboam needed a greater measure of godly discernment, but he did not even recognize just how great his need was. 'The fear of the Lord is the beginning of wisdom' (Prov. 9:10), and when men have not learned to fear the Lord, folly will plague all their dealings with their fellow men. Rehoboam was foolish in selecting his counsellors. As a consequence he was also foolish in responding to his subjects.

If we are to live lives marked by godliness and wisdom, we need to consider the influences which we allow to bear upon our lives. Which friends do we allow to influence us most? Whose example are we seeking to follow? How much are we being influenced by the attitudes and lifestyles being promoted by the secular media? What sort of preaching are we listening to each Lord's Day? Paul speaks very clearly in 1 Corinthians 15:33: 'Bad company corrupts good character.' Christians should seek out churches where the Bible is held in high esteem as the Word of God and its doctrines are clearly taught (1 Peter 2:2), and where godly fellowship is a spur to godliness (Heb. 10:24).

The consequences of taking wrong advice (10:15-17)

Rehoboam's response to a reasonable request stirred his people up to greater resentment. **'So the king did not listen to the people... All Israel saw that the king refused to listen to them'** (10:15-16). 'Surely, there is no point reasoning with this man,' they thought, 'for he is a king who does not listen.' It is a most frustrating thing to talk to someone who does not listen, and who makes it obvious that he is not listening. When marriages break down it is often because husbands and wives have stopped listening to each other. The union between Rehoboam and the ten tribes of his kingdom was never consummated, because he refused to listen.

Rehoboam's words in 10:14 were foolish and inflammatory rhetoric and they provoked an immediate response. The ten northern tribes repudiated their link with the royal line of David and simply **'went home'** (10:16). Later Jeroboam consolidated this rift by establishing himself as ruler of the northern kingdom.

For many years there had been a fault-line between the ten northern tribes and the tribe of Judah, but it was camouflaged. Judah was the largest and most powerful tribe in Israel and many great promises had been given to it (see, for example, Gen. 49:8-12). This tended to make the other tribes suspicious and resentful of Judah's superiority. When David came to the throne, the fact that he was from the tribe of Judah made the rest of Israel wary of accepting him. For seven years he ruled in Hebron, before all Israel acknowledged him as king

(2 Sam. 5:1-5). During David's reign 'a troublemaker named
Sheba' raised the standard of rebellion and his rallying cry in
2 Samuel 20:1 was the same as that of the Israelites in 10:16:

> **What share do we have in David,**
> **what part in Jesse's son?**
> **To your tents, O Israel!**
> **Look after your own house, O David!**

This ancient slogan now returned to haunt the royal line of
David.

Rehoboam's response makes us take note of the power of
the tongue. His insensitive words acted like a crowbar to prise
open this ancient fault-line. The words of Adolf Hitler fanned
the flames of German nationalism in the 1930s, with disastrous consequences. The words of Winston Churchill inspired
the free peoples of the world to resist Nazi aggression. Words
are powerful tools for both good and evil. 'The tongue has the
power of life and death' (Prov. 18:21). 'A gentle answer turns
away wrath, but a harsh word stirs up anger' (Prov. 15:1).
Our words can comfort, encourage, teach and chasten, all to
the glory of God. Let us resolve to guard our lips so that our
words cause no unnecessary offence. Rehoboam's unguarded
words divided his kingdom and resulted in years of civil war.

The significance of the division of the kingdom (10:15,19)

Church history records several important partings of the ways.
In 1054 the eastern and western branches of Christendom re-
nounced each other and went their separate ways. In 1517
Martin Luther nailed his ninety-five theses to the door of
Wittenberg Cathedral and set in motion the Protestant Refor-
mation. Only as we look back on these events do we see their

significance. In the history of Israel Jeroboam's rebellion was an event of equal significance. It is important for three reasons.

1. The northern tribes wilfully rejected the ordinances of God

While we can understand the resentment which had been building up during Solomon's reign and sympathize with the request they presented to Rehoboam, the reaction of the northern tribes in 10:16 can only be described as sinful. It is described in 10:19 as **'rebellion'** (or *pasha*, a word which emphasizes the sinfulness of rejecting God, see 1 Sam. 15:23).

The rebellion of the northern tribes was not simply political; it was spiritual. It was a rejection of two ordinances which the Lord had given to unite his chosen people — the monarchy and the temple. For all his faults, Rehoboam was a descendant of David, and was the one whom God had appointed to sit on David's throne. Jerusalem was the place where the temple was, and it was to Jerusalem that the Lord had commanded the tribes to go to worship. When the northern tribes separated themselves from Rehoboam they also separated themselves from the temple and from the worship of Jehovah. It would not be long before idolatry replaced temple worship (see 11:14-15; 1 Kings 12:26-33).

In the New Testament God's people are ruled by the Messianic King, the Lord Jesus Christ, 'who as to his human nature was a descendant of David, and who through the Spirit of holiness was declared with power to be the Son of God' (Rom. 1:3-4). A succession of mere men who varied in the level of godliness that they displayed has been replaced by a perfect King who reigns for ever. 'Jesus Christ is the same yesterday and today and for ever' (Heb. 13:8). Moreover, Jesus Christ is the temple of the new covenant (John 2:21; Heb. 10:19-20).

Christian believers are no longer citizens of one earthly nation, nor are they obliged to go up to Jerusalem to worship God, but they honour Jesus Christ as King and Saviour. Loyalty to him as our King and a love for his ordinances of religion are tied together, just as the temple and the monarchy were inseparably linked in Israel. We do not worship in the temple in Jerusalem, but we have been given means of grace, such as the reading and preaching of Scripture, private, family and congregational worship, prayer and the sacraments of baptism and the Lord's Supper. If we love the Lord Jesus and acknowledge him as our King, then we will love the means of grace he has given to us. On the other hand, those who refuse to submit to King Jesus show their contempt for him by neglecting the means of grace that he has given. Those who ignore his Word and forsake assembling themselves together for worship will soon grow cold even towards the Lord himself.

2. The defection of the northern tribes was a judgement upon Solomon and his family

'This turn of events was from God, to fulfil the word that the Lord had spoken to Jeroboam son of Nebat through Ahijah the Shilonite' (10:15). This warning is recorded in 1 Kings 11:27-40. Because Solomon had taken many heathen wives and worshipped their gods, his kingdom would be divided after his death and the greater part torn out of the hands of his son. The Lord told Jeroboam that he was to be the Lord's instrument to punish Solomon. Solomon clearly knew that the Lord had given the ten tribes to Jeroboam and resented it.

This does not lessen Jeroboam's responsibility for his sinful actions. He 'made Israel to sin' and he sinned wilfully. God's sovereignty does not deny our free agency, or take away our responsibility for our actions. We can never hide behind God when we sin (see James 1:13-14).

We can, however, take comfort from the knowledge that God is sovereign over the actions of sinful men. Even when they do their worst, God is still perfectly righteous and totally in control of the situation. We see the same sovereign control over the actions of Joseph's callous brothers (Gen. 50:20) and the Jews who crucified our Lord (Acts 2:23).

3. God's covenant was preserved through the southern kingdom of Judah

From this point onwards the book of Chronicles, in contrast to the book of Kings, concentrates almost exclusively on the history of the southern kingdom. The history of Kings records the failings of the northern kingdom as well as the mixed record of the southern kingdom as an explanation of the judgement which fell on all Israel in 587 B.C. The Chronicler focuses on the godly remnant who gathered around the monarchy and who attended upon the ministrations of the temple (the priests and Levites).

This is a calculated reminder that even though God's people may violate God's covenant with them, God himself will never repudiate his covenant. The Lord may chastise his people, but he will never cast them away. The remainder of 2 Chronicles is, in effect, a historical illustration of God's promise to David in Psalm 89:30-37:

> If his sons forsake my law
>   and do not follow my statutes,
> if they violate my decrees
>   and fail to keep my commands,
> I will punish their sin with the rod,
>   their iniquity with flogging;
> but I will not take my love from him,
>   nor will I ever betray my faithfulness.

I will not violate my covenant
　　or alter what my lips have uttered.
Once for all, I have sworn by my holiness —
　　and I will not lie to David —
that his line will continue for ever
　　and his throne endure before me like the sun;
it will be established for ever like the moon,
　　the faithful witness in the sky.

Foolish attempts to frustrate God's decree (10:18 – 11:4)

Rehoboam was not just unwilling to listen to his people; he was slow to learn from experience. Even bitter experience did not teach him to be cautious. He **'sent out Adoniram, who was in charge of forced labour'** (10:18). Presumably Adoniram's task was to force the Israelites back into line. Rehoboam had not counted on their resolve being so strong, and coercion did not work. **'The Israelites stoned him [Adoniram] to death. King Rehoboam, however, managed to get into his chariot and escape to Jerusalem'** (10:18).

When Rehoboam got back to Jerusalem, he set about raising an army to do what Adoniram had failed to do (11:1). **'He mustered the house of Judah and Benjamin — a hundred and eighty thousand fighting men — to make war against Israel and to regain the kingdom for Rehoboam.'** However, it did not come to bloodshed because the Lord intervened to tell him to stop: **'But this word of the LORD came to Shemaiah the man of God: "Say to Rehoboam... 'This is what the LORD says: Do not go up to fight against your brothers. Go home, every one of you, for this is my doing'"'** (11:2-4).

This time there was a glimmer of hope in Rehoboam's response: **'They obeyed the words of the LORD and turned**

back from marching against Jeroboam' (11:4). We are not
told why Rehoboam made this climbdown. We do know, however, that it was joint obedience: 'they obeyed' refers to
Rehoboam and his people. Perhaps Rehoboam's remaining
subjects had had enough of conflict and restrained their king.
Or perhaps Rehoboam was learning to listen to God. If so, he
had come to appreciate two facts.

1. Man proposes, but God disposes

Rehoboam planned to lead an army against the Israelites in
the north, but one word from the Lord put an end to all his
plans. 'Many are the plans in a man's heart, but it is the LORD's
purpose that prevails' (Prov. 19:21). 'In his heart a man plans
his course, but the LORD determines his steps'(Prov. 16:9).
James applies this truth very clearly: 'Instead, you ought to
say, "If it is the Lord's will, we will live and do this or that"'
(James 4:15).

2. It often lakes a long time to learn what listening to God involves

Listening to God is not a natural activity for fallen mankind,
but one which has to be learned by those whose minds have
been renewed by grace. Because we listen so much to the
world or to the desires of our own hearts, we do not have a
sharp ear for what the Lord is saying to us. Only after many
mistakes did Rehoboam learn to listen to God. How can we
avoid making the same mistakes?

Firstly, *by taking heed to God's Word when we hear it.*
This is the obvious place to start. Do you read your Bible
every day? Do you arrive at church each week with your
Bible, eager and ready to follow the preacher's exposition
of God's Word?

Secondly, *by making our plans subject to God's overriding plans.* Do you pray before you make your plans? Or do you make your plans and then set them before God for his blessing? Are your plans flexible in God's hands?

Thirdly, *by seeking out those who can give us godly advice.* Are your closest friends people who love the Lord and walk with him? Are there people you are avoiding because you know they will tell you something you don't want to hear? Do you want flattery or faithfulness from a friend? (See Prov. 27:6).

Fourthly, *by making it a priority to pursue what the Lord wants.*

> Trust in the LORD with all your heart
>   and lean not on your own understanding;
> in all your ways acknowledge him
>   and he will make your paths straight
>
> (Prov. 3:5-6).

When we lean on someone else, our steps are shaped by that person, just like a child beginning to walk, or an elderly person who has lost the power of his limbs. That other person can do with us as he or she wishes. Are you prepared to yield that level of control over your life to the Lord? If so, then you have learned to listen, and to follow the Lord.

8.
Half-hearted leadership

Please read 2 Chronicles 11:5 – 12:16

Rehoboam's reign got off to a bad start. Because he accepted foolish advice he rejected out of hand his people's request that the heavy yoke of forced labour might be eased. As a result he lost control over the ten northern tribes of Israel. Jeroboam established himself, first as their spokesman and then as their king. Rehoboam was left to rule over Judah and Benjamin. Chapters 11 and 12 give us an overview of Rehoboam's reign and God's judgement on it.

In Sellar and Yeatman's mock history of England, *1066 and All That*, everything in English history is summarized in a word: either it was 'a good thing' or 'a bad thing'. We find a similar, striking contrast between the kings of Judah throughout 2 Chronicles. Although the Chronicler's accounts of the kings of Judah are more subtle and complex than those which are given in Kings, ultimately they are all classified as either 'good' or 'bad'.

The Chronicler gave Rehoboam some credit for the good things that he did, but God's verdict is clearly stated in 12:14: **'He did evil because he had not set his heart on seeking the LORD.'** Before we consider the fundamental flaw that ruined Rehoboam and caused so much damage to his kingdom, let us consider some of the positive things that are recorded about his reign.

Rehoboam fortified his borders (11:5-12)

'Rehoboam lived in Jerusalem and built up towns for defence in Judah' (11:5). If you read through the list of garrison towns in 11:6-10 and locate them on a map, you will find that they lie to the south of Jerusalem in the Judean uplands. (The only possible exception is Gath in 11:8, although this may be a Moresheth-Gath which was also in the Judean uplands.) Rehoboam clearly considered that the greatest threat to the security of his kingdom did not come from the northern tribes, but from the south and west. In fact Rehoboam's strengthening of his south-western defences was a timely response to a new threat from Egypt.

Good relations with Egypt had existed during the reign of King Solomon, as a result of Solomon's marriage to the daughter of Pharaoh (see 8:11; 1 Kings 3:1). After Solomon's death this alliance deteriorated. At around the same time, in 935 B.C., the declining twenty-first Egyptian dynasty was overthrown by a Libyan nobleman called Shishak (of whom we shall read more later) who established the Bubastite, or twenty-second, dynasty. This was not the first time that the rise of a new pharaoh in Egypt had spelt trouble for the Israelites (see Exod. 1:8).

Shishak's power base was in Africa and he sought to extend its influence into Asia. To do so he had to come through Judah. Rehoboam was astute enough to recognize this as a very grave threat to his kingdom and to take it seriously: **'He strengthened their defences and put commanders in them, with supplies of food, olive oil and wine. He put shields and spears in all the cities, and made them very strong'** (11:11-12). The Chronicler presents Rehoboam as a man with some of the organizational skills of his father and grandfather.

He received godly Israelites from the north (11:13-17)

The words of Shemaiah the prophet in 11:4 reminded Rehoboam that the northern tribes were still part of the covenant people of Israel. Shemaiah instructed Rehoboam not to lead his army against the Israelites, and pointed out that the northerners were still his kinsmen: 'Do not go up to fight against your brothers.' Moreover there were many godly men and women in the northern territories. God's people lived on both sides of an international boundary, as in many countries today where congregations within the same church worship on different sides of a political border. Although Rehoboam had built fortifications to defend his southern boundary, it appears that he put up no 'ring of steel' to keep out refugees from the north. In fact he encouraged them to join him, and **'The priests and Levites from all their districts throughout Israel sided with him'** (11:13).

The Chronicler takes a special interest in the work of the Levites and their contribution to the spiritual life of God's people. Many of those who returned from exile in Babylon were from the tribes of Judah (the royal tribe) and Levi (the priestly tribe). Out of this remnant would come the one who would be both a Priest and a King for ever. The special relationship that developed between the priestly tribe and the royal line of David during the monarchy was a pointer to the unique office of the Lord Jesus Christ.

The priests and Levites led the northern exiles on their journey south into Rehoboam's kingdom (11:13). They were spiritual leaders among the people of Israel, both in the temple at Jerusalem, and in the communities throughout Israel where they taught God's law and gathered the tithes which supported the temple ministry. They also gave leadership to those from the northern tribes who wanted to separate themselves from

Jeroboam's rebellion and apostasy: **'Those from every tribe of Israel who set their hearts on seeking the LORD, the God of Israel, followed the Levites to Jerusalem to offer sacrifices to the LORD, the God of their fathers'** (11:16). This was just the sort of leadership that Rehoboam failed to give his people. It was wholehearted, sacrificial and centred on God's Word.

The Levites and other Israelites did not just make a short pilgrimage to Jerusalem and then return home. They uprooted themselves, moved their homes and belongings and settled in Judah. This migration involved considerable material sacrifice on their part, because they **'even abandoned their pasture-lands and property'**. God had given an inheritance to each of the tribes in Israel, but to the Levites God gave common land scattered throughout Israel (1 Chr. 6:54-81). No Israelite willingly gave up the land he had received from the Lord (1 Kings 21:3; Lev. 25:23) because it was a token of the Lord's irrevocable gift to his people. However, these Levites made this sacrifice willingly because the worship of Jehovah mattered more to them than their land.

Matthew Henry comments, 'It was a comfort to them that the law so often reminded them that the Lord was their inheritance.' Many years later, Jesus reminded his disciples that those who would serve him must be prepared to make a similar sacrifice: 'If anyone would come after me, he must deny himself and take up his cross and follow me. For whoever wants to save his life will lose it, but whoever loses his life for me and for the gospel will save it' (Mark 8:34-35).

The Levites left their lands in the north because of the apostasy of their nation. Jeroboam had dismissed them from their role as spiritual leaders in the nation: **'Jeroboam and his sons had rejected them as priests of the LORD'** (11:15). When Jeroboam rejected the Lord (who had appointed the tribe of

Levi to its special role, and especially the sons of Aaron to be priests) he also rejected the Lord's servants. In turning away from the Lord Jeroboam also abandoned God's ordinances of worship. There was no place for faithful servants of the Lord in Jeroboam's new order. More accommodating spiritual leaders took their place: **'He appointed his own priests for the high places and for the goat and calf idols he had made'** (11:15).

It must have been painful for these Levites to watch as the people of Israel turned away from the living God to worship false gods who were fashioned after dumb animals. Under Jeroboam's leadership the people reverted to the nature worship of the Canaanites and worshipped **'goat and calf idols'**. The apostle Paul described this foolishness in Romans 1:22-23: 'Although they claimed to be wise, they became fools and exchanged the glory of the immortal God for images made to look like mortal man and birds and animals and reptiles.' Such gods have nothing to say to men, and their influence serves only to degrade those who worship them. In due time the Israelites were to sink even deeper into sin, but before that was allowed to happen these faithful Levites and their families removed themselves from the corrupting influence around them.

Although it is not possible, or necessarily desirable (see 1 Cor. 5:9-10; John 17:15), for Christians today to flee from the sinful world around us, the same principle of separation applies. We need to settle ourselves and our families in locations where we shall be able to attend a Bible-preaching church and enjoy the benefits of godly fellowship. That may involve removing ourselves from church groups where false doctrine is preached or true discipline is not maintained. We should not underestimate the power of false doctrine and godless behaviour to influence us, nor should we expose ourselves to their influence:

'Therefore come out from them
   and be separate'
               says the Lord.
'Touch no unclean thing
   and I will receive you'
             (2 Cor. 6:17, quoting Isa. 52:11).

When the priests and Levites arrived in Judah they brought great blessing with them: **'They strengthened the kingdom of Judah and supported Rehoboam son of Solomon for three years'** (11:17). They strengthened the kingdom by giving wholehearted support to the twin pillars of the southern kingdom — the divinely anointed monarchy and the divinely appointed place of worship. They came south with a greater zeal for the temple and the worship of the true God, after having seen the disastrous slide into idolatry north of the border. The terrible consequences of worshipping false gods had been clearly illustrated to them and they did not want to see a repeat performance in Judah.

We can only speculate as to the other blessings that they brought to Rehoboam's kingdom. When King Louis XIV of France removed the protection afforded to the French Protestants (or Huguenots) in 1685, many thousands of these people fled France to settle in other lands. Many of them settled in Ireland, and brought with them, not just their warm piety, but their skills in linen-making. The departure of the Huguenots not only retarded the French economy for over a hundred years, but it introduced the world-famous linen industry into Ireland. The blessings they brought to the land of their adoption were both spiritual and material. We may imagine that the northern refugees brought similar blessing and Rehoboam was wise to receive them.

He consolidated his family's hold on power (11:18-23)

The Chronicler also takes a keen interest in Rehoboam's family tree (11:18-21). His first wife was **'Mahalath, who was the daughter of David's son Jerimoth and of Abihail, the daughter of Jesse's son Eliab'** (11:18). Jerimoth and Abihail were cousins and their daughter Mahalath was Rehoboam's cousin (see family tree below). Rehoboam's second wife, Maacah, was his favourite: **'Rehoboam loved Maacah daughter of Absalom more than any of his other wives and concubines'** (11:21). She was also his cousin — a daughter, or more probably a grand-daughter, of Absalom, his uncle. According to 2 Samuel 14:27, Absalom is recorded as having only one daughter, called Tamar, so Maacah is generally thought to have been his granddaughter.

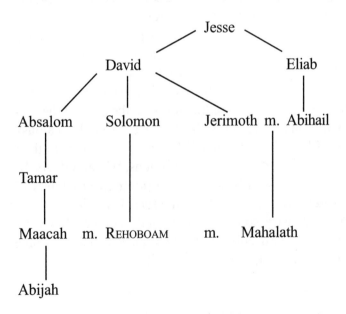

Rehoboam's family tree (see 11:18-21)

The purpose of this rather complicated family story is most probably to point out the thoroughly Davidic nature of the succession. Rehoboam married two wives who were descended from King David, and his heir apparent, Abijah, was descended from David on his mother's account as well as his father's. The importance of a truly Davidic royal line is one of the Chronicler's recurring themes as he looks forward to a great king who will be a son of David.

Rehoboam did his duty in preserving the royal family. He enjoyed the blessing of having **'twenty-eight sons and sixty daughters'** (11:21). Family statistics were often recorded to indicate the extent of God's blessing. The psalmist tells us that 'Sons are a heritage from the Lord' (Ps. 127:3), and certainly Rehoboam knew the Lord's blessing in this respect.

Rehoboam appointed Abijah, the son of his favourite wife, to be his crown prince and heir apparent (11:22). In doing so, he appears to have acted contrary to the principle laid down in Deuteronomy 21:15-17, which requires that if a man has sons by several wives the rights of the first-born must go to the son born first, irrespective of the favour in which the various wives are held. Rehoboam's appointment solved the issue of the succession after his death, but it must have aroused the jealousy of some of his other sons who had their eyes set upon their father's crown. To distract their ambitions, **'He acted wisely, dispersing some of his sons throughout the districts of Judah and Benjamin, and to all the fortified cities'** (11:23). When his sons were spread throughout the country they were less likely to plot mischief, and better placed to achieve some good in the administration of the people.

Rehoboam's fundamental flaw

While we note Rehoboam's strengths we should never lose sight of the ultimate judgement that God passed upon him:

'He did evil because he had not set his heart on seeking the LORD' (12:14). This is not a simplistic assessment of Rehoboam which ignores the beneficial things he did. The Scriptures recognize that unregenerate men and women can perform actions which benefit their fellow men (Luke 6:33; Rom. 2:14-15). Even unregenerate fathers can give 'good gifts' to their children (Luke 11:11-13). From God's perspective these good actions do not look so impressive. God sees the mixed motives and the sinful defects as well. These 'good actions' can never earn God's favour for, as our Lord taught, 'When you have done everything you were told to do, [you] should say, "We are unworthy servants; we have only done our duty"' (Luke 17:10). Compared with the righteous standards of God, even 'The kindest acts of the wicked are cruel' (Prov. 12:10).

The great weakness which spoiled the 'good actions' of Rehoboam was the fact that his heart was wicked: 'He did evil because he had not set his heart on seeking the LORD' (12:14). He did evil because his heart was evil. The heart of fallen man is naturally wicked, and until it is renewed by the grace of God, all its natural impulses will be evil.

Rehoboam's conduct was modified by many godly people around him. No doubt the training that he received from Solomon continued to influence him. There were many godly people within his kingdom — not least the refugees who came from the northern tribes — whose advice would have restrained him. Rehoboam knew what God expected of him. Rehoboam tried to serve the Lord, but his service was never more than half-hearted. 'He did evil because he had not set his heart on seeking the LORD.' This fundamental flaw was exposed with such terrible consequences when Shishak invaded his kingdom.

Complacency had set in (12:1-2)

Everything seemed to be going well for Rehoboam. **'Rehoboam's position as king was established and he had become strong'** (12:1). After a shaky start, the kingdom of Judah got onto its feet again. It enjoyed God's blessing — strong borders and a growing population. Then, as if out of the blue, disaster struck when Shishak invaded. The Chronicler knew that Shishak's invasion did not in fact come out of the blue, for it was God's judgement upon a nation that had grown complacent. Much hard work had been done. The times when Rehoboam was conscious that he needed God were past. He was like the rich fool described by our Lord who thought, 'I will say to my soul, "Soul, you have many goods laid up for many years; take your ease; eat, drink and be merry"' (Luke 12:19, NKJV). He felt quite capable of dealing with the challenges of life on his own, so he himself drifted far from God.

This was God's judgement upon the complacency which grew up as a result of Rehoboam's strong position. After becoming strong, **'He and all Israel with him abandoned the law of the LORD'** (12:1). This in turn made the Lord angry with them: **'Because they had been unfaithful to the LORD, Shishak king of Egypt attacked Jerusalem in the fifth year of King Rehoboam'** (12:2).

God's people should always be aware of this danger when they are surrounded by their success. It may be that they have achieved prosperity or personal advancement in their career; it may be that they have enjoyed academic success; it may even be that they have been greatly used by the Lord in the cause of the gospel. When we begin to bask in the glory of these successes, we cease to depend upon the Lord as we once did. That is the time when we are most vulnerable to satanic attack. It is then that we commit our most grievous sins. King David was a notable example in 2 Samuel 11:1-4.

So, 'Woe to you who are complacent in Zion, and to you who feel secure on Mount Samaria…!' (Amos 6:1).

A formidable military machine (12:3-4)

'Blitzkrieg' is the term that Adolf Hitler introduced into the vocabulary of war. The theory was that a massive concentration of military power, by air and land, would crush everything before it with such speed that organized resistance would be impossible. The same idea lay behind Shishak's campaign in Palestine. He invaded Judah and Israel **'with twelve hundred chariots and sixty thousand horsemen and … innumerable troops of Libyans, Sukkites and Cushites'** (12:3). His armies were so large that even the Chronicler, who normally takes a great interest in quantifying large numbers of soldiers, describes them as 'people without number' (NKJV).

The effect of Shishak's massive troop deployment was swift and effective: **'He captured the fortified cities of Judah and came as far as Jerusalem'** (12:4). Rehoboam's 'Maginot Line' crumbled in an instant, just as the French defences crumbled before Hitler's blitzkrieg in 1940.

Ancient history sheds light upon the events described in this chapter. As well as invading Judah, Shishak overran Israel, Edom and the lands east of the River Jordan. When he returned home from his Palestinian campaign, Shishak constructed a monument at Karnak (near the modern town of Luxor in upper Egypt) to commemorate his victories. Among the 150 towns which he claims to have conquered, there are inscriptions referring to some of the towns listed in 11:6-10 and the Judean town of Megiddo. Archaeological investigations in Megiddo have unearthed a stone slab, bearing an inscription to commemorate Shishak's conquest of the town. It is interesting to note that archaeology substantiates the historical accuracy of this chapter and reinforces the extent of the destruction caused by Shishak's invasion. One historian has commented that this 'blow laid both Israel and Judah low and undoubtedly forced a postponement of their private quarrel'.

A prophetic explanation (12:5-6)

In the midst of this crisis the Lord spoke to Rehoboam: **'Then the prophet Shemaiah came to Rehoboam and to the leaders of Judah'** (12:5). When Shemaiah spoke to Jeroboam and his advisers, he found a pitiable group of men. They were **'assembled in Jerusalem for fear of Shishak'**. 'Huddled' might be a more graphic word to describe them as they hid themselves in their last stronghold, waiting for Shishak to deliver his final, crushing, blow. Rehoboam and his advisers were frightened men who did not know which way to turn. They were not just at a loss with regard to their military strategy; they were spiritually bankrupt. They had no leadership to offer their people. We can only imagine what chaos must have reigned in the streets of Jerusalem as the people waited to be attacked by Shishak's army.

Rehoboam and his counsellors were like the Pharisees who were so roundly rebuked by our Lord in Matthew 16:2-4. They could read the signs of nature, but they could not see the workings of God's hand in their times. Perhaps they knew well enough the reason behind their predicament, but they could not bring themselves to acknowledge it. That is why the Lord sent his prophet Shemaiah to explain their situation to them. **'This is what the LORD says: "You have abandoned me; therefore I now abandon you to Shishak"'** (12:5). The function of God's spokesmen in every age is to point men and women back to God — the God whom they are often trying to ignore.

In 12:1 the Chronicler has already told us that Rehoboam had 'abandoned the law of the LORD'. Shemaiah's words in 12:5 are slightly different, but they say the same thing: 'You have abandoned me.' There are two lessons we can learn from this rebuke.

Firstly, *God and his law are inseparable.* We should not think that God's commands are matters that we can treat lightly. We should not think that we can serve God wholeheartedly if we treat his laws casually. Jesus said, 'If you love me, you will obey what I command' (John 14:15).

Then, secondly, we learn that *open sin begins with secret contempt for God.* We are not told how Rehoboam 'abandoned the law of the LORD'. There is no reference to any acts of idolatry, or murder, or adultery. However, our Lord teaches that each one of these sins begins in the thoughts of the heart (Matt. 5:21-30). Every sinful action begins with a sinful thought, and every sinful thought derives from secret contempt for God's commands. Shemaiah explained this tragic chain of cause and effect to Rehoboam and his counsellors. 'This is what the LORD says: "You have abandoned me; therefore I now abandon you to Shishak."'

Partial repentance and partial deliverance (12:6-12)

The response of the rulers of Judah was encouraging, as far as it went: **'The leaders of Israel and the king humbled themselves and said, "The LORD is just"'** (12:6). They acknowledged that they had done wrong and that God was punishing them for their wrongdoing. This is what King David was forced to acknowledge when Nathan confronted him about his adultery:

Against you, you only, have I sinned
and done what is evil in your sight,

so that you are proved right when you speak
      and justified when you judge

(Ps. 51:4).

They hung their heads in shame and acknowledged that God
was acting within his rights when he sent judgement upon them.
However, there is no evidence of a resolve on their part to do
what they knew to be right, or to change their ways.

Ungodly men and women can (sometimes) see that they
have done wrong and that they are rightly under the judgement of God. Examples from Scripture include King Saul
(1 Sam. 15:30), Judas Iscariot (Matt. 27:3-4) and Esau (Heb.
12:17). God reveals this truth to their minds without necessarily renewing their hearts. Perhaps their actions show re-
morse, or a desire that their lives might have been other than
they were. However, there is no evidence of a desire for spiritual transformation or a willingness to serve the Lord. The
sign of wholehearted commitment in the life of Zacchaeus was
his willingness to make good his evil actions by repaying those
he had cheated (Luke 19:8-10). This was sacrificial repentance! Rehoboam, however, did not 'set his heart on seeking
the Lord'. His repentance was never wholehearted.

Notwithstanding Rehoboam's half-heartedness, the Lord
saw a measure of repentance: **'Since they have humbled
themselves, I will not destroy them'** (12:7). The Lord saw
their humiliation and heard their acknowledgement of sin; therefore he removed the threat of destruction from Jerusalem.
However, we must note the qualified terms of this deliverance: **'Therefore I will not destroy them, but I will grant
them some deliverance'** (12:7, NKJV). The translation 'some
deliverance' is to be preferred over the translation 'soon give
them deliverance' (NIV). The Hebrew phrase literally means
'little deliverance'. The sobering reality is that partial repentance resulted in partial deliverance. God removed the

tribulation that he had brought by the hand of Shishak: **'Because Rehoboam humbled himself, the Lord's anger turned from him, and he was not totally destroyed'** (12:12). Rehoboam was not destroyed, but he was weakened.

There are two indicators that the kingdom of Judah was not the same after the invasion as it had been before.

First of all, *Rehoboam became Shishak's subordinate*. **'They will, however, become subject to him, so that they may learn the difference between serving me and serving the kings of other lands'** (12:8). Shishak did attack Jerusalem and he did carry off treasures from the temple and royal treasuries (12:9). The Lord's deliverance of Judah did not result in their armies enjoying a resounding victory over Shishak, but it did mean that they avoided a humiliating destruction of their city. Other sources suggest that Shishak had to abandon his military campaign in Palestine because of unrest back in Egypt. This may have been the Lord's way of delivering Judah from further humiliation.

However, the stigma of political servitude continued. Rehoboam thought that he could shake himself free from the law of God. God showed him that no one can be a law unto himself. Either he would serve the Lord, or he would serve another master. It is always best to serve the Lord because, paradoxical though it may seem, the greatest freedom is enjoyed by those who submit to the yoke of God's law. When Rehoboam threw off God's law, it was replaced by the yoke of Shishak, and the burden which this imposed was far heavier. This was 'the difference between serving me and serving the kings of other lands'.

Shishak had no love for the people of Israel. He wanted to rule them so that he might extract gold and silver from them. His rule left them poor and miserable. That is how Paul describes the reign of sin in the life of the unbeliever: 'When you were slaves to sin, you were free from the control of righteousness. What benefit did you reap at that time from the things you are now ashamed of? Those things result in death! But now that you have been set free from sin and have become slaves to God, the benefit you reap leads to holiness, and the result is eternal life' (Rom. 6:20-22). What a contrast there is between serving a master who seeks our destruction and serving the Lord who loves us!

Secondly, *Judah's prestige was greatly reduced.* **'So King Rehoboam made bronze shields ... and assigned these to the commanders of the guard on duty at the entrance to the royal palace'** (12:10). These bronze shields replaced **'the gold shields that Solomon had made'** to adorn the walls of the Palace of the Forest of Lebanon (12:9; cf. 9:15-16). Sportsmen are accustomed to think of the gold medal as the highest prize they can win, while the bronze medal goes to the person who comes in third. The change from gold shields to bronze shields was a telling statement about the consequences of Rehoboam's sin. As a result of Rehoboam's half-hearted leadership, Solomon's great empire had been reduced to the status of a third-rate nation.

Summary of Rehoboam's reign (12:13-16)

Rehoboam's reign was a disappointing mixture of good and evil things that had originated in his sinful heart. 'There was some good in Judah', or literally 'good things' (12:12). Among those good things was the survival of the kingdom (12:13). Judah remained as a refuge for those Israelites who sought the Lord, and the temple in Jerusalem remained the place to which Israel came to worship the Lord. Although there was continual warfare between Rehoboam and Jeroboam, Rehoboam died peacefully and passed the kingdom on to his son Abijah (12:16).

These 'good things' were the blessings given by God to preserve his covenant nation. They were marred by the fact that Rehoboam became complacent and abandoned the Lord, and then endured the scourge of warfare and invasion as a result. These bad things go to the heart of what Rehoboam was. They define the legacy he left behind: **'He did evil because he had not set his heart on seeking the LORD'** (12:14).

Why did God bestow any favour on such a king? The answer is found in 12:13: **'He reigned for seventeen years in Jerusalem, the city the LORD had chosen out of all the tribes of Israel in which to put his Name.'** Although Rehoboam was an evil man, Israel remained the covenant people and Rehoboam was their king. He inherited the blessings that the Lord had promised to David and to Solomon and to their descendants. He sat on David's throne and reigned in the city that the Lord had chosen as his own. Outwardly he enjoyed blessings that flowed from the covenant which the Lord had made with his people, even though he was a wicked man.

Many people in our age enjoy the blessings of having had Christian parents or grandparents. Western society is still living off the heritage of a Christian past. The presence of the Christian church in society has exercised a restraining influence on evil and had a blessed effect on the fabric of the community as a whole. The existence of many of our hospitals and charities can be traced back to the convictions of Christian people, even though many who benefit from their care today are not themselves Christians. In all these ways God is showing mercy to a wicked community for the sake of his elect. We should thank God for his mercy, but we should never allow ourselves, or others, to take this mercy for granted. Where God's mercy is acknowledged in a half-hearted way, judgement is sure to follow.

God's covenant mercies to Israel cast light upon Rehoboam's half-heartedness. He had enjoyed the means of grace offered to the men and women of the Old Testament, but he refused to benefit from them. He enjoyed the blessings of knowing God's law and entering God's house, but he did not treasure them in his heart. He is like many people who grow up in a godly home and who know the truth, but who reject it because their hearts are cold towards God. May the Lord deliver us from such coldness.

Signs of half-heartedness

In conclusion let us take note of some of the tell-tale signs which mark half-heartedness.

1. Lack of delight in the blessings that God has given

Do you find that reading the Scriptures, attending worship services and time spent with other believers give you no joy? If this continues month after month then you must examine your heart and ask if it is wholly set upon the Lord.

2. Repentance without renewal

Are you stricken with sorrow when you consider the terrible consequences of your sins, but unwilling to be done with those sins? Sorrow, without a corresponding resolve to replace sinful habits with godly ones, is not genuine repentance. Without genuine repentance, professing believers must ask whether their hearts are wholly set upon the Lord.

3. Enjoyment of God's blessing without growth in grace

Are you content to listen to sermons and memorize the Scriptures without seeing a corresponding growth in your Christian character, service and fruitfulness? Are you praying more fervently than you used to? Is your testimony to Christ more obvious than it used to be? Are you becoming more like Christ? Without this growth in grace you must ask whether your heart is alive for God. Half-heartedness in our own day is just as deadly a spiritual disease as it was in the days of Rehoboam.

9.
Abijah:
God's everlasting kingdom

Please read 2 Chronicles 13:1 – 14:1

The American Civil War was the bloodiest conflict in the history of the United States. More Americans lost their lives in that war than in any before or since. Looking back, it is interesting to note the religious fervour that gripped those on both sides of the conflict. Both the North and the South had godly leaders and praying soldiers in their ranks, and both were tempted to think that the Lord was on their side. Abraham Lincoln was nearer the truth when he said that the issue was not whether the Lord is on our side, but whether we are on the Lord's side! That was the challenge that faced Joshua when he met the Angel of the LORD in Joshua 5:13-14. Joshua asked, 'Are you for us or for our enemies?' To which he received the reply: '"Neither … but as commander of the army of the LORD I have now come." Then Joshua fell face down to the ground in reverence.'

A pressing question in divided Israel was: 'Who is on the Lord's side?' David had ruled Israel as the Lord's anointed. This was obvious to everyone. The Lord had taken the kingdom from Saul and given it to David (1 Chr. 10:14; 17:7,13; 28:4). Solomon was David's appointed successor and reigned as the Lord's anointed (9:8; 1 Chr. 28:5). However, after Solomon's death things started to go awry. Rehoboam followed only half-heartedly in the ways of his father and grandfather.

The ten northern tribes broke away to form an independent kingdom. The Chronicler reminds us that 'There was continual warfare between Rehoboam and Jeroboam' and between their kingdoms (12:15). No doubt both claimed to be the kingdom of the Lord, but which was on the Lord's side? Perhaps many were disillusioned and asked whether the kingdom of the Lord had collapsed altogether?

The Chronicler reminds us that while all the kingdoms of the world belong to the Lord, Judah was God's special kingdom. God's covenant purposes were being worked out through the southern kingdom, which was centred on Jerusalem, and was ruled by the line of King David. For this reason the Chronicler took a special interest in the reign of King Abijah. His account is three times longer than that given in 1 Kings 15:1-8 and it gives us a different perspective on Abijah's reign.

Introducing Abijah (13:1-3)

Abijah became King of Judah **'in the eighteenth year of the reign of Jeroboam'**. In the book of Kings this cross-referencing between the kings of Judah and Israel is very common, but this is the only instance of such a time-reference in Chronicles. Normally the Chronicler relates the history of Judah with barely a mention of the northern kingdom. However, in those tumultuous days after the division of the kingdom, when the relationship between north and south was one of constant conflict, the question could not be avoided: 'Which is the Lord's peculiar kingdom?' The struggle between Jeroboam and the successors of Solomon could not be ignored, because it raised questions that were still being asked many generations later. Had God forsaken Jerusalem? Had the line of David died out? What of the 'son of David'? These were questions that concerned the prophets (Isa. 16:5; Amos 9:11; Zech. 12:7-8), and the Chronicler addressed them by going back into the history of the divided monarchy to demonstrate that, even in the midst of the turmoil between north and south, Judah was still the Lord's kingdom and Abijah was still the Lord's anointed.

The character of Abijah does not come under the scrutiny in this chapter that it did in 1 Kings 15:3. There we read that 'He committed all the sins his father had done before him; his heart was not fully devoted to the LORD his God, as the heart of David his forefather had been.' This stern judgement does not contradict what we read in 2 Chronicles 13. Here we discover that Abijah made a show of piety and devotion to the Lord. While his words were orthodox and impressive, his heart was not. It is Abijah's heart that 1 Kings 15:3 describes. The Chronicler tells us about Abijah's status, rather than his inner worthiness. He remained the one whom the Lord had anointed to rule on the throne of David. The same point is made in 1 Kings 15:4 where we read, 'Nevertheless, for David's sake the LORD his God gave him a lamp in Jerusalem by raising up a son to succeed him and by making Jerusalem strong.'

It was common for these records of the kings of Judah to include the names of their mothers. In Abijah's case this reminds us that he was a true successor to King David. **'His mother's name was Maacah, a daughter of Uriel of Gibeah'** (13:2). Maacah was the favourite wife of his father Rehoboam (11:21-22) and the granddaughter of David's beloved son Absalom. She was the daughter of Absalom's only daughter Tamar (2 Sam. 14:27), who married Uriel of Gibeah. Abijah's Davidic credentials were impeccable.

Abijah's reign was not a long one. It lasted only three years, before he 'rested with his fathers and was buried in the City of David' (14:1). Those three short years were overshadowed by the threat of invasion by his northern neighbour. The chapter describes the battle that took place at Mount Zemaraim (13:4), twenty kilometres to the north of Jerusalem in the disputed **'hill country of Ephraim'** between Judah and Israel. Jeroboam went on the offensive and appears to have had all the trump cards. His armies were twice the size of the armies of Judah (13:3). How would Abijah face this threat? How would his kingdom survive?

Abijah's battlefield speech (13:4-12)

The Chronicler was a most dramatic historian. He took care to preserve the public prayers and speeches of the main players in Israel's history, and to record the drama of the orations as they were uttered. Modern study of the book of Chronicles has noted this feature and sought to explain it. The Chronicler obviously believed in the power of preaching to exhort God's people and the value of public prayer to focus their hearts and minds upon God. Already we have studied the very full records of Solomon's prayers and addresses to the people when the temple was dedicated, also David's prayers and exhortations when he nominated Solomon as his heir. Here in 2 Chronicles 13 is a record of Abijah's speech as two armies faced each other on the field of battle, and perhaps this is the most dramatic oration of them all.

Jeroboam had marched against Judah with an army of 800,000 hand-picked and highly trained men of war. Abijah faced him with an army half that size (13:3) and relied upon the power of persuasion to avoid a potentially disastrous conflict. We are to picture him standing between the two battle lines, appealing for silence, and then reasoning with his opponents: **'Jeroboam and all Israel, listen to me! Don't you know that the LORD, the God of Israel, has given the kingship of Israel to David and his descendants for ever...?'** This was not a message that Jeroboam or his followers wanted to hear; however, we must admire Abijah's courage. His argument was that Jeroboam ought not to press home the attack upon Judah, and he backed up his claim with two reasons.

First of all, he pointed out that *the Lord had appointed the line of David to rule over Israel for ever* (13:5-8). The Lord had made a covenant with David (see 1 Chr. 17:11-14). The kingdom was the Lord's for ever, and it would rest in the hands of David and his sons so long as they were faithful and kept to the terms of God's covenant. That covenant is described in 13:5 as **'a covenant of salt'**. This intriguing expression draws upon the quality of salt as an imperishable chemical. It does not decay itself, and it can be rubbed into food so as to prevent the food from decaying. As a result salt was sometimes eaten in ancient Eastern covenant ceremonies to indicate that the agreements entered into were regarded as binding and unalterable.

In Leviticus 2:13 and Numbers 18:19 we read of salt being added to the offerings which the Israelites offered to the Lord, and this salt was called 'the salt of the covenant of your God'. Commenting on Leviticus 2:13, Gordon Wenham writes, 'To add salt to the offering was a reminder that the worshipper was in an eternal covenant with his God. This meant that God would never forsake him, and also that the worshipper had a perpetual duty to uphold and keep the covenant law.' When Abijah spoke of God's covenant with David as 'a covenant of salt' he was saying that it was an everlasting covenant and that the kingdom had been given to David's family in perpetuity.

In 13:8 Abijah explained the significance of this covenant promise to Jeroboam and his armies. When Jeroboam attacked Judah he was not simply attacking a third-rate little nation; rather he was perpetuating his rebellion against Jehovah: **'And now you plan to resist the kingdom of the LORD, which is in the hands of David's descendants.'** That kingdom was administered by Abijah, but it remained at all times 'the kingdom of the LORD'.

Then, secondly, Abijah drew attention to the fact that *Jerusalem was the home of the true worship of the Lord* (13:8-12). In doing so, he pointed to the Achilles' heel of Jeroboam's great army. Israel had turned its back upon the true worship of the Lord: **'But didn't you drive out the priests of the LORD, the sons of Aaron, and the Levites, and make priests of your own as the peoples of other lands do?'** (13:9). The 'sons of Aaron' were the Levites who had been specially set apart by God to offer sacrifices on behalf of the people of Israel. Not just anyone was eligible to minister at the altar, between the Lord and his people. However, Jeroboam had appointed just about anyone who was willing to do the task: **'Whoever comes to consecrate himself with a young bull and seven rams may become a priest of what are not gods.'**

The deities represented by these golden calves were 'not gods'. They were simply figments of the imagination (see explanation on page 69). These gods have no standard of righteousness by which to restrain their adherents, and as a result their worshippers indulge the worst excesses of their fallen nature. These gods also have no ears to hear, no hands to help and no power to deliver those who cry to them. Abijah urged Jeroboam to pause and consider whether it was wise to venture into battle with his faith resting upon 'what are not gods'.

In contrast to the idolatry being practised in the north, Abijah pointed to the true worship that took place in the temple in Jerusalem. The priests who ministered there were those whom the Lord had appointed: **'As for us, the LORD is our God, and we have not forsaken him. The priests who serve the LORD are sons of Aaron, and the Levites assist them'** (13:10). The sacrifices were those which the Lord had specifically commanded in his laws: **'Every morning and evening they present burnt offerings and fragrant incense to the LORD. They set out bread on the ceremonially clean table and light the lamps on the gold lampstand every evening.**

We are observing the requirements of the LORD our God. But you have forsaken him' (13:11).

We should not be surprised by the importance which Abijah attached to worship in these verses. Worship was obviously a vital part of daily life in Judah. In fact, we might say that worship was Judah's *raison d'être*. It was no accident of history that the temple of the Lord happened to be in Judah's capital city, for the Lord had chosen this people to be his special people and Jerusalem as the place where his name would be glorified. The covenant people were to be a worshipping people. Worship was not a distraction from more important things, or a mere preparation for doing the work of the kingdom. The temple of the Lord was the centre of that kingdom, and its ministrations were to be faithfully maintained.

As Christians we ought to have a similarly high view of worship. God is still jealous to prevent true worship from being replaced by man-made innovations to make it more attractive to worldly people. God still regards worship as one of the primary purposes of his church. It is our great privilege and a great blessing to worship the Lord, and we ought not to regard it as a distraction from evangelism, social witness, personal piety, or doctrinal instruction. All of these are priorities, but our first priority is worship, because our chief calling is 'to glorify God and to enjoy him for ever'.

From Abijah's description of the kingdom, there are three lessons we can learn.

1. Jehovah's lordship applies over everything in church and state

Jehovah was Lord over the government of Judah. He raised up princes and brought them down. He had appointed David to rule; he punished Solomon by dividing the kingdom after his death; he gave two tribes to Rehoboam, and he would not allow Jeroboam to take these from Abijah. Jeroboam had over-reached himself when he sought to defy Jehovah by invading Judah.

The Lord was also sovereign over the religious life of his people. The Lord had taught the Israelites how they were to worship, and who was to lead them when they assembled to offer their sacrifices. Jeroboam therefore overstepped the limits when he appointed priests of his own.

We should not think that the Lord God is content to rule only over 'religious' matters, but is not concerned with the affairs of nations. He is the Lord of all! He has appointed his Son to be both King of kings and our great High Priest. As risen Saviour, Jesus was able to claim in Matthew 28:18: 'All authority in heaven and on earth has been given to me.' God the Father 'has put everything under his feet' (see Ps. 8:6; 1 Cor. 15:27). As a result, Paul tells us that 'We take captive every thought to make it obedient to Christ' (2 Cor. 10:5). There is no part of our lives, whether sacred or secular, that Christ does not claim as his own and which we do not need to surrender to his lordship.

2. It is futile to oppose the lordship of Jehovah

In 13:6 Abijah describes how **'Jeroboam son of Nebat, an official of Solomon son of David, rebelled against his master.'** Abijah explains the special circumstances which allowed Jeroboam to rebel and get away with it: **'Some worthless scoundrels gathered around him and opposed Rehoboam son of Solomon when he was young and indecisive and not strong enough to resist them'** (13:7).

Politicians often talk about putting a 'spin' on events as they unfold. This is the explanation that puts them and their party in the most favourable light. This was the best interpretation that Abijah could put on the events at the beginning of his father's reign. There was a measure of truth in what he said. The legitimate grievances of the people had been exploited by the 'worthless scoundrels' who gathered around Jeroboam. No doubt some of them were more interested in furthering their own ends than in helping the people they claimed to represent. Rehoboam was new to his task and not very sure-footed. It was also said of Solomon that he was 'young and inexperienced' when he came to the throne (1 Chr. 22:5; 29:1), but Solomon at least acknowledged his need to seek godly wisdom. Rehoboam (at the age of forty-one) did not acknowledge his need for God's direction, so Abijah's version of events is less than wholly convincing.

It was Rehoboam's foolishness that allowed Jeroboam to lead the northern tribes astray. However, Abijah was right to point out the essential nature of what Jeroboam and his followers had done — they had rebelled against the Lord. Like the rulers described in Psalm 2:2, they had gathered 'together against the LORD and against his Anointed One', and their rebellion would be similarly short-lived and would end in disaster, because it is always futile to defy the lordship of Jehovah:

> The One enthroned in heaven laughs;
>   the Lord scoffs at them.
> Then he rebukes them in his anger
>   and terrifies them in his wrath, saying,
> 'I have installed my King
>   on Zion, my holy hill.'

We can call to mind the counsel of Gamaliel in Acts 5:38-39, which proved to be truer than he realized: 'For if their purpose or activity is of human origin, it will fail. But if it is from God, you will not be able to stop these men; you will only find yourselves fighting against God.' Jeroboam would soon find that he could not continue this fight indefinitely. Abijah confronted Jeroboam with the awful truth when he said, **'And now you plan to resist the kingdom of the LORD, which is in the hand of David's descendants'** (13:8).

Are you resisting the kingdom of the Lord? Perhaps you are refusing to bow the knee to King Jesus by trying to earn salvation by your own good works. Perhaps you are clinging on to some cherished sin. Perhaps you are stubborn in your unbelief. Perhaps you are resisting the discipline of your local congregation. If so, then you are resisting the kingdom of the Lord which is in the hands of a King far greater than Rehoboam or Abijah. You cannot resist King Jesus for ever, for:

> ... God exalted him to the highest place
> and gave him the name that is above every name,
> that at the name of Jesus every knee should bow,
> in heaven and on earth and under the earth,
> and every tongue confess that Jesus Christ is Lord,
> to the glory of God the Father
>
> (Phil. 2:10-11).

Will you be brought to bow because of his grace, or like Jeroboam, before his sword of judgement?

3. We must appeal to those who resist Jehovah

Abijah saw the tragedy of what was about to happen. Over a million men were being set against each other in battle. Abijah might have echoed the sentiments of Shakespeare's warrior-king, Henry V, when he appealed to the town of Harfleur not to fight him:

> Therefore, you men of Harfleur,
> Take pity of your town and of your people,
> Whiles yet my soldiers are in my command;

Whiles yet the cool and temperate wind of grace
O'erblows the filthy and contagious clouds
Of heady murder, spoil, and villainy.
If not — why, in a moment look to see
The blind and bloody soldier with foul hand
Defile the locks of your shrill-shrieking daughters;
Your fathers taken by the silver beards,
And their most reverend heads dash'd to the walls;
Your naked infants spitted upon pikes,
Whiles the mad mothers with their howls confus'd
Do break the clouds, as did the wives of Jewry
At Herod's bloody-hunting slaughtermen.
What say you? Will you yield, and this avoid?
(*Henry V*, Act III Scene III, lines 27-42).

Moreover, Abijah saw that Jeroboam was rebelling against the Lord and that his rebellion was an offence to God. It was the height of folly. His plans had no chance of succeeding in the face of the Lord. The only thing he could hope to achieve was bloodshed. Abijah pleaded with Jeroboam and his followers not to persist in their foolishness: **'Men of Israel, do not fight against the Lord, the God of your fathers, for you will not succeed'** (13:12).

We have already noted the interest that the Chronicler takes in the speeches and sermons which he records. These often marked important turning-points in Israel's history. They were also powerful appeals that spoke to subsequent generations. Rebellion against God is a serious sin. God does not sit back and watch it happen. God raised up prophets to call sinners back from their rebellion and unbelief.

'Come now, let us reason together,'
   says the Lord.
'Though your sins are like scarlet,
   they shall be as white as snow;

> though they are red as crimson,
>   they shall be like wool.
> If you are willing and obedient,
>   you will eat the best from the land;
> but if you resist and rebel,
>   you will be devoured by the sword'
>
> (Isa. 1:18-20).

> Say to them, 'As surely as I live,' declares the Sovereign LORD, 'I take no pleasure in the death of the wicked, but rather that they turn from their ways and live. Turn! Turn from your evil ways! Why will you die, O house of Israel?' (Ezek. 33:11).

This is the challenge that the gospel presents to men and women today. Sinners are fools and rebels, and destruction is hanging over their heads. John the Baptist preached a warning and alarming message: 'John said to the crowds coming out to be baptized by him, "You brood of vipers! Who warned you to flee from the coming wrath? Produce fruit in keeping with repentance"' (Luke 3:7-8). Stephen warned the Sanhedrin against resisting the message that Jesus Christ is the Messiah (Acts 7:51). Paul warned the men of Athens against resisting the gospel commands of the true and living God (Acts 17:30-31). These warnings were meant to be alarming. Unrepentant sinners are heading for a terrible judgement, and the gospel is meant to arrest their progress so that it may turn them around.

The battle (13:13-15)

When Abijah went into battle his army faced overwhelming odds. Jeroboam had an army of 800,000 'able troops'. Abijah led an army half that size. Jeroboam was a clever and daring tactician. While Abijah was appealing to him to abandon the battlefield, Jeroboam was setting a trap for his army. While Abijah was preaching, Jeroboam was plotting. **'Now Jeroboam had sent troops round to the rear, so that while he was in front of Judah the ambush was behind them. Judah turned and saw that they were being attacked at both front and rear'** (13:13-14). In the face of overwhelming numbers and superior tactics the people of Judah could only rely on the Lord: **'Then they cried out to the LORD. The priests blew their trumpets and the men of Judah raised the battle cry'** (13:14-15).

If the theme of chapter 12 is Rehoboam's *repentance*, the theme of chapter 13 is Judah's *reliance* upon the Lord: 'The men of Judah ... relied on the LORD, the God of their fathers' (13:18). Reliance is simply another word for faith. When we believe someone's assurances we can act in reliance upon them. A friend may invite you to sit down on a chair in his home, but you are unlikely to do so if you see that the chair has an unsteady leg. Only if you believe that the chair can bear your weight, will you entrust yourself to it. This is reliance or (to give it a theological term) faith. The *Westminster Shorter Catechism* describes faith in Christ this way: 'Faith in Jesus Christ is a saving grace, whereby we receive *and rest* upon him alone for salvation, as he is offered to us in the gospel.'

Repentance towards God and reliance upon him always go together. Sometimes people ask, 'Which comes first — repentance or faith?' John Murray answers the question thus: 'There is no priority. The faith that is unto salvation is a penitent faith and the repentance that is unto life is a believing repentance... Saving faith is permeated with repentance and repentance is permeated with faith.' With this kind of faith the people of Judah turned to the Lord in their hour of need and they prevailed against their enemies because they relied upon the Lord. The Chronicler links God's deliverance to the reliance of his people: '**At the sound of their battle cry, God routed Jeroboam and all Israel before Abijah and Judah**' (13:15).

Let us take a closer look at the nature of Judah's reliance upon the Lord: '**Then they cried out to the LORD**' (13:14). The verb is *tsaaq,* which is linked to the root meaning, 'to sound as thunder'. It describes loud exclamations, especially in distress, when help is being sought (e.g., Exod. 3:7; Isa. 33:7). It can also describe laughter. Abraham called his son Isaac (a name derived from this verb) because Sarah, his wife, laughed at the thought that she would give birth to a son. It is a verb that expresses strong feelings forcefully. In the context of 13:14 we notice two aspects of this cry.

1. A cry to God

Judah cried to the Lord, because there was no one else who was able to help. There were no reinforcements. There was no way of escape. There was only certain disaster facing the people of Judah unless the Lord intervened miraculously. First and foremost, faith looks to God and pleads with him for help. Faith seeks to strengthen that vertical relationship between needy people and a powerful God.

2. A call to action

'**The priests blew their trumpets and the men of Judah raised the battle cry.**' In Numbers 10:9 Moses describes how trumpets were to be used in battle: 'When you go into battle in your own land against an enemy who is oppressing you, sound a blast on the trumpets. Then you will be remembered by the LORD your God and rescued from your enemies.' The Lord heard the cries of his people. But the people also heard the rallying call of the trumpets. At the sound of this battle cry the men of Judah took heart. Perhaps they were beginning to panic and looking for a way of escape, but then came the leadership they needed. The colours were raised, orders were given and battle was commenced. 'If the trumpet does not sound a clear call, who will get ready for battle?' (1 Cor. 14:8). The men of Judah got up off their knees, looked their enemies in the face and got on with what they knew they had to do. They did it in the Lord's strength — but they did it. As they rose to the challenge the Lord gave them the victory.

Faith in God is not an excuse for inward-looking piety. Faith involves both of these cries. We cry to God for the strength and wisdom that he gives. Then we cry to the world to defy its arrogant assumptions and to declare God's truth.

The consequences of the battle (13:16-20)

The consequences of the battle were disastrous for Jeroboam. In spite of his overwhelming strength and clever tactics, **'The Israelites fled before Judah, and God delivered them into their hands'** (13:16). Here is a startling reminder that human strength shrivels like a thread before a flame, when we face divine judgement.

> No king is saved by the size of his army,
>   no warrior escapes by his great strength.
> A horse is a vain hope for deliverance;
>   despite all its great strength it cannot save
>   (Ps. 33:16-17).

The people of Judah were able to say, along with David in Psalm 20:7: 'Some trust in chariots and some in horses, but we trust in the name of the LORD our God.'

Jeroboam's army suffered heavy casualties: **'There were five hundred thousand casualties among Israel's able men'**

(13:17). The cream of Jeroboam's hand-picked fighting men lay dead on the battlefield. Their deaths were the result of the rebellion of the northern tribes. Jeroboam and his people were humiliated. The Chronicler's summary was that **'The men of Israel were subdued on that occasion, and the men of Judah were victorious because they relied on the LORD, the God of their fathers'** (13:18).

Defeat was a bitter pill for Jeroboam to swallow. He lost control of a strip of land along his southern border: **'Abijah pursued Jeroboam and took from him the towns of Bethel, Jeshanah and Ephron, with their surrounding villages'** (13:19). It is significant that the town of Bethel should have fallen, in view of what Abijah had said in 13:9 about the false gods that were worshipped there. Although the golden calves were preserved to see another day (see 2 Kings 10:29), they were clearly shown to be unable to preserve the town or the kingdom where they were worshipped.

Jeroboam also lost full control of his territory: **'Jeroboam did not regain power during the time of Abijah'** (13:20). This does not mean that Jeroboam was removed from his throne, but the kingdom that he ruled was a mere rump of what he had ruled before. He did not rule the whole territory of the ten tribes, and within the area that he did control his authority was mortally weakened.

We read in 13:20 that **'The LORD struck him down and he died.'** We are not told how Jeroboam died (either here or in 1 Kings 14:20). He may have died peacefully from an illness, or he may have died a more violent death; we simply do not know. What we do know is that he died as a result of the direct intervention of God: 'The LORD struck him down.' Our times are in the Lord's hands (see Psalm 31:15) both for the purposes of blessing and cursing.

Abijah's last days (13:21 – 14:1)

Even in death there was a pointed contrast between Abijah and Jeroboam. Jeroboam's miserable fate is highlighted by the blessings heaped upon Abijah. Jeroboam's weakness (13:20) is contrasted with Abijah's strength: **'But Abijah grew in strength'** (13:21). The blessings of a large and growing family are mentioned in 13:21 to elaborate the point. Even after death the two men were differentiated. Abijah died leaving his country in peace and was **'buried in the City of David'** (14:1). Those who oppose the kingdom of the Lord will be crushed, while those who are on the Lord's side will be blessed.

In concluding our study of the reign of King Abijah we can remind ourselves that the kingdom of the Lord has been placed in the hands of a greater King than Abijah. Yet, for all his faults, Abijah foreshadows that greater King.

God's kingdom is *an everlasting kingdom*. Peter promises those who make their calling and election sure that they 'will receive a rich welcome into the eternal kingdom of our Lord and Saviour Jesus Christ' (2 Peter 1:11).

God's kingdom is *a worshipping kingdom*. Around the throne there will always be worship. King Jesus reigns over a kingdom of priests who bow the knee in submission and open their mouths in adoration.

God's kingdom is *a victorious kingdom*. There will always be those who oppose the King and they will vent their hatred on the subjects of the king. While they appear to make great strides forward in advancing their evil agenda, their opposition will always be futile. Paul tells us that the Lord Jesus 'must reign until he has put all his enemies under his feet' (1 Cor. 15:25). Are you on the Lord's side?

10.
Asa: a good king stumbles

Please read 2 Chronicles 14:2 – 16:14

In ancient Greece a slave called Aesop was famed for his stories which taught moral lessons. Many of these tales, or fables, are still familiar to people today because they have a message for every age. One of the most popular of them is the story of the tortoise and the hare who decided to compete against each other in a long-distance race. The hare, thinking that victory was assured, started confidently but allowed himself to be waylaid. The tortoise just kept plodding along and eventually came in ahead of the hare. Now there is an encouragement for plodders!

The Scripture records the advice given by King Ahab of Israel to Ben-Hadad, King of Syria: 'Tell him: "One who puts on his armour should not boast like one who takes it off"' (1 Kings 20:11). This is good advice — even though it came from a wicked man. It is easy to begin a project full of enthusiasm, but the greater challenge is to see it through to completion. Some people build the foundations of a house, but they do not have enough money to put on the roof. Others set out to run a marathon, but crumple when they hit the pain barrier. I remember the advice being given at Theological College: 'Remember, the pastoral ministry is a marathon, not a sprint.' The same might be said of the Christian life. Some begin with a flourish, but are not able to say with Paul, 'I have fought the good fight, I have finished the race, I have kept the faith' (2 Tim. 4:7).

The Chronicler's history of the kings of Judah reveals dimensions to their characters which we do not find in Kings. This is what makes Chronicles such a profitable and practical book to study. In Kings we have a more clear-cut and one-dimensional view of kings like Asa, Joash, Uzziah and Manasseh. They were simply good or bad. In Chronicles, however, we find a more complex picture. Good and bad actions are recorded together. King Asa got off to a good start (14:2), but he did not finish as he started (16:7,10,12). He teaches us about our need to persevere in the grace God gives us and to 'finish well'.

In the Chronicler's account of the reign of King Asa there are three themes that come to the fore. Two of them relate to Asa's faithfulness and God's blessing (rest in chapter 14 and reformation in chapter 15), while the final one relates to Asa's unfaithfulness and God's chastisement (reversal in chapter 16).

Rest (14:2-15)

Rest is a blessing from the Lord. It was enjoyed by Asa and his kingdom, at least during the early years of his reign: **'No one was at war with him during those years, for the LORD gave him rest'** (14:6). Asa acknowledged that this was a blessing from the Lord: **'The land is still ours because we have sought the LORD our God; we sought him and he has given us rest on every side'** (14:7). Later, after the covenant renewal festival in Jerusalem, 'They sought God eagerly, and he was found by them. So the LORD gave them rest on every side' (15:15).

The enjoyment of rest was a constant feature of the Lord's covenant faithfulness to the Israelites. Not only did the Lord give them possession of the promised land, he also gave them rest in the land. The land of promise was to be a sanctuary where the people would be free from the distractions posed by heathen nations with their idolatrous practices and therefore better able to devote themselves to serving the Lord. When Joshua led the Israelites into the land he told them, 'Remember the command that Moses the servant of the LORD gave you: "The LORD your God is giving you rest and has granted you this land"' (Josh. 1:13).

This rest was enjoyed in abundance during the reigns of David and Solomon: 'You will have a son who will be a man of peace and rest, and I will give him rest from all his enemies on every side' (1 Chr. 22:9). 'The LORD, the God of Israel, has granted rest to his people and has come to dwell in Jerusalem for ever' (1 Chr. 23:25). When the people were unfaithful to the Lord they were troubled by their enemies and so they lost their rest. Eventually they lost the land as well. However, the prophet Isaiah was enabled to look beyond the exile and predicted that God would again give his people rest: 'My people will live in peaceful dwelling-places, in secure homes, in undisturbed places of rest' (Isa. 32:18).

The rest that Asa enjoyed during the early years of his reign had *a military dimension* (14:1; 15:19). It was a rest from conflict. Civil strife has many destructive consequences. Lives are lost, limbs are maimed, living standards are lowered, social infrastructure is destroyed, attitudes are hardened, deep-seated suspicions are engendered and spiritual life is often adversely affected. Judah was spared these debilitating effects of conflict.

There was also *a spiritual dimension* to Asa's rest. Asa and his people rested upon the Lord. **'Then Asa called to the LORD his God and said, "LORD, there is no one like you to help the powerless against the mighty. Help us, O LORD our God, for we rely on you, and in your name we have come against this vast army"'** (14:11). Because he realized

that he was as helpless as a little child, Asa trusted totally in
the Lord for all the help that he needed. Thus Asa knew the
blessings of rest, even in the exertions of battle. His mind was
at rest, because he was trusting in the Lord.

This peace of mind is what the wicked lack, even when
they prosper outwardly (Isa. 57:21). The godly man is one
who rests in the Lord (Ps. 37:7; 62:1,5; Isa. 30:15). The Lord
Jesus promised rest to those who come to him and take up his
yoke (Matt. 11:28). Although Joshua promised rest to the
Israelites, there is a more blessed rest that is received through
faith in the Lord Jesus Christ. 'Let us, therefore, make every
effort to enter that rest' (see Heb. 4:8-11).

Biblical teaching about the believer's rest draws upon the
Hebrew idea of wholeness or completeness. The popular idea
of rest today is a negative one. After we finish our day's work
we come home and do nothing. That is not rest as the
Scriptures describe it. Rest is not idleness, and resting upon
the Lord is not inactivity. It is an integral part of an active
relationship with the Lord. Resting upon the Lord involves
crying out to the Lord, listening to the Lord and following
wherever he leads. Resting upon the Lord means acting out
our faith with a new-found confidence that is instilled by our
trust in God. Asa was an example of such confident obedience
during the early years of his reign. In chapter 14 we can discern
three areas of activity.

1. Removing heathen altars (14:2-5)

'**He removed the foreign altars and the high places,
smashed the sacred stones and cut down the Asherah
poles.**' These verses echo Moses' command in Deuteronomy
7:5-6, and indicate Asa's desire to be faithful to God's law.
Because the Lord is a jealous God, he will not tolerate even

the symbols of false gods. Asa urged the people of Judah to turn from these false gods and to serve the true God: **'He commanded Judah to seek the LORD, the God of their fathers, and to obey his laws and commands'** (14:4). The genuineness of their faith in God was seen in their willingness to forsake heathen worship. Many years later, the new believers in Thessalonica demonstrated their faith in Christ in a similar way (1 Thess. 1:9).

2. Rebuilding towns and defences (14:6-8)

Oliver Cromwell told his soldiers to trust in God and keep their powder dry. Trust in God did not mean that they could neglect the use of means to bring about a desired end. They would not win the battle if they were careless about their weapons and ammunition. Faith in God does not excuse carelessness, stupidity or laziness (Matt. 25:26-27). That is why Asa set to work strengthening the defences of his kingdom. He was proactive and built up **'the fortified cities of Judah'** (14:6) while the land was at peace. He did not wait until the wolf was at the door before trying to avert disaster. He expanded, trained and equipped his armies so that he had at his command a combined force of 580,000 men. **'All these were brave fighting men'** (14:8).

3. Repelling enemies (14:9-15)

Asa's careful planning was put to the test when **'Zerah the Cushite'** invaded Judah. The Cushites were from Ethiopia, and it is suggested that Zerah was in some way linked to Shishak (of whom we read in chapter 12). Zerah led a formid-able military expedition. The NIV's alternative translation of 14:9, **'with an army of thousands upon thousands'**, is better than the main text which describes Zerah's army as 'a vast army'. As well as many thousands of men, Zerah had **'three hundred chariots'** (the latest in military hardware), while Judah had none. He and his armies advanced as far as **'Mareshah'** (which is in the uplands of south-western Judea). Quite understandably, Asa trembled before such an army. He was **'the powerless against the mighty'**.

Asa's faith in God did not collapse before the onslaught of this great army. He went to the Lord in prayer: **'Help us, O LORD our God, for we rely on you, and in your name we have come against this vast army'** (14:11). Asa relied upon the Lord, but he also recognized his responsibility to act. The Chronicler reminds us that Asa and his people were not in-active when the Lord destroyed Zerah's great army: **'The LORD struck down the Cushites before Asa and Judah'** (14:12). Asa and his army **'pursued them ... carried off a large amount of plunder ... destroyed all the villages around Gerar ... plundered ... villages... They also attacked the camps'** (14:13-15). As the men of Judah went forward, they found that the Lord their God gave them the victory. 'The horse is made ready for battle, but the victory rests with the Lord' (Prov. 21:31). As a result of preparing the horse for battle, Asa enjoyed rest from the Lord.

Reformation (15:1-19)

After a time of God's blessing it is tempting to sit back and take it easy. However, we have seen that resting in the Lord does not involve being idle or taking it easy. 'So, if you think you are standing firm, be careful that you don't fall' (1 Cor. 10:12). The Protestant Reformers of the sixteenth century saw that the church ought to be *reforma semper reformanda* — 'reformed but always reforming'. For this reason the great deliverance described in chapter 14 is followed by the spiritual reformation described in chapter 15. Asa's victory over the Cushites at Mareshah prompted reformation in Judah.

1. Prophetic encouragement (15:1-7)

These verses seem to indicate that Asa was greeted on his return from the battlefield by the prophet Azariah, bearing a message of encouragement from the Lord: **'Listen to me, Asa and all Judah and Benjamin. The Lord is with you when you are with him. If you seek him, he will be found by you, but if you forsake him, he will forsake you'** (15:2). This was a reminder that Asa's victory was from the Lord. God had heard his prayers and had answered them on the battlefield. This was also a reminder of the nature of God's covenant with his people. God's promises to them are couched in terms that require an obedient response. Asa had been faithful as a king over Judah, but there was still a work of reformation to be done. Others before him had not been faithful, and as long as the land was full of idols, the Lord's blessing could not be expected.

The Old Testament prophets were men who spoke from God. Sometimes they made many predictions about the future, but they also spoke about the past and they sought to explain what the Lord was doing in the present. In 15:3-6 the prophet Azariah spoke about Israel's history. These verses describe Israel during the days of the judges, when chaos reigned throughout the land. 'In those days Israel had no king; everyone did as he saw fit' (Judg. 21:25). The political anarchy of those days resulted from the spiritual anarchy of turning away from the Lord.

The lesson of the book of Judges is that when Israel turned to the Lord and cried to him in their distress, the Lord heard their cries for help: **'In their distress they turned to the Lord,**

the God of Israel, and sought him, and he was found by them' (15:4). The lesson for Asa (and every subsequent generation of God's people who find themselves in difficult circumstances) is found in 15:7: **'But as for you, be strong and do not give up, for your work will be rewarded.'** No matter how far God's people have sunk in their distress, they are never beyond God's reach. At times the church seems to be corrupted beyond recovery, but reformation is always possible. This must have brought great encouragement to the Chronicler's generation when the people of Judah struggled to maintain their zeal for God's house.

2. Removal and repair (15:8,16-18)

Asa paid careful attention to the message of Azariah. It brought about a change in his behaviour because it first touched his heart: **'When Asa heard these words and the prophecy of Azariah son of Oded the prophet, he took courage.'** Asa was encouraged by these words because he understood them and they affected him. He came to delight in the Word of God and its call to reformation. He recognized the need for reformation all around him. First of all, **'He removed the detestable idols from the whole land of Judah and Benjamin'**; then **'He repaired the altar of the LORD'** (15:8); and later we read that he brought the dedicated treasures back to to the place where they belonged — the temple of the Lord (15:18).

'Although he did not remove the high places from Israel, Asa's heart was fully committed to the LORD all his life' (15:17). Although these words qualify what we read in 15:8, they do not contradict the statements made there. Asa's clear policy was to remove the idols from Judah, and 15:8 describes how he set out to do this. His work seems to have been like sweeping up leaves on a windy autumn day. So long as the people's hearts were (to use John Calvin's graphic phrase) 'a continual factory of idols', idolatry would be well-nigh impossible to stamp out. There would be no end to the idols and idolatrous shrines until spiritual reformation swept through the hearts and lives of the people.

Asa was determined to remove the influence of idolatry as best he could. We can gauge the strength of his resolve to reform the religious life of Judah from the fact that **'King Asa also deposed his grandmother Maacah from her position as queen mother, because she had made a repulsive Asherah pole'** (15:16). Canaanite Asherah poles were used in fertility rites and it was probably obscene as well as 'repulsive'. This was sin within his own family, where it is always most embarrassing and painful to confront and deal with. Yet Asa did not flinch from this difficult task.

3. Covenant renewal (15:9-15)

In these verses Asa turned from the fabric of Israel's religion to its very core. He sought to turn the people's hearts to the Lord: **'Then he assembled all Judah and Benjamin and the people from Ephraim, Manasseh and Simeon who had settled among them, for large numbers had come over to him from Israel when they saw that the LORD his God was with him'** (15:9). The spectacular victory over Zerah the Cushite at Mareshah had obviously made an impact far beyond Judah. Many Israelites from the northern tribes were so impressed that they came south to seek the protection of King Asa. His prestige was greatly enhanced, so Asa seized the opportunity to gather all those who were willing to seek the Lord, and directed them.

The covenant renewal ceremony in this chapter took place shortly after the victory at Mareshah: **'At that time they sacrificed to the LORD seven hundred head of cattle and seven thousand sheep and goats from the plunder they**

had brought back' (15:11). These animals were part of the plunder taken in 14:13,15. Animal sacrifice was an important part of this covenant ceremony, as it had been with Abraham (Gen. 15:9-11) and Moses (Exod. 24:5-8). When they brought these sacrificial offerings to God the people acknowledged that they were sinners before an angry and offended God. 'Without the shedding of blood there is no forgiveness' (Heb. 9:22), and without forgiveness sinners cannot come into the presence of a holy God, let alone expect blessing from him.

Asa's act of covenant renewal is described in 15:12-15: **'They entered into a covenant to seek the LORD, the God of their fathers, with all their heart and soul'** (15:12). The covenant of grace is a divine initiative in which the Lord approaches sinners to make them his people. The Lord entered into such a covenant with Abraham, and it was an everlasting covenant with his descendants (Gen. 12:1-3; 17:1-8). By its very nature Asa's covenant was a different type of covenant. It was a covenant that the people made among themselves, with a view to serving the Lord more zealously. It was a response to God's covenant of grace and was enabled by God's prior act of mercy. Without God's gracious initiative, such a response would have been unthinkable and impossible. However, because the Lord had made Israel his own special people, this national covenant of reformation was an expression of the people's loyalty to God. In post-exilic times small groups of godly people banded together to do just that (see Mal. 3:16). No doubt the Chronicler wished to encourage his readers to such a movement on a national scale.

Several features of the movement for covenant renewal in Asa's reign call for comment.

Firstly, *the people made themselves accountable to each other in their walk with the Lord.* Of course each person remained accountable to the Lord, and would answer to him on the Day of Judgement. However, they also made commitments to each other which were solemn and binding.

Fellow-Israelites had a right and duty to ask of their neighbours, 'Are you seeking the Lord? Have you forsaken idols?' What a healthy vulnerability! Is there anyone watching out for your soul? How do you take it when someone in your church asks questions about your walk with God? Are you defensive or thankful?

Then, secondly, *the people of Israel gave a national testimony to the truth that Jehovah is the Lord God.* Jehovah was proclaimed to be **'the God of their fathers'**. He was proclaimed as the only true God, the unchanging God, the law-giving God, the creator God, the merciful God, the God who had chosen Israel to be his special people. Their testimony was not just individual, but corporate and public. Hence, **'All who would not seek the LORD, the God of Israel, were to be put to death, whether small or great, man or woman'** (15:13). The people followed the example of Deuteronomy 13:1-18 and 17:2-7, which commanded the execution of idolaters in Israel. These actions resulted from the special status of Israel as church and state combined in the Old Testament economy. No single nation enjoys this status today. However, we are to apply the abiding principles that nations have a duty to confess God's truth by upholding his law, and that the church has a duty to maintain its purity by excommunicating those who deny God's truth.

Then, thirdly, *the people's commitment to serve the Lord was wholehearted.* **'They took an oath to the LORD with loud acclamation, with shouting and with trumpets and horns. All Judah rejoiced about the oath because they had sworn it wholeheartedly. They sought God eagerly, and he was found by them'** (15:14-15). Asa did not have to coerce the people of Israel because the Lord had made them a willing people, by the exercise of his power in their hearts. Their joy and enthusiasm overflowed in covenant renewal. No doubt, the Chronicler would have wished to see a similar enthusiasm in his own day.

Reversal (16:1-14)

Asa lost the blessings of rest and peace within his kingdom. The early successes of his reign were tragically reversed. A series of disasters is recorded, beginning **'in the thirty-sixth year of Asa's reign'**, when **'Baasha king of Israel went up against Judah'** (16:1).

The chronology of Asa's reign calls for some comment. Asa came to the throne after the death of Abijah in 910 B.C. (14:1). There then followed ten years of peace. After those years Zerah invaded Judah from the south. As a result of Asa's victory at Mareshah his kingdom was strengthened and he gathered the people in Jerusalem to renew their covenant with the Lord. This covenant renewal followed shortly after the battle at Mareshah, in the fifteenth year of Asa's reign (15:10). At first glance 15:19 and 16:1 seem to indicate that Baasha's invasion came twenty years later, in the thirty-fifth and thirty-sixth years of Asa's reign,.

The problem with this chronology is that, according to 1 Kings 16:6,8,23, Baasha had been dead for ten years and Omri was King of Israel by this stage. Because the Scriptures are accurate in every detail, including the chronology of events, we cannot accept that this is a 'Bible error'. Even when modern scholars cannot give clear explanations, we should never make the assumption that the Bible is wrong just because we are not in a position to tie up the loose ends of history. Some commentators have suggested that in 15:19 and 16:1 the Chronicler is referring to the thirty-fifth and thirty-sixth years of the kingdom of Judah. The Hebrew phrase would permit such a translation ('the thirty-fifth year of Asa's kingdom').

If this chronology is adopted Baasha's invasion would come the year after the covenant renewal ceremony in Judah, and well within Baasha's lifetime. The problem is that this form of dating is used nowhere else in Chronicles. It also places Asa's reversal precariously close to the spiritual high point of his reign. Yet this juxtaposition of events is true to experience. It is often when we are coming down from the spiritual mountaintop that we stumble and fall into serious sin. Asa reigned for twenty-four years after Baasha's invasion — a total of forty years — and died in the forty-first year of his reign (16:13). These last years were not happy years. They were years of reversal and disappointment.

Reversal became the theme of this second part of Asa's reign because he stopped resting in the Lord his God and started relying on his own strength. This is a trap that believers can all too easily fall into. Paul charged the Galatians with doing this: 'You foolish Galatians! Who has bewitched you? Before your very eyes Jesus Christ was clearly portrayed as crucified... Are you so foolish? After beginning with the Spirit, are you now trying to attain your goal by human effort?' (Gal. 3:1,3). Christ charged the church in Ephesus with doing this: 'You have persevered and have endured hardships for my name, and have not grown weary. Yet I hold this against you: You have forsaken your first love. Remember the height from which you have fallen!' (Rev. 2:3-5). How did Asa fall from a great height and start relying on himself? The answer is found in his response to three challenges.

1. Baasha's invasion (16:1-6)

Baasha wanted to stem the flow of northerners who were leaving his kingdom to settle in Judah. Some wanted political security, but others wanted to worship the Lord at the temple in Jerusalem. Baasha seized Ramah, which was eight kilometres north of Jerusalem and had been the nation's capital in the time of Samuel. This was a serious attack upon Asa's kingdom and its consequences might have been devastating if it had gone unchallenged.

Asa turned to the King of Syria. Ben-Hadad had been an ally of Baasha, but Asa persuaded him to change sides. Asa must have thought himself very clever when he pulled off such a coup. Baasha thought that his northern and eastern flanks were secure because of his treaty with Ben-Hadad, but Asa turned the tables on him.

Asa's plans were *successful*: **'Ben-Hadad agreed with King Asa and sent the commanders of his forces against the towns of Israel'** (16:4). Baasha could not fight on two fronts, so he withdrew from Ramah, as Asa had hoped (16:3,5).

However, there is another light in which we should view Asa's diplomacy. His plans were *costly*: **'Asa then took the silver and gold out of the treasuries of the LORD's temple and of his own palace and sent it to Ben-Hadad king of Aram, who was ruling in Damascus'** (16:2). This money had been dedicated to the Lord's service and it did not belong to Asa to dispose of in that way. Even worse, Asa used the Lord's wealth to demonstrate his own unfaithfulness!

Asa's plans were *deceitful*: **'Now break your treaty with Baasha king of Israel so that he will withdraw from me'** (16:3). Asa won a victory of sorts; however, it was a godless victory. It was gained by his own cunning rather than by relying on the Lord. The hollowness of his victory was explained by a prophet of the Lord.

2. *Hanani's message* (16:7-10)

Hanani showed that, by forsaking the Lord, Asa was going to have to accept second-best: **'Because you relied on the king of Aram and not on the LORD your God, the army of the king of Aram has escaped your hand'** (16:7). There is a clear implication that if Asa had relied on the Lord when Baasha invaded he would not have had to call on the King of Syria for help. As it turned out, the Arameans easily overran Baasha's undefended northern towns, and they expanded their influence further into Israel and even into Judah. If Asa had relied upon the Lord the situation would have been very different. **'You have done a foolish thing, and from now on you will be at war,'** warned Hanani (16:9).

Hanani reminded Asa of God's power by recalling events from the recent past: **'Were not the Cushites and Libyans a mighty army with great numbers of chariots and horsemen? Yet when you relied on the LORD, he delivered them into your hand'** (16:8). The victory over Zerah the Cushite was fresh in Asa's memory, yet he had not learned the obvious lessons of that victory. This is the foolishness of unbelief. It was not lack of proof that led Asa to doubt God's power, but the presence of indwelling sin. How often we are like Peter when he set out to walk on the sea towards Jesus! He had the evidence of his Master's power all around him, yet he shut his eyes to it and looked at the waves instead. When our view of our problems becomes larger and clearer than our view of our God we are liable to fall into the unbelief of Asa.

Hanani used a striking anthropomorphism to describe God's power: **'For the eyes of the LORD range throughout the earth to strengthen those whose hearts are fully committed to him'** (16:9). The Bible frequently attributes human features to God, who is a spirit without physical features. We know that such descriptions must be read figuratively. God does not have organs such as eyes, yet he has the ability to see what no merely human eye can see. He sees 'throughout the earth' and he has insight into the affairs of nations.

The prophet Zechariah reminded the small remnant of Jews who returned to Judah after the exile of this fact (Zech. 4:10). The Chronicler knew how the Lord had worked through Cyrus, King of Persia, to bring his people back to their land of promise.

He had evidence that the Lord's influence was not limited to the land of Judah, for his power ranged 'throughout the earth'. The Arameans, the Libyans, the Persians and every other nation were subject to the Lord who protected his covenant people.

Asa's foolishness went deep. Not only did he lose sight of God's power, he also lost the ability to listen to godly advice: **'Asa was angry with the seer because of this; he was so enraged that he put him in prison'** (16:10). His response to Hanani's counsel was irrational and aggressive: **'At the same time Asa brutally oppressed some of the people.'** We are not told why he oppressed them, but perhaps these were godly people who stood shoulder to shoulder with the prophet. Asa's irrational behaviour was, no doubt, the result of a fierce inner conflict. As he struggled with his conscience he was unable to justify his behaviour, so he threw caution to the winds and sought to silence anyone who might challenge him. Saul the Pharisee acted similarly when his conscience was pricked and responded by persecuting the Christians with great ferocity.

3. *Asa's illness* (16:12)

Illness can be one of the most serious challenges to our faith. Sometimes it brings out the worst in people and unearths doubts that have been ignored for many years. I remember visiting a lady in hospital who was dying of cancer. She knew that her physical condition was terminal, and I suggested that we pray. Her reply came as a shock to me, because she had been a professing Christian for many years. 'What is the point?' she asked.

Asa's **'disease in his feet'** (16:12) may have been gout or gangrene. Whatever its medical characteristics, it presented a serious challenge to his faith. **'Though his disease was severe, even in his illness he did not seek help from the LORD,**

but only from the physicians' (16:12). It was not a sin to seek help from his doctors. The Scriptures teach that God uses secondary means to bring about healing, and doctors have a part to play. Isaiah gave instructions that a poultice of figs should be applied to Hezekiah's boil (Isa. 38:21). Paul advised Timothy to 'Use a little wine because of your stomach and your frequent illnesses' (1 Tim. 5:23), and he spoke positively about 'our friend, Luke, the doctor' (Col. 4:14). In James 5:14-15 (where the verb *aleipho* implies that the anointing oil is for medicinal purposes) the use of means is linked to 'the prayer offered in faith'. Both are commanded by God.

Asa's sin was that he refused to pray the prayer offered in faith. He had sinned so often that he had made it very hard for himself to seek God's favour. His sins had cast up a barrier that was very real in his own mind. As a result he was afraid to pray. This barrier was also an offence to God, and that mountain of unforgiven sin could only be removed by humble repentance. Asa was not yet willing for such a humbling return to God.

Such a spiritual impasse results when faith has become a mere formality, where there is an intellectual assent to the truth of Scripture and the doctrines of Christianity, but there is no daily fellowship with God. When we look to the Lord we are strong, but when we stop looking to God and listening to him, then we start listening to the unsettling voices of the world. So long as Peter looked to his Lord he was able to walk on the waves, but when he looked away, he 'saw the wind, he was afraid and, beginning to sink, cried out, "Lord, save me!"' (Matt. 14:30). We suffer because of our trials only when we refuse to look to the Lord. Perhaps it is stubbornness, perhaps shame or false expectations that have in the past led to disappointment. These sins can reinforce our refusal to cry to the Lord and perpetuate spiritual declension.

Asa's death (16:13-14)

In spite of the disappointments of his last years, Asa was honoured in his death. He was buried in a tomb that he had constructed for himself in the City of David (16:14). This was the most prestigious burial site in Judah. Special mention is made of the fact that the people of Judah **'made a huge fire in his honour'**. Although there was a tradition in Judah of lighting funeral fires for dead kings, this is the only reference in the biblical histories of Israel to such a memorial fire (there is an indirect reference to the practice in 21:19). This is a strong indication that when Asa died he was regarded as a good king who was loved by godly people, in spite of all his faults.

Asa's failings are a sobering thought for believers. Just as David sinned grievously in his adultery with Bathsheba, and just as Peter denied his Lord, so Asa reversed the gains of godly leadership in his early years. The blessings of those early years seem to have been swallowed up in the declension that followed. Asa's example teaches us that it is not sufficient for believers to make a good start; we must also continue well and finish well. 'Abiding' or 'remaining' are translations of the verb *(meno)* that Jesus used to describe what he expects of those who would be his disciples (John 15:1-9). He used the same verb when he said, 'If you *hold to* my teaching, you are really my disciples' (John 8:31). Paul urged Timothy to abide in his teaching and example: 'But as for you, continue in what you have learned and have become convinced of, because you know those from whom you learned it' (2 Tim. 3:14). 'For this very reason,' says Peter, 'make every effort to add to your faith goodness; and to goodness, knowledge; and to knowledge, self-control; and to self-control, perseverance...' (2 Peter 1:5-6).

Asa's example teaches us that mature Christians can be crippled by their besetting sins if they do not master them. We warn young Christians of the sins 'of youth' (2 Tim. 2:22). However, the sins of maturity are just as numerous. In some respects they are more serious, because they make a greater impact on others. Asa's sins as a respected leader made an impact on a whole nation. The sins of maturity can include cynicism, formalism, complacency, hypocrisy, having a form of godliness while lacking its power. We should take as our example the godly Anna, who waited in the temple for the Messiah. 'She was very old; she ... was a widow until she was eighty-four. She never left the temple but worshipped night and day, fasting and praying' (Luke 2:36-37). The psalmist points to the ideal when he describes the righteous who grow into maturity as trees that draw constantly upon God:

> The righteous will flourish like a palm tree,
>   they will grow like a cedar of Lebanon;
> planted in the house of the LORD,
>   they will flourish in the courts of our God.
> They will still bear fruit in old age,
>   they will stay fresh and green,
> proclaiming, 'The LORD is upright;
>   he is my Rock, and there is no wickedness in him'
>   (Ps. 92:12-14).

11.
Jehoshaphat: the danger of bad company

Please read 2 Chronicles 17:1 – 19:3

Jehoshaphat was a model of a godly king, and the Chronicler has a great deal to say about him. Only to Solomon and Hezekiah does he devote more space. Only Josiah is given a more ringing endorsement. Even so, as we shall see, Jehoshaphat had his faults too.

Jehoshaphat's name tells us something very important: it means, 'The LORD is judge.' Jehoshaphat was conscious of the Lord's righteous standards, and he was aware that the Lord would bring his people under judgement if they broke his law. The prophet Joel referred to 'the Valley of Jehoshaphat' (Joel 3:2,12) as the place where the Lord would gather the nations for judgement. The precise geographical location of this valley is not known; neither is any direct link to King Jehoshaphat. However, Joel, who prophesied after the exile, was painfully aware of what Jehoshaphat had known many years earlier — that the Lord will gather all the nations of the world before his throne and judge them according to his law.

Jehoshaphat recognized that Israel was not exempt from God's universal judgement, and he sought to prepare his people for that day. He is regarded by some as having been the most pastoral of all the kings of Judah. With a pastor's heart he led the people to walk in the ways of the Lord. His concern was to teach God's law to his people. This is what makes Jehoshaphat an example of godly leadership. Jehoshaphat as an example is the theme of chapter 17, while his human failings are that of chapter 18.

Introducing the model of a godly king (17:1-6)

The Chronicler introduces each new king with a standard form of words. Often we are told about the death of the previous king, the steps the new monarch took to strengthen his control over the kingdom, the name of his mother, his age and the length of his reign. We should not rush past these introductory verses. They highlight the features of Jehoshaphat's reign that made him a good king.

Jehoshaphat's strengths

Firstly, *he deployed his resources wisely.* He **'strengthened himself against Israel. He stationed troops in all the fortified cities of Judah'** (17:1-2). This was not aggressive sabre-rattling, but a prudent and defensive precaution.

Then, secondly, *he chose his examples wisely.* **'The LORD was with Jehoshaphat because in his early years he walked in the ways that his father David had followed. He did not consult the Baals, but sought the God of his father'** (17:3-4). Within his own family some had served the Lord, but others had not. Jehoshaphat had the wisdom to admire those who were godly and model his life on them.

Thirdly, *he had a wise set of priorities.* **'His heart was devoted to the ways of the LORD'** (17:6). God came first! This is as it should be, for the first and greatest commandment is: 'You shall have no other gods before me' (Exod. 20:3). Jehoshaphat made it his priority to remove idolatry from his kingdom, because the presence of idols distracted his people from the worship of Jehovah.

God's blessings

God rewards those who are faithful to him, and he blessed the faithfulness of Jehoshaphat. Two blessings, both of which were commonly enjoyed by the godly kings of Judah, are mentioned in 17:5.

First of all, '**The LORD established the kingdom under his control.**' This was a fulfilment of God's promise to Solomon (7:18). The Lord subdued Jehoshaphat's enemies and gave him the wisdom and authority to stamp his authority on the machinery of government.

Then, secondly, '**All Judah brought gifts to Jehoshaphat, so that he had great wealth and honour.**' These material blessings are given great significance in Chronicles. They were a sign that God kept his promises and that he was able to bless his people. They were also a sign that those who are faithful to the Lord will be blessed even while they live. These gifts also have a Christological significance. They are typical of the homage that God's people give to the King of kings. To him we present ourselves as living sacrifices (Rom. 12:2).

> Worthy is the Lamb, who was slain,
> to receive power and wealth and wisdom and strength
> and honour and glory and praise
>
> (Rev. 5:12).

Special features of Jehoshaphat's reign (17:7-19)

1. A preaching ministry that taught God's law to the people (17:7-19)

Jehoshaphat sent his officials to travel the length and breadth of his kingdom to teach God's law to the people: '**They taught**

throughout Judah, taking with them the Book of the Law of the LORD; they went round to all the towns of Judah and taught the people' (17:9). This was a serious attempt to influence the spiritual life of the kingdom, from the bottom up. Asa's reformation had been Jerusalem-based. Jehoshaphat sought to make a lasting impact upon all the people of his kingdom by establishing a national network of biblical instruction. We are reminded of Paul's systematic ministry in Ephesus: 'You know that I have not hesitated to preach anything that would be helpful to you but have taught you publicly and from house to house' (Acts 20:20).

The Levites and priests were in the forefront of this movement (17:8). Their role was not limited to ceremonial or sacrificial functions, for they were teachers of God's law to the people:

> About Levi he said:
> '... He teaches your precepts to Jacob
>   and your law to Israel.
> He offers incense before you
>   and whole burnt offerings on your altar'
>
>   (Deut. 33:8,10).

In post-exilic times the role of the Levites became extremely important. Malachi (one of the last of the Old Testament prophets) emphasized the teaching role of the Levites: 'For the lips of a priest ought to preserve knowledge, and from his mouth men should seek instruction — because he is the messenger of the LORD Almighty' (Mal. 2:7).

Some might have thought that they did not need the instruction given by the Levites. 'We can go and listen to the preaching of the prophets!' they could have said. However, the systematic instruction of the Levites on subjects that related to day-by-day godliness was not to be despised. If the people needed it during the lifetime of Elijah, how much more during the age of rebuilding after the exile, when the great prophets had fallen silent!

In our own age we also need systematic instruction from the Word of God. Many people hanker after visions, dreams and other spectacular signs that God is speaking to them. However, the fact that God has withdrawn these gifts does not leave us spiritually impoverished, for he has spoken to us through his Son in the Scriptures (see 1 Cor. 13:8; Heb. 1:1-3). It is through the regular and systematic study of the Scriptures that 'the man of God may be thoroughly equipped for every good work' (2 Tim. 3:16-17).

Jehoshaphat sent out **'his officials ... to teach in the towns of Judah'** alongside the Levites (17:7). These officials lent their weight to the Levites in order to bring about reformation in Judah. This should not come as a surprise because it is always in the best interests of civil rulers to promote national righteousness. 'Righteousness exalts a nation, but sin is a disgrace to any people' (Prov. 14:34). Moreover it is the duty of rulers to promote national righteousness. The civil power 'is God's servant to do you good ... he does not bear the sword for nothing. He is God's servant, an agent of wrath to bring punishment on the wrongdoer' (Rom. 13:4).

National righteousness was best promoted when the Levites and officials (or the civil power and the church) worked together in a relationship of co-operation. One did not dominate the other, but both were pursuing God's standards of righteousness. Matthew Henry points to the abiding significance of this relationship: 'What an abundance of good may be done when Moses and Aaron thus go hand in hand in the doing of it, when princes with their power and Levites with their scripture learning, agree to teach the people the good knowledge of God and their duty!' May God's blessing be poured out upon our nations to turn this lofty ideal into reality.

2. The fear of the Lord fell upon surrounding nations (17:10-11)

Jehoshaphat built up his army and the nation's defences. No doubt his neighbours took note. However, they saw more than merely the military genius of Jehoshaphat. They saw that the Lord of the armies of heaven was with Jehoshaphat: **'The fear of the LORD fell on all the kingdoms of the lands surrounding Judah.'**

These kingdoms included some who were ancient enemies of Israel, such as the Philistines. They **'brought Jehoshaphat gifts and silver as tribute'**. There were also more recent enemies, such as the Arabs, who were nomadic herdsmen: **'The Arabs brought him flocks.'** The presence of Arabs in Palestine can be traced back as far as the ninth century B.C. Their threat to Judah increased after the exile, for Arabs were among the nations who occupied Judah while the land was empty. After returning from exile, Nehemiah found them a threat to his work (Neh. 4:7). It must have encouraged the post-exilic Jews to know that their enemies had been subdued by the Lord before. It is not large armies alone that subdue heathen nations, but the Lord who dwells among his people. The same is true in every age (Zech. 8:23).

3. Powerful defences were built (17:12-19)

Jehoshaphat did not neglect his responsibilities as king on account of the blessing that rested so abundantly upon his kingdom. He followed the example of Solomon by building **'forts and store cities in Judah'** (17:12). He made Jerusalem a garrison city, the headquarters of an army numbering over 1,160,000 men. Jehoshaphat's army was larger than the armies of Asa and Abijah. He was blessed with able and committed generals, whose names are listed in 17:14-18, alongside the numbers of men under their command.

One of them, Amasiah, stands out for special note. In 17:16 the Chronicler, in a brief character sketch, describes the sort of man he was: Amasiah **'volunteered himself for the service of the LORD'**. He was a servant as well as a general. Servant leadership is one of the features of the New Testament church. The apostles referred to themselves and their fellow workers as servants of the Lord Jesus Christ and commended the same attitude to others (Phil. 1:1; Col. 4:7,12; 1 Peter 2:16; 5:2-3). Of course, the greatest example of servant leadership is our Lord himself, who 'took the form of a servant' (Phil. 2:7, NIV alternative reading) and told his disciples, 'I am among you as one who serves' (Luke 22:27).

Amasiah put himself forward to do a task. He was no shrinking violet, inhibited by false modesty. Many people find it easier to mind their own business and leave the work to others rather than volunteer themselves for service. They avoid responsibility in order to avoid criticism. However, God's people should be 'willing ... in the day of [his] power' (Ps. 110:3, AV).

Amasiah offered himself 'for ... service'. Here is an attitude which is essential for real usefulness in God's kingdom. Many people are willing to do the tasks that others will notice and praise, or the tasks that bring status and recognition. How many are willing to do any task, however humble? Paul told those who aspire to leadership in the church that they ought not to seek status but service (1 Tim. 3:1). Much of this service will be humble, unseen and unrecognized. Yet only when we are willing to do this humble work will we are ready for important work. Only when we are willing to take orders will we be ready to issue them.

The mistakes of a human king (18:1 – 19:3)

Ahab was one of the most notorious kings of Israel. His wife Jezebel was a princess from Tyre who introduced new types of idolatry into Israel. Together they brought Israel to a new spiritual low. Ahab also had a baleful influence on the godly King Jehoshaphat. In spite of all the good things recorded about Jehoshaphat in chapter 17, he was waylaid by Ahab. He was a man with feet of clay.

1. Jehoshaphat's alliance with Ahab (18:1-3; 19:2)

This alliance was based upon the marriage between Jehoshaphat's son Jehoram and Ahab's daughter Athaliah (21:6). It was an alliance that was to create many problems for Judah in the years to come, but at the time it was welcomed as a measure to make peace between the two warring kingdoms. The war-weary people of Judah were glad to accept peace at any price.

The alliance between Ahab and Jehoshaphat brought the royal families of Israel and Judah into closer contact, and set the scene for the events of this chapter. **'Some years later he** [Jehoshaphat] **went down to visit Ahab in Samaria.'** Ahab went to great lengths to impress his royal visitor from Judah (18:2). His motive soon became obvious, for he wanted to gain Jehoshaphat's support in a war to recapture Ramoth Gilead from the Syrians (or Arameans). Although this town was historically part of the territory of the tribe of Gad, it lay forty-five kilometres (twenty-eight miles) to the east of the River Jordan and was constantly vulnerable to invasion. It was only 100 kilometres (sixty-two miles) south of Damascus and regularly fought over by Syria and Israel. What started as a family gathering put pressure on Jehoshaphat to ally himself more and more closely with Ahab and all his works.

Perhaps Jehoshaphat clung to the belief that although there were two kingdoms, there was still one covenant nation of Israel. This is suggested by his response to Ahab's request: **'I am as you are, and my people as your people; we will join you in the war'** (18:3). Ahab seems to have played on that notion. Jehoshaphat knew that the Lord had forbidden his people to give their sons and daughters in marriage to the heathen nations, but he no doubt reasoned that the northern kingdom was still a part of Israel, and that he was, therefore, permitted to enter into a marriage alliance with Ahab and his family.

Jehoshaphat had not fully reckoned with Ahab's apostasy. Jehu afterwards rebuked Jehoshaphat for his involvement with Ahab, and showed him the seriousness of what he had done. He 'went out to meet [Jehoshaphat] and said to the king, "Should you help the wicked and love those who hate the Lord?" ' In other words, Ahab and his family were 'those who hate the Lord' and ought to have been treated like the heathen of other nations.

Apostasy is one of the most serious sins. It is worse than unbelief. It is a turning away from truth that was previously believed. It is committed in the face of clear evidence, and in spite of many blessings which illustrate God's mercy. Apostasy is not a sin that the heathen commit. It is committed by those who have tasted the goodness of God (Heb. 6:4-6; 10:26-29). When the sinner rejects God, then God rejects the sinner. Because Ahab rejected the Lord God of Israel, the Lord rejected Ahab and told Jehoshaphat that he ought to look upon Ahab as a heathen king.

When God's people associate with apostasy, they will always compromise their witness. Jehoshaphat presents us with a very pathetic picture in this chapter. He was not an effective witness for truth and for righteousness. Admittedly he did ask that a true prophet of the Lord should be consulted, but that was all he did. He meekly sat by as the false prophets performed their rituals; he allowed the false prophet Zedekiah to slap Micaiah in the face without raising a protest, and he quietly ignored the counsel of the Lord's spokesman. It was impossible for Jehoshaphat to be anything other than ineffective as a standard-bearer for truth because his very presence in Ahab's court had compromised his position. When we once associate with apostasy, we shall find ourselves associating with it again and again until its influence over us far outweighs our influence over it.

2. Jehoshaphat seeks counsel (18:4-13)

Unfortunately Jehoshaphat spoke without thinking when he replied, 'I am as you are, and my people as your people; we will join you in the war' (18:3). He assured Ahab of his support in attacking Ramoth Gilead, and only afterwards thought to seek the Lord's guidance: **'But Jehoshaphat also said to the king of Israel, "First seek the counsel of the Lord"'** (18:4). This brought forth a ready response from Ahab: **'So the king of Israel brought together the prophets — four hundred men'** (18:5). These prophets were the official prophets who ate at Jezebel's table (1 Kings 18:19). They were part of the machinery of state and their main purpose was to reinforce public confidence in the king's decisions. They knew what they were paid to do, and they duly pronounced heaven's blessing on Ahab's decisions. To Jehoshaphat, and indeed to everyone else, it must have been obvious that these were not men speaking as the Lord had directed them.

Jehoshaphat was rather mild in expressing his unease. He did not rebuke Ahab for this blatant attempt to steamroller him into going along with his military plans. Nor did he condemn the heathen practices of these false prophets. Instead he implicitly acquiesced with the religious pluralism of his day when he asked, **'Is there not a prophet of the Lord here whom we can enquire of?'** He wanted the prophet of the Lord to take his place alongside the heathen prophets, as one option among many.

There was indeed a true prophet of the Lord and his name was Micaiah the son of Imlah. He was one of the few who remained to challenge the apostasy of Ahab's kingdom. Consider what Ahab said about him in 18:7.

Micaiah was isolated

Ahab's response to Jehoshaphat's question was: **'There is still one man through whom we can enquire of the Lord.'** In the midst of all those false prophets, Micaiah was the only one who spoke for the Lord. **'All the other prophets were prophesying the same thing. "Attack Ramoth Gilead and be victorious," they said, "for the Lord will give it into the king's hand"'** (18:11). Micaiah was a lone dissenting voice from this chorus of encouragement. He was under great pressure to say what the others had said: **'The messenger who had gone to summon Micaiah said to him, "Look, as one man the other prophets are predicting success for the king. Let your word agree with theirs, and speak favourably"'** (18:12). In such situations today believers can still lose their confidence and think, 'Perhaps I am the one who is mistaken? Could I have misunderstood what God said?' Isolation in a godless world is demoralizing. That is why we need to seek the fellowship of like-minded believers, and above all to keep our fellowship with God.

Micaiah was despised

He was held in contempt by the establishment. Zedekiah, the leader of the false prophets, poured scorn on him in a crude and violent way (18:23). Ahab manifested his dislike in typically childish fashion: **'I hate him because he never prophesies anything good about me, but always bad.'** This comes as no surprise, for there was not much that was good to say about Ahab. He was one of the vilest of sinners in Israel and Micaiah's task was to condemn what God hated. We should not think that Micaiah was a dour misanthrope — he had just not pandered to Ahab's self-esteem. When the Word of God is preached faithfully today and when preachers dare to say what God's Word says about sin, there will be a similar reaction. Until God's Spirit softens their hearts sinners will say, 'I don't like that man. He has nothing positive to say. His preaching is always so negative.'

Micaiah was faithful

He did not crumble under the pressure to agree with the false prophets: **'As surely as the LORD lives, I can tell him** [Ahab] **only what my God says'** (18:13). Even though he was the only one to predict disaster, Micaiah spoke the truth. He knew that God's truth is not settled by a majority vote, but is revealed by the Lord who alone is the source of all truth (Isa. 40:13-14; 55:8-9; Rom. 11:33-36). Even though the world may oppose what God says, 'Let God be true, and every man a liar' (Rom. 3:4). In the modern world we are constantly told that there are no absolutes of truth and error, and that every point of view is, therefore, valid and ought to be given respect. In the face of this world-view Christian believers need to maintain their conviction that only what God says is true.

Micaiah spoke God's truth even though he knew that he would be despised for saying it. He knew that he would suffer simply for being faithful to God. In fact many true prophets in Israel had lost their lives for being faithful messengers of the living God. Micaiah knew that there was one true God and he knew the character of that God. He knew that it was futile to bend his words to the wishes of men, because although men might destroy his body, the Lord had power over his soul. For this reason the Lord Jesus urged his disciples to fear God rather than men (Matt. 10:28). Micaiah was, therefore, unflinching and courageous in warning Ahab and his prophets about the foolishness of their heathen ways and he continued to do so to the very end. We can picture the prophet shouting his stern warning to Ahab even as the guards marched him off to prison: **'If you ever return safely, the LORD has not spoken through me... Mark my words, all you people!'** (18:27).

3. Jehoshaphat is forced to decide (18:14-27)

Micaiah's message to Ahab and Jehoshaphat was clearly not the same as that of the false prophets. When the question was put to him in 18:14, Micaiah mimicked the answer of the false prophets, with the same bitter scorn that Elijah had poured upon the prophets of Baal at Mount Carmel (1 Kings 18:27). Micaiah's reply in 18:14 was obviously ironic, for it provoked Ahab's rebuke: **'How many times must I make you swear to tell me nothing but the truth in the name of the LORD?'** (18:15). A more hypocritical plea for the truth is impossible to find. The last thing that Ahab wanted to hear was the truth from the Lord. Ahab spent his days evading the Lord God of Israel.

However, Ahab did hear the truth from the Lord. It came through Micaiah in a twofold vision. In the first vision Micaiah saw **'all Israel scattered ... like sheep without a shepherd'** (18:16). The direct answer to Ahab's question was: **'Let each one go home in peace.'** God was not going to bless the attack upon Ramoth Gilead. The implications for Ahab were clear, for in ancient times kings thought of themselves as shepherds and their subjects as the sheep under their protection. The Lord had said, **'These people have no master.'** Ahab was being told that he would die in battle and his people would be scattered on the battlefield.

This was also a stern rebuke to Jehoshaphat. Neither he nor Ahab were offering godly leadership to the people of Israel that day. Although both of them sat together on their thrones, there was 'no master' in Israel that day. This is how Israel would continue until the coming of the promised Messianic King. The hearts of godly Israelites longed for such a master to come, and when the Lord Jesus came to his people he was filled with compassion for them 'because they were harassed and helpless, like sheep without a shepherd' (Matt. 9:36). Today we can praise God that his people have a Shepherd who leads them in ways of righteousness (Ps. 23:3). When he leads them into battle, he assures them of victory (Rom. 16:20; Eph. 6:10-18).

Micaiah's second vision was of God's heavenly court (see 18:18-21). Its message was directed especially to Ahab's false prophets. Within themselves they were asking, 'Who does this man think that he is? How can he be the only one that is right, and we all be wrong?' Micaiah's rebuke was a stinging indictment of their deceit. They spoke as they did because they were filled with a lying spirit, designed to lure Ahab to his death: **'A spirit came forward ... and said, "I will entice him... I will go and be a lying spirit in the mouths of all his prophets"'** (18:21).

This vision raises some difficult questions for us. Can we understand Micaiah to say that one of God's elect angels (1 Tim. 5:21), who are described as 'holy' (Rev. 14:10), suggested and executed such a programme of deceit? In spite of what some commentators suggest, this is not an acceptable explanation. The best way of understanding the passage seems to be that one of the fallen angels, 'who did not keep their positions of authority but abandoned their own home' (Jude 6), put this suggestion to God. Although this explanation is not without difficulties, we might find a precedent in Job 1:6, where Satan presented himself before the Lord along with the angels, and proceeded to incite the Lord against Job.

In any event, the Scriptures clearly teach that God is sovereign over the entire host of angels — elect and reprobate, heavenly and fallen, good and evil. God is in control over the actions of sinful and fallen angels, just as he is sovereign over the actions of sinful men. The sinful actions of Joseph's brothers were intended by God, so that many lives might be saved. According to Deuteronomy 13:3, false prophecy is permitted by God to test the faithfulness of his people. And, most notably, Jesus Christ 'was handed over ... by God's set purpose and foreknowledge; and you [that is, sinful men]... put him to death by nailing him to the cross' (Acts 2:23).

God never participates in evil deeds. Wicked men and evil angels are never forced to do what is evil; they supply the evil impetus that makes their actions sinful. John Calvin wrote about this particular instance, 'Whatever men or Satan himself may instigate, God nevertheless holds the key, so that he turns their efforts to carry out his judgements. God wills that the false King Ahab be deceived; the devil offers his services to this end; he is sent, with a definite command, to be a lying spirit in the mouth of all the prophets.'

Ahab and his courtiers were only too glad to hear the message that this lying spirit put into the mouths of the false prophets. We ask, how could they have failed to see through the specious flattery of these false prophets? And how could Jehoshaphat have been blind to the danger he was being led into? The fact that the lying spirit in the mouths of the false prophets was believed makes a telling statement about the prejudices of ungodly men. They want to hear Satan's lies. When they 'suppress the truth by their wickedness' (Rom. 1:18), it is because they need false teachers who will embolden them in their stand against God. As time passes, sinners come to believe their own excuses, and become so darkened in their minds that they lose the ability to tell truth from falsehood.

Thus Ahab, the enemy of God, was only too glad to receive the encouragement of these false prophets.

More perplexing is the fact that Jehoshaphat listened to the advice of the false prophets and rejected the wise advice of Micaiah. Jehoshaphat was a godly man, instructed in the law of God. He had known the sound instruction of the Levites, and should have recognized the truth when he heard it. How could he contemplate going up to recapture Ramoth Gilead after hearing Micaiah's warning? How foolish!

Yet have we not done exactly the same thing? When two paths were set clearly before us, did we not follow foolish advice and stray into the wrong path? So too did Jehoshaphat. He received two conflicting pieces of advice: 'Go up and attack,' and 'Go home in peace.' Which was he to do? Both claimed to be from the Lord, but one was clearly false. Which was it?

The unfolding of events will expose a false prophet. That is the test Moses gave in Deuteronomy 18:22: 'If what a prophet proclaims in the name of the LORD does not take place or come true, that is a message the LORD has not spoken. That prophet has spoken presumptuously.' The penalty for prophesying presumptuously was death (Deut. 18:20). Jehoshaphat, however, did not enjoy the benefit of hindsight, so this test was not available to him. He could, however, have taken into account *the credentials* of these prophets. They were chosen and paid by King Ahab. God had not sent them. They were the sort of men described in Jeremiah 23:32. Only Micaiah was called and sent by God.

Jehoshaphat could have looked at *the lives* of these prophets. They were known sycophants who bowed to the desires of men. Micaiah was a man of God, who sought to speak only what the Lord told him to say.

Jehoshaphat could also have considered *the message* of the prophets. The false prophets had a man-centred message. God was mentioned only incidentally, as a cipher to the plans of

Ahab. These men had not sought the Lord. By contrast Micaiah presents us with a vision of God exalted and sitting upon the throne, as in Isaiah 6:1-7. The God of Micaiah's vision was one to be listened to and obeyed.

Jehoshaphat might also have listened to *the tone* of the prophets. The false prophets did not lack sound and fury (18:23). Zedekiah son of Kenaanah had even prepared a pair of iron horns to illustrate their message. **'This is what the LORD says: "With these you will gore the Arameans until they are destroyed"'** (18:10). Yet there was more sound than substance to their arguments. Was it the very weakness of their arguments that required such a show of force? By contrast, Micaiah's words had a self-authenticating ring of authority. The fact that he really was speaking for the Lord gave him the confidence to proclaim his unpopular message with calmness and dignity.

Zedekiah's only response to Micaiah's vision was a violent outburst and a sneering question. He **'went up and slapped Micaiah in the face. "Which way did the spirit from the LORD go when he went from me to speak to you?"'** (18:23). Micaiah's enigmatic response was: **'You will find out on the day you go to hide in an inner room'** (18:24). The 'inner room' was often the scene of sinister activity (as in 1 Kings 20:30) and indicates an unpleasant end in disreputable circumstances. Before such a prophetic word Zedekiah had nothing to say.

4. Jehoshaphat discovered the consequences of ignoring God's Word (18:28 – 19:3)

Jehoshaphat decided wrongly. **'So the king of Israel and Jehoshaphat king of Judah went up to Ramoth Gilead'** (18:28). He ignored the advice of Micaiah and listened to the advice of the false prophets. To be sure, he must have gone into battle with an uneasy heart. However, the momentum of his alliance with Ahab carried him on into danger, against his better judgement. This is always the danger to which believers expose themselves when they enter a close partnership with unbelievers. This may happen when a young person mixes with the wrong company, or when a Christian chooses as his best friends those who do not love the Lord, or when a believer marries an unbeliever.

Jehoshaphat found that he had a treacherous ally in King Ahab. **'The king of Israel said to Jehoshaphat, "I will enter the battle in disguise, but you wear your royal robes"'** (18:29). Ahab's reasoning must have been obvious to Jehoshaphat. It was common practice for armies to target the commanders of their opponents. By removing the head, the body can become powerless, and this was the aim of the King of Syria: **'Do not fight with anyone, small or great, except the king of Israel'** (18:30). By disguising himself Ahab aimed to ensure that he would not be a target on the battlefield and Jehoshaphat was to serve as a decoy.

In battle Jehoshaphat was in great personal danger (18:31-32). His royal robes were clear for all to see, and the Syrian soldiers turned their attack towards him. Just in time the Syrians realized that they had found the wrong king and Jehoshaphat survived (see 19:1), but not without the special intervention of God: **'Jehoshaphat cried out, and the LORD helped him. God drew them away from him.'** His near escape should have taught Jehoshaphat not to take the Lord's protection for granted. The fact that we are the Lord's people does not mean that we shall be spared from suffering loss on account of our foolishness and carelessness. The Christian leader who is shoddy in his service of God is told by Paul that 'He will suffer loss; he himself will be saved, but only as one escaping through the flames' (1 Cor. 3:15).

Jehoshaphat exposed his armies to defeat at the battle of Ramoth Gilead. Many people in Judah suffered on account of Jehoshaphat's foolish alliance with Ahab. Lives and livelihoods, territory, prestige and integrity were all lost to Jehoshaphat's kingdom. Furthermore Jehoshaphat himself was rebuked by the prophet Jehu: **'Because of this, the wrath of the LORD is upon you'** (19:2). Mercifully, this was not the unquenchable wrath that rests upon the unrepentant sinner. Sometimes the earthly sufferings of sinners are foretastes of eternal torment, but that was not the case here. Jehoshaphat was a godly king from whom the penal wrath of God had been removed. However, the Lord continues to discipline those whose guilt has been removed. King David was a case in point. God had removed David's guilt, but continued to chastise him for his foolishness (2 Sam. 12:13-14). In the same way, Jehoshaphat suffered the consequences of his foolishness for the rest of his earthly life, and other people would suffer, too.

For all his cunning, Ahab was unable to escape Micaiah's prophecy. His treacherous attempt to use Jehoshaphat as a decoy did not work. He was able to hide himself from the Arameans, but not from God. **'But someone drew his bow at random and hit the king of Israel between the sections of his armour... Then at sunset he died'** (18:33-34).

The English translations 'at random' (NIV/NKJV) or 'at a venture' (AV) do not convey the significance of the Hebrew expression *(lethumo)*, which means 'in innocence or simplicity', and indicates that there was no view of the consequences of the action. The humble archer who drew his bow was simply one member of a regiment of archers and had not thought that his arrow might strike the King of Israel. Probably he never knew that he had struck such a decisive blow against his enemy. Yet the sovereign Lord knew every movement of the arrow, for even the seemingly random events of life are directed by him (Prov. 16:33). How foolish it was of Ahab to think that he could evade the hand of God!

Ahab's actions were a deliberate attempt to evade the warning that he had received from Micaiah. However, Micaiah was confirmed as a true prophet of the Lord. Every detail of God's word was fulfilled: Ahab was killed, the people were scattered leaderless over the battlefield and the false prophets were shown to be liars. This was a word from the Lord, and Ahab discovered that God's words never fail. God's warnings never fail, yet many people are still trying to evade God. They go through life hoping that the wages of sin will not turn out to be death. They hope that God will overlook their disobedience and unbelief. These are false hopes, for no one can escape the arm of the Lord.

The sovereign providence of God in the battle at Ramoth Gilead was a two-edged sword. It delivered Jehoshaphat, but it destroyed Ahab. Jehoshaphat was chastened and disciplined, but ultimately he was delivered from danger. Jehu acknowledged that Jehoshaphat was a good man: **'There is, however, some good in you, for you have rid the land of the Asherah poles and have set your heart on seeking God'** (19:3). There was evidence that the grace of God was active in his life. 'Though he stumble, he will not fall, for the LORD upholds him with his hand' (Ps. 37:24). Ahab, however, was a godless man who stumbled and fell to his own destruction. From God's dealings in this chapter, two very different applications can be drawn.

The believer delights in the omnipresence and sovereignty of God. God's people are pleased to know that, wherever they go, the Lord's hand is upon them to keep them and to preserve them. God's people will even pray:

Search me, O God, and know my heart;
    test me and know my anxious thoughts.
See if there is any offensive way in me,
    and lead me in the way everlasting

(Ps. 139:23-24).

They know that all things are being wrought together for their good (Rom. 8:28).

The unbeliever, however, is constantly under God's wrath. Every turn of God's providence is frightening to him, and rightly so. In 'random events' the unbeliever sees the hand of the God whom he has despised and provoked to anger. When the hand of God rests on your life, do you praise him, or are you in fear?

12.
Jehoshaphat: a great deliverance

Please read 2 Chronicles 19:4 – 21:3

It is said that those who do not learn the lessons of history are condemned to repeat its mistakes. This ought to encourage us to read the historical narratives of Scripture. In the history of redemption we meet with men and women who 'ate the same spiritual food and drank the same spiritual drink' as we do. The apostle Paul explains: 'These things occurred as examples to keep us from setting our hearts on evil things as they did' (1 Cor. 10:3,6). As we read 2 Chronicles 19 and 20, we have a sense of history repeating itself during the reign of King Jehoshaphat of Judah.

The previous two chapters have described the encouraging start to Jehoshaphat's reign as well as his disastrous alliance with King Ahab of Israel. We find a similar pattern in chapters 19 and 20. Initially there was a movement for reform based on God's law (19:4-11). This was followed by a demonstration of God's blessing upon Judah, as a result of which **'The fear of God came upon all the kingdoms...'** (20:29; cf. 17:10). However, this was followed by an alliance with the northern kingdom of Israel (20:35-36) and a rebuke from Eliezer, the Lord's prophet (20:37).

Jehoshaphat had learned many lessons during the course of his reign, and he had put them into practice. He had discovered the importance of teaching his people to obey the law of

God (see 17:7-9); therefore he sought to consolidate that work by appointing judges to enforce that law. Jehoshaphat had learned that Jehovah is mighty in battle; therefore he led his people in prayer during a time of national calamity with an enhanced appreciation of the Lord's ability to destroy his enemies.

However, there is a tendency for men to return to their old sins. Paul acknowledged that even in the believer there is a struggle with sin that continues: 'For what I do is not the good I want to do; no, the evil I do not want to do — this I keep on doing' (Rom. 7:19). Jehoshaphat had this problem too. There were some lessons that he found very hard to learn. Because he did not learn from either history or experience, the Lord had to instruct him the hard way.

Jehoshaphat encouraged his people to keep God's law (19:4-11)

Following his disastrous foray onto the battlefield at Ramoth Gilead, Jehoshaphat 'returned safely to his palace in Jerusalem' (19:1). The sobering experience of military defeat left the king a humbled man. To the experience of defeat was added the rebuke of Jehu the prophet (19:2-3).

This hard experience brought Jehoshaphat back to more godly ways. **'He went out again among the people ... and turned them back to the Lord, the God of their fathers'** (19:4). Like a true shepherd, he went out among his people to find out how they lived and to bring back those who had strayed into sin. As he went, **'He appointed judges in the land... He told them, "Consider carefully what you do, because you are not judging for man but for the Lord"'** (19:5-6). He had set up a system of national instruction to teach God's law to the people (17:7-9), but it is never enough simply to hear God's Word; we must also be doers of the Word (Luke 8:18; James 1:22-23). Jehoshaphat wanted his people to be doers of the Word that the Levites had taught them. That is why he appointed judges as he went. Let us take a closer look at these judges and their work.

1. Jehoshaphat established a network of judges to enforce God's law (19:5)

In each town the judges were 'courts of first reference'. Where there was a dispute requiring adjudication the matter went to them first. Then there was a 'court of appeal' in Jerusalem (19:8) to which more difficult cases were brought from the local courts. This appeal court was to be staffed by Levites and priests. Such a court had been established by Moses in Deuteronomy 17:8-13. Moses allowed 'the priests, who are Levites' to hear appeals when 'cases come before your courts that are too difficult ... to judge'. Difficult cases included 'bloodshed, lawsuits or assaults'.

Murder and violent assault were serious crimes that carried serious penalties, in some cases the death penalty. Because of the solemn nature of the penalty it was appropriate to have an opportunity to review the case. 'Lawsuits' were controversial, or borderline, cases. Often a more experienced judge would be able to give a ruling on the issues involved. In 19:10 Jehoshaphat quoted the Mosaic regulations to explain how the Levites ought to hear the appeals that would be brought to them: **'In every case that comes before you from your fellow countrymen who live in the cities — whether bloodshed or other concerns of the law, commands, decrees, or ordinances — you are to warn them not to sin against the Lord.'** The judicial system in Judah was to reflect the character of God. God is a God of truth and justice; therefore the system was to place great emphasis on discovering the truth. That concern carries over into the thinking of Christians today. Paul applies this in the life of the church (e.g., 1 Tim. 5:19-21). In civil society, fairness and the rule of law are principles that are built upon a regard for God's law.

2. *Jehoshaphat recognized the distinction between civil and ceremonial matters* (19:11)

Although Old Testament Israel was both the covenant people and an earthly nation (with a political and legal system), the distinction between civil and ceremonial was maintained. Two presidents were appointed over the appeal courts to advise the judges about matters of legal detail: **'Amariah the chief priest will be over you in any matter concerning the LORD, and Zebadiah son of Ishmael, the leader of the tribe of Judah, will be over you in any matter concerning the king.'** A range of issues was brought to this court in Jerusalem, including criminal convictions and civil claims for damages, and issues touching on the ceremonial law. Amariah supervised the latter, while Zebadiah supervised the former.

The distinction between matters concerning the Lord and those concerning the king became very important during the post-exilic period when the Chronicler wrote his history. There was no longer a king in Jerusalem, but a foreign overlord. In Jerusalem there was a provincial governor who protected the interests of the king, and he would try to restrict the scope of those matters concerning the Lord. Only in 140 B.C., when Simon Maccabaeus was appointed ethnarch and hereditary high priest, were civil and ceremonial functions brought together in the Jewish state. During the intervening years the Levites struggled to hold the people to God's law. They strove to ensure that the demands of heathen kings did not encroach upon the commands of the Lord. They sought to remind the people that the king himself was subject to an even higher King — just as our Lord reminded the Jews of his own day that they were to 'Give to Caesar what is Caesar's, and to God what is God's' (Matt. 22:21).

3. Jehoshaphat reminded the priests and Levites that they themselves were subject to God (19:6-9)

He encouraged the judges to do their work with the utmost seriousness: **'Consider carefully what you do, because you are not judging for man but for the LORD, who is with you whenever you give a verdict'** (19:6). God takes a deep interest in the administration of civil justice (Rom. 13:4). Therefore, in administering justice these men were performing a divinely ordained function. They were to remember that the Lord was watching over them and would call them to account for their decisions: **'Now let the fear of the LORD be upon you. Judge carefully, for with the LORD our God there is no injustice or partiality or bribery'** (19:7). Even less exalted tasks ought to be performed scrupulously because the Lord is watching (Col. 3:22 – 4:1).

4. The message they were to proclaim (19:10)

The message that these judges were to communicate to the people was a simple one: sin must be eradicated from daily life. **'You must serve faithfully and wholeheartedly in the fear of the LORD. In every case that comes before you from your fellow countrymen ... you are to warn them not to sin against the LORD... Do this, and you will not sin'**

(19:9-10). Sin had brought the wrath of God upon their nation, and if the kingdom was to prosper they must wage war against it. A similar goal underlies the gospel of Jesus Christ: 'My dear children, I write this to you so that you will not sin' (1 John 1:8; 2:1). This ought to be our aim. God hates sin, and so should his people. He uses external restraints, such as the police and the courts, to subdue sinful behaviour, but only the saving grace of the Lord Jesus Christ can ever succeed in eradicating sin from human hearts.

5. The purpose of this network of judges — turning the people back to the Lord (19:4)

The system of judges covered the whole kingdom: **'from Beersheba to the hill country of Ephraim'**. Beginning in the deep south around Beersheba, Jehoshaphat moved up through the territory of Judah to the 'hill country of Ephraim'. In so doing he encroached upon territory that had belonged to the northern kingdom. Perhaps in the chaos that followed Ahab's death the authorities in Samaria had been unable to hold onto this part of the kingdom which bordered on Judah, and Jehoshaphat seized the opportunity to expand his own borders. At any rate, Jehoshaphat's purpose was to turn the Israelites back to the Lord, and in this respect he met with a large measure of success. **'Jehoshaphat ... turned them back to the LORD, the God of their fathers.'**

This may refer to idolatrous northerners, or it may refer to the people of Judah who added the worship of other gods to the worship of Jehovah. In either case, there was a reformation which changed lives and resulted in new obedience to God. The word for Jehoshaphat's 'turning them back' is frequently used in the Old Testament to describe repentance. Only the Lord can turn men and women back to himself. The psalmist prayed for this when he said:

> Restore us, O God;
>> make your face shine upon us,
>> that we may be saved

(Ps. 80:3,7,19).

When the Lord turns his people back to himself, their repentance is not superficial or temporary; their salvation is certain. In this work of turning men back to himself the Lord is often pleased to use human instruments. Paul exhorted Timothy to instruct the flock 'in the hope that God will grant them repentance leading them to a knowledge of the truth' (2 Tim. 2:25). Jehoshaphat was such a human instrument, and through his influence real changes took place among the people of Judah. He 'turned them back to the LORD'.

Jehoshaphat led his people to put their trust in the Lord (20:1-30)

An external threat (20:1-4,13)

'After this, the Moabites and Ammonites with some of the Meunites came to make war on Jehoshaphat' (20:1). Jehoshaphat discovered that godliness does not ensure a life without trials. Sometimes it is the very godliness of God's people that makes them targets for God's enemies. In this instance God's enemies were a coalition of nations dwelling to the east of the River Jordan. The Moabites and Ammonites were the nations descended from Lot's daughters. The Meunites were probably Arabs (in 26:7 Meunites are mentioned alongside Arabs during the reign of King Hezekiah; see also 1 Chr. 4:41) who lived a nomadic existence south of the Dead Sea. Together they gathered together **'a vast army'**.

As this army moved north, alarm spread before it. **'Some men came and told Jehoshaphat, "A vast army is coming against you from Edom, from the other side of the Sea"'** (20:2). As the countryside was pillaged and villages torched, messengers brought the terrible reports to Jerusalem. The terrified people sought God's protection: **'The people of Judah came together to seek help from the LORD; indeed, they came from every town in Judah to seek him'** (20:4). Their instinct was like that of sheep when the flock is attacked; they gathered together to seek the Lord. The whole community came together for this sacred assembly: **'All the men of Judah, with their wives and children and little ones, stood there before the LORD'** (20:13).

Those who endured the privations of the Second World War in Britain remember a very strong sense of community spirit. It was, after all, the 'people's war'. The external threat strengthened the sense of national unity, but it did not create it. God's people were united by virtue of their covenant with God. They were united in their need for grace and in their enjoyment of God's mercies. Their unity was cemented as they worshipped together and acknowledged these truths. It is still important that families should gather as whole families to worship God in their homes and in congregational worship. Yes, even the young children should be present when God's people meet.

Jehoshaphat's response (20:5-12)

Jehoshaphat responded to the crisis by taking the initiative. He led the people in prayer. His tone was urgent. Disaster was staring them in the face, but there was no panic in his voice. Jehoshaphat's request was simple: he sought deliverance from his enemies. His approach was bold. He claimed the promises that God had made to Abraham: **'O our God, did you not**

drive out the inhabitants of this land before your people Israel and give it for ever to the descendants of Abraham your friend?' Jehoshaphat quoted directly from the prayer of his ancestor, Solomon: **'If calamity comes upon us, whether the sword of judgement, or plague or famine, we will stand in your presence before this temple that bears your Name and will cry out to you in our distress, and you will hear us and save us'** (20:7,9; cf. 6:24-31).

Does this prayer seem a little presumptuous? Jehoshaphat's prayer would have been overconfident if he had based it on human rights or self-interest. As it was, he based his prayer on the promises of God and the experiences of the covenant people. God had never broken his promises to his people, and Jehoshaphat was certain that he never would. On this basis the king prayed to God for deliverance. He presented five arguments:

1. God's lordship over the nations

'O Lord, God of our fathers, are you not the God who is in heaven? You rule over all the kingdoms of the nations. Power and might are in your hand, and no one can withstand you' (20:6). Jehoshaphat was not afraid of these nations because they were powerless before the Lord. God had created them and he could destroy them.

2. God's promise to Abraham

'O our God, did you not drive out the inhabitants of this land before your people Israel, and give it for ever to the descendants of Abraham your friend?' (20:7). God chose Abraham to be his friend and made a covenant with him and his descendants. An expression of that friendship was God's promise that Abraham and his descendants would dwell in the promised land. God had miraculously given them the land through Joshua. Jehoshaphat rejoiced in the same covenant promise.

3. God's promise to Solomon

The building of the temple in Jerusalem was a sign that Israel had possessed the promised land (20:8), and it was a reminder that God would listen to them when they cried out to him: '**... and you will hear us and save us**' (20:9; cf. 6:28-31).

4. God's despised goodness

God had been merciful to Moab and Ammon in the choice of route taken by the Israelites when they entered into the promised land (20:10-11). Instead of travelling directly from the wilderness to the Jordan crossing at Jericho, they had made a detour into the wilderness. They did not force their way through Moabite and Ammonite territory. Now the Moabites and Ammonites were forcing their way into the land promised to Israel: '**See how they are repaying us by coming to drive us out of the possession you gave us as an inheritance**' (20:11).

5. The powerlessness of God's people

'**We have no power to face this vast army that is attacking us. We do not know what to do, but our eyes are upon you**' (20:12). This was the most persuasive argument of all. God is at his most merciful when his people are at their most helpless. God's mercy overflows when his people are on their knees before him. God's greatness is most clearly demonstrated when his people have run out of strength and his power is demonstrated through their weakness (see 2 Cor. 12:9-10).

A prophetic response (20:14-19)

God's response to Jehoshaphat's prayer was immediate and startling. A voice was heard crying from the body of the assembly: **'Then the Spirit of the LORD came upon Jahaziel ... a Levite and descendant of Asaph, as he stood in the assembly'** (20:14). Although Jahaziel had an honourable lineage that entitled him to serve in the temple, there was nothing that distinguished him from the other Levites. He was standing with everyone else as Jehoshaphat prayed. He was not a great speaker, or an important person, but he had a great message. The Lord uses the things that are nothing to humble those who think that they are something. The Lord conveys his treasure in earthen vessels (see 1 Cor. 1:26-28; 2 Cor. 4:7). Let this humble our pretensions when we are tempted to think our gifts make us indispensable to the Lord.

The fact that Jahaziel was a Levite is, however, worthy of note. It was unusual for the Levites to speak as prophets. However, the book of Chronicles was written after the great prophets had fallen silent. Their words had fallen on deaf ears, and the judgement they predicted had come to pass. But, in his mercy, the Lord had not abandoned his people, and in the post-exilic period the burden of ministry fell upon the Levites who taught the law of God — men like Ezra.

We should not think of these Levites as grey men, with nothing very exciting to say. The Spirit of God spoke through them, just as he had spoken through the prophets. He also spoke through the Levites as they regularly instructed the people in the Scriptures. The ministry of the Levites was not to be despised. Neither ought Christians today to despise the regular ministry of God's Word, for that is how the Lord conveys wonderful promises to his church in our day.

Jahaziel's message promised deliverance: **'Do not be afraid or discouraged because of this vast army. For the battle is**

not yours, but God's... You will not have to fight this battle. Take up your positions; stand firm and see the deliverance the LORD will give you' (20:15,17). Jahaziel's message emphasized the activity of God and the passivity of his people. They were to watch and see what the Lord was going to do, but they were not to fight themselves.

It would be easy to draw the wrong lessons from these verses. In an age of 'laid-back religion' it would be very tempting for some Christians to make this a reason for abandoning our spiritual warfare. For many years it has been taught in some quarters that sanctification comes in the believer's life by 'letting go' and 'letting God' do everything. The 'end of striving' is how the believer ought to win the victory over indwelling sin and besetting doubts. After all, we are told, the battle is the Lord's, and the strength that overcomes is his strength. This, however, is a wrong application of biblical teaching. The faith of God's people is a faith that 'overcomes the world' (1 John 5:4-5). This is not an inactive faith. As believers we are to 'continue to work out [our] salvation with fear and trembling', to 'put on the full armour of God so that [we] can take [our] stand against the devil's schemes', to 'offer [ourselves] to God, as those who have been brought from death to life, and offer the parts of [our bodies] to him as instruments of righteousness' (Phil. 2:12; Eph. 6:11; Rom. 6:13). There is no endorsement of inactivity in these commands. The believer is urged to act alongside the Lord in the co-operative work of sanctification.

Jahaziel's message does not undermine the clear teaching of Scripture that God's people enjoy victory over evil by exerting their God-given strength. The point of his prophecy is not that God's people ought to do nothing. He addressed a situation where they were unable to do anything effective. What ought they to do in such cases? God's people often face overwhelming odds, and they despair as they look at the seriousness of their plight and the poverty of their resources. At such times they face a strong temptation to throw up their hands in despair. Their hearts fail them and their knees give way beneath them in spite of the spiritual armour that they have buckled on.

The purpose of Jahaziel's message was to encourage the people of Judah not to despair: **'Do not be afraid or discouraged because of this vast army'** (20:15). Far from telling the people of Judah to do nothing, he told them to do something: **'Take up your positions; stand firm and see the deliverance the LORD will give you'** (20:17). As they watched they would see the Lord destroy their enemies. The same is true in every spiritual battle. When we go into battle against our temptations and besetting sins, we receive the same encouragement. **'Go out to face them tomorrow, and the LORD will be with you.'**

God's power at work (20:20-25)

'Early in the morning they left for the Desert of Tekoa.' What must the men of Judah have expected as they set out for the desert? Although they had the Lord's assurance that the battle was his and that he would win the victory, they were in the dark about the way in which he would bring this about. What form would that victory take? Jehoshaphat did not know, but he was sure that the Lord knew: **'Listen to me, Judah and the people of Jerusalem! Have faith in the LORD your God and you will be upheld; have faith in his prophets and you will be successful'** (20:20). As if to remind them of this, **'Jehoshaphat appointed men to sing to the LORD.'** Of course, the Lord's people were edified by the words they sang: **'Give thanks to the LORD, for his love endures for ever'** (20:21).

The Lord did not disappoint them: **'As they began to sing and praise, the LORD set ambushes against the men of Ammon and Moab and Mount Seir... The men of Ammon**

and Moab rose up against the men from Mount Seir'
(20:22-23). There is a tantalizing silence in these verses. We
are given no insight into the intrigue that divided and destroyed
this coalition. We have no record of the jealousies and ten-
sions that tore them apart. All we know is that **'They helped
to destroy one another'** (20:23). This disunity was created
by the Lord (20:22).

The men of Judah simply discovered what the Lord had
done when they marched out into the Desert of Tekoa. By the
time they arrived the battle was already won: **'They saw only
dead bodies lying on the ground; no one had escaped'**
(20:24). All that remained for Jehoshaphat and his men to do
was to gather the plunder from the silent battlefield: **'So
Jehoshaphat and his men went to carry off their plunder... There was so much plunder that it took three days
to collect it'** (20:25). What a haunting sight this must have
been! What an eerie silence must have hung over that land-
scape! When the guns fell silent after the great battles of the
First World War, soldiers from both sides went out to retrieve
the corpses which lay scattered over a lunar wilderness.
Nothing was alive — not even the grass. Not even the birds
sang. What must the men of Judah have thought as they walked
among the corpses and thought about what God had done?
Perhaps the words of Balaam came to mind:

> How can I curse
> those whom God has not cursed?
> How can I denounce
> those whom the LORD has not denounced? ...
>
> Edom will be conquered;
> Seir, his enemy will be conquered,
> but Israel will grow strong
>
> (Num. 23:8, 24:18).

They must have pondered on the fact that they had not lifted so much as a little finger to accomplish any of it. Perhaps they remembered David's words in Psalm 110:5-6:

> The LORD is at your right hand;
>   he will crush kings on the day of his wrath.
> He will judge nations, heaping up the dead
>   and crushing the rulers of the whole earth.

God's people in every age are to rejoice in the saving power of God, which is greater than we can ever realize. He saves us without relying on anything we can do. When we were help-less, because we were dead in sins, God took the initiative to save sinners: 'When we were still powerless, Christ died for the ungodly' (Rom. 5:6). Before we loved him, he loved us. Before we trusted him, he drew us. Before we knew of his mercy, he sent his Spirit to enlighten us. Before we could do anything, he had planned and accomplished everything that was necessary for our salvation. Truly, 'Salvation is of the LORD' (Jonah 2:10, NKJV).

However, it is not true to say that Jehoshaphat and the men of Judah did absolutely nothing. Although they did not lay a hand upon their enemies to defeat them, they did look to the Lord. This is evident from 20:20-21. These verses record how Jehoshaphat sent his people out with a right frame of mind. He exhorted them: **'Have faith in the LORD your God and you will be upheld.'** The appointed singers sang the refrain from Psalm 136, a psalm which recounts the Lord's goodness to Israel in the past. He had 'struck down the firstborn of Egypt' (v. 10), 'divided the Red Sea asunder' (v. 13), 'led his people through the desert' (v. 16) and 'killed mighty kings' (v. 18). These were all reasons to give thanks to God. They were also encouragements to trust the Lord as they went out that day.

This is what God expects his people to do. He does not expect them to win the battle by relying on their own cunning or strength. He calls them to look to the Lord and put their trust in him. Faith is the channel by which we receive the promised blessings of God. Faith might be a small pipeline, but it connects the believer to a vast reservoir of strength. What is the helpless sinner to do? He is to look to the cross and believe that there he can find forgiveness. What is the trembling believer to do? He is to look to the Lord who has given him great and precious promises. As C. H. Spurgeon might have said, he is to take out 'the cheque book of the bank of faith' and draw on all the riches that are stored up for him in heaven. Only we can believe. That is what God commands us to do.

Acknowledging what the Lord had done (20:26-30)

Jehoshaphat and his people willingly acknowledged that the Lord had delivered them from invasion. Praise is the theme of these verses. After the three days of collecting plunder and removing it from the battlefield, the people of Judah assembled to praise the Lord. They gathered for this assembly at the **'Valley of Beracah'** (20:26), which was probably near the battlefield. 'Beracah' comes from the verb that means 'to worship' or 'bless'. At the scene of blessing they gathered to bless the Lord for the victory he had given them. They did not become so engrossed with the spoils of victory that they forgot to give thanks to the one who had given them victory. After God has blessed us it is very easy to become more interested in the gifts than the Giver. It is a good practice to pause and give thanks to the Lord as we receive his blessings. Our pause for prayer may only be momentary, but it disciplines us to 'pray continually' and to think as we ought about the Lord.

The people's thanksgiving did not die away as soon as they left the battlefield. **'Then, led by Jehoshaphat, all the men**

**of Judah and Jerusalem returned joyfully to Jerusalem,
for the LORD had given them cause to rejoice over their
enemies. They ... went to the temple of the LORD with harps
and lutes and trumpets'** (20:27-28). Too often God's people
forget his goodness, and what the Lord has done for them, as
they move on to new things, but this was not so in the case of
Jehoshaphat and his people. Their rejoicing in God was not
momentary, but ongoing. Because 'His love endures for ever',
so too must the grateful response of people who have been so
greatly blessed. We need to remind ourselves of the blessings
we have received. We do this by regularly setting aside time to
count our blessings. There is no better way to remember how
God has blessed us than the regular reading of the Scriptures.
They constantly show us how 'His love endures for ever.'

Not only did the people of Judah marvel at the greatness of
Jehovah, even the heathen nations were amazed at what the
Lord had done to the coalition armies: **'The fear of God came
upon all the kingdoms of the countries when they heard
how the LORD had fought against the enemies of Israel'**
(20:29). The facts were incontrovertible. The simple narrative
of events said it all. The acts of God speak for themselves!
They speak even more powerfully when God's people proclaim his greatness with gratitude and admiration, as in 20:26-
28. The men of Judah made sure the whole world heard what
the Lord had done. Yet how often do we keep to ourselves the
breathtaking news of what the Lord has done for us? May he
stir us up to proclaim his greatness!

Jehoshaphat's record was not perfect (20:31 – 21:3)

No doubt we have been blessed to read about God's blessing
upon Judah during the reign of King Jehoshaphat. The faith
and wisdom that he displayed in the face of national disaster
are an inspiration and encouragement to us. This makes it all

the more disappointing to read these verses which conclude
the Chronicler's account of Jehoshaphat's reign.

Not everyone in Judah followed Jehoshaphat's lead (20:33)

Jehoshaphat made sure that the people of Judah were instructed
in the law of God. This, in itself, was unable to eradicate the
sin of idolatry. **'The high places, however, were not removed,
and the people still had not set their hearts on the God of
their fathers'** (20:33). It was Jehoshaphat's aim to eradicate
the false worship that continued at these ancient sanctuaries
and to centralize the worship of Jehovah at the place which
the Lord himself had appointed, the temple in Jerusalem. However zealously Jehoshaphat pursued this goal, it was never
realized. Some of the people continued to worship at the high
places.

Jehoshaphat discovered what many others have proved: that
while it is possible and desirable to suppress ungodly behaviour by instruction and legislation, these means alone cannot
compel a change of heart. Jehoshaphat's actions had removed
some of the high places from the land, but they had not removed idolatry from the hearts of the people. Until that happened idolatry would not be eradicated from the land. How
important is that work of God's grace in the hearts of sinners
which teaches them to hate the sin they once loved! Godly
leaders and teachers may encourage such a change, but only
the Holy Spirit can accomplish it.

Jehoshaphat fell into an old trap (20:35-37)

**'Later, Jehoshaphat king of Judah made an alliance with
Ahaziah king of Israel, who was guilty of wickedness. He
agreed with him to construct a fleet of trading ships.'** Perhaps God's blessing upon his kingdom allowed Jehoshaphat
to indulge in nostalgia. Perhaps he hankered after the days of

Solomon when regular trading expeditions made Israel rich beyond imagination (8:17-18; 9:21-22). Just like Solomon, Jehoshaphat constructed a fleet of 'trading ships' (or 'ships of Tarshish') that was based at **'Ezion Geber'**. To do this he 'made an alliance with Ahaziah king of Israel, who was guilty of wickedness' (20:35).

There was a very important difference between Solomon's venture and Jehoshaphat's alliance. Solomon made use of King Hiram's technology and timber to establish his own enterprise. Jehoshaphat entered into an alliance with Ahaziah that was clearly wrong. Ahaziah was the son of Ahab and heir to his throne. The last time that Jehoshaphat had entered into an alliance with the house of Ahab, he had compromised all his principles. Cravenly, he had followed Ahab into battle at Ramoth Gilead. The alliance with Ahaziah was an 'unequal yoke', for Ahaziah was 'guilty of wickedness'. It was more likely that Ahaziah would lead Jehoshaphat into evil than that Jehoshaphat would be able to lead Ahaziah to do what was right.

God's displeasure with Jehoshaphat's alliance was made clear by the prophet Eliezer: **'Because you have made an alliance with Ahaziah, the LORD will destroy what you have made'** (20:37). Not only did God tell Jehoshaphat that he was displeased with what he had done; he demonstrated his displeasure by destroying the fleet: **'The ships were wrecked and were not able to set sail to trade.'** Jehoshaphat had not learned from the warning of Jehu in 19:2. Therefore he had to receive a double lesson in 20:37 — the word of Eliezer and the wind of destruction. Are we any more willing to listen when God speaks to warn us? Perhaps we wonder why God chastens us so sorely. If that is so, perhaps we need to stop and consider why we are driving God to deal so harshly with us. Could it be that we are refusing to listen to his verbal warnings?

Jehoshaphat's epitaph

When Jehoshaphat's reign came to an end, he was given a good epitaph: **'He did what was right in the eyes of the LORD'** (20:32). Jehoshaphat was a redeemed man, but he has not been presented as a perfect man. His warts have been painted in these final verses. Perhaps an explanation for his imperfections is found in 20:32: **'He walked in the ways of his father Asa and did not stray from them…'** Of course, it was good to have a father like Asa to learn from, for he did many good things. However, Asa too was a mere man. Asa had his failings and imperfections.

The danger of resting upon mere men is that they have feet of clay. We may resolve to learn from their mistakes and reproduce their strengths. However, unless our focus is upon the perfect man, we are more likely to reproduce their weaknesses while wrongly presuming that we have their strengths. For this reason we are urged to look 'unto Jesus, the author and finisher of our faith,' '…till we all come to the unity of the faith and of the knowledge of the Son of God, to a perfect man, to the measure of the stature of the fulness of Christ' (Heb. 12:2; Eph. 4:13, NKJV).

13.
Jehoram and Ahaziah:
dark days in Judah

Please read 2 Chronicles 21:1 – 22:9

The history of God's kingdom has always had its ups and downs. Times of blessing and times of apostasy have alternated with each other. The next section in 2 Chronicles describes dark days in the kingdom of Judah. Outstanding kings were followed in tragic succession by kings who turned away from the Lord. Jehoshaphat was followed by Jehoram, Ahaziah and Athaliah, whose reigns mark successive low points in national depravity. The fifteen years covered by 2 Chronicles 21:1 – 23:21 (Jehoram and Ahaziah reigned for eight years and one year respectively, and Queen Athaliah for a further six years, although her reign will be considered in the next chapter) were days when godly men and women in Judah reached a low point of despair.

There were to be even darker periods to come for the people of Judah, but the Chronicler is keen to show that even in such circumstances the Lord's kingdom has not been vanquished. God is still faithful to his covenant, and his power is not exhausted. Even in the dark days from the death of Jehoshaphat until the overthrow of Queen Athaliah, God preserved David's royal line. So long as there was a son of David to sit upon the throne, there was hope for the people of God.

Common themes in the reigns of Jehoram and Ahaziah

Before we consider the reigns of Jehoram and Ahaziah respectively, let us consider some of the common threads that run through these two chapters.

1. Threats to the royal line of David

The Davidic monarchy was very important to the Chronicler. For this reason, among others, he focuses on the history of Judah rather than that of the northern kingdom of Israel. God had made a promise to David in 1 Chronicles 17:13-14 (see also 2 Chr. 6:16; Ps. 132:11-12) which was to be of great significance for all mankind. The Son whom God would set 'over my house and my kingdom for ever' was, of course, the Lord Jesus Christ who would save God's people from their sins and reign over all creation as the Lord of lords. Preservation of David's line was a demonstration of God's faithfulness to his promise, and loyalty to David's successors was an acknowledgement of God's mercies to Israel.

It is, perhaps, shocking to remember that the human lineage of our Lord included such wicked men as Jehoram and Ahaziah (see Matt.1:8). The result of their evil actions was to threaten the Messianic lifeline that led to Jesus Christ. Four times in these two chapters we read of the royal princes of the house of David being massacred: 21:4, when Jehoram put to death his brothers and rivals; 21:17, when Jehoram's own sons were put to death by an invading army; 22:1, where this second slaughter is described again to explain why Ahaziah became king in Judah; and 22:10, when Queen Athaliah slaughtered the princes of Judah to secure the throne of Judah for herself.

These chapters record Machiavellian manoeuvrings that are worthy of a political thriller. Yet neither the high political drama nor the callous cruelty involved should blind us to the strategic significance of these repeated massacres. They were a threat to the redemptive purposes of God. They have been likened to Herod's slaughter of the children of Bethlehem in an attempt to eliminate 'the one who [had been] born king of the Jews' (Matt. 2:2,16-18). They resulted from the power-lust of godless men and women, but they were directed by the Evil One, who had an even more sinister agenda — the destruction of the Messianic line. He almost succeeded! These were indeed dark days for Judah.

2. The corrupting influence of the house of Ahab

The kings of Judah committed many sins, but only in these chapters are the terrible sins of fratricide and infanticide mentioned with such regularity. This is not unconnected with the fact that Judah had fallen under the influence of Ahab and Jezebel. Ahab was the most notorious king of northern Israel. His wife made the name Jezebel synonymous with immorality and intrigue. In her political system massacre was simply an act of state, to be used by kings when necessity demanded. Idolatry was an instrument of state policy, a means of keeping tight control over a superstitious people.

The policies of Ahab and Jezebel had ruined northern Israel. They were to have a similar influence upon Judah. Both Jehoram and Ahaziah followed the corrupting example of Ahab rather than the godly one set by David (21:6,12-13; 22:3-5). A greater contrast is hard to imagine than that between David and Ahab. David left his kingdom strong, peaceful and ready to serve God. Ahab left his kingdom weak, defeated and demoralized by godlessness. Yet Jehoram and Ahaziah chose to make Ahab their example and follow him to destruction.

The perverse decisions on the part of Jehoram and Ahaziah can be traced back to the actions of a godly man. Jehoshaphat had arranged a marriage between his son Jehoram and Ahab's daughter Athaliah. This is mentioned without much explanation in 18:1. The detail is supplied in 22:3,where we are told that Ahaziah's mother was **'Athaliah, a granddaughter of Omri'**. The Hebrew text literally says that she was 'a daughter of Omri' (the father of Ahab), but we have to understand this phrase in the light of 21:6 which tells us that Ahaziah's father, Jehoram, married a daughter of Ahab. (The Hebrew expression is flexible enough to refer to either a daughter or a grand-daughter of Omri.) Athaliah was the daughter-in-law of King Jehoshaphat, wife of King Jehoram, mother of King Ahaziah and eventually queen of the whole kingdom. Her influence was as wicked as it was powerful.

Why did Jehoshaphat, of whom so much that is good has been written, involve himself in such a foolish alliance? The Scriptures do not tell us why. One commentator put it down to 'Jehoshaphat's desire to think the best of his neighbour, to foster the unity of the two nations, and to overlook inconvenient differences'. But the same writer concludes that 'Subsequent events showed the perils of goodwill without discernment.'

Jehoshaphat's alliance sowed the seeds of disaster. Gardeners have a saying that 'One year's seeding makes seven years' weeding.' That is a piece of lore which has obvious spiritual applications, and they are well illustrated in these chapters. Once sin takes root in our lives it spreads rapidly and is hard to remove. Sins can never be ring-fenced and the consequences contained. Others may still be suffering the painful consequences many years later. God may visit the iniquity of the fathers upon the children of even the third and fourth generations.

Sometimes the consequences are very perplexing for future generations. Children may pick up the sinful habits that their parents have failed to root out of their own lives, and nurture them so that in the younger generation they become deeply rooted weeds of ungodly character. In church life the unacknowledged pastoral cowardice of ministers and elders can blight the witness of a new generation of God's servants. Let us consider what sort of seeds we are sowing for the future. Even men with great gifts and strengths can sometimes leave a terrible legacy for their successors to wrestle with. That was true of Jehoshaphat. In spite of his reformation he left a family poisoned by an unfaithful marriage alliance. The evil of the house of Ahab would have destroyed the house of David had it not been for the covenant mercies of the Lord.

Jehoram (21:2-20)

1. Intrigues within Jehoshaphat's family (21:2-4)

Sons are a blessing from the Lord and the Lord had blessed Jehoshaphat with many of them. Six are mentioned in these verses, and Jehoshaphat was, therefore, able to face death secure in the knowledge that his royal line was secure. He was proud of his sons and gave them **'many gifts of silver and gold and articles of value'**. They were, on the whole, able men, as Elijah testified in 21:13. They were given charge over **'fortified cities in Judah'** and in that way they served their father and the kingdom.

Jehoram was the oldest son and he succeeded his father as king: **'He had given the kingdom to Jehoram because he was his firstborn son'** (21:3). In spite of his position Jehoram behaved like a very insecure man. He saw his brothers as rivals and **'When Jehoram established himself firmly over his father's kingdom, he put all his brothers to the sword along with some of the princes of Israel'** (21:4).

Jehoram's view of the kingship was fundamentally flawed. He saw the throne as a prize to be grasped by any means and to be held at all costs. He lost sight of David's shepherd kingship — a privilege that gives the opportunity to serve others. He majored upon his rights and privileges rather than his responsibilities. He secured his position, but neglected his duty to serve. We do not have to commit murder as Jehoram did to fall into this trap. We can view our privileges within the church of Christ as rights to be claimed whatever the cost. Sometimes people want to get their way, whatever the consequences. They want to win by any possible means. They use the end to justify the means. Remember that Jehoram's goal was a laudable one. He wanted to secure the royal succession. But the end never justifies the means. Let these manoeuvrings within Jehoshaphat's family challenge us to use our privileges for the glory of God.

2. Involvement with Ahab's family (21:5-7)

These verses give the standard introduction to Jehoram's reign. They tell us his age and the length of his reign. His name (Joram or Jehoram) was the same as that of Ahab's grandson (2 Kings 1:17). Sometimes it becomes difficult to avoid confusing the kings of Israel and Judah during this period, because they had the same names. We do not know which Jehoram was the namesake of the other, but we can see that the results of Jehoshaphat's involvement with the house of Ahab were being felt in the house of David.

The impact of this involvement went deeper than the giving of similar names to the sons of the two families. Now that Jehoram was king, his wife Athaliah was queen. She bore a marked resemblance to her mother, Jezebel, and she exercised a powerful influence over Jehoram and his kingdom: **'He**

walked in the ways of the kings of Israel, as the house of Ahab had done, for he married a daughter of Ahab' (21:6). It is impossible for two people to be united in marriage without having a profound influence upon each other. It is only when two people marry in the Lord that this influence is beneficial.

Sometimes a believer will marry an unbeliever in the hope that his or her good influence might win over the unbelieving partner. There are instances when this happens, but in the vast majority of cases the believer is dragged down by the dead weight of an unbelieving partner. That is why the Scriptures forbid an unequal yoke in marriage (2 Cor. 6:14). Athaliah, however, was more than just a dead weight. She was a missionary for the false god Baal. She not only dragged her husband down, but the whole kingdom as well: **'He did evil in the eyes of the LORD.'**

'Nevertheless, because of the covenant the LORD had made with David, the LORD was not willing to destroy the house of David' (21:7). We should not think that this was a sign of weakness or timidity on God's part. The phrase that describes the Lord's unwillingness is also used in Deuteronomy 10:10 to describe Jehovah's unwillingness to destroy the people of Israel after they had worshipped the golden calf at Sinai: 'It was not his will to destroy [them]. "Go," the LORD said to [Moses], "and lead the people on their way, so that they may enter and possess the land that I swore to their fathers to give them."' God's sense of obligation is not imposed upon him by others. It arises out of his own promises. Because of the promises that he had made to Abraham, Isaac and Jacob, the Lord was unwilling to destroy the Israelites in the desert. In a similar way, the Lord was unwilling to destroy even the wicked King Jehoram 'because of the covenant the LORD had made with David'.

The Lord had promised that David would always have a son to sit upon his throne and reign as the anointed of the Lord. **'He had promised to maintain a lamp for [David] and his descendants for ever'** (21:7). The description of God's covenant faithfulness as a 'lamp' for David is unique, but very appropriate for those dark days in Judah. When soldiers went overseas to fight, the families at home would often put lighted candles in the windows of their houses. This was a sign that they looked forward to the day when their loved one would return home. They may have had to wait many years and endure many anxious moments, but their hope kept burning just like the lamp in their window. God's promises kept their faith alive during those dark days of apostasy.

The precise significance of this lamp has been explained in two ways. First of all, it has been interpreted as *a beacon* that stood out on the top of a hill to pass on a message. In that sense David himself was the beacon because of his courage and leadership. In 2 Samuel 21:17 his solders resolved that he ought not to go into battle because they could not afford to lose him: 'Never again will you go out with us to battle, so that the lamp of Israel will not be extinguished.' The line of kings that came from David were also beacons because they reminded the people that God would raise up a son for David who would be an even greater king. Even Jehoram was preserved to be such a lamp.

A second explanation of the significance of this lamp is to be found in *the ritual of the temple*. Every evening a lamp was lit in the temple as a sign that God dwelt among his people (see 13:11). This regular part of the priestly routine continued right through the history of the monarchy, through dark days as well as times of blessing. It was lit during the reigns of good kings like Jehoshaphat, as well as during the reigns of wicked kings like Jehoram. The monarchy itself was a reminder that

God's covenant is 'for ever'. God never abandons his people.
He never breaks his promises.

2. Covenant-breaking and its results (21:8-11)

When the Chronicler lists the outstanding events of Jehoram's
reign, there is little to rejoice over. He lists rebellion, idolatry
and invasion. In eight years Jehoram reversed the reformation
that Jehoshaphat had accomplished during his reign. He '**built
high places on the hills of Judah and ... caused the people
of Jerusalem to prostitute themselves and ... led Judah
astray**' (21:11). The Chronicler's language implies that
Jehoram did not merely lead by example, but compelled his
people to conform to the new official religion.

The idolatry introduced by Jehoram is appropriately described as prostitution. God looked upon the people of Judah
as a nation that he had taken to himself in marriage. They
were to worship him, and him alone. Therefore the sin of idolatry was akin to unfaithfulness in marriage. 'Woe to you, declares the Sovereign LORD. In addition to all your other wickedness, you built a mound for yourself and made a lofty shrine
in every public square. At the head of every street you built
your lofty shrines and degraded your beauty, offering your
body with increasing promiscuity to anyone who passed by...
How weak-willed you are, declares the Sovereign LORD, when
you do all these things, acting like a brazen prostitute! When
you built your mounds at the head of every street and made
your lofty shrines in every public square, you were unlike a
prostitute, because you scorned payment' (Ezek. 16:23-25,
30-31).

To illustrate his relationship with his people the Lord commanded Hosea to take to himself an adulterous wife called
Gomer. Like Gomer the people of Israel had been brought

into a privileged relationship, but they violated it and sought other masters. Gomer did this through sexual promiscuity, while the people of Israel did it through religious syncretism. The result in both cases was covenant violation:

> She has not acknowledged that I was the one
>   who gave her the grain, the new wine and oil,
> who lavished on her the silver and gold —
>   which they used for Baal...
>
> They will eat but not have enough;
>   they will engage in prostitution but not increase,
> because they have deserted the LORD
>   to give themselves to prostitution,
> to old wine and new,
>   which take away the understanding of my people.
> They consult a wooden idol
>   and are answered by a stick of wood.
> A spirit of prostitution leads them astray;
>   they are unfaithful to their God
>
> (Hosea 2:8; 4:10-12).

The result of such unfaithfulness was that the people of Judah became eligible, not for the blessings of God's covenant, but for the curses. Jehoram experienced this punishment when Edom (a vassal kingdom on the south-eastern fringes of Judah) rose in rebellion against him. **'In the time of Jehoram, Edom rebelled against Judah and set up its own king'** (21:8). When Jehoram tried to impose his rule upon them he barely escaped with his life: **'So Jehoram went there with his officers and all his chariots. The Edomites surrounded him ... but he rose up and broke through by night. To this day Edom has been in rebellion against Judah. Libnah revolted**

at the same time, because Jehoram had forsaken the LORD' (21:9-10).

Libnah was part of the Judean heartland (located forty kilometres south-west of Jerusalem) but it too broke free from Jehoram (21:10). Some commentators present this revolt as an opportunistic grab for autonomy, while others see it as a more principled action. Matthew Henry links the revolt at Libnah to Jehoram's programme of state-sponsored idolatry (21:11). 'They shook off his [Jehoram's] government because he had forsaken the Lord God of his fathers, had become an idolater and a worshipper of false gods, and they could not continue subject to him without some danger of being themselves also drawn away from God and their duty.' Whatever the reason for this revolt, we see clear signs that Jehoram's wickedness was inflicting grievous damage on his kingdom.

3. A pointed reminder that God is not idle (21:12-19)

Elijah was the greatest prophet from the prophetic era of the Old Testament. He was raised up by God to challenge the wickedness of Ahab and Jezebel. His sphere of ministry was limited almost exclusively to the northern kingdom and these verses contain the only reference to its influence extending to the kingdom of Judah. Even so he did not appear in person, but spoke through a letter. Some commentators have suggested that the infirmity of old age prevented Elijah from delivering his message to Jehoram in person. However, the account of Elijah's last days in 2 Kings 2 does not present us with a man confined to his home. We do not know why Elijah spoke to Jehoram through a letter. Our thoughts should focus on the message itself.

Elijah told Jehoram what the Lord had said and what the Lord would do. God would display his sovereign power through acts of judgement. Jehoram's actions cried out for God's judgement: **'You have not walked in the ways of your father Jehoshaphat or of Asa king of Judah. But you have walked in the ways of the kings of Israel, and ... led Judah and the people of Jerusalem to prostitute themselves... You have also murdered your own brothers, members of your father's house, men who were better than you'** (21:12-14). His offences were serious, deliberate and prolonged. He had rejected that which was good and sought out that which was evil.

God's judgement upon Jehoram was administered by the Lord himself: **'The LORD is about to strike your people, your sons, your wives and everything that is yours, with a heavy blow'** (21:14). The Lord would not stand idly by and let Jehoram continue in sin. Nor would he leave it to others to punish Jehoram. The wrath of God is not an impersonal principle and the judgement of God is not a mechanical process. The Lord is not idle in the face of evil, but personally active in administering his righteous judgement.

Elijah warned that the Lord's judgement would deliver a very direct blow to Jehoram himself: **'You yourself will be very ill with a lingering disease of the bowels, until the disease causes your bowels to come out'** (21:15). Yet again the Lord was no mere bystander. **'The LORD afflicted Jehoram with an incurable disease of the bowels...'** (see 21:18-19). We cannot be sure exactly what this 'incurable disease' was, except to say that its symptoms were extremely distressing and excruciatingly painful. It was no ordinary disease. We are left in no doubt that the Lord had a message for Jehoram.

Jehoram refused to take any notice of God's message. In this regard he was even worse than his father-in-law, Ahab. At least Ahab had shown some sorrow when Elijah challenged him over his part in the murder of Naboth (1 Kings 21:27-29). Elijah noticed that Ahab had humbled himself, and God's judgement was delayed. Jehoram, however, was hard as stone. We can see that punishment alone, and the threat of punishment, will never bring a sinner to repentance. The rod may terrify, but only the grace of regeneration can bring a sinner to repentance. As we look back upon the hardness of this wicked man who preferred to suffer in silence rather than repent, we can see that the Lord is not powerless. The Lord does not watch helplessly as evil men grow increasingly bold in their wickedness. His judgement brings them to their knees and he is glorified in their destruction.

4. A tragic obituary for a godless man (21:19-20)

The Chronicler's final word about Jehoram is entirely negative. Normally he recounts what happened to mark the end of a king's reign. However, in these verses we are told about three things that did *not* happen when Jehoram died: **'His people made no fire in his honour... He passed away, to no one's regret, and was buried in the City of David, but not in the tombs of the kings.'** He did not value the fellowship of godly men during his life; therefore it did not seem fitting that he should lie alongside men like David, Asa and Jehoshaphat in death. According to Matthew Henry, this was 'ordered by Providence as an intimation of the everlasting separation of the souls of the wicked, after death, from the spirits of just men'.

Ahaziah (22:1-9)

1. The almost total collapse of the house of David

Ahaziah's reign is really a postscript to that of his father, Jehoram. He reigned for only one year and repeated many of the mistakes his father had made: **'Ahaziah was twenty-two years old when he became king, and he reigned in Jerusalem for one year'** (22:2). Ahaziah was the youngest of Jehoram's sons and the only one to survive when Arab raiders attacked Judah and killed all his older brothers. Yet again the royal family of Judah barely survived. It was in danger and weakness that Ahaziah began his reign.

2. The growing influence of the house of Ahab

Quite clearly the power behind the throne was Athaliah, the queen mother. Like her mother, Jezebel, she used every means at her disposal to get what she wanted. She was an evil influence on Ahaziah: **'He too walked in the ways of the house of Ahab, for his mother encouraged him in doing wrong'** (22:3).

Ahaziah surrounded himself with the counsellors who had encouraged his father in his policy of subservience to the northern kingdom. **'He did evil in the eyes of the LORD, as the house of Ahab had done, for after his father's death they became his advisers, to his undoing'** (22:4). The strategic goal of Ahab's dynasty was to unite Israel and Judah in an alliance against the Syrians to the north. Judah's historic claims that the temple in Jerusalem was the only place to worship Jehovah and that the family of David had been appointed to rule over Israel were clearly going to be considered unwelcome and divisive. The only foundation for real unity between the northern and the southern kingdoms was God's covenant with his people, yet theological faithfulness was swept aside in favour of the prevailing *Realpolitik.*

Ahaziah's advisers prevailed upon him to cement the alliance with the house of Ahab: **'He also followed their counsel when he went with Joram son of Ahab king of Israel to war against Hazael king of Aram at Ramoth Gilead'** (22:5).

This was the means of Ahaziah's 'undoing' or 'destruction'. (The same Hebrew word is used in Exodus 12:23 to describe the angel of destruction that visited the homes of the Egyptians on the Passover night.) Ramoth Gilead was the scene of Jehoshaphat's humiliation when he entered an alliance with Ahab. In a twist of irony Ahaziah repeated the same mistake when he fought alongside Ahab's son, at the very same place. He was clearly incapable of learning from the mistakes of others. Unless we are willing to learn from God's Word and to submit to his precepts, we shall continue to fall into the same sins.

Ahaziah walked straight into disaster on account of his alliance with 'Joram son of Ahab'. God had decreed that judgement would fall upon the whole house of Ahab. He had raised up Hazael to be the King of Syria, and Jehu to be the King of Israel, and they were to be God's instruments of judgement. Elijah had been instructed to anoint both of these men for their task (see 1 Kings 19:15-16). When Hazael defeated the north-south coalition under Joram and Ahaziah (in the battle referred to in 22:5-6), discontent among the young army officers boiled over. One of their number, Jehu, set out to kill the whole family of Ahab because of the disgrace they had brought upon the nation.

Jehu gathered many disillusioned Israelites around him and set out to annihilate the family of Ahab. Ahaziah became a target for Jehu's murderous rage while paying a courtesy call on Joram. **'While Jehu was executing judgement on the house of Ahab, he found the princes of Judah and the sons of Ahaziah's relatives, who had been attending Ahaziah, and he killed them. He then went in search of Ahaziah... He was brought to Jehu and put to death'** (22:8-9). His death resulted from his close alliance with the house of Ahab.

3. The constant influence of God

Throughout these dark days the sovereign Lord was in control. Ultimately it was God who brought about Ahaziah's destruction: **'Through Ahaziah's visit to Joram, God brought about Ahaziah's downfall'** (22:7). The book of Kings has much to say about Jehu, God's instrument to scourge Baalism in Israel. The Chronicler, focusing upon the history of Judah, does not have so much to say about him. His focus is upon the Lord who directs all the affairs of men and nations. The hands that brought about the downfall of Ahaziah were Jehu's, but the purposes being accomplished were those of the Lord.

Even in those dark days the godly influence of Jehoshaphat was not forgotten. It was Jehoshaphat's short-sightedness that had helped to bring about these dark days, but the inspired verdict upon his life is that 'The LORD was with Jehoshaphat because in his early years he walked in the ways that his father David had followed' (17:3). Great as his failings had been, the mercies of God were greater still. The Lord permitted Jehoshaphat to be remembered as a good man. All those in Israel who were grieved on account of Ahab's evil influence remembered Jehoshaphat with fondness. Jehu and his followers said of him that he **'sought the LORD with all his heart'** (22:9). They gave Ahaziah's corpse a proper burial, for **'He was a son of Jehoshaphat.'**

The Scriptures encourage us to remember that God uses even the memory of godly men to point to better times ahead. In days of deep spiritual darkness it is good to remember men who have been shining lights in the past. Their godliness can shine through the years to encourage us to keep the faith in the midst of great apostasy. 'The memory of the righteous will be a blessing...' (Prov. 10:7). The memory of Jehoshaphat was a challenge and a rebuke even to a man like Jehu. Through the memory of godly men the Lord reminds us that he will not allow himself to be forgotten.

A kingdom without a king on the throne

The conclusion of 22:9 returns our thoughts to the precariousness of the kingdom after the death of Ahaziah: **'There was no one in the house of Ahaziah powerful enough to retain the kingdom.'** Ahaziah's sons, of whom we shall read later, were infants too young to reign. His brothers and uncles, the princes of Judah, had all been massacred. There was no king to sit on David's throne — but the kingdom continued.

This was also the situation in Judah when the Chronicler wrote. The people had returned from exile in Babylon. The life of the nation was so disrupted and the house of David was so demoralized that there was no one powerful enough to sit on the throne. The characteristic of post-exilic Judaism was that it had the temple, but no king. They were ruled by Persian, Greek and Roman kings. This caused many to ask, 'Has the Lord abandoned us?' The answer was an emphatic 'No!' Although there was no king strong enough to sit on the throne of Judah the kingdom continued — for the kingdom is the Lord's.

The hope for the future was a mystery — a Messianic mystery. God would raise up a true king from the line of King David and he would reveal that king one day. The people could not see who this might be, but the Lord did. As the events that follow Ahaziah's death unfold we shall see that the Lord's anointed was a hidden king. The Lord in heaven knew who would follow Ahaziah on the throne of Judah. However, the people in Judah did not. Here are two very different perspectives on the same situation. The perspective of the people was one of despair because they did not know what God knew. But when we can know what God knows, our hearts are lifted up to rejoice.

As Christians we have the perfect revelation of God's plans which centre on the person of his Son. 'And he made known to us the mystery of his will according to his good pleasure, which he purposed in Christ, to be put into effect when the times will have reached their fulfilment — to bring all things in heaven and on earth together under one head, even Christ' (Eph. 1:9-10).

We often find ourselves looking at God's kingdom from the human vantage-point. We know that the Lord's anointed King is none other than the Son of God himself. We know that all authority in heaven and on earth has been given to the risen Lord Jesus. However, we cannot see him ruling. Indeed we see wickedness appearing to prosper. The writer to the Hebrews put it this way: 'At present we do not see everything subject to him' (Heb. 2:8). That is why the same writer points us to the divine perspective of Psalm 8:

> 'You made him a little lower than the angels;
>   you crowned him with glory and honour
>   and put everything under his feet'...

> We see Jesus, who was made a little lower than the angels, now crowned with glory and honour because he suffered death (Heb. 2:7-9).

The death of the divine Messiah is not to be equated with powerlessness, for by his death the Lord Jesus Christ conquered the power of the Evil One. The ascension of the Lord Jesus is not to be equated with absenteeism, for it is the ascended Christ who has poured out the Holy Spirit upon his people. It is by the power of the Holy Spirit that believing people bring the world into subjection to King Jesus, the rightful King of all. Though we may not be able to see him physically, he is the one 'powerful enough to retain the kingdom'.

14.
The priestly revolution

Please read 2 Chronicles 22:10 – 23:21

Revolution is one of the most explosive words in history —
especially the history of the twentieth century. Karl Marx, the
intellectual father of Communism, believed that beneficial social
progress came through revolutionary struggle as one class
overthrew another. The end result would be a utopian society
in which self-interest would give way to the betterment of all.
The actual results of many revolutionary struggles in recent
times have proved to be rather different.

Revolution is radical transformation. In political terms, a
revolution sweeps away those who have held power and puts
in their place those who previously have been excluded from
power. The effects of revolution are beneficial when wicked
men are removed from power and replaced by men who will
rule righteously. In 2 Chronicles 22:10 – 23:21 the Chronicler
records the events of Jehoiada's priestly revolution. Athaliah,
the wicked queen, was removed from power and a descendant of David was restored to his rightful place on the throne of
Judah.

The revolution in Judah followed a similar development in
the northern kingdom of Israel. There Jehu overthrew the house
of Ahab. This receives only a passing mention in the Chronicler's account of Ahaziah's reign (see 22:7-9). Jehu's

revolution was notably different from events in Judah, and a survey of its distinctive features helps us to see the significance of the events described in this chapter.

First of all, it was *inspired by prophetic, as distinguished from priestly, leadership*. After his flight to Horeb Elijah the prophet was commanded by God to anoint Jehu as king over Israel (1 Kings 19:16). Elijah's successor, Elisha, later sent a prophet to perform the anointing (2 Kings 9:1-13). This prompted Jehu to lead the discontented young army officers in rebellion against Joram, the King of Israel.

Then, secondly, in spite of the prophetic influence, Jehu's revolution was *conducted in a pragmatic and opportunistic way*. Jehu and his comrades conspired and behaved just like the godless men they were. Although they spoke of Jehovah, they were motivated by self-interest and they behaved with great cruelty, causing much bloodshed. The net result of Jehu's revolution was to replace one godless king with another.

Thirdly, by way of summary, we note that Jehu's revolution *resulted in no moral or spiritual improvement* (2 Kings 10:28-31). Israel continued in the sins of Jeroboam, son of Nebat. There was no return to the Lord. There was no seeking out of the Lord's house or the Lord's anointed.

Jehu's revolution was violent and shocking, but it was not radical enough. The causes of Israel's malaise were spiritual, not merely political. It was not enough simply to remove the ruling class that had sustained the house of Ahab without also repudiating the sins of Jeroboam. Jeroboam had rebelled against the house of David and prevented his people from going to Jerusalem to worship in the house of the Lord. Until Israel repented of those sins every effort to make a new beginning would be futile. Yet how often men and women try to get their lives back on track by attacking the symptoms rather than the causes of their sinfulness! They may try to give up smoking or drinking, or they may resolve to be better husbands and fathers, or they may seek to control their furious tempers. However, all their efforts will be in vain until they bow in genuine repentance before God. This means bowing the knee to King Jesus, the Lord's Anointed, and seeking redemption through the gospel.

The difference between Jehu's revolution and that led by Jehoiada was that the people of Judah were willing to have the son of David rule over them, and they sought the Lord in his temple. The events of this chapter focus on the Lord's anointed and the Lord's house. The result was genuine change and God-honouring revolution. Let us follow the events as they unfold.

Rescue (22:10-12)

Athaliah was Queen of Judah. She was also the daughter of Ahab and Jezebel, and through her the worship of Baal had been introduced into Judah. Already we have seen that the link between the families of Ahab and Jehoshaphat had produced disastrous results. Three massacres have already been recorded by the Chronicler (21:4,16-17; 22:8-9). To these Athaliah added a fourth. When the death of her son, Ahaziah, threatened her power base, she set out **'to destroy the whole royal family of the house of Judah'** (22:10). She feared that her power as queen mother would be curtailed if a truly Davidic prince were appointed as regent until one of Ahaziah's sons was old enough to become king in his own right.

One of the princes destined for slaughter was her own grand-child, Joash, the son of Ahaziah. Athaliah had seen her own family wiped out by Jehu and she was determined that she would not fall victim to a similar slaughter in the southern kingdom of Judah. Her instincts told her to strike first. She was willing to stoop so low as to plan the destruction of her own grandchildren in order to preserve her own dynasty.

Her actions invite comparison with those of the pharaoh who ordered the death of every baby boy born to the Hebrew women in order to prevent the Hebrews from becoming a powerful nation in Egypt (Exod. 1:15-16). There is also a parallel with the paranoid reaction of King Herod to reports that one called 'King of the Jews' had been born in Bethlehem. To neutralize the supposed threat to his kingdom, 'He gave orders to kill all the boys in Bethlehem and its vicinity who were two years and under' (Matt. 2:16). In both cases God preserved a special child from the ensuing mayhem. Here, too, God had his chosen child and his agents of deliverance.

The Lord's agent of deliverance was another woman, Jehosheba, the daughter of King Jehoram (22:11). It is possible that Jehosheba was also a daughter of Athaliah, but it is more likely that she was the daughter of Jehoram through another wife, and so was a step-daughter of Athaliah. She was able to rescue her nephew, Joash, before he was murdered along with the other princes. Jehosheba was able to be in the right place at the right time to protect Joash because she was a member of the royal family and because she was married to Jehoiada.

Although Jehoiada is simply referred to as **'the priest'** (22:11), he was most probably the high priest, for that is how the high priest was designated in post-exilic times. He was a man of influence, and through his good offices Jehosheba was able to protect the infant prince in the safety of the temple. At great personal risk she **'stole him away from among the royal princes who were about to be murdered and put him and his nurse in a bedroom... He remained hidden with them at the temple of God for six years while Athaliah ruled the land'** (22:11-12).

Wickedness seemed to have triumphed in Judah. Yet Jehoiada and Jehosheba kept hope alive in their hearts and in their home. Their dwelling would have been in the temple courts and it became a haven for the young prince.

> Even the sparrow has found a home,
>   and the swallow a nest for herself,
> where she may have her young —
>   a place near your altar,
>   O LORD Almighty, my King and my God.
> Blessed are those who dwell in your house;
>   they are ever praising you
>
>   (Ps. 84:3-4).

Blessed, too, were the people of God, for within God's courts dwelt a child upon whose shoulders their hopes rested, even though they did not realize that he was there. Blessed, too, are God's people in every age, because wicked men and hostile powers can never overthrow God's kingdom.

Readiness (23:1-7)

Jehoiada was clearly a significant figure in Judah. As the high priest, he stood at the head of the tribe of Levi. He was in charge of the temple in Jerusalem and supervised the activities of the Levites throughout Judah. As the husband of the late king's sister, he also had a position within the political establishment. He knew how the machinery of state worked. He knew when to bide his time and when to make a decisive move. 'There is a time for everything, and a season for every activity under heaven' (Eccles. 3:1). Jehoiada bided his time for six years while the young prince was growing up in the temple. **'In the seventh year Jehoiada showed his strength'** (23:1).

The strength of both Jehoiada's character and his position became apparent as his plans to reinstate the true king fell into place.

Jehoiada sought the support of the military élite in Judah: **'He made a covenant with the commanders of units of a hundred: Azariah son of Jehoram, Ishmael son of Jehohanan, Azariah son of Obed, Maaseiah son of Adaiah, and Elishaphat son of Zicri'** (23:1). Who were these men? We find similar names in some of the lists of Levites, but there is no evidence that the military commanders were drawn from the tribe of Levi. The 'units of a hundred' were the basic units of Judah's army, and their commanders would have been the junior to middle-ranking army officers. (Interestingly, it was the discontentment of this class which fuelled Jehu's revolution, see 2 Kings 9:11-13.) They had a prominent place in the priestly revolution, but the direction came from Jehoiada.

With the help of these men, Jehoiada set out to gather the support of the people of Judah for the coming revolution. **'They went throughout Judah and gathered the Levites and the heads of Israelite families from all the towns'** (23:2). Jehoiada's goal was to lead the people in the right ways of the Lord. He set out to show them that the royal line of David had not been extinguished and to gather their support for Joash, the rightful king.

It is amazing that the revolution was able to progress undetected and unchecked by Athaliah. This, together with the lack of support that she commanded in 23:14, shows that she must have been a deeply unpopular ruler. She had ruled Judah as if it existed merely to serve the interests of her father's dynasty. Her abuse of power was about to produce a bitter backlash.

Surely too, the providential protection of God enabled Jehoiada to gather support for the house of David unmolested.

Disaster could have struck at any moment. An informer could have betrayed Jehoiada, so that the element of surprise was lost. The life of the infant king could have been betrayed, and the whole project derailed. Men with hot heads and base motives could have allied themselves with the revolution, creating disunity and disarray. Nationalistic hatred for Athaliah could have prevailed over godly loyalty to the infant king. That none of these things happened is a testimony to the fact that God was with Jehoiada.

The outcome of Jehoiada's tour of Judah was a secret constitutional convention in Jerusalem. (Yet again, it is a testimony to God's protection that this body could meet without suspicions being aroused in the royal palace.) This gathering of family leaders set the agenda for the events that followed. **'The whole assembly made a covenant with the king at the temple of God'** (23:3). This covenant followed in a tradition of covenants among God's people by recognizing what God had done for them in his sovereign mercy. God deserves to be acknowledged and honoured, not just by individuals, but by nations as well. Jehoiada led the family heads of Judah in acknowledging that the Lord had appointed Joash, rather than Athaliah, to rule his people.

Although we are not given a great deal of detail about the covenant made at the temple, we are told that it was made **'with the king'** (23:3). We should not imagine that the seven-year-old king was there in person negotiating the terms upon which he would reign. Joash did not make any public appearance until 23:11, when he was brought out to be acclaimed as king and **'They presented him with a copy of the covenant.'** Jehoiada would have acted as Joash's guardian and representative at the constitutional convention. It was his task as a priest to remind the people that God had already set out the terms upon which kings ruled in Israel. Moses had anticipated Israel's request for a king, and in Deuteronomy 17:14-20 he laid down

God's regulations. By implication, these regulations were incorporated into God's covenant with David, confirmed in 1 Chronicles 17:11-14.

At this gathering a plan of action was agreed upon. Athaliah was not going to yield up the throne willingly and there would be a struggle. Planning and prudence were called for if she was to be overthrown and Joash put in her place. They needed a strategy, and the gathering of family heads was the place for hammering out the details. Certainly Jehoiada's words in 23:3-7 indicate that he was acting in accordance with an agreed plan. He reminded the people that the Lord's covenant with David set out the master plan: **'The king's son shall reign, as the LORD promised concerning the descendants of David'** (23:3). The practical outworking of what God had commanded was in the hands of men who sought God's direction and planned accordingly. **'Now this is what you are to do...'** (23:4). This was not presumption or arrogance on Jehoiada's part, but godly leadership.

Let us notice several aspects of Jehoiada's tactics.

1. Everyone knew what they were meant to be doing

The priests and Levites were at the centre of Jehoiada's plans. They were divided into three groups: one on duty inside the temple, another at the royal palace and another at the Foundation Gate (which was most probably a gate into the temple compound, rather than a gate in Jerusalem's city walls). The non-Levite participants in the coup were stationed in the outer courtyards of the temple where the people gathered to present their offerings to God (see 23:4-5). The secret of Jehoiada's leadership was communication. All the people knew exactly what was expected of them. They were in the right place at the right time because Jehoiada told them where to be.

2. Timing

The decisive move against Athaliah was carefully planned. It was to happen at the moment when the **'priests and Levites ... are going on duty on the Sabbath'** (23:4). A large movement of temple personnel would have aroused no suspicion at that hour. The temple courts would have been especially busy on the Sabbath as people came to offer the weekly sacrifices. This provided the perfect opportunity to present the king to his people and avoid arousing the suspicions of Athaliah's guards. This reminds us of the perfect timing of God in presenting his own Son to the world: 'But when the time had fully come, God sent his Son, born of a woman, born under the law, to redeem those under law, that we might receive the full rights of sons' (Gal. 4:4; cf. Luke 3:1-6; Rom. 5:6).

3. Jehoiada showed the men of Judah that their task was a sacred one

He emphasized two priorities.

The sanctity of the temple courts

'No one is to enter the temple of the Lord except the priests and Levites on duty; they may enter because they are consecrated, but all the other men are to guard what the Lord has assigned to them' (23:6). Even in the turmoil of revolution, Jehoiada was concerned that the purity of God's house should not be compromised by soldiers rushing hither and thither. Not even a desirable end could excuse sinful means. Today believers are not bound by the ceremonial laws of purity of the Old Testament. However, we are to be concerned with the purity of our own bodies (1 Cor. 6:19-20) and of the church, which is the body of Christ (1 Cor. 3:16-17).

The safety of the king

This was to be high on the list of priorities of all concerned: **'The Levites are to station themselves round the king, each man with his weapons in hand. Anyone who enters the temple must be put to death. Stay close to the king wherever he goes'** (23:7). Normally the people gathered around the king to enjoy his protection. In other times the king was a strong ruler who subdued threats to his people's safety. The king was God's servant to do his people good (see Ps. 5:11; 91:14). However, these were unsettled times and the Lord's appointed king was a mere infant, himself requiring protection.

Revolution (23:8-11)

Having made his plan, Jehoiada made it work: **'The Levites and all the men of Judah did just as Jehoiada the priest ordered'** (23:8). In human terms, everything depended on the different groups of Levites and soldiers moving into action at just the right time. Under God's direction this is exactly what happened.

Jehoiada's action in 23:9 is significant: **'Then he gave the commanders of units of a hundred the spears and the large and small shields that had belonged to King David and that were in the temple of God.'** Perhaps these centuries-old weapons were the only ones available to Jehoiada and his supporters, but they also helped to bring home to these men the significance of what they were about to do. They were using the weapons of David to restore the son of David to the throne of David.

The weapons stored in the temple were a reminder of better days when David had defeated the enemies of the Lord and his people, in the strength of the Lord God of Israel. When, as a young lad, David went up to fight Goliath with a sling and five stones, he told the giant, 'You come against me with sword and spear and javelin, but I come against you in the name of the LORD Almighty, the God of the armies of Israel, whom you have defied... All those gathered here will know that it is not by sword or spear that the LORD saves; for the battle is the LORD'S, and he will give all of you into our hands' (1 Sam. 17:45,47).

Christians are still engaged in spiritual warfare against the enemies of the King. The weapons that we use are explicitly 'not the weapons of the world' (2 Cor. 10:4). Rather we are to put on the 'full armour of God' that Paul describes so fully in Ephesians 6:10-18: 'Be strong in the Lord and in his mighty power. Put on the full armour of God so that you can take your stand against the devil's schemes...'

The climax of the revolution came in 23:10-11. The young king stood in the centre of his supporters. Jehoiada **'stationed all the men, each with his weapon in his hand, round the king... Jehoiada and his sons brought out the king's son and put the crown on him; they presented him with a copy of the covenant and proclaimed him king. They anointed him and shouted, "Long live the king!"** ' For the first time the people who were assembled in the temple were allowed to catch a glimpse of their king. From now on the king, rather than Jehoiada, was to occupy centre stage.

Four important actions are described here.

1. The fact of Joash's kingship was indicated by his coronation

For many years Joash had been the true king, but hidden. Now his royal status was openly acknowledged as they 'put the crown on him'.

2. The nature of Joash's kingship was indicated when 'a copy of the covenant' was presented to him

This covenant has been variously identified as the Decalogue, the portion of it that governed the national life of Israel, the terms of kingship as set out in Deuteronomy 17:14-20 and the decisions of the gathering of family heads in 23:3. The primary reference is to the covenant made under Jehoiada's direction in 23:3. This covenant paved the way for the restoration of the Lord's anointed to the throne. It is inconceivable that the Lord's anointed could rule on any terms other than those laid down by the Lord himself. Kingship in Israel was 'limited monarchy', for Jehovah alone possessed absolute sovereignty. The presentation of this covenant to Joash was to remind him that the kingdom was the Lord's and that he was to serve the Lord with reverence.

3. The source of Joash's kingship was indicated when he was anointed

Anointing was a sign that the Lord's blessing had come down upon men. Priests and prophets were anointed to indicate that the Lord had filled them with his Spirit to prepare them for ministry. The kings of Israel were anointed to indicate that their authority and power came from the Lord (see 1 Samuel 16:12-13 for the anointing of David, and 1 Samuel 10:1 for the anointing of Saul, who shortly afterwards was endued with the power of the Holy Spirit, which enabled him to serve as king). The king was young and weak, but his strength was to come from the Lord who is almighty.

*4. The rights of Joash's kingship are indicated by the people's
acclamation: 'Long live the king!'*

The people's reaction was instinctive and appropriate. They
were simply acknowledging what the Lord had done. The true
king is entitled to his people's loyalty and affection. Those
who refuse to honour him are rebels. Our Lord referred to the
Jews of his own generation in the parable of the ten minas
(Luke 19:11-27). 'His subjects hated him and sent a delegation
after him to say, "We don't want this man to be our king"'
(Luke 19:14). Jesus Christ is the King of kings whom the Father
has appointed to rule over all creation. Either we acknowledge his kingship, or we are rebels. On which side of the fence
are you?

Reaction (23:12-13)

When God is at work there will always be tell-tale signs. Lives
will be changed and God's people will have something to rejoice about. There was rejoicing in Jerusalem when Joash was
crowned and acknowledged by the people. **'The noise of the
people running and cheering the king'** was to be heard all
over the city (23:12). The sound of rejoicing was to be heard
even in the royal palace, but there the news that the true king
had been crowned was not an occasion for rejoicing.

When God is at work, there will also be a negative reaction
from his enemies. The powers of darkness will not stand idly
by while God rolls back their influence. They will oppose God's
kingdom at every turn. When Athaliah heard that Joash was
alive and sitting on the throne she was not pleased. When she
saw King Joash in the temple she **'tore her robes and shouted,
"Treason! Treason!"'** (23:13). Her reaction was hypocritical. It was she, an interloper into the royal house of Judah,

who had sought to destroy the royal line of David, who had not hesitated to order the murder of the rightful heir to the throne, who was the traitor.

From Athaliah's point of view Jehoiada and his followers certainly were traitors. She represented a kingdom that was diametrically opposed to the kingdom of God. She represented the kingdom of evil which has manifested itself throughout history: when the serpent tempted Eve to eat the forbidden fruit, when Pharaoh sought to enslave the Hebrew people, when Nebuchadnezzar destroyed Jerusalem and carried the people of Judah into exile, when cruel men crucified the Lord of glory and thought that they had overpowered the Son of God, or when Roman emperors cast the early Christians to the lions. The goal of this kingdom is to undermine God's authority wherever possible. Those who serve the true God in any way will be enemies of this evil kingdom.

The kingdom of God and the kingdom of evil are mutually exclusive: 'No one can serve two masters. Either he will hate the one and love the other, or he will be devoted to the one and despise the other' (Matt. 6:24). 'You adulterous people, don't you know that friendship with the world is hatred towards God? Anyone who chooses to be a friend of the world becomes an enemy of God' (James 4:4). Athaliah knew this well. The very survival of the true king was a threat to her position. How much more did his coronation seal her destruction!

There is an application of this principle to the Christian life. No one can continue with a foot in both camps. Either we serve the Lord Jesus, or we serve his enemy. Sometimes people try to sit on the fence because they have grown up in a godly family and many of their friends are believers. They want to keep the respect of these people, but in their hearts they love the things of the world. In secret they pay homage to the Evil One. However, their ungodly behaviour is betraying God. They realize that to make a decisive commitment to Christ will earn them the contempt of their non-Christian friends. These erstwhile companions will call them traitors for abandoning the cause. The cost of discipleship can be costly rejection by the world.

Reformation (23:14-21)

The priestly revolution removed the wicked queen who had caused Judah so much trouble. Her malign spiritual influence had brought God's judgement upon the nation. The climax of the revolution was the coronation of the true king, Joash. However, Jehoiada did not stop with that. Nor would it have been safe for him to have done so. He struck at those who had underpinned Athaliah's idolatrous rule: **'Jehoiada the priest sent out the commanders of units ... and said to them: "Bring her out between the ranks and put to the sword anyone who follows her." ... So they seized her ... and ... they put her to death'** (23:14-15). **'All the people went to the temple of Baal and tore it down. They smashed the altars and idols and killed Mattan the priest of Baal in front of the altars'** (23:17).

The law of Moses had made it a capital offence to commit idolatry in Israel (Deut. 17:2-5). Furthermore, those who taught the people to worship other gods were especially guilty before God (Deut. 13:1-5). Idolatry is like a cancer that cannot be contained; it must be cut out. Moses was aware of the bewitching power of idolatry and warned that it was not to be tolerated: 'If your very own brother ... or your closest friend secretly entices you, saying, "Let us go and worship other gods"... Do not spare him or shield him. You must certainly put him to death' (Deut. 13:6). For this reason the law of Israel meted out such severe penalties for idolatry.

Mattan the priest and Athaliah the usurper queen were especially blameworthy as they had abused their positions of influence to lead the nation into gross idolatry. Their influence was removed by death and in this way the Israelites were given a powerful reminder that the Lord will never tolerate idolatry in any form.

After removing the chief culprits responsible for Judah's national apostasy, Jehoiada set about restoring godliness to national life. This commenced with a national covenant committing the king and the people to **'be the LORD's people'** (23:16). The three parties to this covenant were **'Jehoiada ... and the people and the king'**. Jehoiada stood on a par with the king and the people, perhaps because he acted as the king's representative (Joash being only a boy). Or perhaps it was because Jehoiada acted in a mediatorial role, to bring the king and his people together in covenant relationship with God. In this he foreshadowed the Lord Jesus, who is the mediator of the covenant of grace between God and man (1 Tim. 2:5; Heb. 9:15; 12:24).

The people's promise to 'be the LORD's people' was more than just high-sounding rhetoric. Sometimes our promises can be high-sounding but vague, and they deliver very little in terms of obedient action. The covenant that the people of Judah made changed many aspects of national life, and in particular their worship: **'Then Jehoiada placed the oversight of the temple ... in the hands of the priests, who were Levites, to whom David had made assignments in the temple, to present the burnt offerings of the LORD as written in the Law of Moses, with rejoicing and singing, as David had ordered'** (23:18-19). David had appointed certain men to perform specific tasks for the Lord in the temple, but over the years various rituals of worship had been introduced. In time the worship of Jehovah bore little resemblance to what he had commanded. That is why the church needs constant reformation rather than constant innovation.

There are three features of the reformed worship of the people of Judah that ought to be present in our worship today. At the forefront there was an emphasis on *atonement*. The people dared not come before the Lord without presenting **'burnt offerings'** to atone for their sins. They knew that they had sinned against the Lord, but they also knew that the Lord had opened a way for them to come to him through the shedding of the sacrificial blood for sinners. When we come to worship God, we come as a redeemed people, bought with the blood of the Lord Jesus. Our worship must start with that truth and we must continually rejoice in it.

Secondly, we note the *rejoicing* of God's people. They came **'rejoicing and singing'**. Redemption always leads to rejoicing:

> Praise the LORD, O my soul,
>   and forget not all his benefits—
> who forgives all your sins
>   and heals all your diseases,
> who redeems your life from the pit
>   and crowns you with love and compassion
>
> > (Ps. 103:2-4).

Thirdly, God's people worshipped in *purity*. Jehoiada **'stationed doorkeepers at the gates of the LORD's temple so that no one who was in any way unclean might enter'** (23:19). The role of the doorkeepers was an important one and the Chronicler regularly mentions their work. By their diligence they kept out of the temple people and things that would have defiled the worship of the Lord. We need their alertness to maintain the purity of the church and to maintain our personal purity as we live in the midst of many temptations.

Jehoiada's reformation spread beyond the temple, and entered the royal palace. It was a reformation of church and state: **'He took with him the commanders of hundreds, the**

nobles, the rulers of the people and all the people of the land and brought the king down from the temple of the LORD. **They went into the palace through the Upper Gate and seated the king on the royal throne'** (23:20). The Chronicler was aware of the intimate connection between the priestly tribe of Levi and the kingly line of David. The restoration of the true king was not complete with his coronation in the temple. Only when he was enthroned in his rightful place within the royal palace would he be able to extend his rule over the kingdom. The reformation was not complete until the true king sat upon the throne.

This is a reminder that the Jesus Christ is Lord of all. He is not content to limit his influence to matters often considered sacred, such as personal piety and church life. Secular people are often quite happy to tolerate the Christian faith so long as it pursues its religious activities within church buildings. They will even go so far as to defend the religious freedoms of God's people, so long as they confine the claims of Christ to religious activities. They claim that religious belief is a private matter that ought not to intrude into the public arena. They claim that it is wrong of Christians to 'impose' their morality on society by seeking laws and advocating behaviour which honours God. All of this would be true if the Lord Jesus were merely 'a friend in time of need'. He is far more! He is the Lord of all and must be enthroned in the political life of nations as well as in the spiritual life of the church.

Jehoiada's priestly revolution brought great blessing to Judah. **'The city was quiet, because Athaliah had been slain with the sword'** (23:21). The 'quiet' that Jerusalem enjoyed after the fall of Athaliah reflects the absence of strife that God bestows on a godly nation. Elsewhere this quietness is called 'rest' (14:6,7; 20:30; 1 Chr. 22:9; 23:25). As a result, **'All the people of the land rejoiced.'** When their enemies have been overthrown, then God's people can enjoy peace with security.

'Rest' is the blessedness that God's people enjoy after their enemies have been defeated and so long as they are faithful to his covenant and submit to the rule of his anointed King.

Lessons to learn

1. God preserves his chosen ones through dark and difficult times

Joash was kept from destruction because he had been chosen to rule over God's people. His deliverance was dramatic, but it illustrates a principle that is constantly applied in the lives of God's people. The Lord Jesus Christ was delivered from many dangers, and even from death itself until the appointed time, because he was chosen for a special work (see Matt. 12:18). All God's people are chosen ones. God has chosen his people to enjoy the blessings of salvation and to serve him; therefore we can be sure that he will not disown those whom he has chosen (Rom. 8:33-39).

2. God's people must make preparation for better days

Jehoiada's priestly revolution did not just happen. Jehoiada had a plan, even as Athaliah's death-squads were eliminating the young princes. Jehoiada bided his time during the six long and dangerous years that he and Jehosheba hid Joash in the temple. At the end of that time Jehoiada took his stand. He did all of this because he believed in better times ahead. He really believed that the king's son would reign. Therefore he took those steps towards realizing his prayers.

Jehoiada was rather like a small group of men — less than a dozen in all — who met in a schoolroom every week to pray that God would revive his church in Ireland. These men believed that the Lord answers prayer and they expected better days for the church of King Jesus. In answer to their prayers the Lord sent mighty revival which swept through Ulster in 1859. The Lord prepares his people for blessing by teaching them to expect better days ahead.

3. God himself will have the victory

'The king's son shall reign, as the Lord promised concerning the descendants of David.' The victory belonged to God. His promise of triumph was vindicated. Joash must have appeared a very unlikely king when he appeared before the people of Judah. So too did David when he appeared before Samuel (1 Sam. 16:6-13). And so did Jesus when he was presented to the people of Israel (John 1:11; 18:36). He appeared as a child; he rode into Jerusalem on a donkey; he died an inglorious death on a cross. However, he was the one through whom Satan was defeated and a decisive victory was won on the cross.

4. Godliness exalts a nation

The result of Jehoiada's revolution was peace and blessedness for the nation of Judah. The benefits of ordering their affairs God's way were great. We have already noted that peace was the result of submitting to God's appointed king. Now the people had a king they could rejoice in. They saw the application of the principle in Proverbs 14:34: 'Righteousness exalts a nation, but sin is a disgrace to any people.' Wherever the Lord Jesus is acknowledged as King, there is real and lasting blessing.

15.
Joash: great hopes dashed

Please read 2 Chronicles 24:1-27.

A favourite children's game is 'dressing up'. Some of us can remember playing at being adults when we were children. It must have been an amusing sight for our parents to watch as we dressed up in old coats and hats and shoes that were too big for us, and perhaps they laughed as we walked around awkwardly pretending to be grown-ups. It was funny and ridiculous at the same time. However, it is not so funny when we see the same game of make-believe in the world of adults. When young David went to fight Goliath, and King Saul gave him his armour to wear, David had the sense to know that he could not wear Saul's armour. He was a shepherd lad, not a trained warrior like Saul.

Not everyone has that maturity. People often refuse to accept their own limitations and fail to understand their weaknesses. They try to play a role which they are not able to fill. Instead of filling it, they simply expose their own immaturity and give the impression that they are children dressing up in the cast-off clothes of grown-ups.

King Joash was an example of spiritual immaturity. He ascended to the throne of King David, but he was not a worthy successor. He followed in the footsteps of kings such as Asa and Jehoshaphat and, like them, he tried his hand at reform,

but his efforts were sporadic. His reign, like theirs, was long
— **'He reigned in Jerusalem for forty years'** (24:1) — but
he lacked the stamina to make a lasting impact for good. Joash
came to the throne because of the great courage of Jehoiada
and Jehosheba who hid him in the safety of the temple. However, little of their character rubbed off onto him, and this became apparent as Joash advanced in years.

Joash started well. **'Joash was seven years old when he
became king'** (24:1). Although he came to the throne at a
very young age, he had the support of Jehoiada to back him
up. Jehoiada exercised a powerful influence over the young
king, and while he lived it was an influence for good. The
Lord blessed Joash while Jehoiada was his mentor; however,
when Jehoiada died Joash's immaturity and spiritual weakness became evident. On the surface this is a chapter about
King Joash, but the hero was Jehoiada the priest. He was a
pointer to Christ Jesus as well as being an exemplary father-
figure.

Joash's reforms (24:1-16)

These verses describe the first part of Joash's long reign. The
standard introductory formula is found in 24:1-3. It tells us
how long Joash reigned and the name of his mother. The latter
piece of information is important as Jews trace their ancestry
through their mother rather than their father. Moreover, the
Chronicler's introduction gives the credit for the good that
Joash did to Jehoiada: **'Joash did what was right in the eyes
of the Lord all the years of Jehoiada the priest.'**

Jehoiada's influence upon Joash was significant. **'Jehoiada
chose two wives for him, and he had sons and daughters'**
(24:3). Although we are not told much about these wives or

the children that they bore, the mere fact that the Lord gave them to Joash was a mark of his favour. 'Houses and wealth are inherited from parents, but a prudent wife is from the LORD' (Prov. 19:14). 'Sons are a heritage from the LORD, children a reward from him' (Ps. 127:3). In Joash's case children were a very special reward, for they helped to secure the future of David's royal line. A series of massacres, leading up to Athaliah's purge of the royal family in 22:10, had left the Davidic succession hanging by a very slender thread. Only Joash himself had survived to continue David's royal line and God's covenant with David. This continuity was now more secure as a result of God's blessings upon his family.

The restoration of the temple in Jerusalem was Joash's first priority when he was able to take up his responsibilities as king: 'Some time later Joash decided to restore the temple of the LORD' (24:4). Not only had Athaliah massacred the royal family, but her supporters had almost destroyed the temple of the Lord: **'Now the sons of that wicked woman Athaliah had broken into the temple of God and had used even its sacred objects for the Baals'** (see 24:7). During her reign the temple had fallen into disuse and disrepair because the worship of Baal had supplanted the worship of Jehovah. It seems that Athaliah was not content to see the Lord's house ignored; she wanted to see it desecrated too! She gave a lead to all those who wanted to show their contempt for the living God. The 'sons of ... Athaliah' referred to here may have included her supporters as well as those who were of her own flesh and blood.

We can only imagine to what use the temple courts were put in Athaliah's time. Perhaps they were used to store the property of godless men, as in the time of Nehemiah (see Neh. 13:4-5); or heathen worship may even have taken place in them. We are told that the sacred objects of the temple — including most probably its altars, fire-pans, incense censors, lampstands, plates, trays and other objects — were used in the worship of Baal. Later the Babylonians were to take away these sacred objects and Belshazzar would use the temple cups and bowls in an idolatrous feast described in Daniel 5:1-4. The Lord was deeply offended by this sacrilege and declared his judgement in the message written on the wall by the fingers of a man's hand. He was no less offended by what had happened during the time of Queen Athaliah.

If the degraded state of the temple was a symbol of Judah's apostasy, its renovation was a sign of spiritual renewal. Joash undertook to restore the temple to its former glory and its proper use, but before he could do this he had to raise the funds to carry through the work. **'He called together the priests and Levites and said to them, "Go to the towns of Judah and collect the money due annually from all Israel, to repair the temple of your God"'** (24:5). Joash had in view the half-shekel tax that was levied upon every male over the age of twenty; this levy was to be used 'for the service of the Tent of Meeting' (Exod. 30:11-16). After the temple was built the half-shekel levy continued to be collected for the up-keep of the temple, and after the return from exile Nehemiah reinstated its collection (Neh. 10:32).

The people of Judah had become careless about bringing their dues to the Lord. Their failure to gather the temple levy was more than a mere financial irregularity; it was an expression of their disinterest in the worship of God. While we must always remember that the kingdom of God does not consist of bricks and mortar, the manner in which God's people give to main-tain the buildings in which the Lord is worshipped makes a statement about their regard for him. Even the Levites had become slack and had not given the leadership that they ought (24:5). Joash's words to them were pointed and imperative: **'Do** it now.' The Levites' response was a sad reflection of Judah's spiritual lethargy: **'But the Levites did not act at once.'**

Although the response to Joash's initiative was disappointing, he was not daunted. He summoned Jehoiada and together they devised a plan to raise the money needed to renovate the temple. Joash even appears to have outshone Jehoiada in his zeal to restore the temple. **'Therefore the king summoned Jehoiada the chief priest and said to him, "Why haven't you required the Levites to bring in from Judah and Jerusalem the tax imposed ... for the Tent of Testimony?"'** (24:6). As the chief priest, Jehoiada had the responsibility to oversee the work of the Levites and ensure that they performed their responsibilities. As the king, Joash had overall responsibility for the life of the people and his challenge to Jehoiada was appropriate.

At Joash's instigation, a new approach was taken to collecting the temple tax: **'At the king's command, a chest was made and placed outside, at the gate of the temple of the LORD. A proclamation was then issued in Judah and Jerusalem that they should bring to the LORD the tax that Moses the servant of God had required of Israel in the desert'** (24:8-9). The collection of the temple tax was put on a more voluntary basis. The people brought their dues to the temple rather than having them collected by the Levites. In New Testament times we find a similar form of giving in Mark 12:41 when our Lord observed those who came to pay their dues in the temple treasury (including the widow who gave her all). By this time there were thirteen collecting boxes throughout the temple, all in the shape of trumpets.

The response of the people of Judah to Joash's initiative was most encouraging: **'All the officials and all the people brought their contributions gladly, dropping them into the chest until it was full'** (24:10). When did you last read in the newspapers about crowds of taxpayers thronging around the doors of their local tax office, eager to pay up? These are extraordinary scenes and they are recorded by the Chronicler for our encouragement and edification. We are told that their generosity was not an isolated event: **'They did this regularly and collected a great amount of money'** (24:11). Every time they gave to the Lord they had to walk up the steep road to Jerusalem. For many of the taxpayers this was an all-day journey. Yet the people of Judah 'brought their contributions gladly'.

Paul encouraged the believers in Corinth to give to the Lord with a similar attitude. He urged them to consider what they gave to the Lord's work, and also how they gave: 'Remember this: whoever sows sparingly will also reap sparingly, and whoever sows generously will also reap generously. Each man should give what he has decided in his heart to give, not reluctantly or under compulsion, for God loves a cheerful giver' (2 Cor. 9:6-7).

As a result of generous giving, the work of restoring the temple progressed well. **'The men in charge of the work were diligent, and the repairs progressed under them'** (24:13). The enthusiasm of those who contributed to the repair of the temple appears to have rubbed off onto the **'masons and carpenters'** who carried out the work. After the structural work was completed the temple was equipped with **'articles for the LORD's temple ... and also dishes and other objects of gold'** (24:14). These new articles were required to replace the ones which had been desecrated (or possibly stolen) by the sons of Athaliah. There need be no contradiction between this passage and 2 Kings 12:13, where we read that 'The money brought into the temple was not spent for making silver basins, wick trimmers ... or any other articles of gold...' Both accounts agree that the work of restoring the temple came first and was paid for out of the money collected in the chest outside the temple. This money was not used to furnish the temple until the repair work was completed.

The repair of the temple was not complete until it was restored **'according to its original design'** (24:13). The 'original design' was the plan that God had revealed to David and Solomon when it was first suggested that the temple be built. God did not leave the details of these plans to be fleshed out by human architects, but gave a perfect pattern for his house. 'All this,' David said, 'I have in writing from the hand of the LORD upon me, and he gave me understanding in all the details of the plan' (1 Chr. 28:19; cf. 28:12).

The Chronicler was keen to draw lessons from Judah's history for the edification of his own generation following the return from exile. Blessing had always followed a return to the foundation laid by David and Solomon. The way of blessing was to reform the worship of God's people by clearing away the debris of human inventions and by returning to what God had commanded. In every age the church develops rituals that are intended to make worship more interesting and doctrines that are designed to make the gospel palatable to 'modern' man. The counsel of Jeremiah 6:16 is still relevant:

This is what the LORD says:
'Stand at the crossroads and look;
    ask for the ancient paths,
ask where the good way is, and walk in it,
    and you will find rest for your souls.'

The simplicity of our Lord's doctrine and the worship of the New Testament church are the old paths within which we find God's blessing.

Tragically, the death of Jehoiada brings us to the end of the period of reform at the beginning of Joash's reign. **'As long as**

Jehoiada lived, burnt offerings were presented continually in the temple of the LORD' (24:14). Jehoiada's importance is summarized and emphasized in 24:14-16. He gave great encouragement to those who worshipped the Lord in the temple. He was blessed with a long life, living to the ripe old age of 130 years (24:15). This indicates that he would have been born during the reign of King Solomon and had seen the spiritual state of Judah rise and fall during the succeeding reigns. In fact we read of no one else during the period of the monarchy who lived as long. Joshua had lived to be 110 (Josh. 24:29) and Moses to be 120 (Deut. 34:7). However, we have to go back to the patriarch Jacob (who lived to the age of 147, see Gen. 47:28) to find anyone who lived even longer than Jehoiada. Long life is an evident mark of God's favour (Ps. 91:16). God showed that his favour was with Jehoiada by allowing him to die **'old and full of years'**.

Another mark of Jehoiada's significance is found in 24:16: **'He was buried with the kings in the City of David, because of the good he had done in Israel for God and his temple.'** Jehoiada was the only priest to be buried like a king, because at a critical moment in Judah's history he exercised an influence worthy of a king. It is a tribute to his meekness that, although he took the risks associated with kingship when he overthrew Athaliah, he did not usurp the role of king from the young King Joash. The Lord blessed him by giving him long life. The people of Judah recognized what he had done by giving him a royal funeral. Godliness brings blessing to any nation, and the people of Judah were able to enjoy peace and stable government because of his godly influence.

Good as Jehoiada's influence over King Joash was, there is a serious warning to reflect upon. Jehoiada's influence lasted only as long as his life. Matthew Henry comments: 'Men may go far in the external performances of religion, and keep long to them merely by the power of their education and the influence of their friends, who have yet no hearty affection for divine things nor any inward relish of them.' As the remainder of the chapter unfolds, we shall see how true this was of Joash. His renovation of the temple comes to be seen as a very hollow activity.

Again Matthew Henry comments: 'When he did that which was right it was not with a perfect heart. He never was sincere, never acted from principle, but in compliance to Jehoiada, who helped him to the crown, and because he had been protected in the temple and rose upon the ruins of idolatry; and therefore, when the wind turned, he turned with it.' People may be very zealous about buildings for worship, but less zealous for the Lord himself. Their zeal for buildings may result from a love of material things, or a love of tradition, or a desire to be busy with their hands. The true test of godliness is whether we love the Lord himself wholeheartedly.

We should thank God for the influence of godly men and women who have shared their faith with us. We can learn so much about the Scriptures and about godly living from them. Timothy learned a great deal about the work of the ministry from Paul; Joshua learned the art of leadership from Moses; and we all need such mentors to guide us. However, we need to learn to depend upon God rather than men. Joash never learned to think in a God-centred way independently of Jehoiada. Joash never became a true servant of the Lord. That is why the death of Jehoiada resulted in such a tragic reversal of all the good that had marked the first part of his reign.

Joash's apostasy (24:17-22)

The death of Jehoiada exposed Joash's immaturity: '**After the death of Jehoiada, the officials of Judah came and paid**

homage to the king, and he listened to them. They abandoned the temple of the LORD' (24:17-18). The real Joash now started to step forward, and he was not a very attractive character. He was heartless, fickle and immature. Let us take note of the way he reacted to the new circumstances.

1. He was easily swayed by men

The men who swayed him were the 'officials of Judah', or the court politicians in Jerusalem (24:17). These men clearly had different priorities from those of Jehoiada. To achieve their ends they used subtle persuasion and flattery. They **'paid homage to the king'**. No doubt they paid tribute to Jehoiada's memory, saying that he had done many good things in his day, but the times had changed and new policies were needed. No doubt, too, they encouraged Joash to demonstrate that he was his own man. 'Don't just do what Jehoiada did,' they urged. 'Do something different.' And that is what Joash did. His vanity and immaturity made him into a spiritual weathervane. His principles were those of his most recent counsellor.

2. He was easily separated from God

As a result of this advice, **'They abandoned the temple of the LORD, the God of their fathers, and worshipped Asherah poles and idols'** (24:18). Joash led them back to the dark days of Canaanite fertility religion. The result was the same as it had always been before: guilt and shame were followed by the outpouring of God's wrath upon the people of Israel. Joash's actions indicate that he had no love or reverence for God, nor did he understand the true nature of sin. A renewed person will love God and hate sin. We read of the believers in Thessalonica that they 'turned to God from idols to serve the living and true God' (1 Thess. 1:9). This is true repentance, but Joash did exactly the opposite. He turned his people from the true God to worship idols that were made of wood. His previous profession of loyalty to the Lord was as vacuous as the idols he turned to serve. He was easily turned from his profession of faith in God because it was a false one.

3. He was easily angered by the prophets

The Lord did not allow Joash and his people to abandon the temple without making his displeasure known. **'The LORD sent prophets to the people to bring them back to him'** (24:19). The Lord's rebuke was merciful and aimed to restore those who sinned to a right relationship with God. Joash's sin deserved no mercy, but the Lord called for repentance and offered restoration. Praise God that he is ever merciful, even when he chastises the sins of his people (Jer. 15:19; Ezek. 18:30-32; 33:11; Matt. 23:37). In spite of God's offer of mercy, Joash and his companions did not want to hear any such message. They had set their minds on a course of action which they knew to be displeasing to God.

'Then the Spirit of God came upon Zechariah son of Jehoiada the priest. He stood before the people and said, "This is what God says: 'Why do you disobey the LORD's commands? You will not prosper. Because you have forsaken the LORD, he has forsaken you'"' (24:20). Joash and his advisers did not enjoy hearing these words, and they had every reason to be troubled by them. They knew that they had sinned, and the last thing they wanted to hear was the Word of the Lord. Therefore, **'They would not listen'** (24:19). Here is a further indication that the heart of Joash was very far from God. One of the marks of a renewed heart is love for the Word of God (Isa. 66:2; John 10:4-5,27). Joash did not tremble before God when the Lord spoke to him through his servants the prophets. Instead he reacted as King Ahab had done when he saw the approach of Elijah: 'So you have found me, my enemy!' (see 1 Kings 21:20). Such is always the reaction of an unrepentant heart.

4. He quickly forgot the good that Jehoiada had done for him

One of the prophets to warn Joash about his sin was **'Zechariah son of Jehoiada the priest'** (24:20). Zechariah, like his father, was a fearless servant of God. No doubt he performed priestly duties, but he was also a prophet. **'Then the Spirit of God came upon Zechariah'** (24:20). If we were to translate the Hebrew text of this phrase in a very literal way it would read: 'The Spirit of God clothed himself with Zechariah.' The prophet became like a puppet in the hand of the sovereign Spirit, and the words that he spoke were, in truth, the very words of God. His challenge was a rebuke straight from the mouth of God. Zechariah spoke with boldness and clarity even though to do so put his life in danger.

It was this boldness that cost Zechariah his life. **'But they plotted against him, and by order of the king they stoned him to death in the courtyard of the LORD's temple'** (24:21). In the very courtyard where Jehoiada had presented Joash as a young lad to be crowned as King of Judah, his own son was stoned to death on the orders of the same king. The tragic irony of the situation is staggering: **'King Joash did not remember the kindness Zechariah's father Jehoiada had shown him but killed his son'** (24:22).

Could we ever do such a thing? Yes we could! We owe everything we have to our heavenly Father. Our lives, our bodies, our minds, our families, our health and our wealth all come from his hand. James reminds us that 'Every good and perfect gift is from above, coming down from the Father of the heavenly lights' (James 1:17). Yet how have we respected his Son? Those who will not look to Jesus Christ for salvation are one with those who shouted, 'Crucify him!' If you are not for him, you are against him. Is that how we would acknowledge the goodness shown to us by our heavenly Father?

Zechariah had the last word in this sorry incident. **'As he lay dying...'**, he cried out, **'May the LORD see this and call you to account.'** These words introduce 24:23-27, where we find that the Lord did indeed punish Joash for his evil actions. Perhaps we may think of our Lord's words as he died upon the cross: 'Father, forgive them, for they do not know what they are doing' (Luke 23:34). We may also remember Peter's description of the death of our Lord:

> Christ suffered for you, leaving you an example, that you should follow in his steps.

> 'He committed no sin,
>   and no deceit was found in his mouth.'

> When they hurled insults at him, he did not retaliate;
>   when he suffered, he made no threats

(1 Peter 2:22).

It has been said that these words highlight the contrast between the Old and New Testaments: the one breathes a spirit of vengeance and retribution while the other speaks of forgiveness.

Before castigating Zechariah as a representative of a primitive age and an inferior religion, however, we should remember that our Lord endorsed him (and presumably his words as well) as one of his faithful servants. This was the Zechariah to whom our Lord referred in Matthew 23:35. (Here he is called 'son of Barakiah'. That may be because Barakiah, which means 'blessed by God', was a title given to Jehoiada, or because Barakiah was the father of Jehoiada, and hence the grandfather of Zechariah.) Our Lord mentioned the faithful witness of Zechariah when he indicted the Pharisees for their hypocrisy. They were following in the footsteps of those who had murdered God's servants throughout the Old Testament. From the killing of Abel (who was slain by his brother Cain), through to the murder of Zechariah, God's prophets have been targets for those who are opposed to God. Abel's murder is recorded in the first book of the Old Testament while the book of Chronicles is the last book in the Hebrew Bible, so our Lord was giving an A to Z account of hostility against God's servants.

Nor did our Lord himself refrain from describing the judgement that is due to wicked men (Matt. 24:51; 25:46; Mark 14:21; Luke 17:1-2). Zechariah prayed that the Lord would take note of the injustice that was being done to him and act justly. That is what God's people must do when they see terrible evil in the world. Every year millions of unborn children are killed by abortion. More Christians are being persecuted now for the sake of Christ than ever before. What are God's people to do? If we did not believe that God will do justly, we would despair. There is no more comforting truth than the knowledge that 'The Judge of all the earth [will] do right' (see Gen. 18:25). This comforted the saints in heaven: 'Those who had been slain because of the word of God and the testimony they had maintained ... called out ..., "How long, Sovereign Lord, holy and true, until you judge the inhabitants of the earth and avenge our blood?"' (Rev. 6:9). Zechariah's words were both a statement of fact and a righteous prayer.

Joash's punishment (24:23-27)

It was not long before Zechariah's prayer had an answer. **'At the turn of the year, the army of Aram marched against Joash; it invaded Judah and Jerusalem and killed all the leaders of the people'** (24:23). It was not normal for armies to set out for battle before the springtime, or the 'turn of the year'. When that time came the Lord did not delay to bring judgement upon Joash. Significantly, although the Syrian army brought death and destruction to a great number of people, the Chronicler tells us that it 'marched against Joash'. Zechariah had directed his dying words to the sin of Joash, and it was Joash whom the Lord visited in judgement.

The humiliation of Joash at the hand of the Syrian armies was marked by a series of tragic ironies.

First of all, the Syrian army defeated **'a much larger army'** from Judah (24:24). What a turn around from the victory which Asa had won over the huge army commanded by Zerah the Cushite! (14:9). When the people of Judah trusted the Lord, vast armies could not overcome them, but when they forsook the Lord, then even superior force was powerless to win them the victory.

Secondly, the Syrian army **'withdrew'** and **'left Joash severely wounded'** (24:25). They 'forsook' Joash, leaving him in a wounded condition because he had **'forsaken the LORD'** (24:24). Significantly the same Hebrew verb is used, emphasizing that Joash's weakened state was directly linked to his abandonment of the temple and his refusal to hear the prophets of the Lord.

Thirdly, Joash's demise came about when **'His officials conspired against him for murdering the son of Jehoiada the priest, and they killed him in his bed'** (24:25). We cannot help being amazed at the fickleness of the officials who sought to avenge the murder of Zechariah. They were the men who had advised Joash to abandon the worship of Jehovah, thus inviting Zechariah's denunciation. They were the men who had hatched the plot to kill Zechariah. There is no honour among wrongdoers! This is the twilight zone in which the wicked live. Nothing is certain, except destruction, in a world that has turned its back upon God. Those who join with evil men in their evil schemes are sealing their own destruction.

Fourthly, the burial of Joash was not that of a king: **'So he died and was buried in the City of David, but not in the tombs of the kings'** (24:25). Even in death Joash was snubbed and humiliated. The contrast with Jehoiada is evident. Although Jehoiada was a priest, and not a king, 'He was buried with the kings in the City of David' (24:16). Although Joash was the king, he had lost the respect that was due to his office. A great deal was said about Joash, as the Chronicler records in 24:27. In all these accounts there is a great deal of disappointment. However, the people of Judah had the expectation that one day the perfect King would rule over his people and they knew that then their hopes would not be so cruelly dashed to the ground.

For all his failings, Joash still pointed forward to the King who would restore the temple. Solomon, Zerubbabel and Herod were builders of magnificent temples, but Jesus astounded his generation when he claimed to be the greatest of all the temple-builders: 'Destroy this temple, and I will raise it again in three days' (John 2:19; cf. Mark 14:58). The temple that Jesus would raise was not a structure of stone, for 'The temple he had spoken of was his body.' His body would be nailed to a cross, and after three days he would be restored to life. As a result of the atoning death and glorious resurrection of the Son of God, sinners no longer need to approach God with their animal sacrifices at the altars of an earthly temple.

We are called to come near through the great High Priest of our salvation, the Lord Jesus Christ (Heb. 9:11-12). As a result of coming to God through the Lord Jesus Christ, we become part of a new temple, the church (1 Cor. 3:16-17; 2 Cor. 6:16; Eph. 2:19-22).

16.
Amaziah: reluctant obedience

Please read 2 Chronicles 25:1-28

Can you remember some of the things that your schoolteachers wrote in your end-of-term reports? Sometimes there may have been a straightforward assessment such as 'Excellent', 'Satisfactory' or 'Poor', but on other occasions there may well have been a hopeful comment like 'Shows promise', expressing high hopes that had yet to be realized. We might say that the Chronicler's report on the three kings whose reigns are described in 2 Chronicles 24-26 — Joash, Amaziah and Uzziah — was that they 'showed promise'. Their reigns all started with high hopes, but ended in disappointment. Godly people had looked to these men for good leadership, but did not find what they expected.

Amaziah's reign is introduced in typical fashion in 25:1. We are told that he was twenty-five years old when he came to the throne, and that he reigned for twenty-nine years. These details do not fit easily into the chronology of the reigns before and after Amaziah, or that of the northern kingdom. As a result some commentators have concluded that Amaziah reigned as sole ruler of Judah for only five years before becoming a captive of Jehoash, King of Israel, for nine years as a result of the events described in 25:21-24. It is assumed that Uzziah, Amaziah's son, was then crowned at some time during

the ensuing power vacuum. Afterwards Amaziah was released
from captivity and restored to his throne as co-ruler with Uzziah
for a period of fifteen years after the death of Jehoash (25:25).
With father and son vying for influence within the kingdom,
political instability would have been almost inevitable and 25:27
seems to describe a period of internal exile for Amaziah in
Lachish.

The Chronicler uses a standard formula to assess Amaziah
in 25:2, though there is a slight but significant variation at the
end: **'He did what was right in the eyes of the LORD, but
not wholeheartedly.'** It is hard to see how the first part of
this assessment (that 'He did what was right in the eyes of the
LORD') can apply to the whole of Amaziah's reign. We discover that Amaziah defied the word of the Lord and behaved
with cruelty and arrogance. It is better to take this positive
assessment of Amaziah to describe only the early years of his
reign when he set out to do the work that the Lord had given
him. At that time Amaziah declared that he was going to serve
the Lord. He certainly did some things that were praiseworthy
(25:4,10). However, even from the start he was not wholehearted in his obedience and this became increasingly obvious
as the years passed. Idolatry and pride came to the fore in his
actions.

This encourages us to consider what lies behind the good
actions of men and women. By the grace of God men and
women with ungodly hearts can still perform actions that appear to be good and helpful. We all know of unconverted people
who give money to good causes, who sacrifice time and effort
to help others in need, or who would give us the very shirts off
their backs. Our Lord spoke of fathers who, although they
themselves were evil, knew how to give good gifts to their
children (Matt. 7:11). In 2 Kings 10:30-31 we read of Jehu's
revolution in Israel and the blessing it brought by removing

the family of Ahab from power. Jehu's actions were beneficial, but sinfully flawed. We speak of these actions as 'good works' because they bestow benefit upon mankind, and from our perspective they are certainly beneficial. However, their outward form does not make them 'good' in God's eyes; still less are they meritorious, or able to win his favour.

An excellent analysis of human actions, sometimes known as 'good works', is found in the *Westminster Confession of Faith*: 'Works done by unregenerate men, although, for the matter of them, they may be things which God commands, and of good use both to themselves and to others; yet, because they proceed not from an heart purified by faith; nor are done in a right manner, according to the word; nor to a right end, the glory of God; they are therefore sinful, and cannot please God, or make man meet to receive grace from God' (ch. 16, para. 7). When unregenerate men rely upon their flawed 'good works' to earn a good standing before God, they add insult to their offence to God. So when we become convicted of our sins we discover that 'All our righteous acts are like filthy rags; we all shrivel up like a leaf, and like the wind our sins sweep us away' (see Isa. 64:6).

All this was true of Amaziah. The inspired historian records God's verdict upon his good works. He did what was right in the eyes of the Lord, but not from a perfect heart, or (to translate the Hebrew text literally) 'not from a heart at peace'. Amaziah was not reconciled to God as his Redeemer. As a result of not being at peace with God, he was not even at peace with himself. One part of him knew what he ought to do, while the other wanted to pull away from God. These two forces pulled him hither and thither and made any good that he may have done erratic and short-lived. Even when he did what God wanted, he did it reluctantly. His attitude was sullen and sour. Let us consider what Amaziah did during his reign.

Consolidating his kingdom (25:3-4)

It was a common thing for each new king to strengthen his grip over the machinery of government. He could not take it for granted that those who had served his father would loyally serve him. The circumstances which brought Amaziah to the throne (see 24:25) brought special danger. His father had been killed in his bed (to settle old scores arising from the murder of Zechariah the priest). There were signs that some in positions of authority in the kingdom might not be well disposed towards Joash's son.

Amaziah responded to this threat with firmness and justice, but not vindictiveness. It was entirely appropriate that he should bring his father's murderers to justice. **'He executed the officials who had murdered his father the king'** (25:3). Their actions may have been motivated by anger at Joash's shameful treatment of Zechariah, but there was no excuse for lifting their hands against the king. 'It is mine to avenge; I will repay,' is the word of the Lord in all such situations (Deut. 32:35; Rom. 12:19). David could have claimed the right to avenge himself when he found Saul at his mercy on the two occasions recorded in 1 Samuel 24 and 26. Instead he applied a higher principle of respect for divinely created life and divinely ordained authority by sparing Saul's life. 'I will not lift my hand against my master, because he is the LORD's anointed' (1 Sam. 24:10). Amaziah brought punishment upon the heads of those who lifted their hands against his father, but he also showed mercy.

Amaziah did not treat those who had murdered his father as a vindictive and cruel man might have done. **'Yet he did not put their sons to death, but acted in accordance with what is written in the Law, in the Book of Moses, where the LORD commanded: "Fathers shall not be put to death**

**for their children, nor children put to death for their
fathers; each is to die for his own sins"'** (25:4). A vindictive man, bent on revenge, might have been able to justify
killing the children of the murderers. He might have pointed
to the principle of collective responsibility as an excuse. He
might have cited the example of Achan, who had stolen the
consecrated things from Jericho. 'Then Joshua, together with
all Israel, took Achan son of Zerah, the silver, the robe, the
gold wedge, his sons and daughters, his cattle, donkeys and
sheep, his tent and all that he had, to the Valley of Achor...
Then all Israel stoned him' (Josh. 7:24-25).

The application of this principle may seem very unfair. Why
should God should punish children for the guilt of the fathers?
However, we should note two facts.

First of all, God deals with men and women through *a representative or family head.* His actions are reckoned to be
theirs, for good or for ill. For instance, we are all born as
sinners under the wrath of God because of the actions of our
first father, Adam, and believers are saved from the consequences of their sins because of the actions of Jesus Christ,
their representative in the covenant of grace (Rom. 5:12-17).
If we dismiss this principle as unfair, then we undermine the
possibility of salvation through the work of Christ.

The second fact to note is that the principle of represen-
tation, leading to *collective responsibility*, is a divine principle.
It is a principle that God employs in his dealings with men. It
is his to apply and his to limit. When God saw the possibility
that it might be abused in a vengeful way in the application of
civil justice, he placed a limitation on it. God would apply the
principle of collective guilt according to his perfect wisdom
and holiness. However, God has commanded men to put
another principle to work when they administer justice, that
of individual responsibility. That is why Moses legislated in

Deuteronomy 24:16 that 'Fathers shall not be put to death for their children, nor children put to death for their fathers; each is to die for his own sin.' This is the principle that Amaziah applied in 25:4 when he did not punish the sins of those who had murdered his father.

The Chronicler, no doubt, records this incident because of the significance that the principle of individual responsibility assumed in the post-exilic period. In the aftermath of the exile it was common to hear the people of Israel account for their miserable predicament by pointing to the sins of their fathers. 'We know that we are not perfect,' they acknowledged, 'but the real cause of our problems is the terrible wickedness of past generations.' This enabled them to evade any searching self-examination. They even coined a proverb to express it succinctly: 'The fathers eat sour grapes and the children's teeth are set on edge.' It was this proverb, and the complacency that went with it, that Ezekiel countered in Ezekiel 18:3-4: 'As surely as I live, declares the Sovereign LORD, you will no longer quote this proverb in Israel. For every living soul belongs to me, the father as well as the son — both alike belong to me. The soul who sins is the one who will die.' This is both a principle of fairness and mercy, and it forces us to look to our own sin rather than the failings of others to explain the trials we face.

Campaigning against the Edomites (25:5-12)

Before launching his campaign against the Edomites, Amaziah mustered his army and found that he had 300,000 men (25:5). Although this may sound like a large army, it was considerably fewer than the million men that Jehoshaphat was able to muster (see 17:14-18), or the half a million men in Asa's army (see 14:8). Numerically, at least, Judah's armies were declining from generation to generation.

When Amaziah realized that his army was not as large as he had expected, he sought the help of 100,000 mercenaries from the northern kingdom of Israel (25:6). When he hired these soldiers Amaziah ignored one of the most important lessons that sacred history teaches us. The Chronicler constantly draws our attention to the fact that strength and security do not come from weight of numbers or force of arms; they come from the Lord. Abijah discovered the power of the Lord when he and 400,000 men defeated King Jeroboam's army of 800,000 men (13:3-18; see also 14:8-13; 16:7; 20:15-17, for further illustrations of this 'holy war' principle from the reigns of Asa and Jehoshaphat). When the Lord fought for Israel and when Israel relied upon the Lord, 'Five of you will chase a hundred, and a hundred of you will chase ten thousand, and your enemies will fall by the sword before you' (Lev. 26:8).

Conversely when Israel did not rely upon the Lord, even a vast army would be powerless.

This is what the Sovereign LORD, the Holy One of Israel, says:

'In repentance and rest is your salvation,
    in quietness and trust is your strength,
    but you would have none of it...
    Therefore...
A thousand will flee
    at the threat of one;
at the threat of five
    you will flee away,
till you are left
    like a flagstaff on a mountaintop,
    like a banner on a hill'

(Isa. 30:15-17).

Amaziah, however, trusted in the strength that silver could buy rather than the strength that is found in the Sovereign Lord.

As a result, the Lord threw an unwelcome spanner into the works. He sent a prophet to rebuke Amaziah and tell him, **'O king, these troops from Israel must not march with you, for the LORD is not with Israel... Even if you go and fight courageously in battle, God will overthrow you before the enemy, for God has the power to help or to overthrow'** (25:7-8). We do not know who this prophet was, but his message was consistent with the theology of the other prophets. Victory comes from the Lord, not the arm of flesh. Some commentators call this the 'holy war' theme. If Amaziah relied upon the Lord he would be victorious, even though his army was smaller than that of his enemies. However, if Amaziah relied upon the strength of hired mercenaries he would be defeated, 'even if you go and fight courageously'.

There was also a new message. From the time of Ahab onwards, the northern kingdom came be regarded as virtually a heathen nation. **'For the LORD is not with Israel — not with any of the people of Ephraim'** (25:7; cf. 19:2; 20:37). When those who have professed to serve the true God turn away they have committed the sin of apostasy, and they are to be regarded as separate from the covenant people. The apostle Paul applied this principle when he described the consequences of church discipline (1 Cor. 5:9-11; 2 Thess. 3:14).

Amaziah counted the cost of obeying the prophet's instructions. **'Amaziah asked the man of God, "But what about the hundred talents I paid for these Israelite troops?"'** (25:9). In itself there is nothing wrong with such an exercise. In Luke 14:28-33 our Lord commended the practice of weighing up the implications of obeying the gospel. He told a parable about a king going to wage war: 'Will he not first sit down and consider whether he is able with ten thousand men to oppose the one coming against him with twenty thousand?' It is plain common sense to weigh up the likely consequences of our actions.

Amaziah, however, did not like the sound of what he heard from the prophet. It had cost him a hundred talents (or 3½ tons) of silver to hire the mercenaries from Israel. If he sent them home there was no guarantee that he would get a refund. There was every likelihood that he would lose face, and there was no telling what a band of armed and frustrated mercenaries might do.

There is always a cost to be borne when we commit ourselves to serve God. Many of those who hear the claims of the gospel ask, 'What will it cost if I become a Christian? What will my friends and family think? Will I become unpopular when I tell those friends who were my partners in sin?' As Christians progress in their walk with God they discover more and more of the implications of Christianity, such as witnessing, tithing and mortifying sin. To all these there is a cost. Sometimes we are staggered at what the cost is. That is why we need to keep in mind what the prophet went on to say: **'The Lord can give you much more than that.'**

No one ever suffered loss on account of serving God. Peter believed that he and the other disciples had given up a great deal to become followers of Jesus. In typical fashion he expressed the opinion to Jesus that 'We have left everything to follow you!' Our Lord's reply was equally pointed: 'I tell you the truth ... no one who has left home or brothers or sisters or mother or father or children or fields for me and the gospel will fail to receive a hundred times as much in this present age (homes, brothers, sisters, mothers, children and fields — and with them persecutions) and in the age to come, eternal life' (Mark 10:28-30). Truly God is no man's debtor. No believer should ever feel that he has had a shoddy deal from God. There is no sacrifice that we can make in serving God that is too costly. When the young American missionary William Borden left to serve as a missionary in China he did not consider the cost too great. He in fact never reached China but, as he lay dying of fever in Egypt, he left a note saying, 'No reserve, no retreat, no regrets.' The life that he was about to enter was 'much more' than the one that he gave to the Lord.

Clear as this principle ought to be, it did not convince Amaziah. The prophet's message was unwelcome and he gave only reluctant compliance (25:10). **'So Amaziah dismissed the troops who had come to him from Ephraim.'** No doubt he obeyed less than wholeheartedly. It is true that he did comply with the Lord's instructions and he enjoyed the victory that followed: **'Amaziah then marshalled his strength and led his army to the Valley of Salt, where he killed ten thousand men of Seir...'** (25:11-12). However, his heart was far from submissive, and we see this more and more as the events unfold.

The consequences of foolish decisions (25:13-28)

This last section of the chapter describes the aftermath of Amaziah's campaign against the Edomites. Although Amaziah won the war, he 'lost the peace'. His foolish decisions brought disastrous consequences.

1. The dismissed mercenaries caused havoc on their way home (25:13)

'Meanwhile the troops that Ahaziah had sent back ... raided Judean towns... They killed three thousand people

and carried off great quantities of plunder.' It was easier for Amaziah to dismiss the Israelite mercenaries from his service than to get them out of his territory. After he returned from fighting the Edomites he found that these mercenaries had 'raided Judean towns from Samaria to Beth Horon. They killed three thousand people and carried off great quantities of plunder.' Some commentators suggest that these raids may not necessarily have taken place on their way back from Jerusalem, but may have occurred some time later when Amaziah was embroiled in his Edomite campaign, or perhaps later still. This is suggested by the phrase 'Samaria to Beth Horon', which indicates that they based themselves in Samaria and extended their influence as far back as the Judean town of Beth Horon.

What motivated these raids was the belief of the northern mercenaries that they had been cheated out of their share of the spoils that were taken from the Edomites. In ancient times mercenaries earned more from the spoils of war than from their negotiated fee. Or perhaps they felt that their warlike qualities had been called in question, so they had to let it be known that they really could create havoc.

The destruction they brought was not a consequence of the prophet's command to dismiss the mercenaries. In the final analysis Amaziah and his people were suffering on account of the foolish decision to employ the mercenaries in the first place. Such unstable and ill-disciplined soldiers were always going to be more of a liability than an asset, and the consequences of going to war alongside them would have been even worse. It was an act of unbelief on Amaziah's part to employ them. It was an act of wisdom and mercy on the Lord's part that they were sent home before they were able to inflict any greater damage on the people of Judah. Even in this sorry episode we can see that God really does work all things together for good for the benefit of his people (Rom. 8:28).

2. Amaziah brought back Edomite gods and worshipped them
(25:14-16)

**'When Amaziah returned from slaughtering the Edomites,
he brought back the gods of the people of Seir. He set them
up as his own gods, bowed down to them and burned
sacrifices to them.'** On the face of it this was a very foolish
thing to do. The prophet of the Lord indicated the reason why
in his question: **'Why do you consult this people's gods,
which could not save their own people from your hand?'**
(25:15).

Modern commentators (drawing on more recent studies of
ancient customs) have sought to explain Amaziah's actions. It
was not an uncommon practice for victorious kings to worship (or at least to permit the worship of) the gods of defeated
peoples. Sometimes it was reckoned that if the conqueror stole
the gods of a subject people, they were left defenceless because they no longer had recourse to the deities who had hith-
erto protected them. Sometimes it was reckoned that they had
suffered defeat because their erstwhile defenders had turned
against them; therefore the conqueror owed a debt of gratitude to these gods and it was in his interests to ensure that
they would not likewise desert him. Such thinking was thoroughly pagan and pragmatic. It regards the gods as power-
broking politicians playing games with the lives of their worshippers — betraying and protecting as circumstances and
self-interest demanded.

If these were the reasons why Amaziah worshipped the
gods of the Edomites it shows how thoroughly he had im-
bibed a pagan outlook on life. Amaziah's sin in this regard
stands out in its seriousness. His actions provoked a swift and
pointed response from the Lord: **'He sent a prophet to him'**
(25:15). Whether it was the same prophet who had previously
rebuked Amaziah for hiring the Israelite mercenaries or another

one we are not told. However, on this occasion Amaziah did not offer even token obedience. His behaviour became theatrical and pompous: **'While he was still speaking, the king said to him, "Have we appointed you an adviser to the king? Stop! Why be struck down?"'** (25:16).

These are the words of a man who is unwilling to listen to reason. Clearly Amaziah respected neither the Lord nor his prophets. **'So the prophet stopped...'** The prophet decided not to cast his pearls before swine, as our Lord was later to advise his followers (Matt. 7:6), for reprobate men only multiply their condemnation by their reaction to God's Word. The king had hardened his heart against God's Word and he was handed over to evil. The prophet saw this and said, **'I know that God has determined to destroy you, because you have done this and have not listened to my counsel'** (25:16). While we cannot look with prophetic insight into the hearts of others, we can see similar signs of hardness in those who will not listen to the claims of the gospel. We weep over their lost condition. After we have said all we can, we can only pray that God's mercy will be poured out to soften even the hardest of hearts.

3. Amaziah was humiliated by Jehoash King of Israel (25:17-25)

Amaziah set out on a reckless course of action. He took foolish advice from his counsellors and challenged Jehoash in battle. His message was: **'Come, meet me face to face'** (25:17). This was not a friendly invitation to get to know each other better; it was a challenge to meet on the battlefield. Perhaps Amaziah was filled with a sense of elation after defeating the Edomites and he wanted to advance while morale was high in his army. He may have wanted to humiliate the northern kingdom after mercenaries from Samaria had plundered his own territory. Or he may have suspected that Jehoash had given them support to carry out their raids. Any of these suggestions may be true, but we should not ignore the hand of God in all this, for the Lord put this purpose into Amaziah's heart to bring him to his knees.

Jehoash knew what Amaziah's words meant. He also knew what a war would cost. For this reason he told a parable intending to show that it was not in Amaziah's interests to wage war against him. Jehoash believed that he was in a strong position to face any challenge from Amaziah. Certainly Jehoash's parable does not flatter Amaziah. He is a **'thistle'**, while Jehoash is **'a cedar in Lebanon'**. Jehoash's explanation is clear and pointed: **'You say to yourself that you have defeated Edom, and now you are arrogant and proud. But stay at home! Why ask for trouble and cause your own downfall and that of Judah also?'** (25:19).

Unfortunately for Amaziah, he did not take the advice that was offered to him. He brought about the destruction that Jehoash predicted. The narrative that follows in 25:20-24 describes how this came about. Amaziah and Jehoash met face to face as Amaziah had wanted. They **'faced each other at Beth Shemesh in Judah'** (25:21). The result, however, was not what Amaziah had expected. **'Judah was routed by Israel, and every man fled to his home. Jehoash king of Israel captured Amaziah king of Judah'** (25:22-23). The achievements of David and Solomon were being whittled away as the walls of Jerusalem were destroyed (25:23), the treasures in the temple plundered and the people of Judah taken as hostages (25:24).

4. Amaziah was humiliated at the hands of his own people (25:25-28)

After the death of Jehoash, Amaziah was returned to his kingdom in Judah, and there he lived for the last fifteen years of his life. These last years were neither happy nor glorious, for during them he continued to turn away from the Lord. **'From the time that Amaziah turned away from following the LORD ...'** (25:27). We are not told when this act of apostasy took place, but it may have been when Amaziah started to worship the gods of the defeated Edomites. That was a very public apostasy. Or there may have been an unseen turning from the Lord, and Amaziah's idolatry may simply have been the first public sign of it. It is not uncommon to discover that a public fall into sin has been preceded by many years of secret apostasy. At any rate, there had been a definite and deliberate act of turning from the Lord.

God punished Amaziah by turning the hearts of his people against him: **'They conspired against him in Jerusalem and he fled to Lachish, but they sent men after him to Lachish and killed him there'** (25:27). Lachish was a fortified stronghold forty-five kilometres south-west of Jerusalem. It was one of the last Judean towns to hold out against the Babylonians when Nebuchadnezzar invaded Judah. Here Amaziah sought safety from his own people. Yet he was not to find it. He had lost their respect as well as the protecting hand of God. Only for the sake of his father David was he given the honour of a royal funeral in Jerusalem. **'He was brought back by horse and was buried with his fathers in the City of Judah'** (25:28).

Lessons to learn from the reign of Amaziah

In Amaziah's life we see the instability that destroys the lives of those whose hearts are not fixed wholly on the Lord. Those words in 25:2, 'not wholeheartedly', came back to haunt him time and time again. His early promise gave way to foolishness, defeat and disgrace. In particular Amaziah illustrates two tragic symptoms of spiritual instability.

1. Reluctant obedience is the forerunner of open disobedience

None of us likes to be challenged about our sins. As we have
seen, Amaziah did not relish the prophet's rebuke when he
hired the Israelite mercenaries. There were two inner conflicts
going on in Amaziah's heart when he heard the Lord's command in 25:7-8. One was the struggle to do the right thing. In
this he was victorious, in so far as he did what he was commanded. He sent the mercenaries home. But the other conflict
involved a more intense struggle — to do the right thing for
the right reason, and this was a battle which Amaziah lost. He
did the right thing, but he did so with a heavy heart, brooding
over what it cost him.

When we hear the challenge of God's Word — whether it
is the gospel call to repent and believe, or whether it is a challenge to those who are already believers — we are sometimes
offended. We must take heed to our hearts as well as our
actions. It is not good enough to do the right thing with a cold
heart. That is what Judas Iscariot did for three years as he
followed Jesus. In fact, cold obedience can only last for a time.
We cannot keep it up indefinitely, for our unbroken hearts are
certain to rebel and say, 'Enough of this pretence.' Reluctant
obedience is a certain forerunner of open disobedience, as the
apostle John showed when he described the false teachers of
his day: 'They went out from us, but they did not really belong
to us. For if they had belonged to us, they would have remained with us; but their going showed that none of them
belonged to us' (1 John 2:19). Amaziah's idolatry, arrogance
and self-reliance were like the erupting of a volcano of evil
pent up in his unbowed and unrenewed heart.

2. Foolishness results when God withdraws his favour

The ancient Greeks had a saying that 'Those whom the gods
would destroy, they first make mad.' From a biblical perspective

we can see that foolishness and godlessness are inextricably bound together. According to Psalm 14:1, the 'fool' is someone who has rejected God and who does not allow God to influence his behaviour and thinking. As a result God takes away his kindly restraints and hands him over to even greater depravity (see Rom. 1:21-25). When God withdraws he leaves the fool to continue along the path that he has plotted for himself and that leads on to even greater foolishness. A fool can never see his own folly (Prov. 12:15). Wisdom is always wasted on him (Prov. 24:7).

When Amaziah worshipped the worthless gods of a defeated people and picked a needless fight with a powerful neighbour he marked himself out as a fool. God had withdrawn from him and left him to his own devices. This is emphasized by a play upon the verb 'to take counsel' in 25:16: 'While [the prophet] was still speaking, the king said to him, "Have we appointed you an *adviser* to the king? Stop! ..." So the prophet stopped but said, "I know that God *has determined* to destroy you, because you have done this and have not listened to my *counsel.*" ' (All three expressions in italic type are linked to the same root verb and they make clear that Amaziah made his foolish decision because God had withdrawn and left him to his own devices.)

How can we avoid such foolishness? The answer is to be found in a close walk with God. When we truly seek him he will not withdraw from us. We must be wholehearted in our walk with God. Our hearts must be fixed upon the Lord — unreservedly. Our hearts must be resting upon the Lord totally, and trusting him implicitly. The psalmist says of the man who fears the Lord: 'He will have no fear of bad news; his heart is steadfast, trusting in the LORD' (Ps. 112:7). 'Blessed is he whose help is the God of Jacob, whose hope is in the LORD his God' (Ps. 146:5). In the words of Isaiah:

You will keep in perfect peace
  him whose mind is steadfast,
  because he trusts in you

                                        (Isa. 26:3).

Those whose hearts are resting upon the Lord will want to
be directed in the good and wise ways of the Lord:

Instruct a wise man and he will be wiser still;
  teach a righteous man and he will add to his learning.
The fear of the LORD is the beginning of wisdom,
  and knowledge of the Holy One is understanding

                                        (Prov. 9:9-10).

17.
Uzziah: pride before the fall

Please read 2 Chronicles 26:1 – 27:9

Tragedy is all the more poignant when it spoils something that is good. In classical Greek drama a tragedy was the story of a noble figure, capable of great virtue, who was nevertheless destroyed by a single flaw in his character. That flaw became his 'Achilles' heel'. Similarly in the tragedies of the English playwright, William Shakespeare, the heroes were men like Hamlet (obsessed by a desire for revenge) and Othello (consumed by jealousy). The common feature was that one initially small flaw became an all-consuming and malignant passion. In this sense the life of King Uzziah of Judah was a tragedy.

In the eyes of many historians Uzziah was an outstandingly successful king. He reigned for fifty-two years (787–736 B.C.). For much of that time Jeroboam II (785–745 B.C.) was on the throne of the northern kingdom of Israel. The two kings were at peace with each other and together their reigns are considered to have been a 'golden age' for Israel and Judah. Jeroboam II regained the territory that had been lost to Syria during the reigns of his predecessors Jehoahaz and Jehoash, and the northern boundaries of his kingdom extended as far as those of King Solomon. With peace, trade and industry flourished. Archaeological evidence indicates that many new industries were established at this time and the land of Israel supported a population larger than at any other period of Old

Testament history. In the words of the historian John Bright, 'It was, superficially at least, a time of great optimism.'

However, to most Bible readers King Uzziah is best known in connection with his death. Isaiah dated his prophetic call in 'the year that King Uzziah died'. During the last days of Uzziah's life Isaiah saw a vision of the Lord exalted in glory in the temple: 'In the year that King Uzziah died, I saw the Lord seated on a throne, high and exalted, and the train of his robe filled the temple' (Isa. 6:1). The death of Uzziah came to be regarded as the end of an era in the history of Judah. Thereafter the glory of the kingdom seemed to fade. It pointed out the weakness of human institutions. The great king who had reigned for so long was, after all, only a man. In this context Isaiah was able to draw great consolation from the knowledge that Jehovah is the King who reigns for ever and ever and his reign continues even when human kings die. The king is dead, Isaiah mourned, but long live the King of kings! 'Your throne, O God, will last for ever and ever' (Ps. 45:6).

There was an even sadder aspect to Uzziah's death. As well as indicating human mortality, the circumstances of his death illustrate human sinfulness. Uzziah died as a leper, and his leprosy was inflicted by God as a punishment for his pride. His long and glorious reign was spoiled by one foolish action, which we read about only in this chapter. The account given in 2 Kings 15:1-7 is much shorter and, although it refers to Uzziah's (or Azariah's) leprosy, it does not explain its origin. The historian who wrote Kings leaves us with an unblemished picture of a king who 'did what was right in the eyes of the LORD' (2 Kings 15:3).

As we examine our own lives, and the lives of other Christians, we know that not one of us can live an unblemished life. No, not even the most outstanding Christians have been able to live faultless lives. J. C. Ryle (while preaching on Galatians

2:11-16, which describes how Paul was constrained to rebuke
Peter for inconsistency) illustrates this very point by referring
to the great men of the sixteenth-century Reformation: 'Martin
Luther held tenaciously to the doctrine of consubstantiation…
Melanchthon was often timid and undecided. Calvin allowed
Servetus to be burned. Cranmer recanted and fell away for a
time from his first faith. Jewell subscribed to Roman Catholic
doctrines for fear of death. Hooper disturbed the Church of
England by making too great an issue over the question of
vestments.' So, too, Chronicles presents us with Uzziah, 'warts
and all'. This rings true to our experience of life. We should
not be discouraged to see the fallibility of a biblical hero. Rather,
we should resolve to find out more about our own fallen natures, and in this way learn the lessons to be drawn from the
life of Uzziah.

It is significant that the reign of Uzziah's son, King Jotham,
is described in 2 Chronicles 27 almost as an appendix to the
life of Uzziah in chapter 26. This tells us how Jotham and
others learned lessons from Uzziah's tragic death. Through
our study of these chapters may the Lord teach us to walk
humbly and obediently in reliance upon his grace.

The good that Uzziah did (26:1-15)

When Uzziah came to the throne he was little more than a
boy. At the age of sixteen, he was propelled into a position of
responsibility by the invasion of King Jehoash of Israel. (See
the comment on 2 Chronicles 25:21-24 in the previous chapter.) Jehoash took Amaziah back to Samaria as a captive
(25:23) and a twenty-four-year co-regency followed until
Amaziah died in 775 B.C. For only fifteen of those years did
Amaziah reign alongside Uzziah in Judah.

In 2 Chronicles 26 the name Uzziah (which means, 'My strength in Jehovah') is used. In 2 Kings 15 the name Azariah (meaning 'Jehovah has helped') is used. Both names derive from similar-sounding Hebrew verbs and have similar meanings. They remind us that without the mercy of God we can accomplish nothing. In all probability Azariah was the most commonly used and better known of the two names. During the reign of the Assyrian king Tiglath-Pileser III, Assyrian records refer to 'Azriyau of Yaudi' — another form of 'Azariah of Judah'. It has been suggested that the Chronicler uses the name Uzziah to avoid confusion with Azariah the high priest, who plays an important role in the events of this chapter.

The Chronicler's assessment of Uzziah is positive, but measured: **'He did what was right in the eyes of the LORD, just as his father Amaziah had done'** (26:4). Granted that this is a form of words that the inspired historians commonly use to introduce kings who ruled in Judah, the words are nevertheless significant. Uzziah was a great king whose legacy was beneficial. However, he was one in a line of kings who had feet of clay. Uzziah's father Amaziah and his grandfather Joash had both started well and had accomplished much before stumbling and finishing their reigns in disgrace. The words, 'just as his father Amaziah had done', are a reminder that good men can still sin greatly, and that none of those who serve the Lord can ever afford to rest on their laurels.

During the early years of Uzziah's reign he was guided by Zechariah: **'He sought God during the days of Zechariah, who instructed him in the fear of God'** (26:5). We know nothing of this godly Zechariah except what we read in this verse. It has been suggested that he was a grandson of the courageous priest and prophet who rebuked King Joash in 24:22, although there is no evidence to back this up. However, this suggestion does remind us that King Joash 'did what was right in the eyes of the LORD all the years of Jehoiada the priest' (24:2). Mature believers can have a great influence for good when they act as guides and mentors to those who are younger. The removal of Jehoiada was disastrous for Joash, and the ministry of Zechariah was a stabilizing influence in the early years of Uzziah's reign.

It has been suggested that Zechariah was a prophet. His description as one 'who instructed him [that is, Uzziah] in the fear of God' could also be translated, 'who had understanding in visions of God'. The verb which the Chronicler uses means 'to discern or distinguish' and readily applies to visions or revelations from God. We can think of other prophets from this time (Isaiah, for example) who saw visions of the Lord exalted in glory. An authentic prophet of the Lord was expected to be able to distinguish a true revelation from a spurious one, and so convey what was genuinely the Word of God to others. In this context Zechariah was a good influence upon Uzziah because he was able to teach him what God really said.

Of course, it is never enough simply to hear the Word of God, however pure and clear its exposition may be. God's blessing comes to those who hear God's Word and heed its message. Uzziah was blessed **'as long as he sought the Lord'**. Only then did **'God [give] him success'** (26:5). The Hebrew verb for 'sought' conveys both the idea of devotion to God and that of willingness to do what God commands. To seek the Lord is more than just to ask a question; it is to cast ourselves before him as his servants, saying, 'Here am I. Send me!' As a result of this approach the Lord gave Uzziah 'success'. Let us consider what Uzziah did for the Lord.

1. His work as a military commander (26:6-8)

Uzziah fought against Judah's enemies to the south (Arabs), west (Philistines) and south-east (Ammonites). **'He went to war against the Philistines... God helped him against the**

Philistines and against the Arabs ... and against the Meunites. The Ammonites brought tribute to Uzziah.' The victories he won and the tribute that he received recall the days of David and Solomon. They remind us that Uzziah was one of a line of deliverer-kings leading eventually to the King of kings. The earthly victories of Uzziah and the other kings of Judah were pointers to the eternal victories of King Jesus, before whose throne all nations will bow.

2. His work as a builder (26:9-10)

As well as going on the offensive against his enemies, Uzziah secured the defences of his kingdom: **'Uzziah built towers in Jerusalem at the Corner Gate, at the Valley Gate and at the angle of the wall, and he fortified them.'** This building project was aimed at making his capital a secure fortress.

Further building projects are described in 26:10: **'He also built towers in the desert and dug many cisterns, because he had much livestock in the foothills and in the plain.'** This was the infrastructure that supported agriculture throughout his kingdom. The 'plain' refers to the strip of land along the Mediterranean Sea; the 'hills' are the uplands of Judea, and the 'foothills' are the areas in between. Taken together, these terms describe his whole kingdom in all its diversity and productivity. It is interesting to note that Uzziah was a man of many interests. He was successful in both warlike and peace-time activities. He could tear down, but he could also build up. Herein lay his genius as a good king.

3. His work as an administrator (26:11-15)

During Uzziah's reign a standing army was maintained for the first time in the history of Israel. In these verses it is described as **'a well-trained army, ready to go out by divisions'**. Previously, armies had been raised on a feudal basis. Tribal leaders recruited fighting men from their tribes and clans as need arose in times of national emergency, and when the need disappeared the army was disbanded. Uzziah retained the traditional leadership, for 26:12 refers to **'family leaders'** who were **'over the fighting men'**. However, the army was on constant standby and was **'a powerful force to support the king against his enemies'** (26:13).

A professional army needs good logistical support. This is what Napoleon meant when he said that 'An army marches on its stomach.' To fight well an army needs to be well-clothed, well-fed and well-armed. The provisions described in 26:14-15 show how these needs were catered for. **'Uzziah provided shields, spears, helmets, coats of armour, bows and sling-stones for the entire army. In Jerusalem he made machines designed by skilful men for use on the towers...'** Commentators have described these machines either as offensive weapons designed to project missiles, or defensive structures behind which archers might position themselves. Archaeological evidence suggests that the latter interpretation is more likely to be correct.

Uzziah was blessed by God with many talents and he used them to the full. He had all the strengths that were needed in a great king. In many ways his military power, his building programmes and his economic development remind us of Solomon. Special mention is made of **'Elath'** in 26:2: **'He was the one who rebuilt Elath and restored it to Judah.'** This was to be Judah's trading window on the world, just as it had been in the days of Solomon (8:17).

Uzziah seized the opportunities that God gave him by putting his talents to work. This is how we ought to serve

God. In the parable of the talents our Lord teaches that, whether our talents be many or few, we are to make use of them (Matt. 25:14-30). God gives his blessing to those who exert themselves, and he reproves those who do not: 'Well done, good and faithful servant! You have been faithful with a few things; I will put you in charge of many things... You wicked, lazy servant! ...'(Matt. 25:21,26). Certainly Uzziah was not a lazy servant. However, he fell into another trap.

Uzziah's downfall (26:16-23)

Uzziah followed a pattern that has become depressingly common in the Chronicler's history. Great kings are most likely to fall into sin at the height of their powers. John Dryden once wrote, 'Even victors are by victory undone.' David sinned with Bathsheba as he rested from the heat of battle and left the fighting to Joab. Solomon's heart was led astray by his foreign wives after he had made Judah safe and prosperous. In 26:16 we take note of the same sequence of events: **'But after Uzziah became powerful, his pride led to his downfall.'**

What did Uzziah do? **'He was unfaithful to the LORD his God, and entered the temple of the LORD to burn incense on the altar of incense.'** When the tabernacle and the incense altar were built, God commanded Aaron to burn incense on the altar (Exod. 30:7-10). This ministry was allocated to the priests who were descended from Aaron. 'Aaron was set apart, he and his descendants for ever, to consecrate the most holy things, to offer sacrifices before the LORD, to minister before him and to pronounce blessings in his name for ever' (1 Chr. 23:13). 'The LORD said to Aaron, "Only you and your sons may serve as priests in connection with everything at the altar and inside the curtain. I am giving you the service of the priesthood as a gift. Anyone else who comes near the sanctuary must be put to death"' (Num.18:7; cf. 18:1).

These very clear words in Numbers 18 were a response to the rebellion of Korah, Dathan, Abiram and 250 of the elders of Israel which is described in Numbers 16. These men rejected the leadership of Moses and resented the fact that priestly privileges had been given to the family of Aaron. They, too, wanted to be able to perform priestly duties at the altar (Num. 16:8-11). To demonstrate what God thought of their request Moses told them to appear before the Lord with their censors filled with incense (Num. 16:16-18). The Lord showed his displeasure by opening up the ground to swallow the three ringleaders, and by sending out fire to consume the 250 elders and their censors (Num. 16:31-35). If God had wanted kings or other Israelites to offer incense he would have given them a clear command to this effect.

The principle illustrated in these passages is that God knows exactly what he wants from those who worship him. He has made his wishes clear to us in his Word and there are no details that have slipped his mind. If God had wanted innovative styles of sacrifice he would have said so. If he had wanted Uzziah to minister at the altar he would have made that clear. The fact that there was no command was tantamount to a prohibition.

God still knows what he wants in the worship of the New Testament church. He has not given us liberty to devise forms of worship that are not commanded in the Scriptures. God has commanded us to sing praise, pray, read and preach the Scriptures. Activities such as mime, drama and musical entertainment are legitimate activities in their proper sphere, but not in the worship of God. Applying this principle, the *Westminster Shorter Catechism* answers the question, 'What is forbidden in the second commandment?' as follows: 'The second commandment forbiddeth the worshipping of God by images, *or any other way not appointed in his word.'*

Uzziah's sin was the arrogance of thinking that he knew better than God. His pride was typical of the hubris of men who think that their genius enables them to reform the church to make it more to their liking. In the history of the church it has not been uncommon for civil rulers to invade the workings of the body of Christ. A more recent example was the Scottish king James VI (also known as James I of England). He spoke often of the 'divine right of kings' and believed that this gave him the right to introduce unscriptural ceremonies and institutions into the newly reformed Church of Scotland. One of the ministers of the church at that time was a courageous man called Andrew Melville, and he spoke plainly about the king's place in the church: 'Sir, I must tell you that there are two kings and two kingdoms in Scotland. There is Christ Jesus the king, and his kingdom the Kirk, whose subject King James the Sixth is, and of whose kingdom he is not a king, not a lord, not a head, but a member.' Uzziah forgot that, although he was a king, he was a man under authority.

The courageous man in Uzziah's kingdom was the high priest Azariah. **'Azariah the priest with eighty other courageous priests of the Lord followed him in. They confronted him and said, "It is not right for you, Uzziah, to burn incense to the Lord. That is for the priests, the descendants of Aaron, who have been consecrated to burn incense"'** (26:17-18). They grounded their rebuke on the requirements of God's law. However, their warning served only to provoke a hostile response from the king and to aggravate his guilt. Uzziah **'became angry'** and **'was raging at the priests in their presence before the incense altar in the Lord's temple'** (26:19). At that very moment the Lord struck Uzziah. The king had been given a warning and an opportunity to repent. It was only when Uzziah rejected the warning and refused to repent that God acted in judgement by striking him with leprosy.

The leprosy described here and in other places in the Old Testament may not be the viral infection which doctors today call Hansen's Disease. Commentators and experts are divided on this question. However, we do know that the disease described here was a terrible and feared skin disease. The Hebrew word is derived from a verb meaning 'to strike down' or 'to lay low'. Leprosy was a prostrating and humbling disease. It laid low even the great Syrian general Naaman (2 Kings 5:1). When Miriam opposed her brother Moses, because she coveted his unique position as Israel's leader, God in his anger struck her with leprosy (Num. 12:9-10). Her leprosy was a public humiliation in recompense for her arrogance.

Uzziah was humbled when **'Leprosy broke out on his forehead.'** His raging came to an abrupt halt and his pride was well and truly deflated. The priests did not find it difficult to usher Uzziah out of the temple. **'Indeed, he himself was eager to leave, because the LORD had afflicted him'** (26:20).

For the rest of his life Uzziah lived a life of isolation. **'He lived in a separate house'** — literally a 'house of separation' (26:21). This may have been a sealed-off wing of the royal palace. Henceforth Uzziah was unable to discharge his responsibilities as king. He was unable to meet with his ministers, or sit in the counsels of state to deliberate on official matters. As a result his son Jotham reigned as co-regent (26:21). **'Jotham his son had charge of the palace and governed the people of the land.'**

Uzziah's isolation carried over even into his death (26:23). He was buried, not in the royal cemetery where his ancestors the kings of Judah were buried, but **'near them in a field for burial that belonged to the kings, for people said, "He had**

leprosy."' For the last years of his life Uzziah was a shadow of his former glory and the hopes of his people rested upon his son, Jotham. In spite of Uzziah's failings, there was still hope for the future. The post-exilic generation for whom the Chronicler wrote this history must have been able to take heart from the events of Uzziah's last days. After the exile the monarchy was in an even worse condition. It was worse than discredited — it had disappeared. However, even then there was still hope. The promise of a Son who would reign on David's throne still stood. Even though there was no suitable king, the kingdom had been spared and there was still hope.

More seriously for Uzziah, he was **'excluded from the temple of the LORD'** (26:21). He was not able to join with even the humblest of his subjects when they went up to offer their sacrifices to the Lord. The joys of going up to Jerusalem to worship the Lord are described in Psalm 122:1-2:

> I rejoiced with those who said to me,
>   'Let us go to the house of the LORD.'
> Our feet are standing
>   in your gates, O Jerusalem.

These joys were now denied to Uzziah. The means of grace were for ever cut off from him. His last years must have been miserable indeed.

Uzziah's misery must have been compounded by the knowledge that his shame and isolation all stemmed from one sinful action. He had gone too far and had stepped over the mark when he raged at the priests and refused to heed their warning. How he must have reproached himself when he thought about what he had done! How he must have repeated to himself, 'If only I had not gone into the temple to offer incense in the first place! If only I had stopped when Azariah spoke to

me!' How much Uzziah lost on account of that sinful day —
his dignity, his reputation, his health, his achievements on and
off the battlefield, his authority and, with them all, the joy of
his salvation!

Are there not also times in our experience when we look
back and say, 'If only I had not gone so far!'? It is good for us
to reflect now on the lesson that there is a great deal to be lost
by just one sin. James tells us that although the tongue is a
small part of our bodies, it can do a lot of damage. 'The tongue
also is a fire, a world of evil among the parts of the body. It
corrupts the whole person, sets the whole course of his life on
fire, and is itself set on fire by hell' (James 3:6). One thought-
less or untrue word, one act of marital unfaithfulness or sexual
immorality, one dishonest action can have disastrous consequences. These actions will not rob the true child of God of
his salvation (for our salvation does not rest upon our works)
but they can rob him of the joy of his salvation; they can grieve
the Holy Spirit and cause him to withdraw his fulness from us;
they can divide churches and families; they can spoil our witness and waste our fruitfulness.

The lessons to be learned (27:1-9)

When King Uzziah eventually died he was succeeded by his
son Jotham. As has already been stated, the Chronicler's account of Jotham's reign is presented in the form of an appendix to Uzziah's reign. The Chronicler's purpose was to show
that lessons were learned from Uzziah's reign — both for good
and for ill.

The lessons learned by the people of Judah were destructive lessons, and they led on to even greater evil. In William
Shakespeare's play *Julius Caesar*, Mark Antony says at the

burial of Caesar, 'The evil that men do lives after them; the
good is oft interred with their bones' (Act 3, Scene 2). This
sad analysis of human nature appears to be borne out in the
case of King Uzziah. The people of Judah appear to have forgotten that Uzziah sought the Lord and that, as long as he
sought the Lord, he had enjoyed the Lord's blessing. They
were more inclined to remember his years of absence from the
temple and to emulate his neglect of the means of grace.

The people of Judah also neglected the house of God. Indeed, they took the next step away from God by seeking other
gods. **'The people ... continued their corrupt practices'**
(27:2). Spiritual decline started in Uzziah's reign and Jotham
was unable to halt it. Nature abhors a vacuum and in the absence of firm, godly leadership a nation will slide into a comfortable compromise with evil. Uzziah's paralysed monarchy
lacked the moral authority to give the spiritual leadership that
was needed.

Jotham, on the other hand, learned positive lessons from
his father's reign. He learned to copy his father's strong points.
'He did what was right in the eyes of the Lord...' (27:2).

Jotham built on the good work that his father had done *as
a builder*: **'Jotham rebuilt the Upper Gate of the temple of
the Lord and did extensive work on the wall at the hill of
Ophel. He built towns in the Judean hills and forts and
towers in the wooded areas'** (27:3-4). These projects were
spread throughout his kingdom and contributed to its security
and cohesion.

Furthermore we read that Jotham built upon the good work
that his father had done *as a military commander*: **'Jotham
made war on the king of the Ammonites and conquered
them...'** (27:5). These were the same enemies that Uzziah
had defeated and made into tributaries in 26:8. Although Uzziah
had defeated them, they retained the potential to cause trouble

for Jotham. Even defeated enemies — just like defeated sins — need to be kept in check by constant vigilance.

Jotham also built upon the good work that his father had done *as a spiritual leader*: **'Jotham grew powerful because he walked steadfastly before the LORD his God'** (27:6). Jotham sought the Lord and followed his guidance. In contrast with the three kings who reigned before him — Joash, Amaziah and Uzziah — Jotham did not stumble along the way. He demonstrated stamina in his walk with God. It is important to remember that walking with God is more like a marathon than a 100-metre sprint. It is possible to become weary in doing good, and that is a danger to be avoided (Gal. 6:9).

Jotham learned lessons even from the negative side of his father's reign. In a footnote to 27:2, the Chronicler tells us that Jotham did not follow Uzziah's example in every detail: **'Unlike him** [Uzziah] **he** [Jotham] **did not enter the temple of the LORD.'** Jotham may have inherited Uzziah's power and prosperity, but he did not inherit his pride. He did not repeat his father's mistaken attempt to minister at the altar. Nor did he overreact and turn his back upon the God who had chastised his father. We are not to imagine from these words that Jotham neglected the temple or the worship of Jehovah. Rather, the Chronicler is telling us he was determined not to abuse the temple.

We can learn an important lesson from Jotham's discernment in responding to the example of his father. He sifted the good from the bad. He learned from the good and rejected the bad. As a result of popular psychology many people today regard themselves as hostages to their backgrounds. They blame parents, teachers, siblings, and almost everyone around them, for their own misdemeanours. Abuse is said to beget abuse and neglect is said to beget neglect. There is much common sense in this observation, but when it is pressed to imply that the sins of the parent are inevitably reproduced in the life of the child and therefore excusable in the latter, then we must protest. Sin is never inevitable. It is always the result of free and conscious choices. We sin because we choose to sin. We follow the example of our parents, teachers and role models in society only when we fail to distinguish good influences from evil ones.

By God's grace we are able to break the cycles of sin that run through our families. Jotham was enabled to choose the good and reject the evil because he 'walked steadfastly before the LORD his God'. Close fellowship with God showed him the difference between right and wrong and it strengthened him to choose the right. May we be enabled to choose the right and turn away from what is wrong.

18.
Ahaz: grasping at straws

Please read 2 Chronicles 28:1-27

The names of Bible characters are often more significant than we realize. They tell us about the lives that these people led, or the ambitions they cherished. Jacob was appropriately named 'the deceiver', while Abraham was given his name by God because he would be the 'father of many nations'. King Ahaz also had an appropriate name. It means, 'He grasped.'

Like any other king, Ahaz wanted to strengthen his kingdom and defend his borders, but he was a man who grasped at straws to achieve his goals. He was willing to sacrifice any principle, make any compromise, enter any alliance, serve any god, if only it would strengthen his hand. The only thing that Ahaz was not willing to do was to serve Jehovah, the Lord God of Israel.

Ahaz's reign (734–728 B.C.) was sandwiched between the reigns of two godly kings. His father was Jotham and his son was the great reforming king, Hezekiah. However, Ahaz's reign was one of the most wicked in the history of Judah and under his leadership Judah became perilously similar to the northern Israelite kingdom in the days when Jeroboam son of Nebat had been its king.

'**Ahaz was twenty years old when he became king, and he reigned in Jerusalem for sixteen years**' (28:1). It is not easy to harmonize the dates of Ahaz's reign with those of the reigns before and after, or with other historical events. This has led some commentators to suggest that Ahaz was appointed co-regent with his father King Jotham when he was twenty years old, and that his sixteen-year reign as sole ruler commenced five or six years later. Otherwise he would have been only eleven when his son Hezekiah was born! During his time as king, Ahaz's record was one of continuous wickedness.

Ahaz practised heathen worship (28:1-4)

Ahaz rejected the example and teaching of the godly kings of Judah. He despised the instruction of his father, King Jotham, and he strayed from the pattern set by his illustrious ancestor, King David, who had established his royal line. **'Unlike David his father, he did not do what was right in the eyes of the Lord.'** He looked elsewhere for less inspiring role models: **'He walked in the ways of the kings of Israel and also made cast idols for worshipping the Baals.'** The fact that idolatry had brought disaster to the northern kingdom did not deter him.

Ahaz was an innovator, as Jeroboam I had been in Israel: 'He … also made cast idols for worshipping the Baals.' He experimented with home-grown false religion, but did not stop there. Jeroboam I had made cast idols for the worship of Jehovah, but Ahaz made them for worshipping the Baals. It is typical of the Chronicler to put 'Baals' in the plural to indicate that Ahaz worshipped many false gods. There was a great multiplicity of evil innovations that followed when the restraining hand of Jehovah was cast off. Ahaz **'burned sacrifices in the Valley of Ben Hinnom and sacrificed his sons in the fire'**. These evil practices were forbidden in Leviticus 20:1-5 and Deuteronomy 18:10, and they were to reappear during the reign of Manasseh (33:6; cf. Jer. 7:31-32), but this was their first recorded occurrence in Judah. Ahaz was inquisitive and innovative, but his enquiring spirit invariably led into evil.

Why should this be so? It is not, in itself, a bad thing to have an enquiring mind. It is because man has been created in the image of God, with the capacity to reason and to examine the created world, that he develops new ways of doing things. Sometimes this spirit of enquiry has been put to good use — as for instance, in the progress of medical technology to preserve and enhance life. At other times this spirit of enquiry leads to open rebellion against God, as when the men of Shinar built a tower that reached into the heavens so that they might make a name for themselves (Gen. 11:1-9). When men do not know the power of the living God and the blessings of true religion they very quickly become bored and try to devise something new and better. However, by the very nature of things, there is nothing 'better' than the true religion which has been commanded in the Word of God. Those supposed 'improvements' are always perversions of the truth.

Ahaz was like many people living today in post-Christian societies (especially in the Western world) who are experimenting with Eastern religions and exotic spirituality. (Ironically, at the same time, many in Asia have seen the spiritual and moral bankruptcy of these religions and are turning to Christ in their tens of thousands.) Many are turning to these false religions because they have never known the power of real Christianity. Perhaps for a time they have been exposed to caricatures of Christianity. We might mention churches which have embraced liberalism, which silences the Scriptures and replaces it with religious speculation; or moralism, which obscures the free grace of God behind a religion of good works; or ritualism, which obscures the necessity of a personal relationship with God behind a cloud of external church formalities; or sensationalism, which retreats into a religion of experiences and obscures the power of the truth to make sinners free. The activities of these unscriptural churches have created a vacuum which sends men and women to seek spiritual reality in the strangest of places. The tragedy is that they will not seek Christ unless and until their hearts are renewed by grace.

Ahaz's tragedy is that he ought to have known better. He had examples of true godliness, true salvation and true religion before him since his youth, but his unregenerate heart yearned for something different. Ultimately this is why people seek bizarre substitutes for Christianity. Their hearts are darkened and hostile to God:

> There is no one righteous, not even one;
>> there is no one who understands,
>> no one who seeks after God
>> > > (Rom. 3:10-11; Ps. 14:2).

Ahaz was punished for his faithlessness (28:5-14)

'**Therefore the Lord his God handed him over to the king of Aram... He was also given into the hands of the king of Israel**' (28:5). The alliance between these two kings, Pekah the King of Israel and Rezin the King of Aram (or Syria), is sometimes called the Syro-Ephraimite coalition. We also read of this coalition in 2 Kings 16:5-6. Its impact upon Judah is described in Isaiah 7, and its significance for the northern kingdom lies behind the prophetic message of Hosea 5:8 – 7:16. Before considering the Chronicler's version of events it is worthwhile to set the scene by surveying what we know about this alliance from other Scriptures.

Pekah, King of Israel, and Rezin, King of Aram, were forced to put an end to the feuding between their two kingdoms because of the growing influence of the Assyrian Empire to the east. In the face of a common threat they put aside their differences and concluded a defensive anti-Assyrian pact. Their concern was shared by most of the small nations in Syria and Palestine at the time (it seems that the Edomites and the Philistines were also allied to the Syro-Ephraimite axis), and their fears increased when Tiglath-Pileser III (who reigned from 745 – 727 B.C.) rose to prominence. When he became King of Assyria, Tiglath-Pileser faced simultaneously an internal revolt and threats of invasion from the north, south and east. After he secured the unity and security of his empire, he set out to expand its influence to the west, beyond the River Euphrates. He has been described by John Bright as 'the inaugurator of this period of Assyrian history, and the true founder of her empire ... an exceedingly vigorous and able ruler'.

Pekah and Rezin sought to enlist the help of Judah to resist Assyrian encroachment. Whatever his reasons, Ahaz was not willing to be part of their coalition. Efforts had been made to remove him from the throne and to replace him with a more compliant king, the son of Tabeel (Isa. 7:6). The ensuing political turmoil was the setting for Isaiah's assurance that the plans of Pekah and Rezin would come to nothing:

> Be careful, keep calm and don't be afraid. Do not lose heart because of these two smouldering stubs of firewood — because of the fierce anger of Rezin and Aram and of the son of Remaliah...

> For the head of Aram is Damascus,
> and the head of Damascus is only Rezin.
> Within sixty-five years
> Ephraim will be too shattered to be a people.
> The head of Ephraim is Samaria,
> and the head of Samaria is only Remaliah's son.

> If you do not stand firm in your faith,
>   you will not stand at all

(Isa. 7:4-9).

Furthermore the Lord offered Ahaz a sign that he would be faithful to his promise. Ahaz infamously rejected this offer, but the sign was given nevertheless. 'Therefore the Lord himself will give you a sign: The virgin will be with child and will give birth to a son, and will call him Immanuel... But before the boy knows enough to reject the wrong and choose the right, the land of the two kings you dread will be laid waste' (Isa. 7:14-16).

Isaiah's prophecy of destruction for Israel and Aram came true within only a few years. In a brilliant campaign between 734 and 732 B.C., Tiglath-Pileser conquered the Philistines, left a garrison at the Egyptian border to protect his rear, subdued Israel (2 Kings 15:29-30) and destroyed Damascus (2 Kings 16:9), killing Rezin and deporting most of the inhabitants. It was therefore Tiglath-Pileser's self-interest that moved him to take on the armies of the Syro-Ephraimite coalition, rather than Ahaz's invitation in 28:16.

The Chronicler acknowledges the existence of the Syro-Ephraimite coalition (by mentioning the two kings together in 28:5), but its strategic significance does not loom large in his thoughts. His desire was to present the northern kingdom as an erring segment of the covenant people (but connected to it nevertheless) rather than as one partner in an ungodly alliance. More attention is given to the actions of Pekah, King of Israel, and his people than to their alliance with Aram. This version of events is intended to emphasize the possibility of repentance and restoration for a sinful nation.

Returning to the narrative of Ahaz's reign, it becomes evident that Israel's invasion **'inflicted heavy casualties on him'**

and his kingdom (28:5). Although Jerusalem was not captured
by Pekah (2 Kings 16:5), there was at least one significant
military engagement and **'In one day Pekah son of Remaliah
killed a hundred and twenty thousand soldiers in Judah'**
(28:6). The casualties included several leading people: **'Zicri,
an Ephraimite warrior, killed Maaseiah the king's son,
Azrikam the officer in charge of the palace, and Elkanah,
second to the king'** (28:7). Many more were carried off to
Samaria as captives: **'The Israelites took captive from their
kinsmen two hundred thousand wives, sons and daughters. They also took a great deal of plunder, which they
carried back to Samaria'** (28:8).

The blame for these devastating losses is placed squarely
on the shoulders of Ahaz and those who joined him in idolatry: **'... because Judah had forsaken the LORD, the God
of their fathers'** (28:6). The constant theme of Chronicles is
contained in these words. Those who sin by breaking the covenant that the Lord has made with his people will themselves
suffer the consequences of their actions. There is no hiding
from the righteous judgement of God. Nor can we evade our
responsibilities by pointing to the sins of others. Ahaz was
punished for his faithlessness.

God's judgement was, however, tempered with mercy
(28:9-11). Although the northern kingdom was a sinful kingdom, there were still godly people within its bounds, and one
of them was the prophet Oded. He rebuked the Israelite army
while it was still travelling back to Samaria with its train of
Judean captives. Oded showed them how they had sinned
against God.

First of all, *they had treated the people of Judah with excessive cruelty*: **'You have slaughtered them in a rage that
reaches to heaven'** (28:9). It had been true that **'God ... was
angry with Judah'**, but his purpose was to chasten them, not

to exterminate them. This is always God's purpose when he
administers discipline. This fact has to be kept in mind by
officers of the church when they censure those who have
strayed, and by parents as they discipline their children. The
men of Israel treated the people of Judah as they did because
they had no fear of God. They had no sense of their own sinfulness, which might have tempered their ferocity with the realization that one day they too would face the judgement of
God. Hence Oded's rebuke: **'Aren't you also guilty of sins
against the LORD your God?'** (28:10). Nor had the men of
Israel any sense of God's mercy, which might have inclined
them to treat their **'fellow countrymen'** with mercy. They
behaved as cruelly as the heathen nations around them.

Then, secondly, *they had disobeyed God's law* by enslav-
ing their 'fellow countrymen': **'Now you intend to make the
men and women of Judah and Jerusalem your slaves'**
(28:10). Leviticus 25 regulated the practice of slavery in Israel:
'Because the Israelites are my servants, whom I brought out
of Egypt, they must not be sold as slaves. Do not rule over
them ruthlessly, but fear your God' (vv. 42-43). Quite apart
from the cruelty that was often associated with slavery, it was
an offence to God because the people of Israel belonged to
him and ought to be regarded as his servants. Although Israelites were allowed to sell themselves into slavery in times of
destitution, they were to be released in the seventh year (Exod.
21:2), or the Year of Jubilee (Lev. 25:39-41), whichever came
first, and furthermore no Israelite was to be forced into slavery. Abuses of slavery were a recurring sin throughout the
history of Israel, and Nehemiah had to deal with them in post-
exilic times (see Neh. 5:4-8), so the issue was one that had
relevance for the Chronicler and his readers.

Oded was not the only one to rebuke the leaders of his
people for their cruelty to the people of Judah. His warning in

28:9-11 went unheeded as the victorious procession made its way towards Samaria. **'Then some of the leaders in Ephraim'** (the leading tribe in the northern kingdom) **'confronted those who were arriving from the war'** (28:12). Even in the darkest days of the northern kingdom, during the reign of King Ahab, there were at least 7,000 people who served God (1 Kings 19:18), and one of them was Obadiah, Ahab's chief minister (1 Kings 18:3). A century and a half later there were still such men in Samaria willing to speak out for the Lord.

These godly men pleaded with their leaders not to press on in their wicked ways: **'Do you intend to add to our sin and guilt? For our guilt is already great, and his fierce anger rests on Israel'** (28:13). They may have been thinking of the idolatry that was so widely practised and have been asking their fellow countrymen not to add the sin of slavery to it. Or they may have been struck by the force of Oded's severe warning and have been asking their countrymen not to add the sin of stubbornness to that of disobedience. Those who hear God's warnings and ignore them are guilty of the most serious of sins and will be judged most severely. It would have been better for them if they had never been warned by God at all than to hear and dismiss God's Word. 'Anyone, then, who knows the good he ought to do and doesn't do it, sins' (James 4:17).

The response of the soldiers in 28:14-15 is the most encouraging part of this whole chapter: **'So the soldiers gave up the prisoners and plunder in the presence of the officials and all the assembly.'** This was an evidence that God had not abandoned the people of the northern kingdom. God had spoken to them through his servant the prophet Oded, and they were not so hardened in their disobedience that they were beyond change. They heard God's word and they repented of their sin. The message that this incident taught the Chronicler's generation after the exile was a challenging and exciting one. God was able to restore 'all Israel', and his mercy would not be restricted to the tribe of Judah.

These verses, describing the kindness of the people of Samaria, are significant. They appointed some of their number to clothe **'all who were naked'**. Furthermore, **'They provided them with clothes and sandals, food and drink, and healing balm'**; they put the weak **'on donkeys'** and took them back to **'Jericho'**. We are reminded of the man who 'fell into the hands of robbers' as he 'was going down from Jerusalem to Jericho' in our Lord's parable of the Good Samaritan in Luke 10:30-37. Significantly it was a Samaritan who 'took pity on him' and was a neighbour to the man who 'fell into the hands of robbers'. These people of Samaria in 28:14-15 were fellow citizens in Israel. They were still part of the covenant people and evidence of godliness was to be found among them.

The unfolding of these tragic events shows that there was also mercy for Judah. The southern kingdom had been punished because its people **'had forsaken the LORD, the God of their fathers'** (28:6), and **'because the LORD, the God of [their] fathers was angry with Judah'** (28:9). The result was captivity and temporary exile in Samaria. Peaceful possession of the land of Israel was a covenant blessing that God's people enjoyed so long as they remained faithful to him. When they turned their backs upon God and became covenant-breakers they could not hope to continue to enjoy that blessing. That is why exile became a foreshadowing of the eternal separation from God's mercy that the wicked suffer, and of the temporary chastisement that God's people sometimes endure as a way of bringing them to repentance.

The Chronicler's generation lived in the shadow of a far more devastating exile. In 587 B.C. Nebuchadnezzar captured Jerusalem and took most of its inhabitants to Babylon. It was many years before a remnant would return to rebuild the city

and restore the temple. But they did return! Exile may be a
sign of God's anger, but God does not remain angry for ever:

> The LORD is compassionate and gracious,
>   slow to anger, abounding in love.
> He will not always accuse,
>   nor will he harbour his anger for ever;
> he does not treat us as our sins deserve
>   or repay us according to our iniquities.
> For as high as the heavens are above the earth,
>   so great is his love for those who fear him;
> as far as the east is from the west,
>   so far has he removed our transgressions from us
>
> (Ps.103:8-12).

Even a disaster as great as the Babylonian exile was not
beyond remedy. In his mercy God is able to restore his people
and heal their scars.

> The LORD builds up Jerusalem;
>   he gathers the exiles of Israel.
> He heals the broken-hearted
>   and binds up their wounds
>
> (Ps. 147:2-3).

Sometimes we suffer terribly because of our sins. We may bear
the scars of a sinful relationship, or we may destroy our health
by adopting a sinful lifestyle, or we may cause lasting offence
to others, or we may fall foul of the law and have to pay the
penalty. These are situations that believers sometimes have to
live with, and they are deeply distressing. But the grace of
God is held out to those who will repent and seek the Lord.
The grace of God is able, not just to forgive our sins, but to

restore our lives as well. Addressing the post-exilic generation, the prophet Joel had the same message: 'I will repay you for the years the locusts have eaten' (Joel 2:25).

Ahaz persisted in his unfaithfulness (28:16-25)

Ahaz would not repent and seek the Lord. Sometimes adversity forces sinners to examine their lives and see the error of their ways. This was to be the experience of Manasseh (33:12). The prodigal son, depicted in our Lord's parable, 'came to his senses' while he was destitute, feeding pigs in a foreign land (Luke 15:17-20). However, adversity is not guaranteed to bring sinners to repentance. Ahaz responded to his humiliation at the hands of Pekah, King of Israel, by turning even further from the Lord. Let us consider what he did.

1. Ahaz sought help from the King of Assyria (28:16-21)

The Edomites and Philistines were satellites of the Syro-Ephraimite coalition. **'The Edomites had again come and attacked Judah and carried away prisoners, while the Philistines had raided towns in the foothills and in the Negev of Judah'** (28:17-18). They seized the opportunity presented by Judah's weakness to advance their interests. The gains of the Philistines are listed in 28:18, while 2 Kings 16:6 tells us that the Edomites occupied the strategic port city of Elath on the Red Sea coast. These attacks were God's judgement on Ahaz and Judah. **'The LORD had humbled Judah because of Ahaz king of Israel, for he had promoted wickedness in Judah and had been most unfaithful to the LORD'** (28:19).

Unfortunately Ahaz did not respond by repenting and seeking help from the Lord God of Israel. Instead he turned to the King of Assyria. Strategically this was a foolish move, and a costly one! '**Ahaz took some of the things from the temple of the** LORD **and from the royal palace and from the princes and presented them to the king of Assyria.**' Tiglath-Pileser III did not need a second invitation to get involved in the affairs of Judah. The Philistines and Edomites (as subsidiary members of the Syro-Ephraimite coalition) were his natural enemies and he wanted an excuse to make war with them. Judah too was within his territorial ambitions and it was only a matter of time before the King of Assyria would come to subdue Judah, not to help her.

Ahaz's actions in 28:16 were also a demonstration of unbelief. Jehovah is often described as the helper of his people (Ps. 10:14; 27:9; 118:7; Deut. 33:29; Isa. 50:9). The Chronicler has sought to illustrate this truth through his history (see 14:11; 25:8; 32:8). King Asa was censured because 'even in his illness he did not seek help' from the Lord (16:12). Likewise Ahaz rejected the Lord by refusing to seek his help and by turning to the King of Assyria instead.

Needless to say, Ahaz did not get the help that he had expected. '**Ahaz ... presented them** [his treasures] **to the king of Assyria, but that did not help him**' (28:21). '**Tiglath-Pileser came to him, but gave him trouble instead of help**' (28:20). Ahaz lost his independence and became a vassal of the Assyrian king. This is what happens when we rely upon the arm of flesh. This is how God demonstrates the insufficiency of human resources and the unreliability of men. When we are too proud or stubborn to turn to the Lord for help, all that we achieve is to cut ourselves off from the only help that can bring lasting benefit.

> Oh! what peace we often forfeit,
> Oh! what needless pain we bear,
> All because we do not carry
> Everything to God in prayer!

Have we trials and temptations?
Is there trouble anywhere?
We should never be discouraged:
Take it to the Lord in prayer.
Can we find a friend so faithful,
Who will all our troubles share?
Jesus knows our every weakness;
Take it to the Lord in prayer.

2. *Ahaz sought help from the gods of Syria* (28:22-25)

Ahaz was summoned to Damascus (the new centre of Assyrian influence in the region) to pay homage to Tiglath-Pileser III. **'In his time of trouble King Ahaz became even more unfaithful to the LORD. He offered sacrifices to the gods of Damascus'** (28:22-23). It has been suggested that these 'gods of Damascus' were Assyrian deities whose worship was foisted upon the nations they conquered. However, most historians have concluded from the evidence available that the Assyrians did not force the worship of their gods upon subject peoples, but rather encouraged them to continue worshipping their own gods and to seek their favour.

The gods that Ahaz worshipped were the Syrian deities who, he believed, had helped Rezin to inflict damage upon Judah when the Syro-Ephraimite coalition was at the height of its powers. **'He thought, "Since the gods of the kings of Aram have helped them, I will sacrifice to them so that they will help me"'** (28:23). Did it ever occur to Ahaz that these same gods had been powerless to help Rezin against the Assyrians? Ahaz worshipped them nevertheless, and **'They were his downfall'** (28:23). Still he refused to seek help from the Lord.

Ahaz was not content to worship false gods in Damascus (28:24-25). These verses demonstrate his love of innovation.

He '**set up altars at every street corner in Jerusalem. In every town in Judah he built high places to burn sacrifices to other gods.**' He brought heathen worship into the precincts of the temple in Jerusalem. 2 Kings 16:10-12 describes how Ahaz was so impressed with one of the altars he saw in Damascus that he ordered a drawing to be made so that a replica could be fashioned for use in front of the temple: 'He saw an altar in Damascus and sent to Uriah the priest a sketch of the altar, with detailed plans for its construction. So Uriah the priest built an altar in accordance with all the plans that King Ahaz had sent from Damascus... When the king came back from Damascus and saw the altar, he approached it and presented offerings on it.' Religion flourished in Judah during the reign of Ahaz. New ideas, new gods and new altars multiplied. Some may have thought that these innovations were a sign of progress. In fact they were evidence of spiritual decay.

The consequences of Ahaz's innovations are described in 28:24: '**Ahaz gathered together the furnishings from the temple of the God and took them away. He shut the doors of the LORD's temple.**' In Ahaz's Jerusalem true worship was driven out by heathen innovation. What was meant to supplement the temple soon made the temple redundant. What started out as an alternative to what God had commanded soon became the only form of worship that was tolerated. Truth and error can never cohabit. One will eventually drive out the other.

Ahaz's apostasy illustrates the unstable equilibrium of men and women who have turned their backs on God. Once they cast off God's restraining hand, they descend deeper and deeper into sin. Every experience of life seems to drive them further from God. God's mercy elicits a response of sneering ingratitude. God's judgement evokes vindictive contempt. Typical of this attitude are the words of a man describing the ordeal which befell the Australian city of Darwin when it was destroyed by Cyclone Tracy on Christmas Day in 1974. He boasted with a sneer: 'God tried to kill me, and I beat him.' God laughs at such foolishness and will bring every word and action under his righteous judgement.

God saw this approach to life when he looked upon fallen mankind in the time of Noah: 'The LORD saw how great man's wickedness on the earth had become, and that every inclination of the thoughts of his heart was only evil all the time' (Gen. 6:5). Paul observed the same thing in the Greek and Roman world of his day and described in it in Romans 3:10-18. Apart from the renewing grace of God sinners will always prefer evil to good, even though they are confronted with clear evidence of the destructive consequences of their sins. Men like Ahaz will never be frightened or beaten into repentance. Only the 'new birth' brings about godly change, and only men and women who are new creatures in Christ Jesus will delight in true worship and godly living.

The life of Ahaz summed up (28:26-27)

Nothing good is said about Ahaz in this whole chapter. This is unusual in the Chronicler's history. The same silence is found only in his accounts of Amon and the four very short accounts of the last kings of Judah — Jehoahaz, Jehoiakim, Jehoiachin and Zedekiah. There was something good to say even about such kings as Abijah, Joash and Manasseh.

God's displeasure with Ahaz was demonstrated even on his deathbed: **'Ahaz rested with his fathers and was buried in the city of Jerusalem, but he was not placed in the tombs of the kings of Israel'** (28:27). He did not follow in the ways of David and the good kings of Israel; therefore it was not fitting that he should be buried 'in the tombs of the kings of Israel'.

Ahaz had consistently looked in the wrong places for help. Now in death, when only God could deliver him, he had no one to help. He had no Saviour to guide him through 'the valley of the shadow of death'. He had grasped at straws all his life, and in death he had nothing to cling on to. He demonstrates the tragedy described in Jonah 2:8: 'Those who cling to worthless idols forfeit the grace that could be theirs.' Sinners spend their whole lives chasing shadows and they neglect the salvation that is real. Are you trusting in the Saviour whose help never fails, or are you grasping at straws?

19.
Hezekiah: first steps to reformation

Please read 2 Chronicles 29:1-36

Hezekiah was one of the great kings of Judah. Evidently the Chronicler believed that he was a significant figure in the history of Israel, for he devoted more space to Hezekiah's reign than to any king since Solomon. He has been described as the real hero of the book of Chronicles. The next four chapters describe the twenty-nine years that he reigned in Jerusalem.

Some may find it hard to share our historian's enthusiasm for Hezekiah. He may seem a very remote figure. He is separated from us by the centuries — having reigned some 2,700 years ago. He ruled a far-off country that was very different from our own. Although Hezekiah worshipped the same God as we do, he lived through a different stage in God's plan of salvation. However, what ought to make him of particular interest to us is the fact that he was a reforming king.

Hezekiah came to the throne at a time of great national wickedness and widespread apostasy. Although it is not easy to pinpoint the exact dates of his reign (scholars have two main theories) we will assume, for the purposes of this commentary, that he reigned from 715–687 B.C. and that he came to the throne as king in his own right after a thirteen-year co-regency with his father King Ahaz. The wickedness of Ahaz had poisoned the spiritual life of Judah. The vast majority of the people were coldly indifferent to the things of God. The temple had been closed for lack of interest. Among the few who loved the Lord there was profound hopelessness. Just like the psalmist of a previous generation they might well have asked, 'When the foundations are being destroyed, what can the righteous do?' (Ps. 11:3).

Can you see the similarities with our own day? It is estimated that less than 10% of the population of the United Kingdom attends church. In Australia it is estimated that the figure is less than 5%. In the city where I live there is a large building near the city centre which used to be a church attended by many worshippers. Today it is the venue for a night club. Spiritual apostasy is producing the bitter fruit of national wickedness. Commitment within marriage is considered to be an unattainable ideal. Sexual immorality is not only tolerated, but celebrated. Corrupt business practices that we have traditionally associated with heathen nations are now becoming common in nations formerly known for their Christian principles. Those who campaign to uphold biblical morality are considered by many to be offensive. What can the righteous do?

Sometimes we feel that there is not a great deal that we can do, and we give up in despair. Shortly after passing my driving test I was involved in a car crash. I am thankful to say that I was unhurt, but the car I had been driving was damaged beyond repair. As I walked around the wreckage of the vehicle my first thought was: 'How can I fix this?' It did not take long for me to realize that the mangled remains could not be mended. There was absolutely nothing that I could do to fix it. Panic gave way to despair. That is how many Christians feel as they look at the spiritual state of their nation. But there is something that the godly can do. Hezekiah shows us the way.

As we have already seen, the Chronicler's history is a very practical (as well as a very overlooked) history. It is not just a rerun of the book of Kings. There are significant differences. Chronicles tells us much about Hezekiah that Kings does not.

It was written for the Jews who were living in the land of Judah after the nation had returned from exile. That is why it serves a different purpose from that of Kings.

Let me illustrate. In the aftermath of some terrible disaster (such as an earthquake, or train crash, or outbreak of disease) people often want answers to their questions. Normally they ask two types of question. First of all, they ask, 'Why did it happen in the first place?' Then, secondly, they ask, 'What must we do now to stop anything similar happening ever again?'

The destruction of Jerusalem in 587 B.C. prompted the people of Judah to ask similar questions. The book of Kings was written to answer the first question — it pointed to generations of unfaithfulness. Chronicles was written to answer the second — it points out the sins which God hates and the behaviour which God commends. It is a history for those who want to learn the lessons of the past as they rebuild and reform their nation. It answers the question: 'What can the godly do?' There is something that godly people can do even in the midst of national apostasy. In 2 Chronicles 29 we see how Hezekiah made a start to do just that.

Hezekiah called the Levites to consecrate themselves (29:1-19)

Hezekiah was a young man: **'Hezekiah was twenty-five years old when he became king'** (29:1). He was at the height of his powers and he was eager to serve the Lord. The Chronicler gives us a glowing summary of his twenty-nine-year reign: **'He did what was right in the eyes of the LORD, just as his father David had done'** (29:2). David was the highest and best example of kingship in Israel. He was the king who supremely foreshadowed the royal Messiah. There is no greater tribute that the Chronicler could have paid to a king than to compare him to David. Apart from Hezekiah, only Jehoshaphat (17:3) and Josiah (34:2) are described as walking in the ways of David.

With all the enthusiasm of a young man, Hezekiah wasted no time. He was eager to do what was right. **'In the first month of the first year of his reign, he opened the doors of the temple of the LORD.'** Some commentators argue that this was the very first thirty days of his reign, while others maintain that it was the first month after a new calendar year had commenced. In either case we note that Hezekiah did not waste time. He did not let the years drift by as he bemoaned the state of his nation. He saw the urgency of the situation and he grasped the opportunities that he had as king to do something to turn things around. He acted courageously. May God give us the resolve to be up and doing the things that the Lord puts at hand for us to do.

Hezekiah *focused on the temple* (29:3). The temple ought to have been a symbol of God's presence among his people. Instead it had become a symbol of national apostasy and national shame. It was shut up and desolate. All too often we see derelict church buildings. Sometimes the windows are smashed and the roof has been stripped and the doors are boarded up. In the past congregations of worshippers gathered to praise God in those buildings, but now there is an eerie silence within the ghostly ruins. That was the sight that greeted Hezekiah when he went to the temple. Where would he start to restore the temple to its former glory?

Hezekiah started by *gathering the Levites* (29:4-5). After he opened the decaying doors of the temple, **'He brought in the priests and the Levites.'** The living stones of God's people are always more important than buildings. Hezekiah called together both *the priests* who ministered at the altar (he referred to them specifically in 29:11 when he addressed those chosen by God **'to minister before him and to burn**

incense'), and *the Levites* who assisted the priests in maintaining the temple and its facilities. He challenged them in three ways.

1. A history lesson

Hezekiah made them face up to their past unfaithfulness: **'Our fathers were unfaithful; they did evil in the eyes of the LORD our God and forsook him'** (29:6). During the reign of Hezekiah's father, King Ahaz (whose influence is mentioned later, in 29:19), the temple had fallen into disuse. The Levites and priests had gone along with the prevailing mood of national apostasy. They had left undone those things they ought to have done: **'They turned their faces away from the LORD's dwelling-place and turned their backs on him. They also shut the doors of the portico and put out the lamps. They did not burn incense or present any burnt offerings at the sanctuary to the God of Israel'** (29:6-7).

Furthermore, unwarranted innovations had been brought into the nation's worship. In 2 Kings 16:10-12 we are told of an idea that Ahaz had while he was visiting Damascus to pay tribute to the King of Assyria. There, as we noted in the previous chapter, he saw a heathen altar and ordered Uriah the high priest to build him a replica for use in Jerusalem.

These sins of omission and commission brought God's anger upon the whole nation of Judah, but the people were very slow to learn from God's judgements. Stubbornness and self-righteousness made it difficult for them to imagine that their difficulties were the result of their own sins. Hezekiah's words allowed for no self-deception. He pointed to their sinful history and its tragic consequences: **'Therefore the anger of the LORD has fallen on Judah and Jerusalem ... as you can see with your own eyes. That is why our fathers have fallen**

by the sword and why our sons and daughters and wives
are in captivity' (29:8-9).

2. *His own example* (29:10)

Here are words of personal resolution: **'Now I intend to make
a covenant with the LORD, the God of Israel, so that his
fierce anger will turn away from us.'** Hezekiah's actions
were a response to the mercy that God had shown to Israel in
keeping with his covenant promises. It was God who had taken
the initiative by awakening Hezekiah's heart and opening his
eyes to the needs of his people. Love for God now compelled
Hezekiah to take his stand for the Lord. He expressed himself
in the language of covenant renewal. When he said, 'I intend
to make a covenant with the LORD,' he was not committing
himself to do anything new; he was solemnizing and emphasizing his obligations as the Lord's anointed ruler over the
people of Israel. Even if the Levites were not prepared to stand
with him, Hezekiah was ready to stand up and be counted. He
would say publicly, 'I am for the Lord.'

3. *A plan of action* (29:5)

There were two distinct phases to Hezekiah's plan. First of
all, he said to the Levites, **'Consecrate yourselves'**; then,
secondly, he told them, **'Consecrate the temple of the
LORD, the God of your fathers.'** The order of events, as
Hezekiah sought to overturn many years of spiritual decay,
is significant.

Reformation begins with personal consecration. Before a
surgeon begins an operation he must have clean hands and a
clean scalpel. Before a soldier goes into battle he must have
a clean rifle which will not jam when it is fired. Similarly,

Hezekiah wanted consecrated men for the work of reformation. That is what God wants of his people today so that they can be a force for good in the world. Salt must be salty. Light must be bright. Paul wanted the Philippians to become 'blameless and pure, children of God without fault in a crooked and depraved generation', so that they might 'shine like stars in the universe as [they held] out the word of life' (Phil. 2:15-16). We must be holy. Do we want to see the church revived and our nation reformed? If so, we must ask ourselves questions such as, 'Am I praying earnestly every day? Am I feeding on God's Word every day? Am I regular in family devotions and in attending congregational worship? Am I diligently putting my sins to death?' **'My sons, do not be negligent now, for the Lord has chosen you to stand before him and serve him, to minister before him and to burn incense'** (29:11).

It is amazing what a few godly men can achieve when they consecrate themselves to God. Some of these men are named in 29:12-14. The names of the Levites listed in these verses may otherwise be unfamiliar to us. Our tongues stumble over them as we try to read them aloud. Perhaps our eyes are tempted to skim over them. But we should not pass over them so quickly! The Holy Spirit has recorded the names of these Levites in Holy Scripture so that we might consider them. Lists of God's servants are a common feature in Chronicles. Here we find recorded the names of a few ordinary Levites — you will notice that there were only fourteen of them. However, they were consecrated men.

What an influence they exerted in Jerusalem! Never underestimate what God can do with a few consecrated men. Remember that the missionary endeavours of the New Testament church started with a small band of disciples, but they were consecrated men. Church history provides us with other examples. There were the students at Oxford University in the 1730s who gathered to encourage each other in prayer and Bible study and holy living. They were known as the 'Holy Club', or 'Methodists', because of their disciplined commitment to God. Among these men were John and Charles Wesley and George Whitefield. Through their preaching many thousands were converted during the revivals of the eighteenth century.

Or there were the two Church of England bishops who were burned at the stake in 1555 — Hugh Latimer and Nicholas Ridley. The enemies of the reformation thought that by putting to death the handful of leading Reformers they would silence the preaching of the gospel. Humanly speaking they may have been right, for the evangelical cause had yet to reach the soul of the nation. Yet the death of these martyrs provoked a reaction that their persecutors never thought possible. Latimer encouraged his companion with the following famous words: 'Be of good comfort, Master Ridley, and play the man. We shall this day light such a candle, by God's grace, in England, as I trust shall never be put out.' He was right! That testimony has never been extinguished.

The second part of Hezekiah's plan is described in 29:15-17, where we see how the influence of these consecrated Levites started to bear fruit. Now that they were personally consecrated they were ready to bring about real change. They purified the temple. The task took them two weeks. It took them one week to clear the rubbish from the courtyard so that they could reach the main door of the temple. **'They began the consecration on the first day of the first month, and by the eighth day of the month they reached the portico of the Lord.'** With a path cleared they were able to clear away the debris that had gathered up inside the temple. **'For eight more days they consecrated the temple ... itself, finishing in the sixteenth day of the first month.'** Then they reported back to Hezekiah that their mission was accomplished. **'Then they went in to King Hezekiah and reported: "We have**

purified the entire temple of the LORD... We have prepared and consecrated all the articles that King Ahaz removed in his unfaithfulness while he was king. They are now in front of the Lord's altar"' (29:18-19).

The work of the Levites was more than just a long overdue spring clean. They physically removed accumulated debris and objects of heathen worship. **'They brought out to the court-yard of the LORD's temple everything unclean that they found in the temple of the LORD. The Levites took it and carried it out to the Kidron valley'** (29:16). The Kidron Valley lay at the bottom of a steep slope beside the Temple Mount. Casting out these objects was a sign that they were repudiating false gods and their influence.

Furthermore the Levites reinstated the prescribed temple utensils which had obviously gone missing during the reign of King Ahaz: **'We have purified the entire temple of the LORD, the altar of burnt offering with all its utensils, and the table for setting out the consecrated bread, with all its articles'** (29:18). When the worship of Jehovah was being neglected it was natural that these forks and fire-pans should be lost through carelessness, or sold off on account of greed (29:19). Returning these utensils to their proper use was a sign that the Levites were once more fulfilling their proper function and seeking to serve the true God. They were going to worship God's way. They were going to listen to God's Word. They were going to seek God's way of salvation.

The tragedy of the derelict temple was that the channels of spiritual blessing were blocked. The temple was where God met with his people. There he showed them the way of salvation. There he heard their prayers and forgave their sins. The people went to the temple to cry for mercy. Even far away in the belly of the great fish, Jonah remembered the Lord and his temple and prayed for mercy (Jonah 2:4,7). However, with the temple closed, the well of spiritual blessing had dried up and the means of grace were no longer available to the people. The people were not learning about God. There was little likelihood of sinners being awakened or believers being encouraged. That is why Hezekiah started reformation at the temple and sought to restore the means of grace.

Today there is a great deal of evil in the world that we as Christians are powerless to stop. However, we can begin by looking at ourselves and our churches. We can seek reformation there, just as the Levites did. Is there anything in us that blocks the channels of grace? Does the grace of God flow through us to others? Are our churches gospel-preaching churches? This means more than having evangelical statements of faith and evangelical sermons! Do people hear the gospel from the body of believing people? Do people see the gospel in us? Are we zealous for the gospel? Are we able to articulate the gospel? Do people go away from us saying, 'What a great Saviour!'? If not, then we shall never make much of an impact on the world around us. We cannot do that on our own. Only the grace of God transforming lives through the gospel of Christ can reform nations. Is the debris cleared away so that the grace of God can shine through us to reach others?

Hezekiah called the people to worship the Lord (29:20-36)

Hezekiah did not stop at temple reform. He was eager to carry the reformation beyond the Levites to the nation at large. He showed the same breathless enthusiasm to be active in serving the Lord when he called the whole nation to return to the Lord. **'Early the next morning King Hezekiah gathered the city officials together and went up to the temple of the Lord'** (29:20).

This was a national movement. The 'city officials' were the civil administrators and they too were caught up in the reformation. In recent years it has become fashionable for politicians and public figures to talk about their religious faith. It is even considered good that they have a 'personal faith' to guide them. It seems to make them more compassionate. However, this personal faith must not have too many public implications. Certainly it must not lead them to claim that Christianity is the only true religion, or that biblical morality is to be the basis for the law of the land. Government must be neutral and accepting of all religions, we are told, for the personal faith of individuals cannot be enforced on society. Hezekiah, however, cast neutrality to the winds. He, as king, called his government officials to support and to encourage the true religion of Jehovah. Offerings were made **'for the kingdom'** (for the sins of the royal family), **'for the sanctuary'** (for the sins of the priests and Levites) **'and for Judah'** (for the sins of the ordinary people — 29:21). These sacrifices drew the nation's attention back to the very basics of a right relationship with God. The people had turned their backs on God. They needed to be restored. How could this be brought about?

Hezekiah led the people of Judah back to the temple. A national ceremony of rededicating the temple is described in the rest of this chapter. Three types of sacrifices were offered as part of this rededication ceremony and they point the way towards a right relationship with God.

1. A sacrifice of atonement (29:21-24)

The first sacrifice to be offered as part of this rededication ceremony was called a **'sin offering'**. The king and his officials **'brought seven bulls, seven rams, seven male lambs and seven male goats as a sin offering'** (29:21). The goats were brought before the king and his people, who then **'laid their hands'** on them (29:23). In this way they said, 'We are sinners; we deserve to die; may these animals die instead.' The priests **'slaughtered'** the animals (29:22) and sprinkled the blood on the altar. (According to Leviticus 1:3-5, the worshipper normally slaughtered the sin offering when he brought his animal to the altar. On account of the fact that this was a national ceremony of rededication and repentance, the king and the whole assembly collectively laid their hands on the goat to be sacrificed.)

As a result of the sprinkling of blood the sinner's guilt was taken away. The Hebrew word for the 'sin offering' is derived from the verb meaning 'to cover over'. The forgiveness extended to the sinner is the forgiveness of atonement, which removes guilt. The guilt of the sinner is not covered over only to be revealed at some future date, like skeletons which are liable to come out of the cupboard. No, it is forgiveness purchased by the blood of the substitute. No one can come to God without having had their guilt taken away, and there is no forgiveness until the penalty that sin deserves is paid by the shedding of blood. This principle still holds good. However, today we do not bring bulls and goats to God; rather we look to the cross. Here is the beginning of true reformation, when men and women look to Jesus Christ, 'the Lamb of God who takes away the sin of the world', then lay their hands on him and say, 'Save me, make me clean by your sprinkled blood.'

2. A sacrifice of consecration (29:25-30)

Afterwards the people brought sacrifices that are described as 'burnt offerings'. Hezekiah's order that both burnt offerings and sin offerings be brought is found in 29:24; how the burnt offerings were offered is described in 29:25-30. The significant feature of the **'burnt offering'** is that the whole carcass was consumed on the altar. While only the blood of the sin offering and the fat of the fellowship offering were consumed, all the flesh, bones, skin and inner parts of the burnt offering were given to God. This was a picture of how completely the worshipper consecrated himself to God when he cast himself upon the Lord for mercy.

David, the great sinner who experienced great mercy, described his deep gratitude and total consecration in Psalm 51:19:

> Then there will be righteous sacrifices,
>   whole burnt offerings to delight you;
>   then bulls will be offered on your altar.

Paul describes the only appropriate response to the gospel in Romans 12:1: 'Therefore, I urge you, brothers, in view of God's mercy, to offer your bodies as living sacrifices, holy and pleasing to God.' Examples of this total self-giving are found in the widow of Zarephath, who gave her last oil and flour to prepare a meal for Elijah (1 Kings 17:10-16), and the widow who gave her last mite to the temple treasury (Luke 21:1-4). In 1732 Leonard Dober set out from the Moravian community at Herrenhut in Germany with the intention of taking the gospel to slaves on the Caribbean island of St Thomas. It was not unusual for the Moravians to send missionaries overseas, but what made Leonard Dober so remarkable was his plan to sell himself as a slave so that he could get alongside the slaves who laboured on the sugar plantations of St Thomas. Here was total self-giving to the Lord.

Notice that the Levites did not just stand and watch as the burnt offerings were offered; they sang. This was part of their sacrifice. They gave to the Lord offerings, not just from their flocks and material possessions; they also brought sacrifices from their hearts and from their lips. 'Love the LORD your God with all your heart and with all your soul and with all your strength' (Deut. 6:5) Notice also, in passing, that the Levites accompanied the singing with **'cymbals, harps and lyres'**. These were not used to make the whole spectacle more interesting and enjoyable for those who were there. The instruments were used only as and when God commanded (29:25), and only while the sacrifice was being offered (29:28-29). The instruments were not essential for the singing of praise, but were inextricably linked to the sacrificial system.

3. A sacrifice of thanksgiving (29:31-35)

These verses describe the scale and the zeal of the people's response to Hezekiah's call, which was also a response to God's grace. God's way of salvation had made it possible for this sinful nation to return to him and find acceptance. The working of God's Spirit had inclined their hearts back to God to seek forgiveness. After forgiveness and acceptance the people of Judah acknowledged God's mercy. First of all, the priests offered the great national offerings for the sins of the whole community. Then many individuals offered their own personal tributes of gratitude.

Every year in Britain the second Sunday in November is set aside to remember the sacrifice of those who died fighting for their country. At war memorials throughout the land ceremonies of remembrance are held at which wreaths are laid as tributes to those who died. Wreaths are laid on behalf of the armed forces, ex-servicemen's associations and government bodies, and by local dignitaries. After all these wreaths have been laid, ordinary people lay their personal tributes by the war memorial as they remember a loved one who died many years ago. This is one of the most moving parts of the ceremony. Similarly, the people of Judah brought their personal tributes to acknowledge the grace of God to them and their families. Their tributes are described as **'thank-offerings'**, **'fellowship offerings'** and **'drink offerings'**.

Thank-offerings (29:31)

These were songs of thanksgiving and praise. They were verbal acknowledgements that accompanied the burnt offerings. The word for thank-offering is derived from the Hebrew verb for confessing sin and praising God. Interestingly, Psalm 100 is entitled 'A psalm for giving thanks'. Thanksgiving is an essential part of our worship (see Ps. 95:2). We are to declare that God is great, for he has forgiven our sins.

Fellowship offerings (29:35)

These were animal sacrifices. Only the fat was burnt: **'... the fat of the fellowship offerings ... that accompanied the burnt offerings'**. The remaining portions of the sacrificial animal were shared between the priest and people, so that they could sit down together to eat. In the Scriptures there is no greater way of expressing the fact that two people delight in each other than when they sit down at a common table to eat together. The fellowship offering is a pointer to the fellowship that believers enjoy with their Saviour after redemption is accomplished. When Christ sits down after he has completed his sacrificial atonement (see Heb. 1:3), he enjoys blessed communion with his people. This is the invitation that he issues to his beloved church: 'Here I am! I stand at the door and knock. If anyone hears my voice and opens the door, I will come in and eat with him, and he with me' (Rev. 3:20).

Drink offerings (29:35)

These were offerings of wine that were brought along with the burnt offering (see Exod. 29:40). The offered wine was poured out at the altar. Drink offerings were brought during the major festivals, at new moons, on the Sabbath and on the Day of Atonement (see Num. 28-29). Significantly, too, drink offerings were made during the dedication of a Nazirite (see Num. 6:15-17). Nazirites were people who consecrated themselves to God by taking vows to abstain from wine or anything derived from the vine. They were examples of willing self-dedication to God. The pouring out of the drink offering was a symbol of the servant of God pouring out his life in service to God.

The Christian believer makes the same self-offering when he gives his life to the Lord. In our worship we say, 'You have bought me with your blood; I am yours. Use me in your service.'

Take my life and let it be
Consecrated, Lord, to thee.

Paul certainly looked at his life as an offering poured out to serve his Saviour: 'But even if I am being poured out like a drink offering on the sacrifice and service coming from your faith, I am glad and rejoice with all of you' (Phil. 2:17). 'For I am already being poured out like a drink offering, and the time has come for my departure. I have fought the good fight, I have finished the race, I have kept the faith' (2 Tim. 4:6).

Of the 600 bulls sacrificed (29:33), seventy were from the whole assembly (29:32), while the remaining 530 were brought by private individuals. Of the 3,000 sheep and goats offered

(29:33), 300 were from the whole assembly (29:32), while the other 2,700 were brought by private individuals. This indicated the extent of their new-found zeal for the Lord's house. The priests were overwhelmed by the nation's response. They **'were too few to skin all the burnt offerings'** (29:34). It was the consecrated Levites who were God's men for the moment, **'for the Levites had been more conscientious in consecrating themselves than the priests had been'**.

God was evidently moving in the hearts of his people to bring about such a widespread return to himself. The root cause of this national reformation is indicated in 29:36: **'Hezekiah and all the people rejoiced at what God had brought about for his people, because it was done so quickly.'** It was not Hezekiah, or the people, or their leaders, who had brought about this change in Judah; it was the Lord! When God rends the heavens and comes down among his people great things start to happen.

It is humbling to recognize our own powerlessness to change the world around us. There is so much that we cannot change. But when God moves to revive and reform, then nothing is impossible. Things change more rapidly than we can ever imagine. Revival came to the Scottish parish of Cambuslang in the spring of 1742. For eleven years the parish minister, William McCulloch, had preached the gospel faithfully but had seen little fruit. For the previous year he had preached consistently on the nature and the necessity of the new birth. 'Ye must be born again,' he continually stressed. Yet little appeared to happen until 14 February 1742, when McCulloch preached from the message of John 3:3, 'on which he had been insisting for a long time before'. Thereafter sinners were awakened — so many that McCulloch could not counsel them all. Crowds thronged outside his manse seeking to find peace for their souls. At the July communion season that year over 20,000 people gathered to hear the preaching of the gospel. This was more than anyone in the parish had dared to expect only a few months earlier. God's blessing came very quickly.

When God begins to revive his people he brings about real change in the life of a nation. He brings about changes that we would have otherwise thought to be impossible. In the meantime, what can we do? We begin by consecrating ourselves to serve the Lord.

20.
Hezekiah: the great Passover feast

Please read 2 Chronicles 30:1-27

Mealtimes are important landmarks in our daily routine. They mark out the morning, afternoon and evening times of our day. Many important activities take place around meal-tables. Obviously we are nourished by the food we eat, but we also interact with each other at meal-tables. Businessmen put together deals in the course of meals, politicians network over meals, and families unite around the table at mealtimes. One of the unfortunate results of hectic modern lifestyles is that many families today do not have a time when everyone sits down together to eat and talk without interruption from the television and other distractions. As a result family unity is fragile.

In our church families, too, mealtimes are important. God's people can enjoy rich times of fellowship as they share their food. A great deal of pastoral work can be done very naturally as we sit down to eat together. It should come as no surprise that God uses these times to bless his people.

In New Testament times believers gathered for the Lord's Supper (a sacramental meal) and for love feasts (simple fellowship meals referred to in Jude 12). The kingdom of heaven is described as a great banquet. 'Jesus spoke to them again in parables, saying: "The kingdom of heaven is like a king who prepared a wedding banquet for his son. He sent his servants to those who had been invited to the banquet to tell them to come…"' (Matt. 22:1-3). When our Lord returns in glory his people will sit down with him to partake of the 'wedding supper of the Lamb' (see Rev. 19:9).

In Old Testament times the people of Israel celebrated three great annual festivals. Each of these involved sitting down together to eat.

In the seventh month they celebrated the Feast of Tabernacles, which reminded them of God's goodness to them as they travelled through the wilderness. It was celebrated after the harvest had been gathered, and was a harvest thanksgiving.

In the third month they celebrated the Feast of Weeks, or Pentecost. Pentecost commemorated the giving of the law at Sinai and was celebrated at the beginning of the harvest. As the firstfruits of the harvest were offered to God it was also known as the Day of Firstfruits.

But the greatest of all the feasts was the one which was celebrated in the first month of the year and which was called the Feast of the Passover, or the Feast of Unleavened Bread. It commemorated the night when Israel became a free nation. On that night God overcame Pharaoh's refusal to let the people go and led the Israelites out of slavery in Egypt. Until they had settled in Egypt the Israelites were merely a large family. While in Egypt they were slaves. Now they became the redeemed people of God. In Exodus 19:5-6 Moses explained the significance of what God had done: 'Now if you obey me fully and keep my covenant, then out of all nations you will be my treasured possession. Although the whole earth is mine, you will be for me a kingdom of priests and a holy nation.' The Passover feast celebrated a new beginning in Israel's history, when the nation was consecrated to God to serve him alone.

It is no accident that, in God's providence, reformation came to Hezekiah's kingdom just as it was time to celebrate Passover. Like many other things in Judah, the Passover had been

neglected for a very long time. As we learned in the previous
chapter, Hezekiah set out to turn back the tide of national
apostasy in Judah. He had started by calling the priests and
Levites to consecrate themselves; then he restored the temple
to its rightful place as the focus of the nation's worship, and
here, in 2 Chronicles 30, he called his people to celebrate the
Passover again.

Calling the nation together (30:1-12)

The great Passover Feast at the beginning of Hezekiah's reign
took place in **'the temple of the Lord in Jerusalem'** (30:1).
Some modern commentators have suggested that a centralized Passover was only introduced during the reign of King
Josiah, almost a century later. It is claimed that for many centuries the Passover had been celebrated by Hebrew families in
their own homes and villages in the manner laid down in Exodus
12:1-28, and that a centralized Passover, as prescribed in
Deuteronomy 16:5-8, was a later regulation written into the
Pentateuch to justify subsequent practice. Those who hold to
this hypothesis speculate that the Chronicler uses history to
achieve the same end, by reading back into Hezekiah's time a
practice that had become the norm in post-exilic times.

This idea, of course, rests upon a thoroughly unsatisfac-
tory approach to the Old Testament. The assumption is made
that the Old Testament Scriptures — from the Pentateuch
through to the historical narratives — are a patchwork of fragments which sometimes contradict each other, and that the
writers of Scripture gave more attention to their pet themes
than to historical accuracy. The evidence of Joshua 5:10 (when
the Passover was celebrated in a united national festival just
as the people entered the promised land, as envisaged by Moses
in Deuteronomy 16:1-8) indicates that the celebration of the

Passover at a central, national location was not a later innovation, but can be dated back to the time of Moses. Furthermore, if the Chronicler had been rewriting history to legitimize later traditions it is hard to believe that he would have invented the shortcomings of Hezekiah's Passover, as they are recorded in 30:2-3,15-18.

Hezekiah called the people together to celebrate the Passover **'in the second month'** of the year (30:2). This was one month later than the date prescribed in Exodus 12:2; Leviticus 23:5 and Deuteronomy 16:1 (the fourteenth day of the first month). The Hebrew calendar recognized the significance of the events which took place on the night that God led his people out of Egypt by making the month in which Passover was celebrated the first month of the new year. However, the people in Hezekiah's time were not ready to celebrate the Passover on the fourteenth day of the first month. The priests, in particular, were not ready to do what would be expected of them during the Passover, **'because not enough priests had consecrated themselves and the people had not assembled in Jerusalem'** (30:3).

Hezekiah and the people of Judah were not playing fast and loose with God's decrees when they celebrated the Passover in the second month. They were aware of the Lord's merciful relaxation of the festival timetable in Numbers 9:9-11. In Moses' time there had been some who, for a variety of reasons, were unable to celebrate the Passover with the rest of the nation on the fourteenth day of the first month. 'Then the Lord said to Moses, "Tell the Israelites: 'When you or any of your descendants are unclean because of a dead body or are away on a journey, they may still celebrate the Lord's Passover. They are to celebrate it on the fourteenth day of the second month...'"' This gave those Israelites the opportunity to cleanse themselves in preparation for eating the Passover. The unusual feature of Hezekiah's reformation is that it was

virtually the whole nation and practically the whole priesthood that were unable to eat the Passover. In the merciful
provision of the Lord, the nation was given an extra month to
prepare for the Passover.

Hezekiah called the whole nation of Israel to celebrate the
Passover. **'Hezekiah sent word to all Israel and Judah and
also wrote letters to Ephraim and Manasseh, inviting them
to come to the temple of the LORD in Jerusalem and celebrate the Passover'** (30:1). This was a bold move because
for many years Israel had been a divided nation. As we saw in
chapter 7, about 200 years earlier, just after the death of King
Solomon, the kingdom was divided into two parts. Solomon's
son, Rehoboam, reigned over the two southern tribes of Judah
and Benjamin. In the northern kingdom Jeroboam reigned over
ten tribes, but he refused to let his people travel south to worship in Jerusalem. He set up two shrines at Bethel and Dan,
where he encouraged the idolatrous worship of golden calves.
This religious diversity led to decades of warfare between Israel
and Judah. The rivalry between Israel and Judah came to an
end in 722 B.C. when Samaria was captured by the Assyrians
and the northern kingdom collapsed. However, a legacy of
bitterness and suspicion remained.

It is estimated that Hezekiah's great Passover was celebrated
in 715 B.C., seven years after the Assyrian armies had destroyed the crumbling northern kingdom and carried many of
its people into captivity. (The chronology of Hezekiah's reign
has proved notoriously difficult to establish, but the suggested
dating presumes that Hezekiah reigned alongside his father
King Ahaz from 728–715 B.C., and only in 715 B.C. did he
rule in his own right.) At that time the Assyrian threat cast a
dark shadow over Judah too, and this sets the scene for
Hezekiah's great act of faith. He did not put his trust in a
military alliance, but in the Lord God. Therefore he called the
whole nation back to Jehovah.

'**The king and his officials and the whole assembly in Jerusalem decided to celebrate the Passover in the second month**' (30:2). They knew that their spiritual life was at a very low ebb. '**They had not been able to celebrate it** [the Passover] **at the regular time because not enough priests had consecrated themselves and the people had not assembled in Jerusalem**' (30:3). They resolved that henceforth things would be different. '**A proclamation**' was sent '**throughout Israel, from Beersheba**' (Judah's southernmost town in the Negev) '**to Dan**' (not the territory of the tribe of Dan, but Israel's northernmost town, in territory that today belongs to Syria), '**calling the people to come to Jerusalem and celebrate the Passover to the LORD**' (30:5). '**Ephraim and Manasseh**' (the two leading northern tribes, descended from Joseph, see 30:1) joined with Judah and Benjamin in the south. Unity took the place of hostility among the covenant people when they turned to seek the Lord.

How did this come about? Most probably through the influence of the Scriptures. In the time of King Josiah, it was the rediscovery of 'the Book of the Law' that did so much to encourage spiritual reformation (see 34:15). In chapter 29 large numbers of people, from all over Judah, came together to rededicate the temple (29:20-36). How would these people have been occupied during those highly charged days? Clearly they were rejoicing at what God was doing among his people. They had a heightened awareness of God. They would have been seeking God, talking about God, praying to God, and all these manifestations of renewed spiritual life would have created a thirst that drove them to read the Word of God. Spiritual renewal always leads to a growing love for God's Word.

Church history gives many examples of spiritual renewal producing a greater love for God's Word. One of the early signs that the Holy Spirit had commenced a reviving work in the Scottish parish of Cambuslang in 1742 was a petition signed

by ninety parishioners asking the minister — the Reverend
William McCulloch — to preach an additional, weeknight,
sermon each week. As the revival spread through the parish
many anxious people besieged the manse — even during the
night — wanting to ask about God's Word, so that they might
find comfort for their souls. As they waited for spiritual counsel, many gathered in little groups in the churchyard to read
the Scriptures to each other. There was a similar hunger among
the people of Judah in Hezekiah's day. These people were discovering new things. They must have been saying to each other,
'Here are commands in God's Word that we never knew about
before. We had better make changes to our lives. We have
been slack. We need to seek the Lord so that he might show
mercy to us.' They saw that they had been unfaithful, but they
also saw that there was still a window of opportunity. They
discussed a plan to celebrate the Passover again.

'**The plan seemed right both to the king and to the whole
assembly**' (30:4); therefore they went forward and put it into
practice. This is not to say that they made their plan simply
because it 'felt right'. That is the touchstone for many people
today, including many professing Christians. 'Does it feel right?'
If it does then virtually anything can be justified. Some professing believers have been known to abandon one marriage
partner and marry another simply because 'It feels right to me,
and if it feels right to me then God can't really mind either.'
This is self-centred and unsound thinking and was far from the
minds of Hezekiah and his people.

What these people did was right because God had commanded it in his Word. They had come to a consensus based
on God's Word. They were united in what they were planning
to do because '**The hand of God was on the people to give
them unity of mind to carry out what the king and his
officials had ordered, following the word of the LORD**'
(30:12). Their unity was like that of the early Christians in

Jerusalem of whom we read, 'All the believers were one in heart and mind' (Acts 4:32). It was a unity built upon the teaching of the apostles (see Acts 2:42).

Hezekiah and the people of Judah were zealous in pursuing their plan because they were pulling together. Nothing disheartens God's people like disharmony and disarray. Discordant voices create doubt and cause suspicion. Hezekiah created a situation in which there were no discordant voices by drawing the people into discussion and persuading them of the importance of celebrating the Passover together. He encouraged them, 'Let us seek the Lord with all our hearts.' As a result they reached out to all Israel.

The proclamation that went out to all Israel is quoted in verses 6-9, and the activity of the messengers is described in verses 10-12. Notice the urgency of the invitation: **'People of Israel, return to the LORD, the God of Abraham, Isaac and Israel, that he may return to you who are left, who have escaped from the hand of the kings of Assyria.'** As we have seen, Hezekiah's reformation came seven years after the destruction of the northern kingdom of Israel. Over the years many 'kings of Assyria' had attacked Israel. Among them were Shalmaneser III (859–824 B.C.), Samsi-Adad V (823–811 B.C.), Shalmaneser IV (782–773 B.C.), Tiglath-Pileser III (744–727 B.C., see 2 Kings 15:19-20), and Shalmaneser V (726–722 B.C., see 2 Kings 17:3). Finally Sargon II (who seems to have been the unnamed king of 2 Kings 17:6) captured and destroyed Samaria. With every wave of Assyrian invaders, still more captives were taken into exile, and Israel became more and more depleted. Assyrian records indicate that Sargon II removed 27,270 captives from Samaria. It was indeed a small remnant that had 'escaped from the hand of the kings of Assyria'.

God had warned that he would make the people of Israel 'a thing of horror and an object of scorn and ridicule to all the nations' by taking them into exile if they were unfaithful to him (Deut. 28:37). Moses gave this warning to the people of Israel when God confirmed his covenant with them shortly before his death. This is the warning to which Hezekiah refers in 30:7. The northern tribes sinned by abandoning the temple of the Lord in Jerusalem; hence Hezekiah's call to them in 30:8: **'Do not be stiff-necked, as your fathers were; submit to the Lord. Come to the sanctuary, which he has conse-crated for ever. Serve the Lord your God, so that his fierce anger will turn away from you.'**

Along with these warnings, there was also the promise of restoration, even for those in exile: **'If you return to the Lord, then your brothers and your children will be shown com-passion by their captors and will come back to this land, for the Lord your God is gracious and compassionate'** (30:9). This promise gave hope to Hezekiah and his people when they appealed to their northern cousins to join them at the Passover.

The situation of the northern Israelites was desperate and their need was urgent. The couriers went out as fast as they could, to cover as much territory as possible, **'from town to town in Ephraim and Manasseh, as far as Zebulun'** (30:10). The northern tribes were, after all, still a part of the covenant people. They must be called back to God. Hezekiah's messen-gers went out with great urgency in spite of the scorn they met (30:10).

This will be the response of some in every age when they hear the good news of God's mercy to sinners. Some will hear with gladness, while others will respond with contempt, but God will save his chosen people. **'Nevertheless, some men of Asher, Manasseh and Zebulun humbled themselves and went to Jerusalem'** (30:11). It is the responsibility of God's servants in every age to proclaim the message of God's grace with urgency and faithfulness and recognize that the outcome lies in the hands of our sovereign God. The apostle Paul acknowledged this in his day: 'But not all the Israelites accepted the good news. For Isaiah says, "Lord, who has believed our message?" Consequently, faith comes from hearing the message, and the message is heard through the word of Christ' (Rom. 10:16-17). 'It does not, therefore, depend on man's desire or effort, but on God's mercy' (Rom. 9:16). This is our encouragement and hope.

Hezekiah's messengers went out with urgency in spite of the track record of these northern tribes. They could have said, 'These tribes have already had their chance. They have heard God's Word and they have hardened themselves. Why should we waste time speaking to them?' In fact it was their history, as a privileged but unbelieving people, that made their situation so desperate and the task of the messengers so urgent. The Israelites had been given many warnings and their constant rejection of God's commands had made their guilt even more serious. They had been given much, and much was expected from them. They had sinned in the full light of the prophetic warnings. They had no shred of excuse to cover over their guilt. Their punishment was well deserved. But the offer of grace remained, and there were some who took heed of this final warning: **'Some men of Asher, Manasseh and Zebulun humbled themselves and went to Jerusalem'** (30:11).

Here is a principle that ought to guide our evangelistic witness. We need to follow up 'warm contacts' while they are still warm. These are friends who know the gospel, who have grown up in a Christian home, who are backslidden church members, who have been seekers. These situations present us with opportunities. The longer we neglect them, the harder they become, for their habit of spiritual carelessness becomes harder to break as time passes by. There will come, as our Lord taught, the time when we have to stop casting our pearls before swine (see Matt. 7:6), and when we have to knock the

dust from our feet and move on (Matt. 10:14). In the meantime the awful fate of those who wilfully and knowingly reject
the grace of God as it has been clearly set before them ought
to move us to action.

Cleansing (30:13-20)

Cleansing prepared the way for celebrating the Passover. On
the night described in Exodus 12 when the people of Israel ate
the Passover for the first time, they were preparing to leave
Egypt for good. In just a few hours they would be delivered
from their lives of slavery in Egypt. In fact, the Egyptians compelled the Israelites to leave Egypt as soon as possible, and
their freedom came more quickly than they expected. Pharaoh
ordered them to leave immediately (see Exod. 12:31), and in
the rush they were not be able to make bread with yeast in the
normal way (see Exod. 12:39)

God implanted an important spiritual message in this fact.
Before they celebrated the Passover each year the people of
Israel were to get rid of all yeast from their homes (Exod.
12:18-20). This was a sign of cleansing. In connection with
the Passover, yeast became a symbol of the evil behaviour that
the Israelites had picked up during their stay in Egypt. Even
today, in Jewish homes, all leaven is removed at the beginning
of Passover. A piece of leaven is hidden for the youngest child
to find. The symbolism of cleansing remains.

There are three aspects to the cleansing by which the people
of Judah prepared for the Passover.

1. Physical cleansing

The people who gathered in Jerusalem set about removing
idols from the city: **'They removed the altars in Jerusalem**

and cleared away the incense altars and threw them into the Kidron valley' (30:14). Just as the temple had been purged of the paraphernalia of idolatry in 29:16-17, so too the city of Jerusalem was to be purged. This was an outward expression of repentance. The people were letting it be seen that they had turned their backs on their sinful past. They showed their revulsion at the idolatrous worship which had offended God.

2. Ceremonial cleansing

The priests and Levites set about cleansing themselves in preparation for the tasks that lay ahead. **'The priests and the Levites were ashamed and consecrated themselves and brought burnt offerings to the temple of the LORD'** (30:15). They were the men whom God had appointed to minister in the temple. It was their task to offer the sacrificial lambs and to teach the people regarding their duties towards God. **'They took up their regular positions as prescribed in the Law of Moses the man of God. The priests sprinkled the blood handed to them by the Levites'** (30:16). The blood sprinkled on the altar spoke to the Israelites of how God accepted the death of the substitutionary lamb to release them from bondage to death. And if the sacrifice was to be acceptable to God, then so too must the priests be who offered it.

The priests and Levites were ashamed on account of their lack of spiritual leadership (30:15). They had neglected their duty to be examples to the people, and to teach them the requirements of the law of Moses. They had neglected their duty to keep themselves pure according to the law of Moses. The Mosaic law declared that any Israelite was to be regarded as ceremonially unclean if he touched a dead body (Num. 19:11), or if he came into contact with leprosy (Lev. 13-14), and for a variety of other reasons (Lev. 11; 12; 15). Special rules were given for priests, and if they became unclean they had to purify themselves before they could minister before the Lord (see Lev. 21:1-23). These ceremonial rules were symbolic of God's desire that his people be distinct from the world and devoted to him. God's standards are high. His message is: 'Be holy because I am holy!'

3. Mediatorial cleansing (30:17-20)

The people of Israel — especially those from the north — fell very far short of God's high standards. Years of neglect on the part of the spiritual leaders, and the people they were supposed to lead, were coming to light. Many among the crowds of people who gathered in Jerusalem to celebrate the Passover were ceremonially unclean. **'Since many in the crowd had not consecrated themselves, the Levites had to kill the Passover lambs for all those who were not ceremonially clean and could not consecrate their lambs to the Lord'** (30:17). Those Israelites who were ceremonially unclean ought to have been barred from even eating the Passover meal, but in the excitement of the situation, and in spite of their ignorance of God's law, they came and participated. **'They ate the Passover, contrary to what was written'** (30:18).

The Passover celebration was prevented from becoming a cause of even greater offence to God only when Hezekiah prayed to God on behalf of the people: **'May the Lord, who is good, pardon everyone who sets his heart on seeking God ... even if he is not clean according to the rules of the sanctuary'** (30:18-19). God heard his prayer. **'And the Lord heard Hezekiah and healed the people'** (30:20).

Hezekiah's prayer for the Israelites and God's favourable answer do not provide an excuse for carelessness in matters relating to the worship of God. We should not take this incident as teaching that God does not care what we do, so long as we do it sincerely. God does care about how we live, and how we worship, and how we draw near to him. The whole body of ceremonial laws makes it clear that God attaches importance to what we do when we come near to him. God does not make laws simply to be discarded. He wants us to be precise in seeking to be obedient to his revealed will. If our hearts are right with him we will want to do exactly what he wants, no more and no less. That is why Hezekiah took the matter of these ceremonially unclean Israelites seriously, and he prayed for them. The point to notice is that God is merciful, even to sinners who are not clean. Hezekiah prayed that God would pardon them, even though they were not clean. They had done wrong, but they sought to be right with God. Hezekiah was their representative before God. God heard his prayer and accepted them.

Hezekiah points our thoughts to the King of kings who sits in heaven today and prays for his people. The Lord Jesus Christ is the mediatorial representative of his people: 'Therefore he is able to save completely those who come to God through him, because he always lives to intercede for them' (Heb. 7:25). 'Completely' means that he is able to save any sinner who comes to him — from any sin, and in any age. He is the one and only mediator between unclean sinners and a holy God. Just as those who were unclean were able to enter the temple and eat the Passover, so sinners who put their trust in Jesus Christ can enter heaven and feast with the Son of God. In mercy God offers salvation to men and women who are unclean, and furthermore he offers the signs of salvation — the sacraments of baptism and the Lord's Supper — to sinners who trust in Christ and who are made clean on account of his sacrifice on the cross.

Some will say, 'I am not ready to come to God just yet.' Christ Jesus says, 'Do not wait until you think you have made yourself good enough to come to God. That day will never come! Now is the day of salvation, when those who are unclean are made acceptable in God's sight because I will plead the merits of my death upon the cross.' Remember that 'God demonstrates his own love for us in this: while we were still sinners, Christ died for us' (Rom. 5:8). Some professing believers will hold back from coming to the Lord's Table and say, 'I am not worthy; I am not clean.' God says, 'Yes, you are a sinner, and you are to turn from your sins, but the Lord's Table is a means of grace for sinners who are saved by the shed blood of the Lamb of God, and if you are trusting in Christ then come to the feast that you might grow in grace.'

Celebration (30:21-27)

What makes us celebrate? People celebrate when they get engaged to be married, or when their football team wins a game, or when they get a pay rise. They get together with their friends and let everyone know that they are delighted about their good fortune. The people of Israel and Judah **'celebrated'** the Passover feast (30:21). They got together and expressed their joy. They clearly made a lot of noise in the process. **'The Israelites who were present in Jerusalem celebrated the Feast of Unleavened Bread for seven days with great rejoicing, while the Levites and priests sang to the LORD every day.'** Does their celebration seem a little excessive? Do we celebrate the things of God like this? Do we wake up on a Lord's Day morning and exclaim: 'We are going to go to church today; let's celebrate what God has done for us!' Let's look at what made these people celebrate.

1. The encouragement of Hezekiah

'Hezekiah spoke encouragingly to all the Levites...' (30:22). Hezekiah encouraged the Levites in their work for God. Serving God was a priority for him and he encouraged others to make it a priority too. He explained why he was earnestly seeking reformation in Judah. Hezekiah was willing to give sacrificially from his own possessions to provide sacrifices for the worship of Jehovah (30:24). His enthusiasm was infectious.

2. The uniqueness of the situation (30:26)

'There was great joy in Jerusalem, for since the days of Solomon son of David king of Israel there had been nothing like this in Jerusalem.' A large number of people celebrated the Passover in that first year of Hezekiah's reign. It is an exhilarating experience to be part of a large crowd of worshippers. In Psalm 42:4 the psalmist describes his memories of 'how [he] used to go with the multitude, leading the procession to the house of God, with shouts of joy and thanksgiving among the festive throng'. The 'throng' and the 'multitude' add to the sense of the occasion. However, it was not the weight of numbers that made Hezekiah's Passover such a special occasion. The numbers of worshippers who flocked to Jerusalem were only a sign that this was no ordinary Passover. What made this Passover so special was the coming together of northern and southern tribes to celebrate the festival. Not since the days of the united monarchy in the time of David and Solomon had the northern and southern tribes celebrated together (30:26). That unity was shattered just after the end of Solomon's reign. However, God's covenant promises had been made to the whole nation of Israel, not just to one part of it, and so the coming together of the tribes sparked off rejoicing.

3. The joy of salvation

The people who celebrated the Passover were those whose sins had been forgiven. They had been unclean, but Hezekiah had prayed for them and they had received mercy. They had been accepted by God, even though they were unclean. The Passover was a sign of God's salvation. It was a sign of *the plight* from which the sinner needs to be saved, for it reminded the Israelites of the night when the angel of death passed through Egypt. Death is what every sin and every sinner deserves. It was also a sign of *the substitute who dies in place of the sinner*; for on Passover night the angel of death was turned away from the houses of the Israelites when the lamb was killed. Because the lamb was killed the firstborn son of that house was spared. It was also a sign of *the deliverance that is achieved for sinners*. In place of death there is the gift of life. In place of slavery the people of God enjoy freedom. It was also a sign of *the active participation of the believer*. The Israelites had to take the lamb and kill it and daub the blood on the door-frames. Deliverance had to be actively sought and personally appropriated.

The Passover clearly meant a great deal to those Israelites who celebrated it, because it spoke to them about God's grace to them. Those who gratefully acknowledged the grace of God delighted so much in these things that they celebrated a second time (30:23). **'The whole assembly then agreed to celebrate the festival seven more days; so for another seven days they celebrated joyfully.'**

Christians today rejoice in these same truths. The lessons that were taught to the Israelites in Hezekiah's time, through the Passover, come to perfect fulfilment in the person and work of the Lord Jesus Christ. He is described by the apostle Paul as our Passover lamb: 'For Christ, our Passover Lamb, has been sacrificed. Therefore let us keep the Festival, not with the old yeast, the yeast of malice and wickedness, but with ... the bread of sincerity and truth' (1 Cor. 5:7-8). The Lord's Supper tells the believer about his plight as a sinner condemned to death; his substitute, the sinless Lamb of God; his deliverance from bondage to death and to sin; and his active participation in appropriating the gospel promises through faith in Christ and repentance from sin.

These are the truths most calculated to awaken sinners from spiritual slumber to a sense of their need. These, too, are the truths most calculated to awaken believers to appreciate their privileges and to serve their Lord. That is why the Lord's Supper has often, in the history of the church, been linked with the reviving work of the Holy Spirit. In June 1630 a most unusual communion season was observed in the Scottish town of Shotts. The atoning work of Christ had been set forth with great power by the outstanding preacher Robert Bruce and, as a result, many were eager to hear more when John Livingstone preached the final thanksgiving message on the Monday morning. That morning a 'down-pouring of the Spirit took place' with the result that 500 people saw their lives transformed through the message of that one sermon.

Donald Cargill, the Scottish Covenanter preacher, once described his ministry by saying that he had 'been much in the main things'. The doctrine of the atonement is at the very heart of the Christian faith. Take it out of our churches and what remains cannot be called Christian. When it is proclaimed God's people find that they have a new song in their mouths and a new joy in their hearts. Do you have this salvation to celebrate? If not, then seek it. If so, then join with God's people in rejoicing.

21.
Serving God in everyday things

Please read 2 Chronicles 31:1-21

One of the great landmarks in Paris — to which almost every tourist pays a visit — is the Eiffel Tower. The climb to the very top of the tower involves negotiating 1,760 steps. By the time the visitor has climbed to the top his legs will, no doubt, be weary. However, there is more to follow, for he has to walk all the way back down again, and to do that he will use muscles at the back of his legs that are not often used and which may become very sore. That is why, strange as it may seem, it is often more taxing to come down a mountain than it is to climb up. We stumble more easily when we descend a mountain slope. Sometimes we let our legs run on too fast over the rough terrain. We need to take care not to fall and twist an ankle.

There is a ready application of this principle to the Christian life. After we have enjoyed great blessing from God we need to take care as we return to the routine of daily life. After the Lord's Day comes Monday morning, and we have to put into practice the lessons that we have learned from God's Word. After the spiritual mountaintop come the valley slopes, when we can slip into pride and fall into sin. It is as we come down the valley slope that we discover that truth which remains unapplied is a millstone around our necks rather than a foundation for our feet. After God refreshes and blesses us we have to find our feet again. We are to go forward at a higher level, rather than slip back to old ways.

The people of Israel and Judah had enjoyed a time of spiritual blessing under the leadership of Hezekiah. The temple had been restored to its rightful place at the centre of the nation's religious life. The people had reconsecrated themselves to God and committed themselves to be a nation serving God. The Passover had been celebrated with great rejoicing as a symbol of God's mercy to sinners. The Spirit of God had been poured out in mighty power and the results had been overwhelming. Here in chapter 31 we stand back and look at the fruit.

This is the only way of testing whether a real work of God has taken place, whether in the life of an individual or in that of a community. An outpouring of God's grace will always produce lasting and godly change in the lives of sinners. Among the signs of real change will be ongoing devotion and obedience to God. A group of travelling evangelists came to the town where I used to minister and in two weeks sought to evangelize the community. As a result of their evangelistic efforts they claimed hundreds of conversions. I was asked to visit a dozen or so of these converts. To my dismay, not one of them had any desire to be followed up. None responded to invitations to attend church, or to study the Bible. Some were even reluctant to talk any further about spiritual truth. There was no visible fruit, and sadly the conclusion had to be drawn that there was little real success. In spite of great claims, there seemed to have been no significant work of God.

In this chapter the Chronicler displays the evidence that there had been a real work of God associated with Hezekiah's reformation. The Jewish historian Josephus gives an excellent summary both of the events described in this chapter and their significance: 'After the festival ended, the people went throughout the country and destroyed all pollution from idols. The king also ordered that daily sacrifices be made according to the law and at his own expense. Tithes of all that the ground produced were to support the priests and Levites. Thus they once again returned to their ancient religion.'

There were two signs that a profound change had taken place in the religious life of Israel and Judah. First of all, we read that the people were serious about getting rid of evil: **'When all this had ended, the Israelites who were there went out to the towns of Judah, smashed the sacred stones and cut down the Asherah poles. They destroyed the high places and the altars throughout Judah and Benjamin and in Ephraim and Manasseh'** (31:1). The people were not content simply to go home from the Passover and carry on as before. They were pleased to see the temple functioning again, but they could not abide the thought of rival gods being worshipped in pagan temples nearby. They removed all the paraphernalia of idolatry from the land, and the purge seems to have spread into the territory of Ephraim and Manasseh which had once belonged to the northern kingdom. This became possible because of the Assyrian conquest of Samaria in 722 B.C.

The people's vehemence in purging the land of idols may jar with some modern readers. Some may be offended by the aggressive opposition to evil or by the intolerant approach to the beliefs of others. However, Jehovah is a 'jealous God' (see Exod. 20:5) who is grossly offended by the worship of false gods. On account of his jealousy the Lord commanded his people to 'Break down their altars, smash their sacred poles and cut down their Asherah poles. Do not worship any other God, for the LORD, whose name is Jealous, is a jealous God' (34:13-14). It is also because of the grave danger posed by idolatry to the spiritual life of Israel that God commanded his people to purge the land. In purging the land of idols the Israelites sought to purify the spiritual environment in which they lived. They sought to remove even the opportunity for the seeds of idolatry to sprout again. They wanted to prevent future generations from slipping into the trough from which they had just been lifted.

The second sign that a lasting change had taken place as a result of Hezekiah's reformation is described in 31:2-21 and is the main theme of this chapter. Hezekiah restored a system of ministry to make sure that his people did not slip back into the old ways. He filled the vacuum left by the destruction of the idols by putting better ways in their place.

Hezekiah's 'better ways' were not new ways, but a return to the system of worship that God had already given to his people. He went back to the regulations that God had given to Moses when the tabernacle had been built. In preparation for the time when Solomon would build the temple, God had given King David directions to organize the Levites for their temple ministry. It was to this system (which went back to both Moses and David) that Hezekiah returned. His reformation restored a wide range of seemingly ordinary and mundane activities that related to temple life and worship. As we read this chapter, we may feel that we have come a long way from the mountaintop of spiritual awakening to immerse ourselves in the administrative details of distributing food and money to the Levites. It may seem that there is little of spiritual interest for us in these verses.

However, there is a great deal of instructive teaching in this aspect of Hezekiah's reformation, and it is the very ordinariness of these administrative details that makes them so instructive. After the exile there were many Jews who imagined that they lived in a 'day of small things' (see Zech. 4:10). As a result they entertained low views of God and were lethargic about what they did for him. In fact they did very little for God, either small or great. The temple lay languishing for want of workmen to repair it. Worthless sacrifices were offered to God, because the people despised the worship of Jehovah (see Mal. 1:6-9). The Chronicler wanted God's people to learn the lessons of history and to recognize that little things matter a great deal when we do them for God. Attention to small details leads on to greater things.

What makes the activities described in this chapter so impressive is the fact that they represent lifestyle changes. What is described here is not a momentary flash of zeal, but the putting in place of a system which, if adhered to, would promote practical godliness among God's people. Some people will make great promises to God, and may even carry them through with great zeal for a time. They may impress us with momentary gestures, but they are like the rocky soil in Luke 8:13: 'Those on the rock are the ones who receive the word with joy when they hear it, but they have no root. They believe for a while, but in the time of testing they fall away.' The tragedy is that often their falling away is predictable because they have not put in place the roots of systematic piety to hold them steady when times of testing come. They are irregular in attending the means of grace, in reading the Scriptures and in prayer. They show little inclination to be discipled by more mature believers, or to take an active part in the life of a local congregation.

The fruit that is the sign of a real work of God's grace is also described by our Lord in the parable of the soils: 'The seed on good soil stands for those with a noble and good heart, who hear the word, retain it, and by persevering produce a crop' (Luke 8:15). God's people need a system of ministry that will enable them to know what God's Word teaches, to retain that teaching and to persevere in it. Hezekiah saw the pressing need to put in place a nationwide system of ministry and to maintain it. Two features of his system are described in this chapter: giving to the Lord's work and supporting his servants.

Giving to the Lord's work (31:2-10)

It was good to reopen the temple and to celebrate the Passover, but unless there were men who would keep the temple open and teach the people how to worship God, all these advances would soon be lost. The men whom God had appointed to this task were the priests and Levites. Hence, **'Hezekiah assigned the priests and Levites to divisions — each of them according to their duties as priests or Levites — to offer burnt offerings and fellowship offerings, to minister, to give thanks and to sing praises at the gates of the LORD's dwelling'** (31:2).

The Levites were one of the twelve tribes of Israel — the one which had been set apart to perform a variety of tasks connected with the temple. Those tasks were allocated to the various clans of the tribe in the time of King David, and this allocation can be found in 1 Chronicles chapters 23-26. Some were given the task of helping the priests and maintaining the fabric of the temple; some were treasury officials who looked after the tithes and offerings; some were gatekeepers who made sure that only genuine worshippers and acceptable offerings entered the temple precincts; others were singers who sang praises to the Lord, and there were also other officials who served in a variety of roles.

The family of Aaron had been set apart for an even greater privilege — ministering at the altar of the Lord where sacrifices were offered. In the interests of making sure that priests were constantly available to minister at the altar, the priests were divided into twenty-four divisions, which were rotated to ensure that there was always one division on duty. David had established this system and Solomon had maintained it. However, over the years it had fallen into disuse. Presumably this had happened slowly and gradually, and it was hard to pinpoint a precise time when the system had collapsed. It had happened simply because no one took the initiative to hold the organization together. Kings and people, and the priests themselves, had allowed the religious life of the nation to drift. It was easier to let the nation slumber than to rouse it to action. After all, there was a cost involved in maintaining the temple administration. Animals would have to be sacrificed and tithes would have to be paid, for the Levites would have to be supported. All of this was a cost that the people were not willing to bear, so it just did not happen and the spiritual consequences became evident.

Hezekiah took a personal initiative: **'The king contributed from his own possessions for the morning and evening burnt offerings and for the burnt offerings on the Sabbaths, New Moons and appointed feasts as written in the Law of the LORD'** (31:3). He kick-started the whole process by contributing the animals necessary to commence the daily, weekly, monthly and yearly sacrifices. He followed the example of David in 1 Chronicles 29:2-5, when the king gave generously 'with all [his] resources' to establish the temple. In his generosity Hezekiah set a worthy example for his people.

Hezekiah's example was followed up with a royal command. **'He ordered the people living in Jerusalem to give the portion due to the priests and Levites so that they could devote themselves to the Law of the LORD'** (31:4). This command met with a willing response: **'As soon as the order went out, the Israelites generously gave the firstfruits of their grain, new wine, oil and honey and all that the fields**

**produced. They brought a great amount, a tithe of every-
thing. The men of Israel and Judah who lived in the towns
of Judah also brought a tithe of their herds and flocks and
a tithe of the holy things dedicated to the LORD their God,
and they piled them in heaps'** (31:5-6). The people's generous response was patterned on Moses' words in Numbers 18.
The firstfruits of the produce from the land was given for the
priests (Num. 18:8-13); the tithes were reserved for the Levites
(Num. 18:21); and the Levites brought their own tithes of the
consecrated gifts, which were given to the priests; these constituted 'the tithe of the holy things dedicated to the Lord their
God' (31:6; Num. 18:25-32).

Hezekiah's call to give to the Lord's treasury went out to
the whole nation (31:6). The Israelites from the northern tribes
who were living among the people of Judah responded to the
appeal. This was a further demonstration of the newly restored
national unity of the northern and southern tribes. Hezekiah
saw a great response to his initiative, and the priests and Levites
were able to bring back an encouraging report: **'Since the
people began to bring their contributions to the temple of
the LORD, we have had enough to eat and plenty to spare,
because the LORD has blessed his people, and this great
amount is left over'** (31:10). Hezekiah and his officials rejoiced: **'They praised the LORD and blessed his people'**
(31:8). The people were to be commended for the good that
they had done. Their contributions were very visible **'heaps'**.
Their generosity was outstanding, and calls for further
comment.

1. The cause of their generosity

The explanation for the generous response of the people of
Judah to Hezekiah's appeal is not hard to find. It was the result
of spiritual awakening. They realized what God had done for

them, and they were thankful. The message of the great Passover feast had sunk in. Like the psalmist, they were asking,
'How can I repay the LORD for all his goodness to me?' (Ps.
116:12). Of course, no man can ever begin to repay the debt
that he owes to God his Creator and Redeemer, but the believer's love for God prompts him to give his all to the Lord.
Jesus explained the same principle in Matthew 10:8: 'Freely
you have received, freely give.' When Paul exhorted the Corinthians to give to the Lord's work, he grounded that appeal
on God's goodness: 'Remember this: Whoever sows sparingly
will also reap sparingly, and whoever sows generously will
also reap generously. Each man should give what he has decided in his heart to give, not reluctantly or under compulsion,
for God loves a cheerful giver... Thanks be to God for his
indescribable gift!' (2 Cor. 9:6-7,15). Thankfulness that 'God
so loved the world that he gave his one and only Son' is what
makes God's people generous in returning their tithes and offerings to him.

2. The consequences of their generosity (31:10)

As a result of the firstfruits and tithes which were brought into
the Lord's treasury, the priests and Levites were freed from
the demands of earning a living so that they could devote themselves to doing the Lord's work in the temple. As the Chronicler put it, they were allowed to 'devote themselves to the
Law of the LORD' (31:4). This involved, first of all, doing what
God's law commanded and offering sacrifices and, secondly,
devoting themselves to studying and teaching the law of God.

The priests and Levites were not to be content with simply
being in the temple to perform the sacrificial rituals in a mechanical fashion. These men were to be devoted to God and
to his Word. They were to be like the psalmist who could say:

Oh how I love your law!
　I meditate on it all day long.
Your commands make me wiser than my enemies,
　for they are ever with me.
I have more insight than all my teachers,
　for I meditate on your statutes.
I have more understanding than the elders,
　for I obey your precepts

(Ps. 119:97-100).

The example of their lives was to lift the spiritual tone of the nation. They were to be able to teach others as a result of their close study of God's law (see Mal. 2:7).

In their role as men devoted to the study of God's Word they are a pattern for the Christian ministry in the New Testament. Paul describes the role of men who are set apart from other activities to devote their time and energy to the study of Scripture. Their 'work is preaching and teaching' (1 Tim. 5:17), and they do not '[get] involved in civilian affairs' (2 Tim. 2:4). Their calling is to be '[workmen] who [do] not need to be ashamed and who correctly [handle] the word of truth' (2 Tim. 2:15) so that they are ready to 'preach the word ... in season and out of season' (2 Tim 4:1-2). This is a full-time work which requires full-time support and for this reason the practice of tithing ought to be a minimum standard to guide our giving to the Lord's work. We continue to bring our tithes and offerings to the Lord for exactly the same reason that Hezekiah called upon the Israelites to do so — for the support of God's servants and for the spread of the gospel.

3. The confirmation of God's promises

When the people started bringing in their tithes, there were 'heaps' (31:6), and a **'great amount'** was **'left over'** (31:10).

What had previously been unimaginable now became a reality when people took God's Word at face value and obeyed it. The Chronicler clearly saw a lesson for those Jews after the exile who were not so generous when it came to bringing their tithes to the Lord. In Nehemiah 13:10-11 we read about Nehemiah's dismay when he learned that the Levites had had to go back to their fields and abandon their temple ministry because the tithes were not being gathered in. This was the reason why the temple was not rebuilt as quickly as it should have been in post-exilic times, nor subsequently properly maintained as a place of worship. Many thought that the people did not have the resources to restore the temple. But there was enough — if only God's people would obey the Scriptures.

Malachi challenged the Jews of his generation with the promise: ' "Bring the whole tithe into the storehouse, that there may be food in my house. Test me in this," says the LORD Almighty, "and see if I will not throw open the floodgates of heaven and pour out so much blessing that you will not have room enough for it" ' (Mal. 3:10). In Hezekiah's time the people did just what God commanded, and God amazed them with what they gathered in for the ministry of his temple. The same amazing principle holds true today, for God is no man's debtor. A tithing church is a church that will be blessed by God and will be used by him to extend his kingdom. It has been awakened to its privileges and to its responsibilities.

Supporting the Lord's servants (31:11-19)

This was the second feature of Hezekiah's administrative reforms. A system was put in place to gather the gifts of God's people and to distribute them among the priests and Levites.

Firstly, at Hezekiah's command, *storehouses were prepared* to receive the tithes and offerings as the people brought them in (31:11-12). The extent of God's blessing was such that special preparation had to be made to receive it. God's people must always exercise careful stewardship in their handling of God's good gifts so that they are not wasted or frittered away.

Secondly, *supervisors were appointed* by Hezekiah to administer these storerooms, and **'Conaniah, a Levite,'** was put in charge of this department. The measure of importance that Hezekiah attached to temple administration is shown by the fact that he had appointed a government official called Azariah (who is probably to be distinguished from 'Azariah the chief priest' as this was a common name among the Levites) to take charge of the temple and report directly to him. The list of the other Levites who worked with Conaniah is found in 31:12-13. Again we notice that the names of these otherwise unknown Levites are recorded for us because their work, however humble, was important to Hezekiah and to the Lord.

Thirdly, *a group of distributors was appointed* to allocate provisions among the priests and Levites (31:14-15). Again they are all listed by name, and they worked under the direction of **'Kore son of Imnah the Levite'**.

Fourthly, *guidelines were issued* to show how the offerings ought to be distributed. All the priests were given an allowance (31:15). Both serving and retired priests (**'old and young alike'**) received maintenance from the temple treasury. Interestingly, the young sons of the priests, aged three and over, also served in the temple and they too were given an allowance (31:16). They were following in the footsteps of young Samuel, who from the age that he was weaned from his mother was given to the Lord to serve in the tabernacle at Shiloh (1 Sam. 1:24-28; 3:1). Some might have asked, 'What is the value of having such young children there?' Clearly these young sons of the priests were there for a purpose. Young as they were, they were learning to serve God. They were being prepared for a life of service. This almost hidden historical detail shows the importance of those formative years in a child's life. Never underestimate what a child can learn at that stage. Scripture teaches believers to have high hopes for their children and to train them from a very early age.

While the sons of the priests received an allowance from the age of three, the same provision was given to the Levites only when they reached the age of twenty years: **'and likewise to the Levites twenty years old or more'** (31:17). It is not made clear why the descendants of Aaron were treated differently from the other Levites. From the time of Moses the family of Aaron was regarded as especially privileged in view of its priestly responsibilities. They were the only Levites who ministered at the altar. With these special responsibilities went special privileges. This principle was challenged by Korah when he rebelled against Moses and Aaron, and at that time the Lord defended the special status of the family of Aaron (Num. 16:8-11; 17:1-12).

The distribution of the offerings to the priests and Levites was to provide for their families as well: **'They included all the little ones, the wives, and the sons and daughters of the whole community listed in the genealogical records'** (31:18). A man is duty-bound to provide for his own family (see 1 Tim. 5:8) and this principle demands that those who work for the Lord must be enabled to support their families. Special care was taken to ensure that the Levites who lived and ministered in remote countryside locations were not to be left out (31:19). Although the setting for their ministry was in the villages of Judah rather than the temple in Jerusalem, they were teaching the people the precepts of God's law, and 'The worker deserves his wages' (see 1 Tim. 5:18; Luke 10:7).

The characteristic of the Levites who administered this system was *faithfulness*. See how this theme recurs: **'Then they faithfully brought in the contributions, tithes and dedicated** gifts' (31:12). They **'assisted [Kore] faithfully in the towns of the priests'** (31:15). **'For they were faithful in consecrating themselves'** (31:18). The essence of their faithfulness was dependability. These men had been asked to do a job, and they did it. The task that was assigned to these officials was not as important as that of the priests, nor was it as public as that of the Levites who taught the people. Still, Hezekiah did not come back to find the work undone. Conaniah may have thought that he had a less important task to perform than Azariah the chief priest, but it did not affect the *way* he did his work. These stewards did their work faithfully by applying themselves even to mundane tasks.

Dependability, or faithfulness, is what the Lord expects of his people when they have been given a task to do. Those who are called upon to serve the Lord ought to do it wholeheartedly. In the parable of the talents, the master (representing our Lord in the final judgement) commends the servant who has taken his talents and used them to the full: 'Well done, good and faithful servant! You have been faithful with a few things; I will put you in charge of many things' (Matt. 25:21). 'It is required that those who have been given a trust must prove faithful' (1 Cor. 4:2). Every child of God has been given a trust. God has given us talents. We have been given opportunities to use those talents within the church and in our secular activities. The responsibilities that have been given to you may be as simple as tidying a room, or being at church each week, but others are relying on you. Are you faithful? Do you do them well? Are you faithful in little things?

Jesus set out a principle in the parable of the talents which Paul developed in 1 Timothy 3:13: 'Those who have served well gain an excellent standing and great assurance in their faith in Christ Jesus.' Those who serve well in little things can go on to be trusted with greater things — but not before! If a person is neither able nor willing to be faithful in little things then he is not ready for more important things. Moreover, he will always be discontented. Those who serve well in little things and then go on to do greater things for God gain 'great assurance' because they can look back and see the objective signs of God at work in their lives.

The example of Hezekiah (31:20-21)

Hezekiah, too, provides us with a marvellous example of faithfulness: **'This is what Hezekiah did throughout Judah, doing what was good and right and faithful before the Lord his God. In everything that he undertook in the service of God's temple and in obedience to the law and the commands, he sought his God and worked wholeheartedly. And so he prospered'** (31:20). We can see why the Levites were so faithful — they had a faithful role model! Their king did exactly what God told him to do, and he did it 'wholeheartedly'. Notice the combination of two things that are sometimes considered to be opposites: self-discipline and spontaneity. Hezekiah set up a system and stuck to it with a spirit of self-discipline. He worked his system with wholehearted devotion.

Many people today value spontaneity and despise discipline. Some professing Christians are of the opinion that discipline produces cold, formal religion. In the interests of sincerity, they say, they will do only what they feel prompted to do at any given moment. However, Hezekiah's spontaneity flourished in the midst of self-discipline.

That was true of the early Methodists in England. They were given the nickname of 'Methodists' because they aimed to be methodical in their piety. They set aside times each day when they would pray and read their Bibles. They set aside whole days for prayer and times for visiting the sick or those in prison. They wrote journals recording how their plans worked out. Fellowship or class meetings were carefully planned by John Wesley to include times of praise and prayer, thanksgiving and testimony. Does this sound regimented? Perhaps so, but from these fellowship groups came spontaneous outpourings of love and praise to God, charity to their brothers and sisters in Christ and evangelistic outreach to the lost. God's grace bore lasting fruit in this disciplined setting.

The lesson of this chapter is that we need to discipline ourselves to be godly. God's people in every age need to be systematic in their giving to the Lord, reading of Scripture, attending church and witness to society. We need the discipline that comes from being attached to the visible church, which provides us with a system of ministry and ongoing nurture from the means of grace. This is the key to fruit that lasts.

22.
Hezekiah: troubled times

Please read 2 Chronicles 32:1-33

There are two sides to Hezekiah. So far, as we have followed the Chronicler's account of his reign, we have seen only one — Hezekiah the reformer. He was a man of God who sought to bring his people back to the ways of true righteousness. Inevitably there was also another side, because Hezekiah served God as king of his covenant people, and we now come to look at Hezekiah the politician, a man caught up in the turbulent events of his time.

The accounts of Hezekiah's reign in 2 Kings 18-20 and Isaiah 36-39 major on this aspect. They both recount in great detail the threat posed to Judah by the Assyrians, how Hezekiah responded and the arrival of the envoys from Babylon. Only incidentally do they describe Hezekiah's reformation of Judah's worship.

It is on account of his opposition to the Assyrian king, Sennacherib, in the year 701 B.C., that Hezekiah is often best remembered. The Assyrians kept detailed accounts of their dealings with other nations, and especially of their military campaigns, and some of these have been discovered by archaeologists. One of the best known is the Taylor Prism (a hexagonal column of stone on which is recorded the events of Sennacherib's reign) which is kept in the British Museum in

London. It records the Assyrian version of Sennacherib's invasion of Judah as follows: '... as for Hezekiah the Jew, who did not submit to my yoke, forty-six of his strong walled cities, as well as smaller cities in their neighbourhood ... I besieged and took ... himself, like a caged bird, I shut up in Jerusalem, his royal city... As for Hezekiah, the terrifying splendour of my majesty overcame him ... and his mercenary troops deserted him.' As we shall see, not every claim that Sennacherib made ought to be taken at face value. In spite of his insulting language, he obviously took Hezekiah seriously.

Secular historians, such as the Greek historian Herodotus and the Jewish historian Josephus, have also written about Hezekiah's stand against Sennacherib. The English poet Lord Byron made the events of this chapter famous in his often memorized poem, 'The Destruction of Sennacherib':

The Assyrian came down like the wolf on the fold,
And his cohorts were gleaming in purple and gold,
And the sheen of their spears was like the stars on the
sea,
When the blue wave rolls nightly on deep Galilee.

Clearly Hezekiah faced troubled times as well as enjoying periods of spiritual awakening, and that is the theme of this chapter. This may strike us as something of an anticlimax after the glowing accounts of reformation in Judah: **'After all that Hezekiah had so faithfully done, Sennacherib king of Assyria came and invaded Judah'** (32:1). Faithfulness was the key word in 31:20-21. Hezekiah was faithful in everything that he did, whether great or small: 'This is what Hezekiah did throughout Judah, doing what was good and right and faithful before the LORD his God.' He was systematic, dependable and wholehearted in serving God. Some may have asked, 'What good did his faithfulness do him? Did God protect him from trouble?' The short answer is that his faithfulness did not prevent him having to face troubled times.

In fact it was Hezekiah's faithfulness to the Lord that made him vulnerable to attack. According to 2 Kings 16:7-8 his father, King Ahaz, had pursued a pro-Assyrian foreign policy. Ahaz opposed the Syro-Ephraimite coalition and Judah became an Assyrian vassal state. This had religious implications (see 2 Kings 16:10), for Assyrian-style innovations had entered the religious life of Judah. This was a sign of Judah's political subordination. So when reformation transformed the worship of the people of Judah and when Hezekiah took a leading role in promoting that reformation, the Assyrians became uneasy. Hezekiah knew that he was setting out on a collision course, and that sooner or later there would be trouble. He knew that being faithful to God carried a cost.

Hezekiah's experience is also the experience of many Christians. Our Lord warned: 'In this world you will have trouble' (John 16:33). This trouble is often a direct result of serving him (see John 15:18-20). James was equally realistic: 'Don't you know that friendship with the world is hatred towards God?' (James 4:4). The reverse is also true, for friendship with God brings hostility from the world. It is when we are faithful that the world hates us. The world loves compromised Christians who will join them in their wickedness. It is the faithful believer that ungodly people cannot tolerate.

Sometimes believers are tempted to feel bitter when they face trials that are a direct result of their faithfulness. They feel cheated and let down by God. If we are ever tempted to think like that, let us remember Hezekiah. God does not promise that we shall be spared trouble. He promises to deliver us in times of trouble. Let's consider how God delivered Hezekiah.

Hezekiah's preparation (32:1-8)

These verses describe the precautions which Hezekiah took when it became clear that his country was in danger. He saw trouble coming and prepared for it. He saw that faithfulness to God carried a cost, but he did not moan about it. Instead he got ready to face it. He put his trust in the Lord, but he took practical steps as well. Prayer and precaution go together. Matthew Henry draws an important lesson: 'Those that trust God with their safety must use proper means for their safety, otherwise they tempt him, and do not trust him.' Hezekiah did three things.

1. He secured the water supply (32:2-4)

Palestine is an extremely dry land. Water is in very short supply and without it armies will die of thirst. Hezekiah sought to cut off water supplies from the invader and secure them for his own people inside the fortress in Jerusalem: ' "**Why should the kings of Assyria come and find plenty of water?" they said.**' Near Jerusalem there are two sources of water: one at En Rogel, several kilometres to the south, and another at Gihon, just outside the city walls in the Kidron Valley. Bringing that water into the citadel presented a challenge to the engineers of the day, but they succeeded by cutting a channel through solid rock to bring water up into Jerusalem. The task required '**a large force of men**'. There were two groups of workmen cutting through solid rock and meeting each other in the middle to create a tunnel which was 533 metres long. Today visitors to Jerusalem can still wade through Hezekiah's tunnel. It was one of the marvels of ancient engineering.

2. He repaired the defences of Jerusalem (32:5)

'**Then he worked hard repairing all the broken sections of the wall and building towers on it.**' A wall with a hole in it is no defence, so it was imperative that the holes in the wall be repaired. Hezekiah then doubled his defences: '**He built another wall outside that one and reinforced the supporting terraces of the City of David.**' Hezekiah's plans were very similar to those of King David when he first secured Jerusalem as a fortress (see 1 Chr. 11:8). This casts a very positive light on all that Hezekiah did, for he was a worthy successor of that great king and, like him, pointed forward to a greater King who is a sure defence for all who put their trust in him.

3. He taught the people to trust the Lord (32:6-8)

Hezekiah '**encouraged them with these words: "Be strong and courageous. Do not be afraid or discouraged because of the king of Assyria and the vast army with him, for there is a greater power with us than with him..."**' Hezekiah knew that military precautions alone were not enough. Isaiah 22:8-11 describes exactly the sort of precautions that Hezekiah took, but warns against making them a substitute for trusting in the Lord. Later Hezekiah would trust in these precautions to his great peril. Apart from God stone walls and metal shields are worthless. All the precautions that the people of Judah could take would not save them if God were against them; yet all the might of Assyria could do them no harm if God were with them. '**And the people gained confidence from what Hezekiah the king of Judah said.**'

Assyria looked like a powerful nation, but all it had to rely upon was the '**arm of flesh**'. Judah had the Lord to help them. What a contrast! Who would be in the shoes of Sennacherib? Hezekiah urged the people to remember the greatness of the

Lord. We have a similar encouragement in 1 John 4:4: 'You, dear children, are from God ... the one who is in you is greater than the one who is in the world.' Often we are tempted to forget this and we need to be reminded just how great is the Lord our Protector. Elisha prayed in 2 Kings 6:16-17 that God would open the eyes of his servant to see the power of God displayed around them both. When we see that our strength comes from him, then nothing can alarm us.

Satan knows our weak spots and sets out to undermine our confidence in the greatness of God. He is happy for us to acknowledge it in theory so long as we deny it in practice. He is happy for us to say to ourselves, 'God did things like this in the past, but he does not act like this today... God may do great things, but we cannot depend upon him, so we will not try anything too risky.' Hezekiah urged his people to stand up to Sennacherib and to stand firm, because **'With us is the LORD our God to help us and to fight our battles.'** This is a truth that prompts us to action. Faith in God leads to action. William Carey's motto makes that principle memorable: 'Expect great things from God. Attempt great things for God.'

Sennacherib's propaganda assault (32:9-19)

Sennacherib's army was camped near Jerusalem at Lachish. Most of Judah had been overrun and only the royal citadel at Jerusalem left in Hezekiah's hands. Before launching a full-scale military attack Sennacherib tried a more subtle approach. He attempted to destroy the morale of the people of Judah by waging a propaganda war. In 32:10-15 we find a summary of his message. Hezekiah had just urged his people to put their trust in the Lord, but Sennacherib set out to undermine that trust: **'This is what Sennacherib king of Assyria says: On what are you basing your confidence, that you remain in**

Jerusalem under siege? When Hezekiah says, "The LORD
our God will save us from the hand of the king of Assyria,"
he is misleading you, to let you die of hunger and thirst.'
    The thrust of Sennacherib's message was twofold. First of
all, he asked, 'Why should the Lord save you?' **'Did not
Hezekiah himself remove this god's high places and
altars...?'** (32:12). Secondly, he asked, 'Even if he wanted
to, how could the Lord save you? Haven't the Assyrian armies
destroyed many nations? Their gods didn't save them'
(32:13-15). The assumption was made that every nation had
its god (or gods) and that when a nation's armies were defeated it was because their god had also been defeated. These
nations and their gods are listed in more detail in Isaiah
37:12-13: 'Did the gods of the nations that were destroyed by
my forefathers deliver them — the gods of Gozan, Haran,
Rezeph, and the people of Eden who were in Tel Assar? Where
is the king of Hamath, the king of Arpad, the king of the city
of Sepharvaim, or of Hena or Ivvah?' Sennacherib concluded
his list of conquests with a calculated insult to Jehovah: **'How
then can your god deliver you from my hand? ... How
much less will your god deliver you from my hand!'**
(32:14,15). In Sennacherib's eyes Jehovah counted for even
less than the already defeated gods of his subject nations. How
insulting!
    Sennacherib and his propaganda machine made one fatal
miscalculation (32:19). He thought that Jehovah was just like
any of these false gods. He thought that Jehovah could be
worshipped in the same way as heathen people worshipped
their false gods. He thought that Jehovah was content to be
worshipped as one of many gods, that Jehovah and Baal and
Ashtoreth were all worshipped at the same altar. Jehovah's
response to this idea was an emphatic rebuttal. There is one
true and living God (Deut. 6:4) and as a consequence there is

only one acceptable way to worship him — according to his revealed will. God had made it clear that there was one place at which he was to be worshipped and one temple at which sacrifices were to be offered (see Deut. 12:1-7). Far from offending the Lord when he destroyed the 'high places and altars', Hezekiah was faithfully applying God's law.

Sennacherib made another mistake by thinking that Jehovah was as powerless as these false gods. Isaiah mocked such gods and the person who serves them:

> He cut down cedars,
>> or perhaps took a cypress or oak.
> He let it grow among the trees of the forest,
>> or planted a pine, and the rain made it grow.
> It is man's fuel for burning;
>> some of it he takes and warms himself,
>> he kindles a fire and bakes bread.
> But he also fashions a god and worships it;
>> he makes an idol and bows down to it.
> Half of the wood he burns in the fire;
>> over it he prepares his meal,
>> he roasts his meat and eats his fill.
> He also warms himself and says,
>> 'Ah! I am warm; I see the fire.'
> From the rest he makes a god, his idol,
>> he bows down to it and worships.
> He prays to it and says,
>> 'Save me; you are my god.'
> They know nothing, they understand nothing;
>> their eyes are plastered over so that they cannot see,
>> and their minds are closed so that they cannot understand
>>> (Isa. 44:14-18).

The psalmist also indicted the foolishness of idolatry:

> The idols of the nations are silver and gold,
> made by the hands of men.
> They have mouths, but cannot speak,
> eyes, but they cannot see;
> they have ears, but cannot hear,
> nor is there breath in their mouths.
> Those who make them will be like them,
> and so will all who trust in them
>
> (Ps. 135:15-18).

These were the only gods that Sennacherib knew. It is little wonder that he had contempt for them. But the Lord God of Israel was different. He is the Creator of the heavens and the earth. He is described by Isaiah as the one who 'sits enthroned above the circle of the earth... He brings princes to naught and reduces the rulers of this world to nothing' (Isa. 40:22,23). He is beyond comparison with any created thing. He is the Lord of hosts who directs the armies of heaven. He could easily destroy the army of Sennacherib. That is why the people of Judah laughed at Sennacherib's foolish words: 'The Virgin Daughter of Zion despises you and mocks you...' (see 2 Kings 19:21).

Sennacherib's propaganda was a tissue of lies, but note that his foolish slanders were wrapped up in just enough truth to make them dangerous. They may have been believable to some, or confusing to others. They may have caused some to ask, 'Might there be something in what he says?' It was true that Hezekiah had destroyed all those altars, and it was also true that Assyria had conquered all those kingdoms. To some those arguments may have sounded like common sense. And even if his reasoning did not convince them, the self-confident tone of Sennacherib's message might have swayed some of the people of Judah.

Today there are still those who are confident, arrogant and insolent in their hostility to God. They have arguments which sound so convincing, and we feel intimidated by them. They present a worldly wisdom that sounds like practical common sense. Sometimes they launch an outright assault on the Christian faith. They ask, 'How can you believe in such a God when you look at the trouble spots in the world? How can you believe in the Bible when it is full of mistakes? How can you talk about salvation when I know people who claim to be saved and they are just as nasty and dishonest as the next person?'

Sometimes they plead for us to accommodate Christianity with what the reasonable man in the world might accept. They say, 'You had better tone down what God's Word says if you want to get converts, because people don't like that sort of message and you will drive them away. You had better find new ways of getting people into church because people do not want to listen to plain Bible preaching. You should not expect too much commitment from people today because modern life is just too hectic.'

All of this sounds like practical and realistic common sense, but it is the wisdom of the world. It is like the reasoned arguments of Sennacherib. It is like the logic of the Sadducees, which our Lord cut down to size in his discussion with them in Mark 12:24. These were the learned intellectuals of our Lord's time and they brought forward a difficult situation which they thought would make the doctrine of bodily resurrection untenable. 'Jesus replied, "Are you not in error because you do not know the Scriptures or the power of God?"' If Sennacherib had known the Scriptures, he would have known that, far from offending God by destroying these idolatrous altars, Hezekiah was obeying God. If he had known the power of God, he would never have spoken of the Lord in the same breath as the gods of the other nations. He would have covered his mouth in shame and terror.

How are we to see through the clever propaganda of our day? We are to immerse ourselves in the Scriptures and to listen to what God says. We ought to let our minds become so saturated with a godly way of thinking that the wisdom of the world clearly stands out for what it is — utter foolishness. When we do that we shall see that all the teachings of Scripture fit perfectly together and that everything God commands has a good reason lying behind it. As we spend time getting to know God better through his Word, we shall also come to see how great our God is. Nothing is impossible to those who claim his promises.

God's powerful deliverance (32:20-23)

God silenced Sennacherib's boasting in a most amazing way: **'The Lord sent an angel, who annihilated all the fighting men and the leaders and officers in the camp of the Assyrian king'** (32:21). Additional details are found in 2 Kings 19:35, where we learn that 185,000 men died at the hand of the angel of death that night. Secular historians have struggled to explain this miracle. According to Josephus, 'God had sent a terrible plague on the Assyrians and 185,000 had died.' Herodotus put forward an almost laughable suggestion: 'A multitude of field mice which by night devoured all the quivers and bows of the enemy, and all the straps by which they held their shields... Next morning as they commenced their fight great numbers fell as they had no arms with which to defend themselves.' Lord Byron's poetic description of that night's events is much more to the point:

And the might of the Gentile, unsmote by the sword,
Hath melted like snow in the glance of the Lord.

It is important to notice that this happened in answer to prayer: **'King Hezekiah and the prophet Isaiah ... cried out in prayer...'** (32:20). Prayer has a very important place in God's plans. God acted to fulfil his sovereign purpose, but he also put it into the hearts of Hezekiah and Isaiah to pray earnestly. Prayer laid the foundation for their calm confidence as they faced Sennacherib's threat. A captain of a sailing ship once had a sarcastic passenger who was extremely antagonistic to Christianity. When a fierce storm blew up the passenger remarked to the captain, 'Why don't you pray to that God of yours?' The captain's reply was calm and simple: 'While you were sleeping I was praying. Now that you are panicking I have a ship to sail.' He was able to face the storm calmly because he had already entrusted his life and his ship to the Lord in prayer.

God answered Hezekiah's prayer in a way that Hezekiah could never have imagined, by sending the angel of death to smite the Assyrian army (32:21). Even more amazing is what we read next: **'And when he** [Sennacherib] **went into the temple of his god, some of his sons cut him down with the sword.'** This took place some twenty years later in 681 B.C. God answers our prayers and brings judgement upon his enemies in the long term. Many years after the Second World War we still read in the newspapers about war criminals being pursued and called to account for their atrocities. The passage of time and the advance of years do not lessen the determination of those who seek to bring them to justice. God is equally zealous to bring his plans to fulfilment. Those who mock and reject God will not just walk away. They will stand before the God they despised.

Those who pray should not think that their prayers are futile because they do not see the answers after only a few years. God will answer the prayers of his oppressed people (see Rev. 6:10). He will answer the prayers of those who seek that his will may be done and that his kingdom might be established on earth.

The problems of success (32:24-33)

In these verses we come to the end of Hezekiah's life. What ought to have been a glorious finale is a rather disappointing account of failure. The lesson we learn is a perplexing one: serious problems follow success. These verses provide a summary of Hezekiah's successes. He enjoyed riches (32:27). He left behind many buildings (32:28-29). Among the things he constructed were landmark projects such as the tunnel that brought water from the Gihon spring to the pool of Siloam (32:30). The Chronicler also records Hezekiah's devotion to God (32:32) and the affection of his people (32:33). However, his successes became a snare to him. Two in particular are singled out for special mention.

1. Hezekiah's answered prayer (32:24-26)

'In those days' refers to the days before Sennacherib's invasion. In 32:24 there is a very brief account of Hezekiah's illness, prayer and deliverance. More information is found in 2 Kings 20:1-11, and the Chronicler assumes that his readers are familiar with this earlier account of Isaiah's warning, Hezekiah's prayer, God's reprieve and the sign to confirm that the Lord's hand was in it.

The Chronicler takes up the account at this point in 32:25, telling how Hezekiah responded to the kindness that God had shown him. He was proud and did not respond as he ought to have done. He took God for granted. **'Therefore the LORD's wrath was on him and on Judah and Jerusalem.'** God's wrath came in the form of Sennacherib's invasion. Not only did Hezekiah suffer the consequences of his pride, but his people suffered as well. Only when Hezekiah **'repented of the pride of his heart'** was 'the LORD's wrath' taken away.

2. Hezekiah's spreading reputation (32:31)

In 32:23 we read that after the humiliation of Sennacherib, 'Many brought offerings to Jerusalem for the LORD and valuable gifts for Hezekiah king of Judah. From then on he was highly regarded by all the nations.' Among the visitors there was a delegation from Babylon. The Babylonians worshipped the sun and were very interested in any unusual developments in the heavens. Matthew Henry comments, 'The sun was their god; they came to enquire concerning the favour he had shown to Hezekiah, that they might honour him whom their god honoured.'

The Babylonians were also enemies of Assyria and Sennacherib. They wanted Hezekiah as an ally and they wanted to weigh up what sort of a man he was, how strong he was, and where his strengths and weaknesses lay. Hezekiah was put under the magnifying glass and at that crucial moment God left him. This is not to say that God is not omnipresent, for at all times God is present in every place. But at that moment God did not give Hezekiah a clear and specific revelation of his will. He left the king to work out for himself what he ought to do. Hezekiah should have known what to do for he had been instructed in the Word of God and he had already seen God at work. He knew that the real strength of his kingdom lay not in his treasure, but in the Lord.

God's purpose was to test how well Hezekiah had learned that lesson, and especially to see whether he would remember it under pressure. God, of course, did not need to discover the true state of Hezekiah's heart, for he already knew it, but he wanted to reveal to others — not least to Hezekiah himself — what his heart was really like.

The results of God's test were disappointing: **'Hezekiah's heart was proud and he did not respond to the kindness shown him.'** He showed the Babylonians around his storehouses so that they might see his wealth, and he showed them around his armouries so that they might see his military power (see 2 Kings 20:13). Little, if anything, was said about the Lord, and it fell to the prophet Isaiah to point out Hezekiah's unfaithfulness (2 Kings 20:14-18). Hezekiah took the credit for himself when he described his success in worldly terms. That is why the Lord judged him. There are lessons for us to learn from Hezekiah's failings.

First of all, *take care when you are enjoying success.* Hezekiah became complacent when he was at the height of his powers. That is a feature of human nature. It is when we are successful in our careers, climbing the corporate ladder, making money in business, in the winning sports team, passing examinations, that we most need to take care. Take care that you are not carried away by 'the worries of this life, the deceitfulness of wealth and the desires for other things' (Mark 4:19). According to our Lord's interpretation of the parable of the sower, these are the thorns that choke out the growing seed. Or we might remember the farmer in another parable, whose ground produced a bumper crop. It was not during the months of hard work and eager waiting that he became complacent. It was when his harvest was too big to store in his barns that he said to himself, 'You have plenty of good things laid up for many years. Take life easy; eat, drink and be merry.' God's response was: 'You fool!' (Luke 12:19-20).

We need to take especial care when we enjoy success in the Christian life. When we have committed our lives to the Lord, and are assured of our salvation, and after we have seen off several temptations and are overcoming sin and are growing spiritually, and when others think highly of us, and when we can see fruit from our witness and we feel happy and secure — that is when Satan will strike with deadly effectiveness. If we do not take care our fall will be swift and serious.

Secondly, *the consequences of complacency are serious.* We might not rate complacency as a very serious sin, like murder or adultery. After all, isn't it just a sin of the thoughts? When we are complacent we imagine that we do not actually do anything; we just forget to do something. When we know that we have become complacent we sometimes say to ourselves, 'I can soon snap out of it.' But stop and look at the consequences of Hezekiah's complacency. He took God for granted, and as a result he stopped thinking straight. He took the credit for himself, and stopped pointing others to God. As a result, 'The LORD's wrath was on him and on Judah and Jerusalem.' Devastation and captivity ruined the lives of many. As we saw, Sennacherib's armies were destroyed and Jerusalem was spared, but much damage was done.

There was, however, worse to come. Although Hezekiah repented and **'The LORD's wrath did not come upon them during the days of Hezekiah'** (32:26), judgement did come eventually. This is elaborated in 2 Kings 20:16-19: 'Then Isaiah said to Hezekiah, "Hear the word of the LORD: The time will surely come when everything in your palace, and all that your fathers have stored up until this day, will be carried off to Babylon. Nothing will be left, says the LORD. And some of your descendants, your own flesh and blood, that will be born to you, will be taken away, and they will become eunuchs in the palace of the king of Babylon.' These were the tragic consequences of Hezekiah's complacency.

One of the most common mistakes a golfer will make is to lift his head just as the club is about to hit the ball. That momentary look away from the ball spoils the whole swing. It is even more important for a trapeze artist in the circus to keep his focus. If his attention slips for just one moment as he swings from one crossbar to the other, he will fall. He is unlikely to be killed, because he will fall into the safety net, but his act will be spoiled. The same is true of a believer: 'Though he stumble he will not fall, for the LORD upholds him with his hand' (Ps. 37:24). However, his witness will often be spoiled. This is the consequence of becoming complacent in our walk with God, cool in prayer, blasé about doctrine, irregular in attending church, forgetful to return thanks to God and neglectful of our duty of self-examination and repentance.

Serious as these consequences are, they are often worse for those who come after us. Those who suffered most from Hezekiah's complacency were his children and his people's children. Remember that when we begin the slide, those who come after us often continue it to their destruction. When a godly example is not set in the home, or godly standards are not maintained in the church, or others are turned away from Christianity because our religion is cold and formal or lax and careless, then it is those who follow after us who suffer most from our complacency.

Thirdly, *regard every blessing from God as precious.* That is what Hezekiah forgot to do. Every ounce of silver in his treasury and every day that he lived were from God. Of all people, Hezekiah ought to have known that. He had faced death during his serious illness and because of the direct intervention of God his life had been extended for a further fifteen years. But the same is true of each one us. Everything we have has been given to us from God.

I have noticed how Christians in Australia thank God for the rain. That has been a new idea for someone who grew up in the British Isles, where Christians thank God for every hour that it does not rain! However, both rain and sunshine are from God. 'He causes his sun to rise on the evil and the good, and sends rain on the righteous and the unrighteous' (Matt. 5:45). 'Don't be deceived, my dear brothers. Every good and perfect gift is from above, coming down from the Father of the heavenly lights' (James 1:16-17). Because every gift that God gives is good, it is precious. God's gifts include our health, our families, our homes, our jobs, our minds, our abilities and talents. As Christians we should look at all these things in life in a new way because we see God's hand in them. We appreciate them because he has given them to us.

Moreover, we ought to have a special appreciation of every day that God has given to us. We are not in this world for ever. Our lives are like a mist, and all too soon they will end. But God has given us today. That is why Paul urges us to make the most of every opportunity (Eph. 5:16). For those who are not yet saved this is still a day of opportunity; don't waste it. 'I tell you, now is the time of God's favour, now is the day of salvation' (2 Cor. 6:2). Don't make any more plans until you have made your peace with God (James 4:13-14).

For believers, each day is also a day of opportunity to serve God, and every second of it is precious. Today is a day to do as much as we possibly can. He has saved us and he gives us this day so that we might show him our gratitude. George Whitefield once asked a group of ministers if it were not a comfort to them to know that soon they would go to their rest. William Tennant Jr. was uncomfortable with what Whitefield had said: 'No sir, it is no pleasure to me at all, and if you knew your duty it would be none to you. I have nothing to do with death; my business is to live as long as I can, as well as I can, and to serve my Lord and Master as well as I can, until he shall think proper to call me home.' Yes, every day of our life on earth is precious!

Fourthly, *our silences dishonour God.* When the envoys came to ask about the miraculous sign, it was a demonstration of God's power over nature that drew them. Yet Hezekiah gave them a demonstration of his own power, and said not a word about God. This is what dishonoured God. This was what offended our Lord when only one out of the ten lepers that he had healed returned to say 'Thank you'. 'Were not all ten cleansed? Where are the other nine?' (see Luke 17:17-18).

Do you see God's hand in the good things that you have? Do you appreciate them because God has given them to you? If so, say so. Say so in prayer and in witness to others. Don't be silent when others ask about the mercy of God, or when others start to talk about God, or when others deny God, or when others praise you for the blessings that God has given you. Christian people enjoy many blessings that unbelievers do not have. The lives of Christian people will be holding together where those of unbelievers will be falling apart. Believers have faith and hope where believers have doubt and uncertainty. Don't take the credit for what God has done for you; speak out for God!

Sometimes people may say to you, 'I really admire your faith.' Our reply should be that it is not our faith that sustains us; rather it is the God in whom our faith rests. Let me express this point theologically: it is not the exercise of my faith that sustains me, but the object of my faith, the Lord Jesus. After the home of an elderly lady was burgled she received a visit from a Victim Support volunteer. She told her visitor that she was not afraid to stay on her own in her home because she knew that the Lord was her protector. The visitor was profoundly impressed by that testimony. God was honoured because one of his people refused to be silent and was willing to give the credit for her courage to God. Are you willing to do the same?

23.
Manasseh and Amon:
the worst of men

Please read 2 Chronicles 33:1-25

People are often fascinated by sheer wickedness. Newspaper editors know that 'Good news is no news,' because most people are not interested in other people's good news. It is the bad news that grabs our attention and makes the headlines. Popular newspapers are more likely to contain stories about corruption, dishonesty, violence, cruelty, sex and perversion than about honesty, kindness, purity and uprightness. Recently I went to the local library to do some reading about the history and culture of Cambodia, a country that has a long history and a fascinating culture; but all I could find were books about Pol Pot and his 'killing fields'. A bizarre manifestation of this fascination is the way in which, not so long ago, in the United States of America, a mass murderer on 'death row' became a celebrity and received fan mail.

Why should this be so? Perhaps it is because people like to gaze at the darker side of their own personalities, kept safely at a distance, or perhaps because they like to reassure themselves that they are not so bad after all. Or it may be nothing more sophisticated than a perverse fascination with evil. But none of these explains why the Chronicler gives this account of King Manasseh and his son Amon. They were wicked men who took wickedness to new and unprecedented levels in Judah.

The lives of Manasseh and Amon are wedged in between the accounts of two good kings — Hezekiah and Josiah. These two men undid all the good work that Hezekiah had done and left a dreadful mess for Josiah to clear up. Our hearts sink when we read about them. Most of the chapter is devoted to the fifty-five-year reign of Manasseh (687–639 B.C.), while the two-year reign of Amon (639–638 B.C.) is described in only five verses. It is not simply the length of Manasseh's reign (the longest of any king in the history of Israel) that makes him noteworthy, but the fact that his sins were regarded as making the exile of the people of Judah inevitable.

Manasseh's sin brought God's judgement upon Jerusalem more than a century after his death. 'The LORD said through his servants the prophets: "Manasseh king of Judah has committed these detestable sins. He has done more evil than the Amorites who preceded him and has led Judah into sin with his idols. Therefore this is what the LORD, the God of Israel, says: I am going to bring such disaster on Jerusalem and Judah that the ears of everyone who hears of it will tingle..."' (2 Kings 21:10-12). 'Surely these things happened to Judah according to the LORD's command, in order to remove them from his presence because of the sins of Manasseh and all he had done, including the shedding of innocent blood. For he had filled Jerusalem with innocent blood, and the LORD was not willing to forgive' (2 Kings 24:3-4). Manasseh's sin was the straw that finally broke the back of God's patience and mercy.

'Manasseh was twelve years old when he became king' (33:1). He was born during the fifteen 'additional' years that the Lord gave to Hezekiah (2 Kings 20:6). Perhaps, by this stage of his life, Hezekiah was too old and ill to nurture his son properly. At any rate, Manasseh showed no evidence that he was influenced by his father's godly example — at least not in his early years. Why, therefore, does the Chronicler dwell on the life of Manasseh? Let me suggest two reasons.

Firstly, to show us that *God's people can never afford to sit back and take for granted the privileges of God's blessing.* Each generation must fight anew its own battles and grasp afresh the power of God's truth. This lesson is well illustrated in the book of Judges. When the people of Israel sinned, the Lord allowed them to suffer oppression at the hands of their neighbours. When they cried out to the Lord for deliverance, he raised up judges to rescue them. However, after each judge had called the people back to the Lord there was another time of falling away, and another time of oppression at the hands of Israel's enemies to oppress the people again, until once more their distress drove them to cry out to the Lord, who once again answered by sending a deliverer.

Mao Tse-Tung's distinctive form of Marxism envisaged society in a state of constant revolution. Constant, frenetic revolutionary activity would, he claimed, purge society of its evils. The result of Mao's ideology was the disastrous 'Cultural Revolution' of the 1960s and 1970s, which, in time, exhausted the people of China and burned itself out. Similarly, church history shows us that there is no such thing as constant revival in a sinful world. The history of the church in every age is a cycle of revival and falling away. After times of blessing old sins come back with new vigour and there is a great need for spiritual watchfulness. After the Protestant Reformation of the sixteenth century, Martin Luther reminded his followers that a reformed church will be *semper reformanda* (always reforming). After Hezekiah's reformation the people of Judah stopped reforming and started following Manasseh's wicked lead. Why? Where were the spiritual watchmen? They had evidently failed to do their work!

There is a second reason why the Chronicler tells us about Manasseh. He records something that the writer of Kings does not. He tells us about *Manasseh's repentance and restoration.* Manasseh became a reforming king — yes, even Manasseh!

Against the black darkness of Manasseh's sin we see the power of God's saving grace.

The Chronicler often describes long life as a gift from God indicating his mercy and favour. This raises the question: how could it be that the most wicked of the kings of Judah ruled longer than any other king and enjoyed a relatively long life compared with most of those who came before and after him? This question remains unresolved in the account in the book of Kings, which is primarily concerned with explaining the eventual destruction of Jerusalem in 587 B.C. However, the Chronicler was greatly concerned to promote godly conduct from day to day and sought to show that blessings are enjoyed by those who are faithful to the Lord. Manasseh ruled so long because, eventually, **'He sought the favour of the LORD his God'** (33:12). Amon, on the other hand, serves merely to re-inforce this lesson, by way of contrast: **'He did evil in the eyes of the LORD, as his father Manasseh had done... But unlike his father Manasseh, he did not humble himself before the LORD'** (33:22-23).

The seriousness of Manasseh's sin (33:1-10)

1. He returned to the sins of the past (33:2-6)

Manasseh restored the sinful practices that his father Hezekiah had suppressed. They are listed here: **'He rebuilt the high places his father Hezekiah had demolished...'** (33:3). God had commanded his people to worship him at a central lo-cation (Deut. 12:1-7). However, Manasseh encouraged the establishment of many shrines throughout the land. He encouraged the worship of many false gods (take note of the plurals here): **'... he also erected altars to the Baals and made Asherah poles. He bowed down to all the starry hosts**

and worshipped them' (33:3). His worship of false gods spilled over into the temple: **'He built altars in the temple of the LORD... In both courts of the temple of the LORD, he built altars to all the starry hosts'** (33:4-5).

Manasseh's wickedness took a sinister new turn: **'He sacrificed his sons in the fire in the Valley of Ben Hinnom, practised sorcery, divination and witchcraft, and consulted mediums and spiritists. He did much evil in the eyes of the LORD, provoking him to anger'** (33:6). It is not possible to identify with precision which of the valleys in the vicinity of Jerusalem was the Valley of Ben Hinnom, but in the Old Testament it was associated with the most detestable practices of idolatry. During the lifetime of Jeremiah a shrine to Molech was erected here and Josiah later defiled it. The Hebrew phrase for the Valley of Hinnom *(ge Hinnom)* became *Gehenna* in Greek, a description for hell. In this awful place the most despicable of sins were committed by Manasseh and his people. Children were sacrificed to demon-gods and the occult was openly practised.

These were not new sins. The Canaanites had practised them for many centuries. That was why the Lord put them out of the land. When the Lord God led the Israelites into the land to possess it as the covenant people he gave them laws to suppress these activities. 'Do not give any of your children to be sacrificed to Molech, for you must not profane the name of your God. I am the LORD' (Lev. 18:21). 'Let no one be found among you who sacrifices his son or daughter in the fire, who practises divination or sorcery, interprets omens, engages in witchcraft, or casts spells, or who is a medium or spiritist or who consults the dead. Anyone who does these things is detestable to the LORD, and because of these practices the LORD your God will drive out these nations before you' (Deut. 18:10-12).

Manasseh did not heed these warnings in the law of God. In fact he went back in history to find the inspiration for his wickedness: **'He did evil in the eyes of the LORD, following the detestable practices of the nations the LORD had driven out before the Israelites'** (33:2). Other kings merely looked back a generation or two to the sins of their Hebrew forbears. Manasseh went back to the sins of the Canaanites, who had lived in the land before Joshua possessed it. If their sins had been offensive to the Lord, the sins of Manasseh were no less so. The consequences for Israel would be as serious as they had been for the Canaanites. The Israelites too would be removed from the land.

Manasseh's headlong rush to copy the evil practices of the Canaanites was foolish and disastrous. He broke down the barriers of national righteousness that restrained evil in society. As you may know, Holland is a country that has been reclaimed from the sea over many years. Much of it lies below sea level and the sea water is kept back by a system of dykes, canals and pumping houses that have been built up over generations. The survival of the country depends on maintaining these dykes intact. One hole will allow the water to flood in and overwhelm the whole system.

A nation that has enjoyed the preaching of the gospel and the influence of God's Word over the generations is like that. God's law has built up commonly accepted norms of public morality: respect for honesty at work, respect for honesty in business, respect for marriage and family, respect for the lives of the ill, aged and unborn, respect for the Lord's Day as a day of rest. We all benefit from the common acceptance of these norms because they hold back a flood of evil. But they can very easily be dismantled, and once they are destroyed it is very difficult to re-establish them. Foolish decisions and ungodly laws can so easily breach the dyke and allow a flood of evil to sweep in over society. That is what is happening in many countries today.

The dykes of Christian morality are being dismantled and being replaced by a new morality — one that is sponsored by godless academics, politicians and churchmen. This new morality is based on human speculation rather than divine revelation, on shifting situational ethics rather than moral absolutes, on preferences rather than convictions. In the end it is the weak who suffer, as in the time of Manasseh. Then it was his own children who suffered the terrible cruelty of being sacrificed in the flames of pagan gods. Today the ones who suffer are unborn babies whose lives are aborted before birth, children who are robbed of the security of their childhood because of family breakdown and many forms of abuse, or the old and the ill whose lives are treated as of little worth and ended by so-called 'mercy killing'. They will suffer more and more until the church is revived and national righteousness is restored.

Manasseh dismantled the patterns of godliness that Hezekiah and others had so painstakingly built up. He restored the sins that Hezekiah had suppressed. Oh, the terrible foolishness of sin!

2. His sinfulness became defiant (33:4,7-9)

'**He built altars in the temple of the LORD, of which the LORD had said, "My Name will remain in Jerusalem for ever,"**' and '**... I will not again make the feet of the Israelites leave the land I assigned to your forefathers, if only they will be careful to do everything that I commanded them concerning all the laws, decrees and ordinances given through Moses.**' Notice the symbolism of Manasseh's act. He set up idols right under God's nose and in defiance of all that God had said to his people.

In 33:4,7 the Chronicler refers to the promises that God had made to Israel when the temple was dedicated: 'I have chosen and consecrated this temple so that my Name may be there for ever. My eyes and my heart will always be there'

(2 Chr. 7:16). Manasseh's actions were an open demonstration of his contempt for the mercy that God had shown to his people by dedicating such a place of worship. Furthermore he demonstrated his contempt for God's exclusive claims upon Israel. This was defiant covenant rejection. This was provocation. Manasseh's rebellion against God was not a quiet rebellion, but an insult hurled publicly into the face of the Most High.

Manasseh and his people sank to depths that had never been plumbed before: '**...they did more evil than the nations the LORD had destroyed before the Israelites**' (33:9). They had been warned: '**The LORD spoke to Manasseh and his people, but they paid no attention**' (33:10). This wickedness was all the more serious because Manasseh and his people had to shut their ears tightly against God's Word so that they could press ahead in their evil with their consciences unassailed. For such men the most serious judgement is reserved.

The punishment of Manasseh's sin (33:11)

Here is the turning-point of the chapter. Manasseh had heard the warnings of 33:8: 'I will not again make the feet of the Israelites leave the land ... if only they will be careful to do everything that I commanded them...' If they did not heed God's warnings then punishment would follow, and it did. Manasseh became a slave of the King of Assyria: '**So the LORD brought against them the army commanders of the king of Assyria, who took Manasseh prisoner, put a hook in his nose, bound him with bronze shackles and took him to Babylon**' (33:11).

Historians argue over the exact circumstances described in 33:11. Under what circumstances might the King of Assyria have taken Manasseh to Babylon?

Some place the events of 33:11 in the reign of Esarhaddon (681–669 B.C.). R. K. Harrison explains: 'Since Babylonia was a vassal of Assyria, and Esarhaddon was in the process of rebuilding Babylon, which his father had destroyed, it is probable that the visiting rulers were shown the magnificence of the restored city before being allowed to return home.' This makes Manasseh's visit to Babylon appear more as a sightseeing tour than a chastisement at the hand of the Lord.

Others place the events of 33:11 in the reign of Esarhaddon's son and successor, Ashurbanipal (669–627 B.C.), and link it to the revolt of Shamash-shum-ukim, the subordinate King of Babylon, which started in 652 B.C. Not much is known about this revolt, though it is thought that Manasseh may have allied himself with the rebel Babylonians. This revolt unsettled the whole Assyrian empire, and resulted in a crackdown upon states whose loyalty was suspect. Ashurbanipal was keen to show Manasseh that rebellion was not a good idea, so he brought him to Babylon, to show him the place where the rebellion had been crushed.

Suffice it to say that Manasseh's experience was not pleasant. It made a profound impression on him. He took a new look at himself and he did not like what he saw.

1. Manasseh saw the nature of his sin

It had made him *a slave.* Sin is a powerful addiction. It starts with small forays into ungodly behaviour that the sinner thinks he can control, but soon he finds it harder and harder to control his sinful behaviour, and his craving for sin comes to dominate his life.

Perhaps you think that this analogy is rather far-fetched and does not have much relevance to your own life. You may ask, 'What has Manasseh got to do with my life? I am not doing the things he did — worshipping idols, killing children, dabbling with the occult, and so forth. Why be so paranoid about sin?' The fact is that if we leave our sin alone, it grows bigger and bigger until it enslaves us. 'Don't you know that when you offer yourselves to someone to obey him as slaves, you are slaves to the one whom you obey — whether you are slaves to sin, which leads to death, or to obedience, which leads to righteousness?' (Rom. 6:16). Unless we are servants of the Lord Jesus we are still slaves to sin, and Manasseh illustrates what a terrible slavery that is.

2. Manasseh saw the seriousness of his sin

What a sorry sight he was, with **'a hook in his nose'** and bound **'with bronze shackles'**! What a humiliation for his family and for his kingdom! It is hard to believe that this pitiful man was the successor of David and Solomon. How could the kingdom fall so low? The Lord brought this about because he took Manasseh's sin very seriously. God hands men over to the consequences of their sins:

> Not so the wicked!
>   They are like chaff
>   that the wind blows away.
> Therefore the wicked will not stand in the judgement,
>   nor sinners in the assembly of the righteous.
> For the LORD watches over the way of the righteous,
>   but the way of the wicked will perish
>
> (Ps. 1:4-6).

3. Manasseh saw the consequences of his sin for others

His exile was only a foretaste of the exile that his wickedness would bring upon Judah a century later. It is sobering to be reminded that when we sin it is not only ourselves that we hurt. Others around us, or who come after us, also suffer. Manasseh was the king and the representative of his people. His actions influenced and affected them. As he suffered the shame of being taken as a slave to Babylon, he was able to get a foretaste of what his children would suffer. But there was a gracious side to God's dealings with Manasseh.

The forgiveness of Manasseh's sin (33:12-17)

Even more breathtaking than Manasseh's sin is his repentance. More amazing still is the demonstration of God's mercy to him. God's grace shines like a jewel against the black backdrop of Manasseh's life. What lessons can we learn?

1. God speaks to sinners through distress

'In his distress he sought the favour of the LORD his God' (33:12). We do not always listen when we are called. For example, we may be called to the dinner table when the meal is ready, but because we are watching an interesting programme on television, or busy doing something else, we do not hear. Again comes the call to sit down at the meal table. This time we hear, but grunt a reply. The third time there is no call, simply a silent jab in the ribs. We know that we dare not delay any longer, or else our meal is likely to be given to the dog! The more caught up we are with our television programme, or whatever else it is that we are doing, the harder it is to get our attention. The same is true when we are slaves to sin. The more we are caught up in our sin, the less attentive we are to the Word of God and the harder God has to prod us in the ribs, so to speak. C. S. Lewis has said, 'Pain is God's megaphone to speak to a deaf world.' Sometimes it is only when we are in distress that we are willing to listen to God and to repent.

2. God is moved by humble prayer

'**And when he prayed to him, the** Lord **was moved by his entreaty and listened to his plea...**' (33:13). It is humbling to realize that the God who never changes is moved by the entreaty of men. God brings about changes in response to our prayers. The Lord who is a solid rock is moved by our prayers. The God who cannot tolerate sin cannot turn away a broken sinner. God does not contradict his own nature, but he shows his everlasting mercy. This is what he had promised in 7:14: '... if my people, who are called by my name, will humble themselves and pray and seek my face and turn from their wicked ways, then will I hear from heaven and will forgive their sin and will heal their land.'

3. God restores those who repent

'**Afterwards he rebuilt the outer wall of the City of David, west of the Gihon spring in the valley, as far as the entrance of the Fish Gate and encircling the hill of Ophel; he also made it much higher. He stationed military commanders in all the fortified cities of Judah**' (33:14). The walled defences of Jerusalem and Judah had been reduced to rubble by the Assyrian invaders, but after Manasseh repented they were rebuilt. This is how God 'healed their land' in faithfulness to his promise in 7:14. This reminds us that both our sin and our repentance have consequences that reach far beyond our personal walk with God. 'Righteousness exalts a nation, but sin is a disgrace to any people' (Prov. 14:34). Here is a clear example of how repentance exalted the broken-down fortunes of Jerusalem.

4. Manasseh's life showed that his repentance was real

This was not a superficial change in Manasseh's life. His repentance stemmed from a knowledge of God. He **'humbled himself greatly before the God of his fathers... Then Manasseh knew that the LORD is God'** (33:12-13). He didn't just moan about his miserable condition; he did something about it. He cried out to God asking for forgiveness: **'He sought the favour of the LORD his God'** (33:12). But the most telling evidence that Manasseh was serious about turning his back upon sin was his willingness to put right the wrongs that he had done. **'He got rid of the foreign gods and removed the image from the temple of the LORD... Then he restored the altar of the LORD and sacrificed fellowship offerings and thank-offerings on it'** (33:15-16). Here is the sign that Manasseh's repentance was real. He set about undoing what his sins had accomplished. He did what he had sinfully neglected to do.

Works of repentance are never the foundation of our salvation, but they are the signs that our salvation is genuine. They are 'fruit in keeping with repentance' (Matt. 3:8). True repentance involves not only a resolve to live a new life, but also receiving from God a new heart, which means that we now hate our old way of living and grieve over the sins which we have committed. It is impossible both to hate our sins and to continue in them at the same time. Change will be manifested in the lives of those who repent. This was very evident in the life of Zacchaeus, the cheating tax-collector. When salvation came to his house he stood up and told the Lord, 'Look, Lord! Here and now I give half of my possessions to the poor, and if I have cheated anybody out of anything, I will pay back four times the amount' (Luke 19:8).

5. No one is too wicked to be saved by the grace of God

Manasseh was the worst of all the kings of Judah, but God's grace reached down into the gutter and raised him up. The people of Judah went into exile because of Manasseh, yet he himself was not beyond the reach of God's grace.

Remember Peter, who denied his Lord (Luke 22:54-62). Remember David, the adulterer and liar and murderer and coward (2 Sam. 11:1-27). Remember Saul, the Pharisee and persecutor (Acts 8:1,3). 'Even though I was once a blasphemer and a persecutor and a violent man, I was shown mercy' (1 Tim. 1:13). We can understand why Ananias was reluctant to visit him (Acts 9:13-16), and why the Jerusalem believers were at first unwilling to receive him (Acts 9:26). Paul explains God's purposes more fully in 1 Timothy 1:14: 'The grace of our Lord was poured out on me abundantly, along with the faith and love that are in Christ Jesus. Here is a trustworthy saying that deserves full acceptance: Christ Jesus came into the world to save sinners — of whom I am the worst.'

It should not surprise us that God should save such a man as Saul or Manasseh. It should give us hope for ourselves. If God can save a Saul or a Manasseh, then he can save anyone, and if he can save anyone then he can save me. Do you believe that?

Some worry about the unforgivable sin (Matt.12:31; 1 John 5:16-17). 'What is it? Have I committed it?' It is important to remember that the only sins which are not forgiven are those that are not repented of. 'Blasphemy against the Holy Spirit' is the persistent refusal to hear his offers of mercy. There is no one who is too sinful to be offered mercy through the Lord Jesus Christ. So, when you hear his gospel offer, do not harden your heart. Repent and believe, for 'Everyone who calls on the name of the Lord will be saved' (Acts 2:21).

Postscript: King Amon (33:21-25)

Sometimes we say, 'Like father, like son,' and the phrase seems appropriate when we read about Manasseh and his son Amon. Their similarities are pointed out in 33:22: **'He did evil in the eyes of the LORD, as his father Manasseh had done. Amon worshipped and offered sacrifices to all the idols Manasseh had made.'** This is a sad postscript to the life of Manasseh, a man who demonstrated God's amazing grace and such evident repentance. Amon continued in the sins of his father, rather than following his father in repentance.

This demonstrates the power that sin can hold over the lives of men. For this reason God commanded the people to remove every trace of idolatry from the land of Canaan when they went in to possess it: 'This is what you are to do to them: Break down their altars, smash their sacred stones, cut down their Asherah poles and burn their idols in the fire' (Deut. 7:5). The very paraphernalia of idolatry was likely to prove a snare to them, so they were to leave nothing to rise up and tempt them. However, it is not easy to root out idolatry, even at the best of times.

Manasseh's reformation was not a thorough reformation and the sins that he had encouraged for decades were not rooted out in the few years of godly living that were allowed to him before he died. Much as Manasseh might repent of his sin, he could not alter the fact that it had been committed, or undo its effects. The insidious influence of his idolatry lived on through his son Amon. It is true that God's grace heals the wounds of our sins, but it does not always remove the scars. We rejoice that an alcoholic who has destroyed his body through a life of sinful drunkenness can come to God and find peace within his soul, but we also have to acknowledge that the damage done to his liver may remain. The damage that Manasseh's sins did to his son remained — and increased.

In two respects Amon differed from his father. First of all, he differed from his father *in his death*. He lived a short life: **'Amon was twenty-two years old when he became king, and he reigned in Jerusalem for two years'** (33:21). He died a violent death: **'Amon's officials conspired against him and assassinated him in his palace'** (33:24). We do not know why they conspired against him. It may have been because they were offended at his idolatrous behaviour, or it may have been because of a palace power struggle. We do know that their actions were sinful (see 1 Sam. 24:6). We also know that they were brought to justice (see 33:25). A higher justice was also being administered because God was able to use their sinful actions to bring his judgement upon Amon.

Secondly, Amon differed from his father in that *he did not repent*. This was a crucial point of difference, and the Chronicler highlights it: **'But unlike his father Manasseh, he did not humble himself before the LORD; Amon increased his guilt'** (33:23). This is why Amon and Manasseh died so differently (one violently after a short life, the other peacefully after a long life) after having lived so similarly. The lesson of Manasseh's life is that the grace of God is offered to the worst of men and can transform the most wicked of lives. Both men lived wicked lives, but Amon would not repent.

We should not see Amon as a helpless victim caught up in a vortex of national apostasy. True, his father's lifestyle had been an unedifying influence upon him, but 'Amon increased his guilt.' He did this by the lifestyle choices he made. He had seen the two sides of Manasseh's life and he selected the evil example to follow. God held him fully accountable for his actions.

From time to time we meet people who blame God for their predicament in life. 'God dealt me a difficult hand. It has been too hard for me to live a Christian life, when I am surrounded by such wickedness and hardships,' they say. But God gives us no room for such fatalism in our thinking or living. We all make decisions and we are accountable to God for them. Amon died in sin because 'He did not humble himself', and as a result he 'increased his guilt'. Let the example of Amon make us resolve to make every effort to 'hear his voice'. 'Let us, therefore, make every effort to enter that rest, so that no one will fall by following their example of disobedience' (Heb. 4:7,11).

24.
Josiah: seeking God

Please read 2 Chronicles 34:1-33

Many people today describe themselves as 'seekers'. They are looking for something in life but have not yet found it. They are not sure what they are seeking, with the result that often they do not find it. Still, they keep looking. Some churches target people whom they call 'seekers'. They offer 'seeker-friendly services' which are stripped of traditional Christian phraseology and features (such as the sermon or the offering) in the hope that they will attract seekers from the world. But they forget that there is 'no one who seeks God' (Rom. 3:11) until God himself draws them; and when God draws sinners, it is not self-fulfilment or entertainment they seek, but God himself. They will be satisfied with nothing less than his Word. They will find their spiritual home among people who have an exalted view of God and his truth.

King Josiah stands out as a man who sought after God. This is the theme of 2 Chronicles 34. Josiah was the last good king of Judah. His reign offered Judah her last chance to avoid impending judgement. Josiah was a reforming king who aimed to transform national life in Judah, but first of all he sought to know the power of God in his own life.

In his allegorical description of the Christian life, *The Pilgrim's Progress*, John Bunyan followed the travels of Christian from the City of Destruction to the Celestial City. Here is how he describes his first sight of the pilgrim: 'I saw a man clothed with rags standing in a certain place, with … a book in his hand, and a great burden on his back. I looked and saw him open the book, and read therein; and, as he read, he wept and trembled; and not being able longer to contain, he brake out with a lamentable cry, saying, "What shall I do?"' As we shall see, this is an excellent description of Josiah — a man with a book in his hand and a burden on his heart. Above all he sought God.

Seeking God is a lifelong commitment (34:1-13)

Josiah became king when he was only a boy and he ruled Judah for thirty-one years, from 640–609 B.C.: **'Josiah was eight years old when he became king, and he reigned in Jerusalem for thirty-one years.'** Throughout those years Josiah made it his priority to serve the Lord his God. **'He did what was right in the eyes of the LORD and walked in the ways of his father David, not turning aside to the right or to the left.'** When a ploughman sets out to plough a straight furrow through a field he fixes his eye on a distant object and does not turn to the right or the left. Provided he has fixed his eye on an object that does not move, his line will be straight. That is what Josiah did. He fixed his eye on the Lord, and all his life he served God.

Notice that Josiah started to seek God early in life: **'In the eighth year of his reign, while he was still young, he began to seek the God of his father David'** (34:3). Josiah was a young man, sixteen years old, when he started to get serious about seeking God. At the time other young men of his generation might have been getting serious about keeping fit, or getting drunk, or finding excitement in their lives, he was serious about God. At that time others were worshipping a whole range of false gods in the hope that one of these deities might be able to answer their prayers. In the ancient world people thought of religion in the same way that businessmen today think of an investment portfolio. They diversified their assets so that if one investment failed, they would have others to fall back on. To some it may have seemed that Josiah was foolishly 'putting all his eggs in one basket'. He sought only Jehovah, 'the God of his father David'. But he sought him with all his heart.

Who encouraged Josiah to seek the Lord? Certainly not his father, Amon. Could it have been his grandfather, a repentant Manasseh, who died when he was six? This is possible, but we have no indication in Scripture. No mentor is mentioned. It was God who drew him, sovereignly, irresistibly and early.

It should not surprise us that God should act in this way. We remember that Jesus said, 'Let the little children come to me, and do not hinder them, for the kingdom of God belongs to such as these' (Mark 10:14). On that occasion Jesus was speaking of infants, children even younger than Josiah. In Ecclesiastes 12:1 the Preacher exhorts: 'Remember your Creator in the days of your youth, before the days of trouble come...' God wants us to seek him as soon as we possibly can. God would rather have a whole life devoted to him from childhood than half a life devoted to him after a dramatic adult conversion. It is said that C. H. Spurgeon once reported to a friend that the previous Lord's Day he had witnessed two and a half conversions. The friend replied, 'What do you mean — two adults and a child?' 'No,' replied Spurgeon, 'two children and an adult.'

It is important to remember this lesson if you were converted as a child, and sometimes think that you do not have a glorious testimony about what the Lord has done in your life. Your conversion is no less a work of amazing grace than that of Saul of Tarsus, the persecutor turned preacher, or John

Newton, the former slave-trader who wrote the words of 'Amazing Grace'. This is an encouragement to parents to pray for the conversion of their children while they are still young. Parents are appointed to be mentors to their children in the faith. They are to have godly expectations for them. They are to expect them to be even more zealous Christians than they themselves have been.

The example of Josiah has a message for even the youngest person who might be reading this book. You are not too young to commit your life to the Lord, and the sooner you do it, the better.

Notice too that Josiah regularly moved on to new stages of spiritual growth. Notice the sequence of events in 34:3-13. In the twelfth year of his reign Josiah started to purge Judah and Jerusalem: **'In his twelfth year he began to purge Judah and Jerusalem of high places, Asherah poles, carved idols and cast images.'** Then in the eighteenth year of his reign he repaired the temple. **'In the eighteenth year of Josiah's reign, to purify the land and the temple, he sent ... to repair the temple of the LORD his God'** (34:8). It is clear from this account that reformation was well under way and that the temple was already being repaired when the 'Book of the Law' (which prompted Josiah's Passover celebrations in chapter 35) was discovered. The account in 2 Kings 22 puts the spotlight on the discovery of the scroll rather than the personal initiative of Josiah, but the chronologies are easily harmonized.

As we follow the progress of reformation during Josiah's reign, we notice that he did not try to do everything that needed to be done all at once. That would have been impossible. He would have burned himself out if he had tried. However, as he grew in grace Josiah moved on to face new challenges and to advance the work of the Lord. What we should notice is that he was not content to rest on his achievements. He was not content to seek God, find peace with God and then go to sleep.

He sought to know God, then to obey God, then to glorify God more and more.

Josiah set himself progressive goals and targets. First of all, he wanted to be a man *walking in a right relationship with God*. He wanted to be a man who could say to Jehovah, 'My Lord and my Saviour'. But he also wanted to be a man in an *obedient* relationship with God. Josiah set out to purify his kingdom from the idolatrous practices that had become so common in Judah. As the king, he could not turn a blind eye to what was happening around him, as if public righteousness were no concern of his. He set out to remove the 'high places, Asherah poles, carved idols and cast images', and as he attempted to do this he realized that he had set himself a mammoth task. He saw new needs and formulated new goals (34:8). In order **'to purify the land and the temple, he sent Shaphan son of Azaliah and Maaseiah the ruler of the city, with Joah son of Joahaz, the recorder, to repair the temple of the Lord his God'**. If there was going to be national reformation, the temple would need to be repaired and restored to its proper use.

Seeking God is not an isolated event, but a lifetime of spiritual growth and rededication. If you have committed your life to the Lord, the next step is to ask, 'Am I growing in the Christian life?' That was the thrust of Paul's prayer for the believers in Colosse: 'We have not stopped praying for you and asking God to fill you with the knowledge of his will through all spiritual wisdom and understanding. And we pray this in order that you may live a life worthy of the Lord and may please him in every way: bearing fruit in every good work, growing in the knowledge of God' (Col. 1:9-10). As you look back over recent years, can you see progress? As you move through the stages of life (childhood, teenage years, adulthood, marriage, parenthood, middle age, old age), are you responding to the challenges of these new situations, or are you just living the sort of Christian life that you learned to live as a child? At each new stage we need to keep growing, or we shall stagnate.

Notice that *Josiah's personal faith had public implications*. Josiah was not content to seek God in the privacy of his palace, and leave untouched all the evils in his kingdom that so offended God. He did not seek God simply to find personal self-worth and self-fulfilment, but because God sought him and called him to be his servant. Jehovah is glorious and worthy of all honour, and that is why the evils listed in 34:4-7 were so offensive to Josiah. The **'high places'** were hills with shrines or altars on the top, traditional places of worship since Canaanite times. **'Asherah poles'** were symbols of the fertility goddess. **'Carved idols and cast images'** were specifically condemned in the second commandment (Exod. 20:4). **'Baals'** were idols derived from the old Canaanite religions, and were a frequent snare to the people of Israel.

Josiah launched the most thorough attempt ever made to eradicate these heathen practices: **'These he broke to pieces and scattered over the graves of those who sacrificed to them. He burned the bones of the priests on their altars.'** His actions fulfilled the warning of the unnamed prophet in 1 Kings 13:2 who had told Jeroboam that his experiment with idolatry would bring the Lord's wrath on Israel. The Lord would destroy his altar: 'O altar, altar! This what the LORD says: "A son named Josiah will be born to the house of David. On you he will sacrifice the priests of the high places who now make offerings here, and human bones will be burned on you." ' It comes as no surprise therefore that the influence of Josiah's reformation reached into the territory of the former northern kingdom. **'In the towns of Manasseh, Ephraim and Simeon, as far as Naphtali ... he tore down the altars**

**and the Asherah poles and crushed the idols to powder
and cut to pieces all the incense altars throughout Israel'**
(34:6-7).

Nor could Josiah rest content while the temple of the Lord
remained in a state of disrepair (34:8-13). In 34:8 he gave an
order to his officials **'to repair the temple of the LORD'.** Just
as Hezekiah had nurtured the true religion, so Josiah took steps
to make sure that the divinely ordained institutions of worship
were maintained. Needless to say, Josiah could not do all this
on his own, so he enlisted the help of others. Shaphan and
Maaseiah were the royal officials who had control of the public coffers (34:8) and they took money to Hilkiah, the high
priest, who had charge of the temple (34:9). Hilkiah in turn
passed this money on to the Levites who supervised the repair
of the temple (34:10), and they paid the workmen who did the
repair work (34:11).

The fact that we ought not to lose sight of as we read the
Chronicler's account of these administrative details is that
Josiah's faith had public implications. It started with a young
lad seeking God, but the consequences affected national priorities and national finances. We may not be in a position to
exercise this kind of influence on the priorities and policies of
our governments, but our faith can still have public implications.
We are called to be witnesses to nations (see Matt. 28:18-20).
We are called to withdraw from the evil practices of the world
around us and to protest against them. Our calling to be 'the
salt of the earth' and 'the light of the world' (Matt. 5:13,14) is
fulfilled only when our private faith becomes a public, and
sometimes unpopular, stand for righteousness. When we take
a public stand for righteousness our good deeds will not simply
be a private matter, for 'men' will 'see your good deeds and
praise your Father in heaven' (Matt. 5:16).

Seeking God involves learning to listen to him (34:14-32)

There is little point in asking a question if we do not listen to the answer. Yet that is what we sometimes do when we seek the Lord in prayer. Dutifully we bring our petitions to God, but as we rise from our knees we are not filled with a confident expectation that God will answer them. We ask for guidance, but we are not alert to God's reply. We speak to God, more to get a burden off our chest than because we know his presence. Sometimes, therefore, we are startled by the way God answers our prayers. This need not be the case if we train ourselves to listen to the Lord.

For many years Josiah sought the Lord, but in the eighteenth year of his reign God directed him in a most dramatic way: **'While they were bringing out the money that had been taken into the temple of the Lord, Hilkiah the priest found the Book of the Law of the Lord that had been given through Moses'** (34:14).

What was this 'Book of the Law'? The most likely suggestion is that it was the book of Deuteronomy, which often describes itself as 'this Book of the Law' (see Deut. 28:61; 29:21; 30:10). However, in Joshua 1:8 and 8:31 the phrase 'this Book of the Law' most probably refers to all five books of Moses. Some have suggested that it was indeed the whole Pentateuch that was discovered and brought before Josiah. However, as the book was read in its entirety twice in one day (according to 2 Kings 22:8,10) this seems unlikely.

Others have put forward the idea that the 'Book of the Law' contained only portions from Deuteronomy, such as chapters 27 and 28, which describe the curses that fall upon those who disobey and the blessings that come to those who obey the covenant. The problem with this suggestion is that it presumes Deuteronomy was composed of a series of smaller books or fragments which were brought together during the reign of

King Josiah. There is no evidence that Deuteronomy is such a gathering of fragments, and there is much to commend the unity and integrity of it as a book written by Moses. This book came to Josiah in its integrity and was read aloud in his presence.

The discovery of this book gave fresh impetus to the reformation that Josiah had already initiated in Judah. The contents of Deuteronomy suggest that it was this 'Book of the Law'. Deuteronomy told the people of Israel that they were to worship God at one central location. God's people were not to worship as the surrounding nations worshipped, and they were to worship only as God commanded. These are themes central to Deuteronomy (Deut. 12:1-7,32) and they were vitally relevant to Josiah's day.

Furthermore the book of Deuteronomy pronounced curses upon the people of Israel should they ever repudiate God's covenant with them: 'However, if you do not obey the LORD your God and do not carefully follow all his commands and decrees I am giving you today, all these curses will come upon you and overtake you... Then the LORD will scatter you among all nations, from one end of the earth to the other' (Deut. 28:15,64). Such a solemn warning would surely explain Josiah's startled response to the reading of the 'Book of the Law'.

How such a part of the Old Testament Scriptures came to be lost must amaze us, because every word of God is 'precious' (Ps. 19:10) and we are assured that his statutes 'stand firm' (Ps. 93:5). In one sense the Word of God was never lost during those years of apostasy in Judah. It remained in the hands of God's people, but it was never opened. It lay gathering dust in a temple storeroom, just as it may have lain in many homes in Judah. It was not totally lost, but it no longer figured in the thinking of the people.

This is how it was in Europe during the Middle Ages, when the Scriptures were kept from the people and even the clergy did not read them. Most parish churches did not even possess a copy of the Bible, and hardly anyone had the opportunity to read it. Thereafter the rediscovery of gospel truth that took place at the time of the Reformation was built on the work of Bible translators such as William Tyndale. Tyndale expressed his life's ambition in a debate with one of his Roman Catholic opponents: 'If God spare my life, ere many years I will cause a boy that driveth the plough to know more of the Scripture than thou.' God answered Tyndale's dying prayer to 'Open the King of England's eyes' in 1538 when Henry VIII, the King of England at the time, ordered that a copy of the Scriptures be placed in every parish church in England. The Word of God was being rediscovered, or rather restored to its rightful place.

The disappearance of God's Word from the consciousness of the people of Judah indicates that the spiritual state of Judah was at a very low ebb. It was a further sign of how far they had drifted from God that the Scriptures were no longer read. It is an indication that this state of affairs had been going on for a very long time. The officials who were meant to teach God's law to the people had forgotten even that this scroll was in the temple. This was a major contributing factor to Judah's national decline. Josiah and his courtiers were in for a shock when they read the words of this long-hidden scroll.

How was 'the Book of the Law' rediscovered? As he was discharging his responsibility to pay the workmen who repaired the temple, Hilkiah found it. He then passed it on to Shaphan, the royal secretary, whose responsibility it was to report on all that had been done to repair the temple. This is described in 34:16-18: **'Then Shaphan took the book to the king and reported to him: "Your officials are doing everything that has been committed to them."'** Then, almost as an aside, he mentioned the Book of the Law that had been given to him. Notice that it was as they carried out their God-given work that they discovered further guidance. This reminds us of the words of Abraham's servant, Eliezer of Damascus, when he went to seek a wife for Isaac: 'I being in the way, the Lord led me' (Gen. 24:27, AV). God does not direct us when we sit doing nothing. He directs us when we are following the leads he has already given us.

Notice also that God's direction to Josiah could very easily have been overlooked. The 'Book of the Law' was just a dusty old scroll, lying in a corner of the temple. It could very easily have been swept aside by these men who were doing an important task for the Lord. They were restoring the house of the Lord, not preserving ancient relics, and in their excitement they might easily have missed the importance of the scroll. That would have been a tragic loss. But that is what busy Christians often do today. They are busy with church life and meetings; they enjoy fellowship with other believers; perhaps they are out every night of the week attending Christian activities; but they hardly ever take time to read the Bible for themselves. If they do read it, they rarely take time to feed upon it and listen carefully to the Lord as they read. That is why Bible-believing Christians need to learn to be Bible-reading Christians. We need to learn to listen to God as he speaks in his Word, for listening is not as easy as we think. God does not always answer us as we expect. God often answers us in surprising ways. Certainly Josiah and his courtiers got a surprise when they read the 'Book of the Law'.

What became of this rediscovered book? **'Shaphan read from it in the presence of the king'** (34:18). When Josiah heard it read he listened long and hard, and he was devastated. **'When the king heard the words of the Law, he tore his robes'** (34:19). Josiah realized that all the reforms which had taken place during his reign to date had only scratched the surface of his nation's apostasy. Perhaps the king might have been expecting a pat on the back to congratulate him for his zeal and faithfulness. However, instead of a commendation he and his people received a stern warning from the Word of God. He was reminded that, as well as being guilty of sins of commission by setting up heathen idols, they were guilty of sins of omission by failing to observe the ordinances of divine worship prescribed in the 'Book of the Law'.

We can learn from Josiah's response, for there are two ways of responding to God's directions.

One way of responding to an uncomfortable challenge from God's Word is *evasion*. We reason to ourselves: 'There must be some mistake here. This book in interesting, but not very relevant to us today.' We plead, 'Be reasonable! These idol-worshippers can't be completely wrong. Some of them are very sincere people.' Perhaps we may try to argue along prag-matic lines: 'We have done our best, and we should not push people too far. They have built up their traditions, and they have to be respected.' Where the will to obey is lacking, a loophole will always be found to get around God's Word.

The other way of responding to the challenge of God's Word is *submission*. We say, 'God has spoken and we will listen — even if our traditions demand one thing and God's Word another.' This was the challenge that faced Martin Luther when he was called before the Holy Roman Emperor in 1521 and charged with disrupting the empire on account of his 'hereti-cal' teaching. Luther was warned that he was challenging the pope, the councils of Christendom and a thousand years of church tradition. This fact weighed heavily upon Luther's mind, but he was faced with a stark choice between the authority of Scripture and that of tradition. His response gave expression to the Reformation motto of *Sola Scriptura*: 'I do not accept the authority of popes and councils, for they have contradicted each other and my conscience is captive to the Word of God.'

When we bring God's Word to bear on the habitual sins of our lives and our churches and our communities, we shall find ourselves in situations like that which confronted Josiah, where many vested interests are challenged by the Word of God. Many times it would be easier just to close the Bible and pretend that we have not heard what is taught in it. However, for the Christian this is never an option. We should always be willing to come back to Scripture, acknowledge that we have been wrong, and make the necessary (if painful) changes. Let's take a closer look at how Josiah responded to God's Word.

1. With grief and horror

'He tore his robes' (34:19). Josiah was horrified that for all those years God had been dishonoured and his Word had been ignored: **'Great is the Lord's anger that is poured out on us because our fathers have not kept the word of the Lord'** (34:21). God's Word had made an impact on his soul and Josiah saw the horror of his sins.

2. With a hunger to find out more

He issued the following decree: **'Go and enquire of the Lord for me and for the remnant in Israel and Judah about what is written in this book that has been found'** (34:20-21). Josiah's servants went to a prophetess called Huldah for further direction from the Lord (34:22). This was unusual in Old Testament times, but not unknown. Miriam (Exod. 15) and Deborah (Judg. 4) were also prophetesses. The fact that God spoke through prophetesses in times when godly men were in short supply does not indicate that this ought to be a regular practice. Nor ought we to use this instance to justify the exercise of a teaching ministry by women within the church. How do we square this fact with the principle expressed in Paul's injunction, 'I do not permit a woman to teach or to have authority over a man; she must be silent,' in 1 Timothy 2:12? We are to remember that not everything described in Scripture is commended. We are to acknowledge that there are passages in Scripture which appear difficult to reconcile with other passages. In those cases we take our lead from the clear teaching of the more straightforward passages in Scripture. The lesson we learn from these verses is that Josiah saw danger and went to God for direction. He turned to God for guidance — not to men.

The message from Huldah was a mixed one. There was a message of ultimate disaster for Judah: **'I am going to bring disaster on this place and its people — all the curses written in the book that has been read in the presence of the king of Judah'** (34:24-25). But there was also a message of present deliverance for Josiah: **'Tell the king of Judah, who sent you to enquire of the LORD, "This is what the LORD, the God of Israel, says concerning the words you heard: Because your heart was responsive and you humbled yourself before God when you heard what he spoke against this place and its people, and because you humbled yourself before me and tore your robes and wept in my presence, I have heard you, declares the LORD"'** (34:26-28).

Josiah knew that it was never too late to hear God's Word and repent, however depressing the situation around us may be. However heavily the skies may be laden with God's judgement, it is always worthwhile to preach God's Word and call men and women to repentance. Fatalism ought to have no place in the thinking of the people of God. God's Word is always powerful:

So is my word that goes out from my mouth:
  it will not return to me empty,
but will accomplish what I desire
  and achieve the purpose for which I sent it
                                        (Isa. 55:10-11).

It always does good. Although its warnings may terrify us, if we heed them God will hear us and deliver us from disaster.

3. With a desire to bring his people to repentance (34:29-32)

Josiah was a powerful leader among his people. He **'called together all the elders of Judah and Jerusalem. He went up to the temple of the Lord... He read in their hearing all the words of the Book of the Covenant... [He] stood by his pillar and renewed the covenant in the presence of the Lord...'** The covenant that Josiah renewed was the everlasting covenant that God had made with his people. God had made that covenant with Abraham and it had been renewed many times since (see Deut. 29; Josh. 24; 1 Chr. 17; 2 Chr. 15:14; 23:16). Israel was a nation greatly blessed by God, and with those blessings came great responsibility. God's covenant proclaims both promises and warnings to his people. Josiah sought to impress both of these upon the collective consciousness of his people by making a solemn covenant before the Lord. He 'renewed the covenant in the presence of the Lord'.

God's covenant is not made with individuals in isolation. God called Israel to be his chosen *nation*. As a community they were to enjoy the blessings of God's mercy and shoulder the obligation to honour him in all that they did. That is why Josiah was not content simply to renew his personal covenant with the Lord. His next step was to call his people to do the same. **'Then he made everyone in Jerusalem and Benjamin pledge themselves to it; the people of Jerusalem did this in accordance with the covenant of God, the God of their fathers'** (34:32). This national commitment was the next appropriate response to God's covenant of grace.

Nations today do not have a unique relationship with God, as the nation of Israel had in Old Testament times, but they are blessed by God. Nations are under the sovereign rule of Jesus

Christ, the mediator of the covenant of grace, and they are to acknowledge his authority. The example of Josiah and his people was an inspiration for the people of Scotland in 1638 during a time of spiritual awakening when they acknowledged *in writing* their duty to honour Christ. This they did when they signed the National Covenant of Scotland in Greyfriars Church-yard in February 1638. Many godly citizens did exactly what Josiah and his people did. They heard God's Word and called their fellow citizens to acknowledge God. Let's pray for such national awakenings in our lands today.

But let us begin with ourselves. Have you begun to seek the Lord? Are you seeking God daily? Are you listening to him and following him? The psalmist was able to say in Psalm 85:8, 'I will listen to what God the LORD will say...' Is that true of you?

25.
Josiah: the last opportunity

Please read 2 Chronicles 35:1-27

Sometimes when you go down to the beach, you may see a sign warning about dangerous currents. This means that you will have to be careful if you go into the water to swim, especially if the tide has turned. Even a strong swimmer can swim with all his might, but still make little headway against the tide, while a weak swimmer will be swept away. In many ways King Josiah was like a man swimming against the tide. He was one of the greatest of the reforming kings of Judah. He was upright and courageous; he set his face on seeking God, 'not turning aside to the right or to the left' (34:2). However, the times were against him. The moral and spiritual tide had turned. Manasseh's sin had made judgement inevitable for Judah.

In chapter 34 the Chronicler described how Josiah sought to turn back the evil of his time. As a young man he sought the Lord his God and he attempted to purify his kingdom. His reforms were given added impetus by the discovery of the Book of the Law. Josiah listened to the reading of the long-lost scroll as he had never listened before. What an impact it made on him! Already he knew that Judah's idolatry was an offence to God, and perhaps he was tempted to pat himself on the back for trying to remove it. Any danger of Josiah's allowing himself the luxury of self-congratulation was blown away by what he heard read. He came to see Judah's sins of omission, as well as their sins of commission. For generations they had failed to keep the Passover, and Josiah resolved to observe it at once. That is the theme of 35:1-19.

Josiah's Passover (35:1-19)

The Feast of Passover, or Unleavened Bread, was an annual celebration, held every year on the fourteenth day of the first month of the Jewish calendar. **'This Passover was celebrated in the eighteenth year of Josiah's reign'** (35:19). This was the same year that 'the Book of the Law' had been found during the renovation of the temple. Because the Passover was celebrated so early in the calendar year it has been suggested that Josiah's Passover preceded the discovery of 'the Book of the Law'. This is not necessarily so, as in all probability Josiah's regnal year did not begin with the calendar year, and his eighteenth year on the throne would have reached over to a new Passover season. We should regard Josiah's Passover as one of the results of the discovery of 'the Book of the Law'.

The Passover Feast had first been celebrated when the Lord God brought the Israelites out from slavery in Egypt. They were to take a year-old lamb which was without blemish, they were to kill it at twilight and they were to sprinkle its blood on the sides and tops of the door-frames (Exod. 12:5,6,7). In time, when the Passover was a regular celebration, it was followed by a seven-day festival during which no bread made with yeast was to be eaten. This was known as the Feast of Unleavened Bread.

After the Israelites settled in the promised land, the Passover was celebrated centrally by the whole nation at Jerusalem. Looking forward to the time when there would be a temple in Jerusalem, Moses gave this instruction: 'You must not sacrifice the Passover in any town the LORD your God gives you except in the place he will choose as a dwelling for his Name. There you must sacrifice the Passover in the evening, when the sun goes down, on the anniversary of your departure from Egypt' (Deut. 16:5-6). That is why the tribes of Israel went up to Jerusalem to celebrate the Passover.

These features were faithfully reflected in Josiah's Passover: **'Josiah celebrated the Passover to the LORD in Jerusalem, and the Passover lamb was slaughtered on the fourteenth day of the first month'** (35:1). Throughout the rest of this account of Josiah's Passover the Chronicler reminds us that Josiah earnestly sought to observe the Passover correctly — **'as is written in the Book of Moses'** (35:12), **'as prescribed'** (35:13). Indeed, **'The entire service of the LORD was carried out for the celebration of the Passover and the offering of burnt offerings on the altar of the LORD, as King Josiah had ordered'** (35:16). Josiah was devoted to doing exactly what the Lord had commanded his people to do, 'not turning to the right or to the left'. He made sure that on this occasion there were none of the loose ends about which Hezekiah had needed to make special intercession (see 30:2-3,17-20).

All of this ought to be of interest to Christians today, because our Lord celebrated the Passover on the evening that he offered himself to die on the cross. On that evening of anxious waiting he prayed to his Father, 'Father, the time has come. Glorify your Son, that your Son may glorify you' (John 17:1). In the upper room, as he ate with his disciples, our Lord took the cup of blessing and the bread used in the Passover feast to symbolize his shed blood and his broken body when he died on the cross to make an atoning sacrifice for sin. In doing so our Lord transformed and renewed the Old Testament Passover into the New Testament sacrament of the Lord's Supper.

The main difference is that the work of Christ is now presented more clearly in the Lord's Supper, where he is set before us as a Saviour who has already died, rather than as a promised Saviour who was still to die. In the Lord's Supper the Lord's people look back upon his death and forward to his return (1 Cor. 11:26).

Josiah's zeal for the Passover teaches us to value the privilege of coming to the Lord's Table. Some have over-emphasized the significance of this sacrament. Ritualists within the Roman Catholic Church and other churches teach that the sacraments automatically convey grace, and have made the reception of the Lord's Supper a means of salvation rather than a means of grace. The Reformers correctly stressed the fact that the Lord's Supper conveys blessing only to those who exercise saving faith.

Some Protestants overreact in the opposite direction. You may hear some say of the Lord's Supper, 'It is only a sign; it does not save.' They are right in saying that it does not save us, but it is not a trivial ritual! The Lord's Supper is an inestimable privilege and when properly observed (by believing people and accompanied by the preaching of the Word and prepared hearts) it has the potential to revive and refresh the church. Matthew Henry commented: 'Religion cannot flourish where that Passover is either wholly neglected or not duly observed; return to that, receive that, make a solemn business of that affecting binding ordinance, and then, it is to be hoped, there will be a reformation in other instances too.'

Josiah went back to basics by celebrating the long-neglected Passover Feast. He was careful to do what generations of God's people had done. He did what Moses, Joshua and Hezekiah had all done, but his celebration of the Passover was unique: **'The Passover had not been observed like this in Israel since the days of the prophet Samuel; and none of the kings**

of Israel had ever celebrated such a Passover as did Josiah'
(35:18). We shall consider some of its distinctive features.

1. The possibility of a fresh start

After an open-air service I once got into a conversation with a
half-drunk man who started to tell me about his woes. His
wife had left him; his family did not want to know him; he had
taken to drink, and his life was a mess. In the course of our
conversation I gave him an evangelistic leaflet entitled *A Fresh
Start*. He took a look at its title and sighed, 'That's what I
need.' That is what many sinners say. It is also what some
Christians say. The Passover is a reminder that, with God, there
is the possibility of making a fresh start. The Passover reminded
the people of Israel of a time when they were slaves in Egypt
and their situation seemed hopeless. However, God brought
them out of Egypt and made them into a free nation. He gave
them a fresh start.

That is also the significance of Josiah's command in 35:3:
**'Put the sacred ark in the temple that Solomon son of David
king of Israel built.'** It is not clear why the ark had been
taken out of the temple in the first place. It has been suggested
that previous kings (with no love for the worship of Jehovah)
had removed it. Or perhaps it had been removed to let the
workmen do their job when Josiah ordered the repair of the
temple. Or it may have been that the ark was being carried
around like a talisman, as happened when Eli was the high
priest and his wicked sons took it into battle (see 1 Sam. 4:3-6).
If that were the case it might explain Josiah's words when he
went on to say, **'It is not to be carried about on your
shoulders.'**

Another suggestion is that the ark had been removed from
the temple at Josiah's command to allow a symbolic

re-enactment of 2 Chronicles 5:2-14, when the ark had been installed in the inner sanctuary of the temple during the temple dedication ceremony. Having the ark of the covenant in the Most Holy Place was the symbol of God's presence among his people. The ark was a wooden box, overlaid with gold, and containing two stone tablets on which were written the law of the covenant. After the tabernacle had been constructed the ark was placed in the inner sanctuary (Exod. 40:20-21) and the glory of the Lord filled the tent (Exod. 40:34). It was not the ark of the covenant that protected the people, but the Lord of the covenant, who dwelt among them. The ark was a reminder of his presence according to the terms of his covenant. That covenant was summarized in the promise of 2 Chronicles 7:14-16, where God promised to hear his people and heal their land, if they looked to 'this place'. Josiah's action took them back to that place and that promise.

Yes, those were dark days in the history of Judah. God's judgement hung like a thundercloud over the nation on account of Israel's sin. Yet God's covenant with them was an everlasting covenant of mercy. Even then, as Josiah called the people to repentance, there was the possibility of a fresh start. The same possibility lies before each one of us. You may have sinned terribly and you may have let the Lord down, but remember there is always the possibility of a fresh start.

2. The preparation of spiritual leaders

Josiah **'appointed the priests to their duties and encouraged them in the service of the LORD's temple'** (35:2). It is typical of the Chronicler to record what the priests and Levites did to strengthen the spiritual life of Judah. The Levites were men **'consecrated to the LORD'** who served God by instructing the people (35:3). In 35:4-5 we see how Josiah prepared them to exercise spiritual leadership in Judah — he *appointed* them and *encouraged* them: **'Prepare yourselves by families in your divisions, according to the directions written by David king of Israel and by his son Solomon.'** Each Levite clan had a special task allocated to it. Some were gatekeepers, some were treasurers, some were musicians and others administered the temple sacrifices. Each one knew his task because it had been determined before his birth. Josiah was in effect saying to the Levites, 'You know your task. Now get on with it.'

In 35:6 one additional task was given to the Levites: **'Slaughter the Passover lambs ... for your fellow country-men, doing what the Lord commanded through Moses.'** The ritual they followed had been prescribed by Moses. However, the role of the Levites (slaughtering the Passover lambs for the people) only went back to the reign of King Hezekiah. At Hezekiah's Passover the Levites slaughtered the lambs because the people who came from northern Israel were ceremonially unclean (30:17). This state of national unpreparedness to celebrate the Passover was equally prevalent, even in Judah, during the reign of Josiah. It was accepted that the Levites were to slaughter the Passover lambs for each family. Josiah and his circle of advisers could not turn the spiritual condition of the nation around on their own. They needed able men to whom they could delegate tasks of spiritual oversight. This was the lesson that Jethro taught Moses in Exodus 18:17-23. Without the enthusiastic participation of the Levites, the Passover would not have been celebrated in Judah. Therefore they were 'encouraged' by Josiah.

The church still needs spiritual leaders. That is why our Lord 'gave some to be ... pastors and teachers, to prepare God's people for works of service, so that the body of Christ may be built up' (Eph. 4:11-12). These are men appointed by

Christ to teach God's Word, to administer the sacraments, to nurture and to discipline God's people. This work is important work and, like the work of the Levites, it is to be done in the way that God has commanded in his Word. Also like the work of the Levites, it is to be done by men appointed by Christ. It is demanding work, and work that requires training and encouragement.

3. The provision made by Josiah and his officials

The statistics of 35:7-9 are worth examining. They tell us that Josiah contributed 30,000 sheep and 3,000 cattle (35:7); that the leaders of the priests gave 2,600 sheep and 300 cattle (35:8); and that the Levites gave 5,000 sheep and 500 cattle (35:9) for the Passover sacrifices. This made a total of 37,600 sheep and 3,800 cattle. This is what made Josiah's Passover stand out as special from those that had gone before (35:18). It was special on three counts.

First of all, it was remarkable because of *the numbers of animals sacrificed*, which far exceeded the sacrifices offered even at Hezekiah's Passover. At that time a total of 17,000 sheep and 2,000 cattle were slaughtered.

A second distinguishing feature was *the correctness of the celebration*. There were none of the irregularities that had to be overlooked in Hezekiah's time.

The third factor was *the personal generosity of Josiah*, which, in turn, inspired the priests and Levites to contribute generously themselves. The total value of the animals exceeded several million pounds.

Yet even this generosity pales into insignificance beside the generosity of the Lord Jesus Christ, who gave himself as our

Passover Lamb: 'Greater love has no one than this, that he lay down his life for his friends' (John 15:13). 'For you know that it was not with perishable things such as silver or gold that you were redeemed ... but with the precious blood of Christ, a lamb without blemish or defect' (1 Peter 1:18-19). The fact that salvation is freely offered does not mean that it is cheap. It was costly to buy and it is precious to those who have received it.

4. The people's participation without enthusiasm

The generosity of Josiah camouflages something quite worrying. Normally each family provided its own lamb. That is how it was on that first Passover night, but not at this Passover, for Josiah provided all. The people of Judah simply turned up and ate. It was all too easy for them. Everything was done correctly, but throughout these verses it was the Levites who did it. The people are not mentioned until 35:17: **'The Israelites who were present celebrated the Passover at that time.'** Those who could be bothered to turn up celebrated the feast! A favourite phrase in Chronicles is 'all Israel'. Often it describes the collective actions of the covenant people, but it is noticeably absent here.

We start to see the weakness of Josiah's reformation. It was his personal project, but his people were lukewarm in their support. Josiah did too much for them. He carried their responsibilities, and as a result he encouraged them to be complacent. Those who truly love the Lord will want to give themselves to serving the Lord. They will not be content to watch others giving sacrificial service to the Lord without following their example. This was not the case among the people of Judah at the time of Josiah's Passover. Josiah's reformation had been superficial. It had changed some habits, but it did not change hearts. Jeremiah saw that, and called the people to a more thorough reformation:

> Break up your unploughed ground
> > and do not sow among thorns.
>
> Circumcise yourselves to the LORD,
> > circumcise your hearts,
> > you men of Judah and people of Jerusalem,
>
> or my wrath will break out and burn like fire
> > because of the evil you have done —
> > burn with no one to quench it
>
> > > > (Jer. 4:3-4).

Of course, only God can turn back the tide of national wickedness. However great, or gifted, or zealous individual men might be, they can never do it on their own. A minister was walking through the town where he ministered when he saw a crowd gathering. At the centre of the commotion he saw a member of his congregation in a drunken stupor. A man in the crowd asked, 'Isn't that one of your converts?' To which the minister replied, sadly, 'Yes, that is one of my converts. If only God had converted him it might have been different.' The changes that God makes in the lives of men are lasting and profound, while the changes that we ourselves make will always be superficial, by comparison.

As we look at ourselves we should ask, 'Are we God's converts?' Do we have just a form of godliness, or do we have the power as well? Do we have just a correct form of doctrine and worship, or do we have enthusiasm for it as well? Do we love the Word of God, the praise of God, the worship of God and the people of God? Do we love God when no one is watching over us? We each need to test our own hearts. We need to seek the Lord and serve him wholeheartedly.

The fall of a good man (35:20-27)

Every good story has a surprise. The Chronicler often has a surprise for us when we read about the kings of Judah. We were surprised at the way Hezekiah's reign concluded. We might never have thought that Manasseh would end his reign as a repentant and forgiven man. Josiah, too, surprises us. He was one of the most outstanding examples of piety among the kings of Judah, but there is a surprise for us as we consider his death. He died on the battlefield just before he reached his fortieth birthday. Josiah's life and death warn us against resting on the achievements of a godly life. We are to persevere in serving the Lord right to the end.

1. The setting of Josiah's fall

'**After all this...**' (35:20) refers to the years of extensive reform in Judah. It had all begun with Josiah seeking the Lord when he was sixteen years of age and covers his purging idolatry from among the people, restoring the temple, returning to God's law and celebrating the Passover. Josiah went further and achieved what Hezekiah had sought to do: he shut down the shrines and high places throughout Judah where false worship took place. In his short lifetime he accomplished a great deal.

We also need to remember Josiah's weakness. The reformation was his reformation. The people were not really with him. They participated, but without enthusiasm. He carried the whole burden on his shoulders, and the people were willing to let him. He did far too much himself, and fostered complacency in others. He was like a rector who developed the habit of going to a certain railway bridge in his parish every afternoon to watch the 4.10 p.m. express train to London rush past. Some of his parishioners were concerned when they became aware of this habit and asked him why he did it. His reply was that this train was the only thing in the parish that moved without his pushing it. Here was a typical example of pastoral inability to delegate. The result for pastor and people was frustration and exhaustion.

Josiah was like a doctor on call for many hours on end. Tragically some doctors work impossibly long hours and the strain affects not only themselves and their families, but their patients as well. As a result of exhaustion they can make fatally bad decisions. That happened to Josiah. He was physically, emotionally and spiritually exhausted, at the very time when he needed a clear head and a steady hand to steer his people through turbulent times. All around Judah empires were crumbling and new powers were rising, and Josiah was caught up in the turmoil when **'Neco king of Egypt went up to fight at Carchemish on the Euphrates'**.

On 9 November 1989 the Berlin Wall was torn down and the way was opened to German reunification. This was one of the clearest signs that the Soviet Union was losing its grip on eastern Europe. Some years later the American president at the time, George Bush, commented that this incident was 'the most dicey of my presidency'. Only the personal friendships between the world leaders of the time and steady diplomacy prevented a violent reaction to what happened in Berlin. Josiah was living though a similarly volatile and unstable time.

The Assyrian Empire (Judah's traditional enemy) was collapsing and the Babylonians were advancing from the East. In 612 B.C. they captured Nineveh, the Assyrian capital. After the Assyrians regrouped at Haran the Babylonians attacked again in 610 B.C. The Assyrians regrouped again at Carchemish, in an effort to retake Haran. To the west, Egypt moved to pick up the crumbs from the crumbling Assyrian Empire. When the Egyptians realized how rapidly the Babylonians were advancing from the east, they tried to prop up the Assyrian Empire as a buffer between themselves and Babylon. That is why Neco, the Egyptian pharaoh, marched out to support the Assyrians in their efforts to recapture lost territory. It was a futile campaign and the combined forces of Egypt and Assyria were eventually defeated at Carchemish in 609 B.C. Unfortunately (in his eagerness to see Assyria crushed) Josiah failed to foresee how vulnerable the Assyrian position was. He tried to stop Neco before he could reach the Assyrians and was defeated at Megiddo.

Strategic analysis should have told Josiah to stay out of this quarrel between the Egyptians and the Babylonians. So too should the principles of God's Word. 'Starting a quarrel is like breaching a dam; so drop the matter before a dispute breaks out' (Prov. 17:14). 'Like one who seizes a dog by the ears is a passer-by who meddles in a quarrel not his own' (Prov. 26:17). So too should the prophecies of Scripture, which pointed to Assyria's inevitable destruction. However, an even clearer warning should have warned Josiah to avoid a quarrel with Pharaoh Neco.

2. The warning of Josiah's fall (35:21-22)

'Neco sent messengers to him saying, "What quarrel is there between you and me, O king of Judah? ... God has told me to hurry; so stop opposing God, who is with me, or he will destroy you." ' Evidence from ancient inscriptions seems to indicate that Neco had made a prior request for passage through. Josephus records that 'Neco sent a messenger to him, explaining that he only wanted free passage on his way to Euphrates. But Josiah ignored the request and prepared for battle.' This was not an invasion of Judah and in 35:21 Neco protests that he had no hostile intentions towards Josiah. He was attacking another kingdom — 'the house with which I am at war' — and he had done this at God's prompting. This must have caused some consternation and puzzlement on the part of a godly man like Josiah. But still he failed to heed the warning not to attack.

Neco's claim raises several questions. How could he have claimed to speak for God? Perhaps it was a false claim, like that of Sennacherib's field commander in 2 Kings 18:25. Perhaps, but not necessarily. God had revealed himself to heathen kings before (Gen. 41) and would do so again (Dan. 2; 4). God had spoken through a wicked man like Balaam (Num. 23:7-12,18-24; 24:3-9,15-19). According to 35:22, the Chronicler accepted Neco's claim as true. Josiah **'would not listen to what Neco had said at God's command'**. Josiah ought to have heeded Neco's warning.

How ought Josiah to have recognized that Neco's claim was true? It did sound a suspiciously convenient thing for Neco to say. Josiah must have been confused. On the one hand, God had said that Assyria was going to be judged, and Neco's support for Assyria seemed to be frustrating God's purposes. On the other hand, Jeremiah and other prophets spoke of Egypt as an unreliable ally, and warned against entering into an alliance with her. This might have encouraged Josiah to adopt an anti-Egyptian stance. There may have been a word of confirmation from one of the prophets to back up Neco's warning, but the Scriptures give us no evidence in support of this suggestion. In any event, God's Word always carries the ring of truth. Josiah ignored it, and the inspired historian regards him as blameworthy and careless.

What ought Josiah to have done in this confusing situation? He should have sought further direction from the Lord. The irony is that Josiah was renowned for his reverence for God's Word. When he heard it read in 34:18-21 he recognized it, obeyed it and sought further guidance. When he heard this word from the Lord he failed to heed it (perhaps understandably) and failed to ask for further guidance. This second failure is what we find hard to fathom. He ought to have sought the Lord before launching an attack on Neco. This is what we ought to do when we are unsure about some doubtful project. Perhaps it is a suggestion our friends have put to us, or a plan that we have made. If our consciences are not clear, we should say 'No!' A little caution can protect us from a lifetime of misery, or a lifestyle of sin. We should always stop and seek the Lord first.

3. The details of Josiah's fall (35:23-24)

Josiah went into battle against Neco at Megiddo in northern Israel. Four features of Josiah's death are worthy of our attention.

Firstly, *he went into battle in disguise*: **'Josiah ... disguised himself to engage in battle'** (35:22). Perhaps he was more worried by Neco's warning than he admitted.

Secondly, *he was shot by archers* (35:23).

Thirdly, *he was laid in his chariot to die.* 2 Kings 23:29 makes it clear that Josiah died on the battlefield at Megiddo. This appears at first sight to contradict the Chronicler's account in 35:23-24, as some translations punctuate the verse in a way which gives the impression that Josiah died in Jerusalem. This is not necessarily so, however, for the Chronicler's account does not specify where Josiah died — simply that he did die and was buried in Jerusalem.

Finally, *he was brought back to his palace for burial.*

These details are significant. They would have struck a chord in the memories of those who first read this history, for they were Jews who had a detailed knowledge of their Bibles. They would have been struck by the parallels with the death of King Ahab, the most wicked of all the kings of Israel (1 Kings 22:29-40). They would have been appalled at the comparison.

We know, of course, that Josiah did not die in the same spiritual condition as Ahab, but the details of his death show that he died *like* Ahab. He died as a sinner. His death reminds us that good men can fall, and forfeit some of the blessings that could be theirs. In 34:28 God had promised that Josiah would be 'buried in peace' and that his 'eyes will not see all the disaster I am going to bring on this place and on those who live here'. God kept this promise, in that Josiah did not live to see the destruction of Jerusalem by the Babylonians. He was buried in his own city by his own people, but his death was not a peaceful one. Josiah died a tragic death because he did not follow God's directions. He suffered the consequences of covenant unfaithfulness, and he suffered them within his own lifetime. This 'immediate retribution' is a feature of God's justice to which the Chronicler often draws our attention.

As we think of Josiah's fall, it is sobering to remember that there is no sin which we ourselves are not capable of committing. However old we are, or however far we have advanced in the Christian life, there is never a point at which we can say, 'I have successfully passed through that minefield; there is no more temptation for me.' Good men can fall into sin. The higher they climb, the harder they fall, and the more people they hurt when they fall. It is sobering to be warned by Josiah's fall. Tragedy results when good men fall.

4. The response to Josiah's fall (35:25-27)

The response to Josiah's death was twofold.

First of all, there was *grief*: **'Jeremiah composed laments for Josiah, and to this day all the men and women singers commemorate Josiah in the laments'** (35:25). Although these laments were written down, they were not preserved in Scripture and they are lost to us today. Writing in the first century A.D., Josephus refers to a lament which Jeremiah composed for Josiah's funeral and 'which has survived to this day', but he does not quote from it. Nor are any of these laments contained in the book of Lamentations, which describes Jeremiah's grief after the destruction of Jerusalem in 587 B.C.

Secondly, the people recorded their *gratitude* (35:26-27). Josiah's good works were recorded. His devotion to God, his obedience and his reforms are also referred to here. There was sincere mourning for Josiah because he was a genuinely good man and he had done a great deal for Judah. In fact he offered Judah her last opportunity to repent and to avoid God's judgement. After Josiah died the history of Judah was a steady decline into destruction.

If only the people of Judah had mourned while Josiah lived! Human nature is inclined to miss a good man only after he is dead. People are more inclined to lament their misery than their sin. Tragically, this was mourning tinged with self-pity rather than true repentance. It challenges us to mourn for our sin now so that we might be able to rejoice later. Don't carry on in sin until it is too late; mourn now for your sin. Jesus said, 'Blessed are those who mourn, for they will be comforted' (Matt. 5:4). Paul did not regret the grief he caused the Corinthians by his hard words of rebuke: 'Now I am happy, not because you were made sorry, but because your sorrow led you to repentance... Godly sorrow brings repentance that leads to salvation and leaves no regret, but worldly sorrow brings death' (2 Cor. 7:9-10).

But let's return to Josiah himself, for there are two more lessons to learn. First of all, there is a reassurance: a good man may fall, but he will not be utterly cast down. Josiah fell, but he was still the Lord's. 'Though he stumble, he will not fall, for the LORD upholds him with his hand' (Ps. 37:24). 'The

LORD upholds all who fall and lifts up all who are bowed down' (Ps. 145:14). This is *the preservation of the saints*, a work of God's sovereign grace.

Secondly, we receive an exhortation, not to fall, as Josiah fell, at the end of his life. We are to press on in the Christian life so that we might live well and die well. This is *the perseverance of the saints*, a work of the believer which is enabled by the sovereign grace of God. It is excellently summarized in chapter 17 of the *Westminster Confession of Faith*: 'They whom God hath accepted in his beloved, effectually called and sanctified by his Spirit, can neither totally nor finally fall away from the state of grace; but shall certainly persevere therein to the end, and be eternally saved.'

Here is the goal that we ought to aim for, that our testimony to God's working in our lives will still be flourishing when we are old and tired, ill and dying, and that we might die like Stephen rather than Josiah. 'Stephen, full of the Holy Spirit, looked up to heaven and saw the glory of God, and Jesus standing at the right hand of God...' (Acts 7:55). A close friend of Dr. Martyn Lloyd-Jones visited him just before his death. As he left Lloyd-Jones asked his friend to pray that he might enjoy an 'abundant entrance' into the everlasting kingdom, 'in the full assurance of faith ... in the full sail of faith'. This is a worthy goal for which to live and die.

How are we to pursue this goal? By holding fast to the truths we have believed and by seeking fresh fellowship with Christ every day. 'Guard the good deposit that was entrusted to you — guard it with the help of the Holy Spirit who lives in us' (2 Tim 1:14).

26.
The end of an era

Please read 2 Chronicles 36:1-23

It is not easy to serve God during times of spiritual darkness when everyone else seems to be turning their backs on God. It is hard to be the odd one out, the one who always seems to be out of step with everyone else. It is then that we feel, most acutely, the pressure to conform to the ways of others. It is distressing to see that the God whom we love so dearly is so rudely dismissed by those who despise him or simply want to ignore him. Sometimes, too, the pressure of unbelief around us can fuel our doubts and fears. Perhaps we are tempted to ask, 'If God is the Lord, why do so many deny him? If Christianity is true, why do so many reject it?'

The Chronicler describes such times in this final chapter of his mammoth history of Israel, which recounts the last days of the kingdom of Judah. The northern portion of the kingdom had already disappeared from the political map when the Assyrians captured Samaria in 722 B.C. At that time Hezekiah was king in Jerusalem, and his godly influence and that of men like him turned God's wrath away from Judah for well over a century. The influence of these reforming kings of Judah gives us great encouragement. We can think of God's promise to Abraham in Genesis 18:32 that 'for the sake of ten' he would not destroy the wicked cities of Sodom and Gomorrah. What a difference even a few godly men can make! A small number can have a profound influence on the life of a nation, if they are consecrated to the Lord and their lives are like salt and light. Hezekiah and Josiah were men like that.

However, in 609 B.C. Josiah died, and no one took his place of moral leadership in the kingdom. During the twenty-two years between the death of Josiah and the destruction of Jerusalem in 587 B.C. Judah was ruled by four weak and wicked men — Jehoahaz (36:1-3), Jehoiakim (36:4-8), Jehoiachin (36:9-10) and Zedekiah (36:10-16). In the brief accounts of their reigns we see what happens when men turn their backs on God. Firstly, God permits them to turn away from him. Secondly, God permits them to suffer the consequences of their sins. But thirdly, God does not turn his back on his people. These lessons are illustrated in the three main sections of this chapter.

Rapid decline (36:1-16)

The history of Judah has been like a roller-coaster. Hezekiah took over at a low point and started a great reformation. Gradually integrity was restored to national life and Judah regained her independence and respect. These gains were lost during the reign of his son, Manasseh, although at the end of his reign Manasseh repented and there was a minor reformation. These gains were rapidly lost again during the reign of Amon. The reign of Josiah saw another period of reform, but this was brought to an abrupt end when he died at the battle of Megiddo. Now we are coasting into the final plunge, and 36:1-16 summarize briefly the reigns of the four kings who followed Josiah.

Jehoahaz (36:1-3)

Jehoahaz was Josiah's younger son. According to 36:1, he was the people's choice to succeed Josiah in preference over Jehoiakim: **'The people of the land took Jehoahaz son of**

Josiah and made him king in Jerusalem in place of his father.' He followed Josiah's popular anti-Assyrian and anti-Egyptian policy, but he did not follow Josiah's godly example by putting his trust in the Lord. The Egyptians considered Palestine to be within their sphere of influence (now that the Assyrian Empire had been forced to relinquish its control of the area) and could not tolerate a hostile power so close to its border. So when the Egyptians came to remove Jehoahaz there was no one to whom he could turn.

As a result Jehoahaz reigned for only three months before being taken to Egypt as a hostage (36:4). There he was imprisoned as an example to others who might oppose Egyptian ambitions, and he may have been the prince for whom Ezekiel lamented in the following words:

> Take up a lament concerning the princes of Israel and say:
>
> What a lioness was your mother
>   among the lions!
> She lay down among the young lions
>   and reared her cubs.
> She brought up one of her cubs,
>   and he became a strong lion.
> He learned to tear the prey
>   and he devoured men.
> The nations heard about him,
>   and he was trapped in their pit.
> They led him with hooks
>   to the land of Egypt
>
> (Ezek. 19:1-4).

The prophet Jeremiah warned that Jehoahaz would never return to his homeland (see Jer. 22:11-12, where he is referred to by the name Shallum). The people also suffered on account of his anti-Egyptian policies, because a heavy levy was imposed on Judah, which placed a further burden on the economy.

Jehoiakim (36:4-8)

Jehoiakim was Josiah's eldest son. However, it was not his birthright that secured his succession, but the Egyptians. **'The king of Egypt made Eliakim, a brother of Jehoahaz, king over Judah and Jerusalem and changed Eliakim's name to Jehoiakim'** (36:4). Before long he transferred his allegiance to the Babylonians, as their influence was in the ascendant. In all probability this switch followed the Babylonian victory over the Egyptian-Assyrian alliance at Carchemish in 605 B.C. which left Palestine and Syria open to Babylonian penetration.

The precise meaning of 36:6 has been disputed: **'Nebuchadnezzar king of Babylon attacked him and bound him with bronze shackles to take him to Babylon.'** Some historians claim that Jehoiakim himself was taken to Babylon in chains. This would coincide with the first deportation of Judean exiles in 605 B.C., which is mentioned in Daniel 1:1-3. However the lack of additional evidence to indicate Jehoiakim's personal removal to Babylon has led some to suggest that this was a token binding to indicate Jehoiakim's vassal status.

To the end of his days Jehoiakim remained a political opportunist. After Pharaoh Neco won a costly victory over the Babylonians in 601 B.C. Jehoiakim changed sides again and rebelled against Babylon (see 2 Kings 24:1). This antagonized Nebuchadnezzar and made Babylonian retribution a certainty. Jehoiakim died just as Nebuchadnezzar and his armies arrived at the gates of Jerusalem bent on revenge.

Other aspects of Jehoiakim's reign are mentioned in the Scriptures. He lived luxuriously and built spacious palaces, while at the same time his people suffered deprivation and injustice (Jer. 22:13-17). He was a cruel ruler who was responsible for the murder of the prophet Uriah (Jer. 26:20-23). In marked contrast to his father Josiah, he burned the scroll on which Jeremiah recorded the Lord's condemnation of his sins (Jer. 36:1-32). He restored hideous idolatry to the temple of the Lord in Jerusalem (see Ezek. 8:15-16), undoing the reformation that had taken place during the reign of Josiah. These are described as **'detestable things'** in 36:8.

Jehoiachin (36:9-10)

Jehoiachin was the son of Jehoiakim. He came to the throne just as the Babylonians arrived to punish his father in late 598 B.C. He was eighteen years old when he became king. In some Bible versions there is a marginal note informing us that most Hebrew manuscripts read 'eight' rather than **'eighteen'** (36:9). If this were the correct reading this verse would contradict 2 Kings 24:8 which clearly states that Jehoiachin was eighteen when he became king. However, as there is manuscript evidence to indicate that 2 Chronicles 36:9 should also read 'eighteen', most scholars accept that the 'eight' was a copyist's error which crept into a number of manuscripts, and that the original text (which was kept free from all error by the Holy Spirit) was in perfect agreement with 2 Kings 24:8 in giving his age as eighteen.

Jehoiachin reigned for the 100 days that the Babylonians laid siege to Jerusalem. The city fell to Nebuchadnezzar in March 597 B.C. and many of its inhabitants were taken to Babylon as exiles. Among this number were Ezekiel and his companions, who dated their exile from the captivity of King Jehoiachin (see Ezek. 1:2). Jehoiachin himself was taken as a royal hostage but after a time he was elevated to a privileged position within the Babylonian court. 'In the thirty-seventh year of the exile of Jehoiachin king of Judah, in the year Evil-Merodach became king of Babylon, he released Jehoiachin from prison... He spoke kindly to him and gave him a seat of honour higher than those of the other kings who were with him in Babylon' (2 Kings 25:27-28; Jer. 52:31-32).

Zedekiah (36:10-16)

Zedekiah was another son of Josiah, although the Hebrew text of 36:10 describes him as Jehoiachin's 'brother'. The Hebrew language allows more flexibility to the use of terms which describe family relationships than English does, and Zedekiah was in fact Jehoiachin's uncle. His original name was Mattaniah, but the throne-name Zedekiah was given to him by the Babylonians when they made him king. This was a constant reminder that he was no more than a Babylonian vassal.

The Babylonians had already taken captive the leading members of the noble families of Judah (men like Daniel, and his three faithful companions, see Dan. 1:6), so it was men of inferior calibre that surrounded Zedekiah to advise him. Jeremiah tells us that he was a weak man caught between Babylonians on the one side, and a nationalistic faction among his advisers on the other, which sought to regain national independence through an alliance with Egypt. Jeremiah and other faithful prophets warned Zedekiah not to rely on Egypt, but to look to the Lord who alone was able to preserve his people through the uncertain times ahead.

For his faithfulness Jeremiah was regarded as a Babylonian collaborator (Jer. 37:12-13) and treated shamefully (Jer. 37:15; 38:6). Zedekiah oscillated between despising Jeremiah and seeking his counsel: 'Neither he nor his attendants nor the people of the land paid any attention to the words the LORD had spoken through Jeremiah the prophet... Then King

Zedekiah sent for him and had him brought to the palace, where he asked him privately, "Is there any word from the LORD?" ' (Jer. 37:2,17; cf. 38:4-5,7-10,14-28).

Eventually Zedekiah rebelled against Babylon. This was a sinful breach of his treaty of alliance with Nebuchadnezzar (2 Kings 24:20; Ezek. 17:13-21). The results for Judah were disastrous (as the Chronicler records in 36:17-21). Zedekiah's fate is described in 2 Kings 25:5-7: 'The Babylonian army pursued the king and overtook him in the plains of Jericho. All his soldiers were separated from him and scattered, and he was captured. He was taken to the king of Babylon at Riblah, where sentence was pronounced on him. They killed the sons of Zedekiah before his eyes. Then they put out his eyes, bound him with bronze shackles and took him to Babylon.'

The Chronicler does not dwell on the details of these four reigns or the personalities of these four kings. He gives us four very similar, and very compact, accounts. In essence we are told two things about these kings: they did evil and they were puppets of foreign kings. They are like four objects we might glimpse from a moving train. We barely have time to see them, let alone take in their details or distinguish them. They are simply milestones marking out the rapid decline of Judah. By means of these short repetitive summaries the Chronicler makes the point that Judah was in rapid decline.

Political decline

After Josiah's death and defeat at Megiddo Judah ceased to be a free and independent nation. Judah was a puppet, first of Egypt, then of Babylon. Jeremiah tells us about the internal politics of Judah at that time. The picture is one of indecision and intrigue, treachery and violence, paralysis and panic. It bears a marked similarity to the last days of the Third Reich as the allied armies closed in on Berlin. Within the Führer's bunker the atmosphere was confused and acrimonious, leading to the eventual suicide of Adolf Hitler and his mistress, Eva Braun.

Social decline

There was not just one king who did evil and was a puppet of foreign powers, but four. A trend was established. By Zedekiah's reign we see that this trend was not limited to the king: **'Furthermore, all the leaders of the priests and the people became more and more unfaithful, following all the detestable practices of the nations'** (36:14). Having rejected God, they wanted to remove every reminder of him from their minds: **'But they mocked God's messengers, despised his words and scoffed at his prophets'** (36:16).

Even when God spoke to them in mercy (36:15), they longed to silence his prophets. How irrational, and how destructive! **'The wrath of the LORD was aroused against his people and there was no remedy'** (36:16). A collective momentum had built up, and in their lemming-like recklessness they rushed towards destruction. This is why post-Christian societies (such as Britain, America and Australia) are more resistant to God's Word and more blatant in their wickedness than non-Christian societies (such as China and India). When a nation has enjoyed a heritage of Christian knowledge and gospel preaching, its people know that their wilful ignorance is a sin. This is a terrible truth to acknowledge, so once wilful sinners have turned their backs on God they are determined to get as far away from him as they can. Notice that, in his wisdom, God permits them to go their own way.

Spiritual decline

Underlying all of this was a rejection of God. Their hearts and their evil actions were a reflection of this rejection (36:16).

The jokes of their comedians, the opinions of their academics, the schemes of their politicians and the alliances forged by their diplomats were all a reflection of this rejection of God. The whole spectrum of social, cultural and political life was in decay because it had no foundation, and it had no foundation because God was not in their thoughts.

Can you see the parallels with our modern world? From the music of our popular culture to the value systems of our politicians there are clear signs of decay. This is because God is not at the foundation of the way our societies think or live. Notice again that God permits this to happen. He speaks in mercy, but he does not step in and compel people to listen to his Word. Sometimes we panic and ask, 'Why doesn't God step in and do something?' God did then, and he still does — but his intervention doses not always take the form that we expect.

Retribution (36:17-19)

Rapid decline continued until its terrible conclusion. In 36:17-21 the Chronicler records what God did: **'He brought up against them the king of the Babylonians...'** The sword was in the hand of Nebuchadnezzar, but the purposes being fulfilled were those of the covenant Lord of Israel. He permitted the people of Judah to suffer the consequences of their own actions. Let's consider what Nebuchadnezzar did.

1. Nebuchadnezzar massacred the people of Jerusalem, young and old (36:17)

He **'killed their young men with the sword in the sanctuary, and spared neither young man nor young woman,**

old man or aged'. Moses had warned that when the covenant people forgot their Lord, and his wrath began to burn against them, terrible judgement would follow: 'In the street the sword will make them childless' (Deut. 32:25). There was no refuge, not even 'in the sanctuary' of the temple. They had turned their backs on God and now they found out what life without God is like. Here is a terrible reminder that the wages of sin is death (Rom. 6:23).

2. Nebuchadnezzar carried off the treasures of the temple (36:18)

'He carried to Babylon all the articles from the temple of God, both large and small, and the treasures of the LORD's temple and the treasures of the king and his officials.' The 'treasures of the king' were carried off in fulfilment of Isaiah's warning to Hezekiah in 2 Kings 20:16-17. This is a reminder that pride bears bitter fruit. The 'treasures of the LORD's temple' included the cups, bowls, plates and other implements that were used to bring offerings to the Lord. They were made of silver and gold because they were made for the service of the Most High King. They were a tangible link to the days of Solomon when the kingdom had reached its zenith of wealth and power.

They were also made to be used during those times when God and his people came together. David had described those times of fellowship in Psalm 23:5 in terms characteristic of table fellowship:

You prepare a table before me
  in the presence of my enemies.
You anoint my head with oil;
  my cup overflows.

However, the covenant-breaking people of Judah wanted no fellowship with God, so God cleared the table and took its vessels from them. They were taken to Babylon where they would be used in the service of a heathen god (Dan. 5:2-3).

3. *Nebuchadnezzar destroyed Jerusalem* (36:19)

'They set fire to God's temple and broke down the wall of Jerusalem; they burned all the palaces and destroyed everything of value there.' The destruction of the whole city of Jerusalem was full of symbolism for the covenant people. Jerusalem was the place to which they came to pray because of the promise contained in 7:15: 'Now my eyes will be open and my ears attentive to the prayers offered in this place.' Jerusalem was 'Mount Zion, the city of the Great King' (Ps. 48:2). It was the focal point of God's covenant blessings. But his people had turned their backs on their King. By their actions they had made the temple and the city redundant, so God destroyed them both.

4. *Nebuchadnezzar exiled the people* (36:20)

If the city of Jerusalem was the focal point of the nation's covenant blessings, the land of Israel was the field on which those covenant promises were played out. The land had been a gift from God, promised to Abraham (Gen. 12:7; 13:14-17; 17:8), and claimed by Joshua (Deut. 30:5; Josh. 1:6). God had called Abraham from Ur of the Chaldees so that his descendants might be separated unto the Lord and enjoy the land of Canaan (Gen. 12:1; 15:7; Neh. 9:7-8). But the people would not serve God in the land of promise, so they were removed from it and they served Nebuchadnezzar in a foreign land. Significantly, they were exiled to Babylon, or Chaldea, the land out of which Abraham had been called to become the father of the covenant people. Their exile is clearly portrayed as the consequences of covenant unfaithfulness.

5. Nebuchadnezzar gave the land rest (36:21)

According to the law of Moses, the land was to be given one year of rest in every seven as a further application of the creation principle of sabbath rest (Lev. 25:1-7). Because God, the Creator, rested on the seventh day, his creatures were to rest as well. The seventh day was consecrated as a holy day and the seventh year was a fallow year for the land. This was something the people had failed to do, in spite of the clear warnings of Leviticus 26: 'For the land will be deserted by them and will enjoy its sabbaths while it lies desolate without them. They will pay for their sins because they rejected my laws and abhorred my decrees' (v. 43; cf. vv.32-35). Just as the sabbath principle was integral to the enjoyment of covenant blessings, so the same principle was an integral part of the imposition of covenant curses. **'The land enjoyed its sabbath rests; all the time of its desolation it rested.'**

Each of these actions of Nebuchadnezzar represented a warning ignored. God's warnings had been ignored so often and so blatantly that by this time there was 'no remedy' (36:16), at least not for that generation of Israelites. God cleared the promised land of its people for seventy years. The span of a whole human life would pass before they would return. This is a serious matter to consider. We are reminded that it is possible for those who hear the Word of God to harden their hearts to the point where there is 'no remedy'. This is not because God runs out of mercy. Rather it is because men become so set in their sinful ways that God hands them over to continue unchecked in their sin.

This is the challenge to those who hear the warnings and the offers of mercy in God's Word: do not harden your heart against God. Sometimes when people hear God's Word it makes them uncomfortable and they ask, 'Why do I have to listen to this?' Their prayer, in effect, is: 'God, leave me alone.' Sometimes God does just that. He troubles them no more. He lets them face the consequences of their sins. They carry on through life like the men and women on board the *Titanic*, as it sailed through seas as calm as a millpond. They were eating and drinking, laughing and dancing as they ploughed at full speed into an iceberg. Sinners who push the call of God's Word out of their minds so that they might pursue the pleasures of this life will one day plough into the iceberg of God's judgement.

Take heed if you hear God's Word calling you to repentance. Let it be a timely warning for you. Take heed, especially, if you are unconcerned about how you will face God on the Day of Judgement. Take care if you have not a care in the world about spiritual things, for God will break into the tranquillity of your life suddenly and violently.

Restoration (36:22-23)

This chapter concludes on a note of promise. The seventy years would come to an end. The land would receive its rest. The people would be restored. This was promised by God through the prophet Jeremiah (36:22; cf. Jer. 25:12; 29:10). **'In the first year of Cyrus king of Persia, in order to fulfil the word of the LORD spoken by Jeremiah...'** This was prompted by God as he moved in the heart of Cyrus.

> **... the LORD moved the heart of Cyrus king of Persia to make a proclamation throughout his realm and to put it in writing:**

**'This is what Cyrus king of Persia says:
"The Lord, the God of heaven, has given me all the
kingdoms of the earth and he has appointed me to
build a temple for him at Jerusalem in Judah..." '**

This is one of the most amazing illustrations of God's sovereign foreknowledge. Over a century before Jeremiah, Isaiah had spoken about Cyrus (see Isa. 44:28; 45:1-6,13). Isaiah warned the people of Judah that God would judge them and remove them from the land because of their sins. However, the prophet looked beyond the exile to restoration. He foretold that God would use a most unlikely person to deliver his people — Cyrus, a future king of the then insignificant Persian kingdom:

He is my shepherd
    and will accomplish all that I please;
    he will say of Jerusalem, 'Let it be rebuilt',
    and of the temple, 'Let its foundations be laid.'
This is what the Lord says to his anointed,
    to Cyrus, whose right hand I take hold of
to subdue nations before him...
I will go before you...
For the sake of Jacob my servant,
    of Israel my chosen,
I summon you by name
    and bestow on you a title of honour,
    though you do not acknowledge me.
I am the Lord, and there is no other;
    apart from me there is no God.
I will strengthen you,
    though you have not acknowledged me,
so that from the rising of the sun

to the place of its setting
men may know that there is none besides me.

God had prepared a role for Cyrus and had foretold what that role would be. God put it into Cyrus' heart to do what he had declared he would do. One of the first things that Cyrus did when he conquered Babylon in 538 B.C. was to give an order that the temple in Jerusalem be rebuilt: 'The LORD, the God of heaven, has given me all the kingdoms of the earth and he has appointed me to build a temple for him at Jerusalem in Judah' (36:23; see also Ezra 1:1-4 for a fuller account of Cyrus' decree).

The Chronicler's history was written to encourage those who had returned to Jerusalem after the exile. What a blessing it must have been for them, after those seventy years, to see how God's hand had been at work in the life of their people! After seventy years in captivity they were a chastened people, but they were also very easily discouraged. They were just a tiny nation. They were surrounded by powerful enemies (see Neh. 4:1-15; 6:1-14). Their work was difficult (see Neh. 4:10). But the last words of this history are: '… **may the LORD his God be with him, and let him go up.'**

As they struggled against hostility, hunger, exhaustion and a host of other problems that beset them, they could remember that God had moved empires to bring them back to the land of promise and to rebuild their temple in Jerusalem. The Lord Almighty was the God they served and he desired to be worshipped in his house in Jerusalem.

For Christians today, our focus is on a new and very different temple. When the third Jewish temple was destroyed by Roman armies in A.D. 70, God gave no indication that the temple was ever to be rebuilt. In fact the temple was part of the Old Testament economy that was described by the writer to the Hebrews as 'obsolete and ageing' and which would 'soon disappear' (Heb. 8:13). It was 'only a shadow of the good things that are coming' (Heb. 10:1). Our Lord himself pointed to the day (even sooner than its destruction in A.D. 70) when the magnificent temple in Jerusalem would be rendered redundant: ' "Destroy this temple, and I will raise it again in three days." The Jews replied, "It has taken forty-six years to build this temple, and you are going to raise it in three days?" But the temple he had spoken of was his body' (John 2:19-21).

The Son of God who was born of a virgin is the person in whom God and man come together. His death on the cross is the means whereby sinful men can draw near to a holy God and know the blessings of forgiveness. The Lord Jesus is the only mediator through whom we can come near to God in prayer. He is our temple, our sacrifice and our High Priest. 'Therefore, brothers, since we have confidence to enter the Most Holy Place by the blood of Jesus, by a new and living way opened for us through the curtain, that is, his body, and since we have a great priest over the house of God, let us draw near to God with a sincere heart in full assurance of faith, having our hearts sprinkled to cleanse us from a guilty conscience and having our bodies washed with pure water' (Heb. 10:19-22).

Although we do not worship at a temple in Jerusalem, and the work of Christ is complete, requiring no additions from us, the lesson for us is the same as it was for those returning exiles. Even in times of spiritual darkness, God will not allow himself to be ignored.

The rulers of nations are in his hands, just as they were in the times of Nebuchadnezzar and Cyrus. God used Nebuchadnezzar to administer judgement and he used Cyrus to administer mercy, but they were both subject to his sovereign lordship. Evil men are in his hands. They are never in control of this world, and they will never escape the just judgement of God.

God's chosen people are also in his hands. He will never allow even one of them to be lost. Even when they live in the midst of a wicked generation and a godless world, they are 'sealed with this inscription: "The Lord knows those who are his"' (2 Tim. 2:19). Even when they seem to disappear from the face of the earth, they are still in God's safe hands. He will gather his people to himself. 'I give them eternal life, and they shall never perish; no one can snatch them out of my hand' (John 10:28).

A wide range of excellent books on spiritual subjects is available from Evangelical Press. Please write to us for your free catalogue or contact us by e-mail.

Evangelical Press
Faverdale North Industrial Estate, Darlington, Co. Durham, DL3 0PH, England

Evangelical Press USA
P. O. Box 84, Auburn, MA 01501, USA

e-mail: sales@evangelicalpress.org

web: http://www.evangelicalpress.org